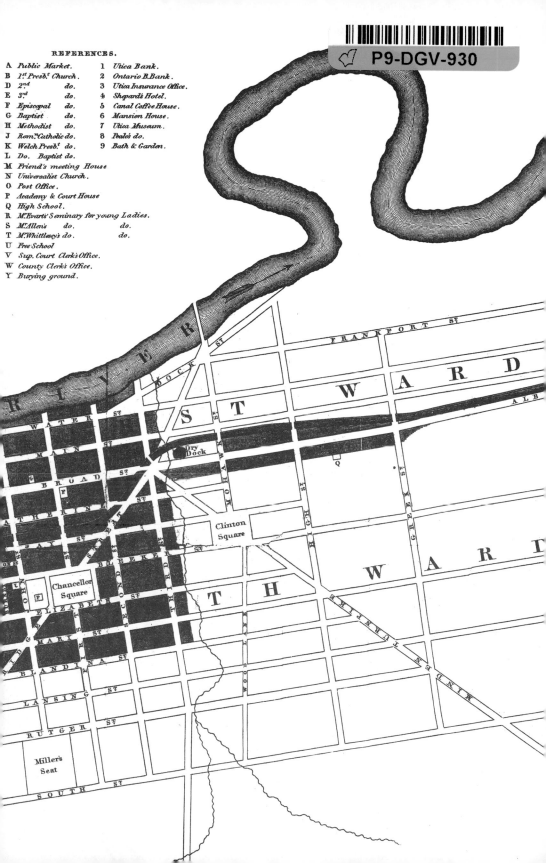

REFERENCES.

A *Public Market.*
B *1st Presb.t Church.*
D *2nd   do.*
E *3.d   do.*
F *Episcopal   do.*
G *Baptist   do.*
H *Methodist   do.*
J *Rom.n Catholic do.*
K *Welch Presb.t do.*
L *Do. Baptist do.*
M *Friend's meeting House*
N *Universalist Church.*
O *Post Office.*
P *Academy & Court House*
Q *High School.*
R *Mr Evarts' Seminary for young Ladies.*
S *Mr Allen's   do.   do.*
T *Mr Whittlesey's do.   do.*
U *Free School*
V *Sup. Court Clerk's Office.*
W *County Clerk's Office.*
Y *Burying ground.*

1 *Utica Bank.*
2 *Ontario B. Bank.*
3 *Utica Insurance Office.*
4 *Shepard's Hotel.*
5 *Canal Coffee House.*
6 *Mansion House.*
7 *Utica Museum.*
8 *Peale's do.*
9 *Bath & Garden.*

Vignettes
of
Old Utica

John J. Walsh

John J. Walsh

UTICA PUBLIC LIBRARY, UTICA, NY

1 9 8 2

Printed by Dodge Graphic Press, Inc., Utica, NY USA

FOREWORD

The Utica Public Library is pleased to publish one of the Hon. John J. Walsh's many writings on local history, "Vignettes of Old Utica", as a contribution to the Sesquicentennial Celebration of the City of Utica. For the Utica Centennial of 1932 the Library published *Utica: Village and City   A Bibliography of the History and Life of Utica,* which has served local scholars well over the past 50 years. It is the hope of the Trustees and Staff of the Library to update that volume in the near future. We are especially pleased that Judge Walsh's writings are, in large measure, based on painstaking research done over the years in the local historical archives of the Utica Public Library. The reader is invited to consult the other writings of Judge Walsh in the Library's collection.

The publication of this volume has been made possible by generous grants from:

> The Gannett Foundation
> The Clothing Bureau Trust Fund of the Utica
>   Foundation, Inc.
> Teamsters Union Local 182 of Utica and
>   Central New York
>   President, Rocco DePerno, Sr.
> United Food and Commercial Workers District
>   Union Local One
>   President, Joseph Talerico

to whom grateful acknowledgement is made, not simply by the Board and Staff of the Library but by the present and future citizens of the City of Utica.

PREFACE

These sketches of the notable men and women and interesting events of old Utica were written in the hope that Uticans today will take pride in the accomplishments of the sturdy and courageous men and women of various ethnic and religious backgrounds who faced danger and privation to transform the wilderness of Old Fort Schuyler into a modern city.

In the process they developed means of transportation; constructed the telegraph system of the State; established newspapers; organized the Associated Press; opened California with the Overland Mail; created the American Express Company; supplied the country with textiles, clothing, knit goods and shoes; and were in the vanguard of the social movements for temperance and the abolition of slavery.

This book is the combined effort of a score of people to whom I am indebted for its publication. The Utica Public Library sponsored and four organizations have provided grants for its publication.

In the editing and selection of material to be included, I wish to express my sincere appreciation to Doctor Eugene Nassar of Utica College, to Frank Scalise and Ann Curtin, and to Mario Mannella and the staff of Dodge-Graphic Press, Inc.

I hope that the reader will enjoy this volume as much as I have enjoyed collecting the material.

February 1982   John J. Walsh

About the author . . .

John J. Walsh is a native Utican, a graduate of Hamilton College and the Albany Law School of Union University. He was elected a member of the New York State Legislative Assembly from Oneida County from 1937 thru 1940. Elected City Judge of Utica in November 1940, he served in that position for eighteen years, until elected in November 1958 as Oneida County Judge. As County Judge, he served in that position from January 1st, 1959 until his retirement on December 31, 1979.

In 1966 he was elected a delegate from the 44th Senatorial District to the 1967 New York State Constitutional Convention in which he was a member of the committee on the Judiciary and Labor and Civil Service.

Judge Walsh has for a long time been interested in the history of Utica and has written and lectured on the subject. He is a member of the Board of Trustees of the Utica Public Library and has been appointed by the Mayor as Historian for the Sesquicentennial of 1982.

TO
Mary and Maryrose
and
TO THE MEMORY OF
Michael Joseph
and my parents,
Michael and Margaret McKernan Walsh

TABLE OF CONTENTS

OLD FORT SCHUYLER

THE Indians called the Mohawk River TE-NON-AN-AT-CHE, "the river flowing through mountains." Like most Indian names it was extremely descriptive. The Mohawk is the only river that cuts a passage through the rock wall of the great Appalachian plateau, extending unbroken from the St. Lawrence valley to Georgia. Beginning at its source on the desolate slopes of Mohawk Hill, just north of the present boundary of Oneida County, the stream slowly descends southward through the upland area of Lake Delta to the present city of Rome. At this point, it makes an abrupt turn eastward to mingle its waters with those of the Hudson. Prior to the present century, it made a U-shaped turn immediately west of Bagg's Square to touch the present northerly edge of the railroad tracks before continuing its eastward journey. The river was shallow at this point, providing a fording place for the old Indian trails from the north and the east to the south and the west.

The early Dutch from Fort Orange (Albany) followed these Indian trails to trade for furs and the early English colonists recognized that the river and the trails afforded an easy approach for raids along the valley by the French and their Indian allies from Canada. As a result, they erected a series of fortifications from Schenectady to Rome, where Fort Stanwix formed the western bastion.

About 1758, the English erected a fortification, called Fort Schuyler to protect the crossing at Utica. It was not as formidable as Fort Stanwix and was never known to have been garrisoned as a fort. It consisted of a block-house just north of the present Main street near the Union Station. The plan of the old fort was recently discovered in Albany and a copy is now on display at the Oneida Historical Society in the Fountain Elms. There is some doubt as to whether it was named for Colonel Peter Schuyler, of New Jersey, who commanded at Oswego, or Colonel Philip Schuyler, of Albany, uncle to General Philip Schuyler of the Revolutionary War. It is now generally believed that it was named for the New Jersey commander. The old fort had fallen into disuse before the time of the Revolution but it is said that General Nicholas Herkimer stopped there on his return from the

1

historic Battle of Oriskany, of which George Washington said that "here Herkimer first reversed the gloomy scene of the opening years of the Revolution."

The few travelers who came by soon after the Revolution found the old fort largely in ruins. The Indians called the spot "TWA-DAH-AH-LO-DAH-QUE" — "ruins of old fort". The future site of Utica was called U-NUN-DA-DA-GES — "around the hill", referring to the hills which surround the city.

John George Weaver, together with three others, Christian Reel or Reall, after whom Reel's Creek is named, Marcus Damuth and George G. Weaver settled on the north bank of the Mohawk river, opposite the fording place in the spring of 1773, two years before the outbreak of the Revolution. The annual overflow of the Mohawk at the end of the first season drove these early settlers from the bank of the river to the brow of Deerfield Hill. Here they built log cabins, cleared the land of trees, planted crops and remained three years until the summer of 1776 when the little settlement was broken up by an Indian raid from Canada.

Of the Indian tribes, the Oneidas were the friendliest and often enjoyed the hospitality of the Weavers. One of the Oneidas was surprised by a raiding party and learned of their plans to attack the Deerfield settlement. He warned Weaver and the little group of the impending attack and the settlers fled to Stone Arabia down the valley. For some time thereafter, they remained at the Stone Arabia fort, but returned daily to cultivate their crops. On one such occasion, Weaver was captured by the hostile Indians and taken to Canada. He was transported to England and remained there until exchanged for one of Burgoyne's soldiers toward the close of the Revolution.

With the establishment of peace, all four of these original settlers returned to Deerfield where the numerous descendants of the Weavers played important roles in the development of the town and Oneida County. George M. Weaver, the son of George M. Weaver and grandson of John George Weaver was born January 15, 1788 and claimed the distinction of being the first white male born in the vicinity of Utica. Christian Reel built his cabin on the bank of Reel's Creek and Captain Damuth built his on what was to be the northwest corner of Trenton avenue and the River road. This was finally torn down in 1875.

2

Except for the Deerfield settlers on the north side, there were only four original pioneers on the south side of the river. These original holdings were by lease. John Cunningham had a piece of land on the ground of the later Bagg's Tavern. George Damuth had a twenty-one year lease from Rutger Miller of land a few rods west of the old fort, near first street. Jacob Christman occupied land a few rods west from Cunningham and a man by the name of McNamee built a log cabin near the present State Hospital grounds. None of the original settlers remained long in the vicinity.

Leslie W. Devereux described the log cabins of that period in the "Utica Daily Press" for March 3, 1932:

"The original log cabins were built of basswood, the spaces between being filled with moss and covered with bark. The front was from 12 to 20 feet high, sloping toward the rear, the lower end being but a few feet from the ground.

"Around the cabins, a space of about one-eighth of an acre had been cleared of trees and the lumber not used for the houses had been burned to the ground. This made the soil a rich loam good for crops and did away with the necessity of plowing. Here corn, potatoes and turnips were planted. The few cattle belonging to the community were allowed to roam wild in the woods, a bell attached to the neck of one of them, so that their whereabouts could be easily discovered.

"The log cabins were small and contained but a single room. Although the bark roof shed rain quite well, there were always leaks and it was often necessary, when eating or sleeping to move from under a spot that dripped water. A mud and stick chimney and stone hearth provided a place for cooking and was the only means of heat in winter. The floor was made of basswood logs, split and partially hewed on one side and then spotted down. A hole dug under the floor served as a cellar where dried corn, potatoes and other supplies were kept in winter. In order to reach this storeroom, it was necessary to take up one of the flattened logs from the floor. At first the doorways were covered only with blankets, but later, boards were hewn from logs, fastened together with rough cleats, with wooden hinges, and wooden catch and latch raised by a string. The door was fastened by a pin inside when the occupants wished to secure it. But in general, except when away from home or fearing an Indian raid, the latch string was always out, and travelers were always welcome to the rough hospitality.

3

In return they retailed what news they possessed, which was greedily received.

"The furniture consisted of a rough table made of logs hewn on one side, with four rough legs to support it. Three-legged stools of the same finish were the only seats. Beds were made from two logs set parallel on the floor with rough slats across with hay or evergreen boughs for a mattress. Covers — and clothes for that matter — were made from skins and dressed hides until it was possible to own sheep and shear, pick, card, spin and weave wool."

The area around the old fort formed a part of a tract of land of 22,000 acres granted in 1734 by the King of England to several persons, for the benefit of William Cosby, the Governor of Colonial New York. In default of the payment of arrears of quit rents, it was seized and sold at auction in 1772 by the Sheriff of the Colony to Philip Schuyler, for the joint benefit of himself, General John Bradstreet, Rutger Bleecker and John M. Scott. This tract of land was known as Cosby Manor and included a large part of the present downtown Utica.

Rutger Bleecker was a wealthy resident of Albany and in 1786, his son, John R. Bleecker made a survey of the property and divided it into 106 great lots, some on the north and some on the south side of the Mohawk river, each about 1000 feet wide and about three miles in length. These great lots were assigned individually to the four owners in groups of three. On the south side of the river between Bagg's Square and Mohawk street was the property of Bleecker and his heirs; and between Bagg's Square and Varick street belonged to the heirs of Bradstreet.

General Bradstreet had devised his share to his two daughters, Martha and Agatha. Martha who died unmarried willed her portion as follows: one-third to her sister Agatha; one-third to the children of her half brother, Samuel; and one-third to her half-sister Elizabeth. The executor of the original Bradstreet will was Sir Charles Gould, who, by the terms of the will, was authorized to sell and dispose of the land. Sir Charles sold the land in the Cosby grant between 1790 and 1794 to the settlers there.

For a period of thirty years these settlers were compelled to defend their titles against a litigious woman named Martha Bradstreet. Martha was a daughter of Major Samuel Bradstreet and was born on the Island of Antigua, West

4

Indies in August 1780. In Ireland in 1799 she married Matthew Codd and came with him to America and they settled in Utica. Their marriage was a stormy one and finally ended in a divorce obtained by her lawyer, Aaron Burr. For a quarter of a century thereafter, she laid claim in the courts to a large portion of Utica. The settlers were forced to defend their claims to title and eventually they were successful. It was but one indication of the difficulties encountered by the early residents in establishing their homes and laying the foundation of the great city that was to replace the little hamlet of Old Fort Schuyler.

THE PIONEER MERCHANTS OF OLD FORT SCHUYLER

PERHAPS the first person to recognize the possibilities for trade at the site of the old fort was Peter Smith, the father of the well-known abolitionist, Gerrit Smith. Peter Smith was a native of Rockland county and was born in 1768. Apprenticed at the age of sixteen as a clerk in the importing house of Abraham Herring & Co., he remained with them three years. He then opened his own store at Fall Hill, a few miles below Little Falls. About 1789 he moved to Old Fort Schuyler and bought the log house of the widow Damuth for a few pounds of tea and put up a log store on what was later to be the site of Bagg's Tavern. He soon built another store near the lower end of Main street, near which he erected a handsome two story dwelling on the corner of Main and Third streets. This house he occupied for a few years and then it passed to James S. Kip and later to Judge Morris S. Miller.

Peter Smith thus became Utica's first merchant, but the major portion of his trading was done with the Indians for furs. When John Jacob Astor came here in search of pelts, the two men became partners and both became millionaires.

Together they journeyed on foot between Schenectady and Old Fort Schuyler, stopping at the various Indian settlements to pick up the furs. Smith became acquainted with the language of the various tribes and earned their respect and friendship.

Although the law prevented him from buying land outright from the Indians, about 1794 he obtained proprietary rights from the Oneidas of a tract of land containing about fifty thousand acres, stretching from Syracuse across Madison county into the town of Augusta in Oneida county. He did this by leasing the tract, at first called New Petersburg, afterward Peterboro, from them for 999 years. This grant was later confirmed by the State of New York. In March 1797, Gerrit Smith, his son, was born in Utica at the Smith residence then on Broad street beyond the old Gulf. In 1806, Peter Smith moved his family to Peterboro and his son eventually inherited the vast lands. Peter Smith died in Schenectady on April 17th, 1837.

In 1787, Henry Salyea, of whom little is known, entered into an agreement with John Post for the sum of one hundred dollars, to surrender to him on the first day of April following, his lease from Rutger Bleecker of a lot near the ford of the Mohawk adjoining those of Cunningham and Damuth.

In the spring of 1790, Post sailed up the Mohawk river from Schenectady with his wife and three children. It took him eight days to make the trip. Of Dutch extraction, Post had been a soldier in the Revolution and had been present at the surrender of Burgoyne at Saratoga and later Cornwallis at Yorktown. For some years previous, in connection with a Mr. Martin of Schenectady, he had engaged in trading with the Indians, especially in the purchase of ginseng, an herb with a long fleshy root found in the woods. He exported large quantities of the herb to China where it was highly prized as a remedy for the plague, being much superior to the Chinese variety. He also purchased furs and skins and came here for that purpose. He built a house on the west side of Genesee street, near Whitesboro and kept goods for sale at his house, consisting of spirits, tobacco, blankets, ammunition and beads and trinkets. In 1791 he erected a store immediately north of his house at the Square where he conducted his business. Post soon became a prosperous merchant and he erected a warehouse of wood on the bank of the

Mohawk, three stories high, which he later replaced with one of brick.

His daughter, Mrs. Petrie some years later told Pomroy Jones for his "Annals and Recollections of Oneida County" (1851):

> "As ours was the first house which could accommodate travellers, a sign was put up, though reluctantly, and my father kept tavern no longer than until some one with means, could be prevailed upon to leave a more privileged place to settle here, for the sole purpose of keeping a tavern. As the place was then much resorted to, my father sold lots to mechanics and traders. The first settlers were men wanting in energy and enterprise, and he re-purchased the lots from them, and soon sold to others, who also proved inefficient in building up the place which my father fancied, in due time, would command much trade. Again he repurchased the lots, and he did not wait long before he, a third time, sold them to such men as became permanent residents and acquired a competency."

Giving up the tavern-keeping, John Post continued his store with great financial success and was about ready to retire and enjoy life comfortably when one of his pretty daughters married Giles Hamlin. This ambitious young man joined the firm and urged Post to embark upon an expanded wholesale business. Hamlin went to New York city and purchased on credit huge stocks of merchandise. He proceeded to sell this to small retailers in the neighboring settlements, taking in return their promissory notes. On May 16, 1803, the Utica "Patriot" announced in its columns:

> "John Post & Giles Hamlin under the firm name of Post & Hamlin, have commenced business at the store formerly occupied by said Post, where they are just opening for sale an elegant assortment of dry goods, groceries, crockery, hard and hollow ware, which will be sold at the most reduced prices for prompt pay only."

Disaster occurred on the morning of February 4, 1804, when perhaps the first fire of importance in the little settlement broke out in the store. The "Columbian Gazette" of February 4, 1804 reported:

> "An alarming fire broke out in this village on Saturday last, between the hours of two and three. It commenced in the store of Post and Hamlin, and was so far advanced before it was discovered that their clerk had only time to secure a part of the account books, some silver money, and make his escape through a window."

7

The fire occurred at a very unfortunate time and resulted in Post's financial ruin. His own creditors began demanding payment and without his account books, he could not collect what was owed to him. Since Post was an honorable man, he divested himself of all his real property and assets, to pay his debts. A broken man, he retired to a farm in Manlius, New York where he died in 1830. His only monuments are the old-fashioned box stove used in his store, now the property of the Oneida Historical Society and the shabby street named after him behind the Paul building on Elizabeth street.

Watts Sherman came to Utica from Newport, Rhode Island and was a carpenter by trade. He was not a particularly skilled mechanic and to make ends meet, his wife, Olivia, kept a small shop on Main street where she sold cake and beer. In 1802, Sherman formed a partnership with Arnold Wells, who furnished the capital to open a store. Sherman was a shrewd and ambitious man and became a successful merchant. Because Sherman was a little too ambitious for Wells, the latter left the business. The store was on Genesee street, a little below what was later to be Broad street and afterward nearly opposite Catharine street. He died in 1820.

Talcott Camp was born in Durham, Connecticut in 1762. Around 1796, he was in New York city where he met William G. Tracy of Whitesboro who brought with him a barrel or two of silver coins, the usual medium of exchange at the time, for the purchase of goods he needed. This market appealed to Camp and he came here for a visit in the fall of 1796. He returned in the spring of 1797 and opened a store for the sale of goods. He was successful and soon disposed of his interest and engaged in the purchase and sale of real estate. He was prominent in village affairs and died in 1832, at the age of seventy.

In 1797, Silas Clark and William Fellows kept the largest store in the hamlet, on the north side of Whitesboro street, near Division. Silas Clark was an excellent horseman and a Major of militia. He died at the early age of 37. It is said that his death was caused by wearing tight boots while on parade, which produced an inflammation of the leg. After Clark's death, William Fellows became associated with Moses Bagg, Jr., until John Camp, the eldest son of Talcott Camp, purchased Mr. Fellow's interest. The firm of Bagg & Camp kept their store in a building next to Bagg's Tavern on the north. When Bagg withdrew from the business, the firm became John Camp & Co. and the store was moved to Genesee street, opposite Catharine. John Camp died in 1867 at the age of eighty.

One of the foremost merchants of early Utica was Bryan Johnson, a native of England who arrived at old Fort Schuyler on July 4th, 1797. He established himself in a small building on Whitesboro street, near what was later to be Division street. His policy was to sell merchandise at the lowest prices, and to buy country produce at the highest. He was soon joined from England by his son, Alexander B. Johnson and the two gained considerable property and real estate. Mr. Johnson's residence was originally over his store, but in 1800 he bought and reconstructed a house standing a little farther west on the opposite side. He retired in 1808 and died on April 12th, 1824 at the age of seventy-five.

The firm of Kane & Van Rensselaer had a successful business at Canajoharie. As their business began to decline, they would hail the boats passing down the Mohawk with wheat and potash, in order to ascertain to whom the freight belonged. Learning that the merchandise in both directions belonged to Bryan Johnson, they determined to share in the same trade here. Thus was developed a business rivalry that continued as long as Johnson remained in business. The "Columbian Gazette" of July 10th, 1800 contained the following announcement:

> "Archibald Kane and Jeremiah Van Rensselaer, Jr., under the firm name of Kane & Van Rensselaer have opened a house in Utica, where may be had a general assortment of dry goods and groceries on moderate terms."

Jeremiah Van Rensselaer, Jr. was the son of General Robert Van Rensselaer, of Claverack, who fought in the Revolution. He settled in Canajoharie in 1795 and with Archibald Kane established a business. While Kane remained in Canajoharie, Van Rensselaer with the assistance of his brother, James came to Utica and opened a store on Genesee street on the corner of what was to become Broad street. A few years later, when Broad street was laid out from Genesee to John street to complete the road which originally ran east from John street, it became necessary to turn the store half way around to prevent its encroachment upon the new street. This was accomplished by placing a cannon ball in the center as a pivot, after which it could be swung into place.

Archibald Kane's brother, John had an extensive business in New York city and by reason of that fact, Kane & Van

Rensselaer had facilities for importing goods and shipping and selling produce that few of their competitors possessed, and they did an extensive business. After John Post's retirement, their chief rival was Bryan Johnson and the two firms conducted a price war, freely advertising in the weekly papers.

Mr. Van Rensselaer built an elegant mansion on what was then the outskirts of the village. This was on the east side of Genesee street and included the area later embraced by Devereux, Charlotte, Blandina and Genesee. The main entrance was by a large driveway at what is now the junction of Genesee and Devereux. The house was a wooden one, painted white, with two oval wings and located some hundred feet from the street. It was approached by a circular driveway to the right and left. In the rear were the stables and a beautiful garden.

Then Kane & Van Rensselaer encountered the rocky commercial period which followed the resumption of specie payments after the War of 1812-15. It caused the collapse of the John Kane firm in New York city and with it fell the associated businesses in Canajoharie and Utica. Resuming business alone, Mr. Van Rensselaer tried to carry on but at length was forced to close. He sold his home to Nicholas Devereux and about 1825 moved to Canandaigua, where he died in 1828.

John Corish Devereux was born in Enniscorthy, County Wexford, Ireland on August 5th, 1774, the son of Thomas and Catharine Corish Devereux, a wealthy and prominent family. The family name is of French origin and tradition has it that when William the Conqueror, Duke of Normandy, invaded England in 1066, Robert DeVereux, the younger son of the feudal owner of Evreux accompanied him and settled in Ireland, with grants from the Crown. During the century that followed, the Devereux family, Catholic in religion, was respected and honored by the Irish and when the Irish, prompted by the American and French revolutions, struck for independence from England in 1798, Thomas Devereux added his voice and financial means to the cause. When the rebellion was crushed, great retribution was visited upon the family in the loss of their lands and fortune to the Crown. Around 1796 or 1797, their son John C. Devereux came to America and a few years later to the little village of Utica.

On November 8th, 1802, he advertised that he had

10

"opened an assortment of dry goods and groceries at the store lately occupied by John Smith" at Bagg's Square. John C. Devereux soon became a successful merchant and he brought his brothers, Luke, Nicholas and Thomas to help in his business. Nicholas Devereux was born in Ireland in 1791 and came to this country in 1806 to join his brothers John C. and Luke in the business. Luke left Utica in 1814 and went to Natchez where he died of yellow fever in February 1818. Thomas Devereux arrived in Utica from Ireland in 1810 and operated the Utica Distillery, later the Gulf Brewery, where he sold "excellent Whiskey in exchange for cash, wheat rye or store hogs." When Thomas returned to Ireland, Nicholas advertised the distillery for sale in March 1815.

John Devereux retired from active management of the business and Nicholas continued the firm as "N. Devereux & Co.". John C. Devereux's earlier home was on Main street, but near the close of the War of 1812, he erected the house at the corner of Broad and Second street where he lived until his death December 11, 1848. Nicholas Devereux was a successful merchant and became the owner of the handsome Jeremiah Van Rensselaer residence on Genesee street, which he later laid out for building lots.

EARLY TRAVEL AND TRANSPORTATION

THE Mohawk was navigable for boats of small tonnage from Schenectady to Fort Schuyler. The rapids at Little Falls presented difficulties and prior to 1795, it was necessary to unload the boats and pull them through the rapids by means of ropes from the bank. In 1795, an association incorporated by the State and known as the "Inland Lock Navigation Company" constructed several locks at Little Falls. This improvement permitted the boats to move without unloading and enabled the passage of larger boats.

The earlier boats were Canadian batteau, and capable of carrying one and half to two tons upstream and five tons downward. They were called three-handed or four-handed boats according to the number of men who propelled them. The boats were propelled by the members of the crew by means of pike poles. These were generally from eighteen to twenty-two feet in length with a sharp pointed iron affixed to the lower end. The upper end had a large knob called a "button" which could be placed against the shoulder. Within the boat on each side was fixed a plank running fore and aft, with a number of cleats nailed across it, for the purpose of giving the polemen a surer footing during the hard poling over the rapids. The men, after setting their poles against a rock, bank or the bottom of the river and placing their right or left shoulder, according to the side on which they were poling, then fell down on their hands and toes, crept the whole length of the gang-boards, and sent the boat forward. It was an extremely laborious task and only those of great strength could manage these poles with any kind of advantage. The crews considered themselves fortunate if they made ten miles in one day. Occasionally, when the wind was favorable along the straight stretches of the river, a sail could be hoisted. Most of the merchandise brought to Fort Schuyler came by these boats. Later, John Post had boats constructed, propelled by oars, carrying twenty passengers.

In the years before the Revolution, there existed the Sackett's Harbor turnpike, a military road between that place where a garrison was stationed and Albany. The section through what is now Deerfield is now known as the "River Road". When hostilities ceased, caravans moving westward followed this old road to Deerfield and then turned south toward Bagg's Square through a wallow of mud, mire and boulders. Westward from Utica, as early as 1790, a "road" was opened by William and James Wadsworth on their way to the Genesee river, where they planted a settlement.

In the summer of 1792, the inhabitants petitioned the State to furnish financial help in building a bridge across the Mohawk at the ford. The State was slow in acting, and the residents became impatient and held a "bridge-building" of their own. The result was a wooden one at the foot of Second street. French agents who stayed with John Post in November 1793 described the bridge in their journal:

"This bridge, built after the English manner, is in the arc of a circle, with a very moderate curve, and is supported

12

by beams placed like a St. Andrew's Cross, and covered with plank. The bridge has already bent from the curve intended and inclines to the oval, an effect due as much to the framing as to the quality and smallness of the timbers, which are of pine and fir. The main support which they have put in the middle would rather tend to its entire destruction when the ice is going off. The abutments are of timber, and are also settled from miscalculation of the resistance, the one on the south side being built upon ground that is full of springs."

The prediction of the French agents was an accurate one and within a few months the bridge was swept away. Apollos Cooper became a resident here in 1795. He was a carpenter and builder by trade and he undertook to build a new bridge, this time at Bagg's Square. Moses Bagg in his "Memorial History of Utica" wrote:

"A peculiarity of this bridge consisted in the long covered avenue of trestle work that led down to it, reaching back half way to Main street, a proof that the river bank was then much lower than at present and the bridge in consequence more difficult of approach. This bridge had a stone abutment in the center, and was more substantial than its more immediate predecessor. Mr. Cooper was also the artificer of Hamilton Oneida Academy, the precursor of Hamilton College."

This second bridge was succeeded in 1810 by a third "covered" bridge, built by Captain Joseph Pierce, of Deerfield.

In 1794, the State Legislature appointed three commissioners to lay out a road from Utica to Canandaigua, to be known as the "Genesee road". This was not immediately constructed and a Colonel Williamson who travelled through the State in 1797 described it as no better than "an Indian trail".

In 1800, the Seneca Turnpike Company was chartered by the State and work was commenced on a new road, beginning at Bagg's Square. With the help of volunteers, the first mile was soon constructed running up Genesee street, and eventually extended through New Hartford, Kirkland, Vernon and Oneida Castle.

Jason Parker was born in North Adams, Massachusetts in 1763 and came to New Hartford in 1794 with his wife Roxanne and their children. He purchased and operated two farms, but when his health failed, he was advised to relinquish farming and engage in some less arduous occupation. He removed to Utica where the only employment he could find was that of post rider between Whitestown and Canajoharie. It was his task to carry the mail pouch on horseback when the road was passable. When it was not, he tramped through the mud and snow with the pouch slung over his back. After a short time, he decided to open a stage line to carry the mail and from this humble beginning, he developed a business which during his lifetime grew to be one of the largest transportation companies in the State. In the "Western Sentinel" of September 23, 1795 can be found the following advertisement:

> "Parker's Mail Stage from Whitestown to Canajoharie. The mail leaves Whitestown every Monday and Thursday, at 2 o'clock p.m., and proceeds to Old Fort Schuyler the same evening; the next morning starts at 4 o'clock and arrives at Canajoharie in the evening; exchanges passengers with the Albany and Cooperstown stages and the next day returns to Old Fort Schuyler. Fare for passengers $2.00, way passengers four cents per mile. Fourteen pounds of baggage gratis — 150 weight rated the same as a passenger. Seats may be had by applying at the post office, Whitestown, at the house of the subscriber, Old Fort Schuyler, or at Captain Roof's, Canajoharie. August 1795. Jason Parker."

Jason Parker first lived in a small log cabin on Main street, a little west of First street, but as his business grew, he opened an office in the basement of Bagg's Tavern and moved to the south side of Whitesboro street, near Seneca, his carriage and blacksmith shop and stables being adjacent. By 1799, he and his partner, Moses Beal, were operating the mail stage twice weekly between Schenectady and Utica. In 1802, Jason Parker announced that "a stage for the conveyance of the mail and those who wish to travel by stage will start from Utica for Onondaga twice a week." In March 1803, Mr. Parker petitioned the Legislature to grant him the exclusive right to run stages from the village of Utica to the village of Canandaigua for the term of ten years, stating that "the present emoluments are inadequate to reimburse the expenses by the proprietors."

The following year, an act was passed granting to Jason Parker and Levi Stephens the exclusive right for a period of seven years of running a line of stages for the conveyance of passengers, at least twice a week, along the Genesee road or Seneca turnpike, between the villages of Utica and Canandaigua. They were required to furnish four good and substantial covered wagons or sleighs, and sufficient horses to run the same. The fare was not to exceed five cents per mile, and they were to run through in forty-eight hours, accidents excepted. They were forbidden to carry more than seven passengers in any one carriage, except by the unanimous consent of said passengers. If four passengers above the seven applied for passage they were obliged to fit out and start an extra carriage for their accommodation; any number less than four might be accommodated by paying the rate of four.

Jason Parker gradually improved his eastern runs so that by the fall of 1810, the stages between Utica and Albany ran daily and the next year another line, operating three times a week, was added to the daily lines. The western line was extended in 1811 to Buffalo and Niagara Falls. Jason Parker had come a long way from his post rider days.

Parker had competition from Joshua Ostrom, the son of Judge David Ostrom, who began to operate stage lines to Albany. This competition was demonstrated by newspaper advertisements in 1811. On January 11th, 1811, Parker advertised:

> "Eight changes of horses. The mail stage now leaves Bagg's, Utica, every morning at 4 o'clock. Passengers will breakfast at Maynard's, Herkimer, dine at Josiah Shepard's, Palatine, and sup (on oysters) at Thomas Powell's Tontaine Coffee House, Schenectady. Those ladies and gentlemen who will favor this line with their patronage may be assured of having good horses, attentive drivers, warm carriages, and that there shall not be any running or racing of horses on the line."

A week later, Ostrom announced that he was prepared to "go through in one day, unless extreme badness of the travelling render it utterly impossible" and assured the passengers that they would have "the liberty of breakfasting, dining and supping where, when and on what they pleased." Ostrom, however, was not able to compete with Parker and went out of business, leaving the monopoly of staging to Parker & Company from 1812 to 1821.

In later years, when competition again appeared, Parker obtained the services of two other great pioneers of transportation, Theodore S. Faxton and John Butterfield. When Parker died on September 28, 1830, he had eight stage lines running daily east and west through Utica, and twelve daily and semi-weekly north and south.

In stage coach days, as the stage approached a village, the

driver would blow his horn. The object was to notify the hostlers at the stables to make ready the relay team of horses and the landlord of the tavern that meals should be spread for the passengers. The horses were Morgans, nervy, sure-footed and strong. The drivers were men of great physical strength. The whip was a stick of finely polished hard wood, four to five feet long, to which was attached a lash ten to twelve feet in length, and on the end of the lash a finely braided silk cracker. The later stage coaches weighed 2200 pounds and carried eleven passengers with their baggage. The flavor of stage-coach travel in the early days was captured in an article in the "Utica Daily Observer" in 1878, written by Ned Spicer:

> "The heavy, big-wheeled, fat-bodied old vehicle rocked and rolled, and pitched into the bog holes with a stately bow, and with creaks and groans was pulled out again along through woods, through fields, and across streams on bridges of logs and turf, and through valleys that were hemmed in by deep forests of hemlocks and pine. The driver's long whip with a flourish was launched at the ears of the lagging leaders and without touching them as it cracked overhead in the clear, crisp air, infused the old animals with all the ardour of youth. What a change! Naught is left now of the old coach. It has passed away, and with it the driver, whose rich fund of anecdote, and wit and jollity, is only left to us in the musty books that, laid away in garrets and dark holes under stairways, tell such quaint stories of olden times. No more is heard the crack of the long whip, the richness of the horns, the rattle of the harness, the creaking of the springs."

In 1923, while workmen were digging trenches in lower Genesee street for a new sewer, relics of old Utica were uncovered. The "Utica Saturday Globe" of August 18, 1923 reported:

> "This was the discovery of the plank road which once covered Genesee street. The road is about five feet below the level of the present pavement. A particularly good idea of the old-time street pavement may be found in the excavations in front of J. B. Wells store. What is being brought up are logs which formed the foundation of the plank road and pieces of the plank. Along the trench runs a series of chunks of plank driven into the earth, which looks like a row of sheathing. The logs are soft on the surface from being water soaked, but they are far from decay. The pieces of planking which are several feet square, are also well preserved."

16

PIONEER TAVERNS AND INNKEEPERS

PRIOR to the year 1800 taverns began to spring up in the little hamlet to accommodate the growing stream of pioneers which had already begun to wend its way westward. Although these rude early structures lacked the most ordinary conveniences, they did afford a rough hospitality and fare. Since most of the early travelers arrived here by horseback, ox drawn carts or by stage coach, the pioneer tavern owner had to provide barns, stables and a shed for animals. In addition, to alleviate the rigors of the road and the inclemency of the weather, a bar room became a necessary adjunct to a well kept establishment.

In March 1788, Major John Bellinger, who was at Herkimer's side at the Battle of Oriskany, came to old Fort Schuyler. He built a rude hut of boughs without a side until he could construct a small one and a half story frame house, the first of its kind here. This was placed at the rear of a lot at the southwest corner of Whitesboro and Washington streets. In later years, the corner itself was occupied by the Bethesda (Welsh) church which in 1870 was taken over as a Jewish synagogue, the House of Israel.

For a time, Bellinger managed the farm which adjoined the house and, like all the other residents, gave temporary shelter to travelers. He found this occupation less arduous and more profitable than farming, and proceeded to erect a larger wooden building across on the north side of the road to Whitesboro. This became the first regular inn in the hamlet.

First known as the "Bellinger Tavern", it was later known as the "New England House". His sign, a custom of the old taverns, was a spread eagle with a scroll in its beak, bearing the motto, "E Pluribus Unum." This caused considerable comment and his nephew, Nicholas "Honnickel" Smith, was once asked its meaning and he replied, "Dat means mine unkle geeps de pest tavern in Utica."

Nicholas Smith's parents were Mohawk Dutch and among the earliest settlers in the valley. When Nicholas was eleven months old, his parents were pursued by some Indians and fearing that they would be overtaken, hid the boy in a hollow hemlock log. There he was found the next day by some white

17

men, his parents having been massacred by the savages. Brought to Utica, he grew to manhood and served during the War of 1812 and was known thereafter as "Colonel" Smith. His son, William Bellinger Smith was born July 20, 1824 in the family home on the east side of Washington street, just above Whitesboro street. William Bellinger Smith died in Utica on September 23, 1916 at the age of 92 years.

The innkeepers' recognizance for the town of Whitestown, which included Fort Schuyler, lists John Bellinger and John House, among others, as posting a bond in the sum of $150 with the condition of the undertaking,

> "that you will not during the time you keep an inn or tavern, keep a disorderly inn or tavern, nor suffer or permit any cock-fighting, gaming or playing with cards or dice, or keep any billiard table or other gaming table or shuffleboard within the inn or tavern by you to be kept, or within any outhouse, yard or garden belonging thereunto then this recognizance to be void, otherwise to remain in full force."

When John Bellinger died in 1815, the tavern was taken over by his son John and his nephew. They lacked his interest in the business and by 1820, Theophilus Lombard became the proprietor. As the century progressed, the old "New England House" ceased to be a fashionable hostelry. After a series of landlords, it was taken over in 1859 by Isaac Van Wormer, who renamed it "Van's Hotel."

On March 16, 1863, shortly after three o'clock in the morning, fire broke out and gained considerable headway before it was discovered. The firemen were called, but the hydrants in the vicinity were frozen and it was necessary to draw water from the Erie Canal, some distance away. The building was completely destroyed, leaving only the barn in the rear. In 1869, the old barn was leveled and dwelling houses were built on the site.

Another pioneer tavern owner was John House who opened his inn on the southeast corner of Genesee and Main street, facing Bagg's Square. Little is known about him as he remained here only a short time and by 1802 his tavern was kept by others.

In 1792, Gurdon Burchard, a native of Norwich, Connecticut came to Utica. He was a saddle and harness maker, and occupied a lot fronting on Whitesboro street, on the south side, reaching through to Genesee street. A gore of land on the southwest corner of Genesee and Whitesboro streets was later to become the building known as "Dudley Triangle". About 1810, Burchard abandoned his trade and opened a tavern on the southeast corner of Burchard Lane, known as "The Sign of the Buck". This he conducted until his death on August 17, 1832, at the age of 64, he and one of his daughters dying of cholera during the epidemic which visited the city that year. The old tavern was destroyed in the great fire of 1837 which destroyed most of the buildings on lower Genesee and Whitesboro streets.

When Moses Bagg, of Westfield, Massachusetts sailed up the Mohawk river with his wife and two sons in the autumn of 1793, he was not very much impressed by the area and stayed instead at Middle Settlement during the winter. He changed his mind and came back on March 12, 1794. He opened a blacksmith shop on Main street, a little east of the Square. His house was a log structure described by his grandson, M. M. Bagg as "a shanty made of hemlock boards nailed to the stubs of trees, and stood directly on the corner; and this he opened for the accommodation of travellers."

Finding it was more profitable to fit rooms to visitors than shoes to horses, in 1795 he put up a two story wooden building on the same site and kept it as a tavern until his death in September 1805. For the next two years the tavern was kept by George Tisdale and the first elephant ever seen in Utica was exhibited in Tisdale's yard in 1806-07. Then Moses Bagg Jr. took over the tavern and continued his father's tradition as a congenial host. It was rather a small building and when the first Board of Canal Commissioners came to Utica in July 1810 to make a preliminary survey for the Erie Canal, only two of the commissioners, Stephen Van Rensselaer and Gouverneur Morris with their servants could be accommodated and the rest of the commissioners were required to seek quarters elsewhere.

In 1812, Moses Bagg Jr. decided to build a large hotel on the same site. In 1792 Joseph Ballou had come from Rhode Island and purchased a lot on the southeast corner of Main and John streets. He built a red brick building and store there, occupied by his son, Jerathmel Ballou, a merchant. When his father died in 1810, Jerathmel took over the property and when Moses Bagg decided to build his new hotel, Jerathmel purchased and moved across to his property the old wooden Bagg's tavern. He made additions to it in 1817 and it was opened as a public house by Amos Gray. It was afterwards kept by Cyrus Grannis who was successively a packet boat captain, merchant and tavern owner and he called the place "Union Hall".

In March 1870 it was known as the "Northern Hotel", leased by Jeremiah Shaw from the then owner, Theodore P. Ballou. On March 12th of that year, it was destroyed by fire. When first discovered, the blaze was confined to the eastern wall and garret over the sitting room fronting on Main street but the fire gained headway and destroyed the old hostelry. The "Utica Morning Herald" the next day wrote:

> "The old hotel has gone; peace to its ashes. More sightly structures may occupy the ground where it once stood; but some years must pass before they become as venerable as was the Northern Hotel."

On November 2, 1795, the agents of the Holland Land Company purchased a lot on the northerly side of Whitesboro street just west of the Square and within two years, proceeded to erect the first brick structure in the village. The contract was given to Samuel Hooker and his son, John, who were the only residents competent to undertake so substantial a structure. They secured the brick from Heli Foot, of Deerfield. The building was started probably in the year 1797 and was finished near the close of the year 1799. The land selected was swampy and considerable difficulty was experienced in laying the foundation. When completed it was a square three-storied building with a four-sided roof. It was opened in December 1799 and the first proprietor, Philip J. Schwartz announced to the public that

> "the hotel in the village of Utica is now open for the reception of such ladies and gentlemen as choose to honor the proprietor with their patronage."

It was an imposing structure for the time and loomed above all the story-and-a-half wooden houses of the village. Upon the front was displayed in chiseled letters, "Hotel", which no subsequent painting was able wholly to obliterate. Thus it was for years known as "the Hotel." Practically all of the large dancing parties in the village were held there. The "Saturday Globe" of December 6, 1902 thus described these affairs:

> "In the second story was a large ballroom with a spring floor, where were held all the fashionable parties and assemblies of the day. At one end was a wooden screen, cut out to represent trees and groves in a sort of Forest of Arden effect. At the sound of the music the dancers emerged from behind these trees and when the graceful

gavottes or scarf dances were finished, they disappeared into the leafy shades. The room was lighted with candelabra and sconces filled with wax candles. In those days the balls began at 7 o'clock and continued until midnight."

Not long after the opening of the hotel, a street was opened southward from it and intersected the Genesee road at what was then the upper part of the village. This it was hoped would divert the travel from the west and bring it directly to the doors of the hostelry. This street was naturally given the name of "Hotel Street". Whitesboro street was widened to permit the four and six-horse stage coaches to turn around in front of the Hotel, a situation which is still noticeable to the present day.

The development and improvement of the stage coach lines to the east and west and the building of the Erie Canal diminished the importance and patronage of the "York House" as it was known after 1814. There was a succession of landlords until 1861 and in October of that year a fire broke out in the shed of the York House and despite the valiant efforts of the volunteer firemen, only the brick walls and a part of the tenement house remained standing. While some historians contend that the old hotel still stands on Whitesboro street, it was actually replaced in 1863 by a new building, called at first, "Fuller's Hotel." From 1902 to 1913, it was used for private residence purposes, except for the years 1905-06 when George W. Head & Co. used it as a warehouse. After 1914 it was occupied by Lester J. Start Co. Inc. as a wholesale grocery warehouse.

As early as May 1811, a new tavern keeper, Jonathan Hedges installed himself in a wooden building that stood on the west side of Genesee street, about opposite Catharine street and which with its yard and stables to the north and rear of it, covered the ground now occupied by a block of stores. Hedges did not stay long and was followed by other landlords. About 1810, Levi Cozzens came from Providence, Rhode Island to Utica to work as a tanner for James Hopper. Then he became the proprietor of the "Old Stage Coach Tavern" in New Hartford. About 1820, Cozzens took charge of Hedges' Tavern and remained there some years. When he left, the old tavern was closed and was moved to Seneca street as a double house, to be replaced by the business block on Genesee street.

Of all these pioneer taverns, Bagg's was to have the most

21

lasting effect upon Utica and it continued for well over a hundred years until 1932 when it finally closed and was torn down. To the original brick hotel built in 1812-15 in the center of the lot. Moses Bagg added additions on either side until including the old Bleecker House to the north, Bagg's Hotel occupied the entire east side of the Square. From 1825 to 1828, it was conducted by Abraham Shepard, a native of New London, Connecticut as "Shepard's Hotel". In 1828, Moses Bagg returned to the hotel and took as his partner, Alfred Churchill, who became the sole proprietor in 1836. In the last years of the 19th century, Thomas R. Proctor was the proprietor and he developed the old hotel into the finest in this part of the country.

After the construction of the Erie Canal, the attention of tavern owners turned southward along Genesee street.

THE EARLY RELIGIOUS SOCIETIES
1800-1832

T HE inhabitants of Old Fort Schuyler represented a number of ethnic groups and a variety of religious preferences. The only existing society up to the year 1801 was the United Society of Whitestown and Old Fort Schuyler, organized in 1793 and presided over by Rev. Bethuel Dodd. In 1797, as the number of Presbyterians in the village increased, Pastor Dodd began to preach here frequently. When he could not, sermons were read by Talcott Camp, Hiel Hollister, Solomon P. Goodrich and others, while the singing was led by Nathan Williams and Richard Kimball. These church services were held in the old school house which stood on the south side of Main street, about midway between First and Second streets, with its end to the street and its longer side facing the highway. As a place of worship, this building was used until the completion of Trinity Church in 1806, when, for a brief period, the two congregations alternately worshipped in the latter edifice.

By the end of the 18th and beginning of the 19th century, the only sizeable immigration to Utica consisted of the Welsh. By 1798, quite a number of Welsh arrived here and the newcomers held a prayer meeting as one of the first public events, thanking the Almighty for a safe arrival. A deeply religious people, the first regular church organization in Utica proper was formed by them.

On September 12th, 1801, twenty-two persons of Welsh descent, who were Baptists, met in the log cabin of John Williams, upon the road to Whitestown, opposite the present State Hospital grounds. They formed the "First (Welsh) Baptist" Church. The society met at first in a log cabin on Varick street, near what was later to be the Globe Woolen Mills. In 1806 they erected a chapel on Hotel street on ground that was later to give way to the Erie Canal. Then the chapel was removed to the west side of Broadway, a short distance below Liberty street. The services were held in the Welsh language and continued for many years, the congregation reaching nearly 300 persons at one time. But the location of the church as the city advanced became unpopular and many of the Welsh speaking people died, while the younger Welsh preferred to go to the English speaking churches. After 1885, the church continued but services and preachers were sporadic. Finally the "Utica Daily Press" of April 21, 1904 reported:

> "The first Welsh Baptist Church of Utica, the oldest church organization in the city met last evening, in the church building on Broadway and did what it has been the intention of the members to transfer the church property to the Tabernacle Baptist Church, for the reason that the society of Tabernacle Church is the daughter, so to speak, of the Welsh church. The church building is now in good condition and the auditorium is pleasant and inviting. It is a frame building and stands on a good sized lot. At the rear of the church is a large shed where the farmers from the country drove and kept their horses while attending services and it is the only church in town, probably, that is fitted with such an appendage."

The second regular church organization was formed on January 1st, 1802 as a Congregational or independent church by the people of Welsh descent. In 1801, ten Welsh Congregationalists residing in Utica united with the Presbyterian society in Whitestown. They were followed by several new arrivals shortly thereafter and at a meeting in a private residence on Main street, it was decided to form a separate society. It consisted of some twenty to twenty-five persons and their first pastor was the Rev. Daniel Morris, a bookbinder by trade, who arrived here in 1802. It was he who arranged for the binding of the first book printed in this country in the Welsh language. This church was the Welsh Congregational Church, later to be known as Bethesda. Until 1804 the congregation worshipped in private homes, but in that year, they erected a small frame house on the southeast corner of Whitesboro and Washington streets, which was the first church completed in the village. This edifice served for thirty years as a place of public worship, being replaced by a larger church of brick on the same site. This was opened on January 1, 1836.

In 1862, a dispute arose within the church organization and seventy members withdrew and formed the Second Congregational Church, purchasing the old Grace (Episcopal) Church on the corner of Columbia and Broadway for services. A reconciliation was effectuated shortly thereafter and the two congregations united to build a new brick church on the west side of Washington street, just south of Pearl street which opened in 1872. Services continued in Welsh for many years with the number of Welsh-speaking residents declining to the degree that it was necessary to alternate with English services. In 1963 because of a smaller congregation, Bethesda merged with Plymouth as Plymouth Bethesda Church at Oneida Square.

In 1803, "The First Presbyterian Society of Utica" was formed and after the death of Rev. Mr. Dodd in 1804, the Rev. James Carnahan preached alternately at Whitesboro and Utica until 1812. In 1807, the Utica Society completed its first house of worship, on the corner of Washington and Liberty streets. The lot was given by John Bellinger on the condition that he should have a pew in the new church. In 1813, the fifty-seven members of the church who resided in Utica were constituted a separate church under the name of the "First Presbyterian Society".

Dr. Bagg in his "Memorial History of Utica" described this first church building:

"In 1815 it was elongated by the addition of about one-quarter of its length and this, with a porch at the end, somewhat marred its architectural proportions. Within it was still more unique, for its sentry box of a pulpit was perched against the wall in the middle of the north side

24

and had a canopy or sounding board above, while the
pews for the most part so placed as to look one-half
westward and one-half eastward, a few square ones
being immediately in front of the pulpit and a few long
ones under the chorister's gallery on the south side."

As the congregation grew, it became necessary to plan for
a larger church. In 1826, Philip Hooker, of Albany, submitted the plans and the foundations were laid on the west side
of Washington street just below Liberty, some twelve feet
north of the old church. The new church was a substantial
one of brick, 72 feet by 106 with a steeple 208 feet high. The
church was dedicated on November 8, 1827 at a total cost of
$30,000, with an organ fifteen by ten feet in dimensions and
having twelve stops, at a cost of $4,000. Until 1850, this Ionic
edifice surpassed any church structure in Central New York
and its spire could be seen for miles around.

The Rev. Philander Chase, afterwards Bishop of Illinois
was on his way westward when he visited Utica in 1798 and
collected the few Episcopalians then resident in the hamlet.
He urged them to form a religious society to read the prayers
each Sunday. From that time to 1803, lay leaders conducted
the services on alternate Sundays in the old Main Street
school house. In 1803, John R. Bleecker gave a lot 100 feet
front by 127 feet deep on Broad street, running through to
Catharine street for the new church. Philip Hooker, of Albany made the plans and construction was completed in
1810. It stood back in the lot and was entered through what
was called "Church Lane", now First street, by taking down
the bars of a fence that enclosed the whole lot. Corn was
planted in the yard and the approach to the church was
through a lane of Indian maize. Professor Walter E. Fowler,
long time choirmaster in 1927 thus described the old edifice:

"The interior of the church was considered a marvel of
completeness in those early days. The pulpit was elevated several feet above the floor, the chancel enclosed
by a circular railing and the communion table, supported by four fluted columns about four inches in
diameter, stood before the pulpit. The clergyman ascended two or three steps into the church from the
vestry, where he read the opening sentences and continued the service. In reading the lessons, he ascended
three or four steps more to the reading desk. The choir
sang a psalm, during which the minister passed down
into the vestry. He reappeared through a door back of
the pulpit, robed in a black silk gown, ascended to the
pulpit and preached the sermon.

"All the woodwork, outside and inside, including the walls and ceiling, were painted white. The pews were in the old country style and most of them were owned and furnished by the different subscribers. Owners had keys to the pews and these, when not in use were locked against any intruder. The church was heated by two stoves placed in front with pipes running along the ceiling to the back of the church, and even with this arrangement, it was very cold in extreme winter weather and some members brought in foot stoves in order to offset the cold. Three large oil lamps furnished the illumination. The silver communion service supposedly came from New York, the inscription on the plate being 1824.

"Very often as many as fifteen Indians and their squaws attended service dressed in beautiful ornamental garments with moccasins, embroidered in beads and quills and their hair gathered in a knot, from which feathers of bright colors depended. After the galleries were put in, the Indians sat up there at the right side of the church, always attentive and reverent worshippers."

For more than a century, until 1922, Old Trinity welcomed the pioneering families of Utica. In that year the dwindling congregation united with St. Andrew's on Faxton street.

Methodism in Utica dated from the early days of the village. At first the few members in Utica were attached to the church that was located on the road to New Hartford. Around the year 1808 Solomon Bronson, a member began to hold meetings in a school house on lower Genesee street on the east side near Catharine. Later, a school house was built at the corner of Elizabeth street where Grace church now stands. This was known as the "Dixon School House" and regular services were held there until 1816. In that year, a regular church was incorporated. The old church in New Hartford was sold for 5,000 bricks which were used to erect a chapel on Main street in Utica. This was on the west side of the "gulf" on land donated by Rutger Bleecker.

This chapel was in use until 1826 when it was decided to build a new edifice on the south side of Bleecker street, between Charlotte and Burnet streets. James B. DeLong, the noted abolition leader and a member of the church donated the land. This church was renovated in 1855. In the fall of 1866, the Bleecker Street Methodist Church united with the State Street Methodist Church, formed in 1847. The First

Methodist Episcopal Church was the result. The old building was sold to Mooney & Howe, tobacco manufacturers.

By the year 1817, the Presbyterians, Welsh Baptists, Episcopalians, Congregationalists and Methodists had active churches. A number of new churches were formed between that date and 1832, when Utica became a city.

In 1819, seventeen English-speaking members decided to separate from the Welsh Baptist Church on Broadway, where the services were conducted in the Welsh language. With permission, they formed the Second Baptist Church of Utica, generally known as the Broad Street Baptist Church, the predecessor of Tabernacle Baptist Church. The new group purchased a lot on the north side of Broad street near the corner of John and built a wooden frame building, 50 by 120 feet in size. In 1847, the old building became too small and a new brick church was erected on the same site. The old wooden structure was moved back toward Main street and was used for a short time as a theater.

The new brick building was built in the Doric order. The front was somewhat similar to the Dutch Reform Church, with a portico with two columns. In June 1864, the church society voted to vacate their house of worship and remove to a more central location. The United States Court Room in the City Hall on Pearl street was secured as a place of worship until a new church could be erected. In October of that year, the church was incorporated as the "Tabernacle Baptist Church" and on August 3, 1865, the cornerstone was laid for the new church on the corner of Hopper and King streets.

John C. Devereux was the pioneer in the movement to establish the first Roman Catholic Church west of Albany, and the fourth in New York State. Through his efforts, Father Michael O'Gorman came to Utica and on January 10, 1819 said Mass in the old Court House and Academy on Chancellor Square. On January 25th, 1819, a meeting was held in the home of Devereux and "The First Catholic Church in the Western District of New York" was incorporated. Father Farnan became the first pastor and his residence was a small wooden house on the east side of the Square.

Three parcels of land, ninety feet on John street and one hundred on Bleecker street were donated by Judge Morris S. Miller. The congregation at that time did not exceed thirty persons, and the donations of the Irish laborers and tradesmen were of necessity small. John C. Devereux and his brother Nicholas donated $1,125 to start the church.

Edward Crane, a carpenter born in England, lived in Utica at the time and he undertook to design and build a church for the Catholic congregation. He had given much study to architectural design and in 1821 erected on the corner of John and Bleecker streets, a church building at variance with the traditional square, wooden meeting house. Thomas W. Seward in a lecture before the Oneida Historical Society in 1887 said:

> "The front of the first St. John's Church with its Tudor doorway, mullioned windows, engraved clustered columns, foliated window gables, and its gracefully outlined open spire, was a gem."

Another of Utica's historic church buildings was the one erected on the southwest corner of Bleecker and Charlotte streets in 1826. Edward Crane was asked to design and build this church for the Second Presbyterian Church, organized in 1824, as an offshoot of the First Church, whose congregation had outgrown the small church on Hotel street. Crane was hampered by the size and shape of the site and had to modify the design which he had used for St. John's church. He was forced to perch his steeple partly on the pediment of the main building, and partly on the smaller and lower pediment of the projecting vestibule. Nevertheless, it was a very imposing building. For many years, the clock in the steeple was the official city clock.

On November 21, 1825, a Universalist Society was organized in Utica and held its services first in the old Academy at Chancellor Square until the society purchased from Nicholas Devereux a lot on the south side of Devereux street, just east of Genesee street in 1828 and built thereon a church building. In the course of time, the society became involved in financial difficulties and to satisfy its creditors, the church was sold. In July 1844, the Westminster Presbyterian Society was organized and it purchased the Devereux street church which it enlarged and materially improved. On March 10, 1853, at midnight, the steeple of Westminster Church was discovered to be on fire and in spite of the valiant efforts of the volunteer firemen, it was soon a heap of rubbish. The Universalist Society did not revive until the late 1840s.

The Dutch Reformed Church in Utica grew out of the missionary efforts of Rev. John P. Spinner, pastor of the church at Fort Herkimer in 1801. He preached in Utica in private homes and in the Baptist Church on Broad street. In 1824-25, services were held on alternate Sundays in the

Methodist Chapel on Main street. In 1828, the Rev. John F. Schermerhorn came to Utica and organized a society. Abraham Varick and George M. Weaver, Jr. were chosen elders. A site was selected on the southeast corner of Broad and John streets, owned by Samuel Stocking, for which he was paid the sum of $500. On June 26, 1829, a contract was made with James McGregor to lay the stone and brick for a building, 74 by 54 feet, to be called the Dutch Reformed Church. The rate was five shillings per perch and for laying brick, eighteen shillings per thousand. The building was completed in June 1830, at a total cost of $19,986, exclusive of upholstering and the organ. On October 26, 1830, the Reformed Church was organized with 46 members.

For thirty-six years, the congregation worshipped there and then decided to move uptown to be closer to its members. The site chosen was on the northwest corner of Genesee and Cornelia streets and the last service in the old church was held October 14, 1866. While its new church was being built, services were held in the United States Court Room in the City Hall. The old church building was used for various purposes for a few years, including a headlight factory and then was sold to the wholesale grocery firm of Crouse, which proceeded to raze the building about 1870 and erect a business block thereon.

In February 1830, Robert J. Jones, Evan Roberts, Richard H. Hughes and Evan Ellis asked permission to withdraw from the Welsh Congregational Church and form a Calvinistic Methodist Church in Utica. Permission was granted and they began to meet in a little school house on Bleecker street. In March 1831, the "Moriah Welsh Calvinistic Church" was organized and a small church was built at No. 11 Seneca street, which was replaced by a larger one in 1847. When this site was selected, nearly all of the Welsh people in the city lived east of Genesee, south of Whitesboro and north of the Erie Canal. Later in the century, they became scattered throughout the city, many moving up into Corn Hill. Accordingly, they built in 1882 a new church on the corner of Dakin and Park avenue. The religious designation of the church was changed to "Moriah Presbyterian Church" in later years.

THE VILLAGE OF UTICA
1798-1817

O N April 3rd, 1798 the Legislature created the "Village of Utica". The name had been chosen at a meeting of the inhabitants held at Bagg's Tavern. The debate was long and heated. Some favored retaining the name of Old Fort Schuyler; others favored an Indian name such as Skenandoah, the great Oneida Chief who had been friendly during the Revolution; still others thought a national hero such as Washington was appropriate. Finding agreement impossible it was resolved to decide the name by lot. Each person deposited the name he preferred written on a slip of paper and placed in a hat. There were thirteen names in the hat and the first slip drawn contained the name of "Utica".

This was the suggestion of Erastus Clark, born in Lebanon, Connecticut in 1763. He graduated from Dartmouth College, was admitted to the Bar, and came to Old Fort Schuyler in 1797. He was a classical scholar and the name of the long dead city in North Africa, the rival of ancient Carthage, appealed to him. It was thought that the Phoenicians built Utica about 1100 BC, about 27 miles northwest of Carthage, near the Gulf of Tunis, about halfway between the modern cities of Tunis and Bizerta. In the days of its glory, Utica was almost as powerful as Carthage. When the Roman legions invaded North Africa during the Third Punic War, Utica accepted Roman rule and became the capital of the Roman Province of North Africa. It was also an important religious center. During the 600s conquering Arab tribes plundered the city and destroyed it. The younger Cato was the defender of ancient Utica.

The Rev. Timothy Dwight, president of Yale College made a trip through New York State about this time and wrote about the new village:

> "Utica, when we passed through it, was a pretty village containing fifty houses. It is built on the spot where Fort Schuyler formerly stood. Its site is the declivity of the hill which bounds the valley of the Mohawk and here slopes easily and elegantly to the river. The homes stand almost all on a single street parallel to the river. Generally those which were built before our arrival were small, not being

intended for permanent habitations. The settlers were almost wholly traders and mechanics and it was said that their business had already become considerable. Their expectations of future prosperity were raised to the highest pitch, and not a doubt was entertained that this village would at no great distance of time become the emporium of all the commerce carried on between that ocean and a vast interior."

All the early records of the village were destroyed in the fire of 1848, except the tax roll for 1800 which listed a total tax of $40.00, John Post being assessed the highest amount, $2.00. The only streets in the little village were Main, Whitesboro, Genesee and Hotel streets, to which was added in 1804, the lower portion of Seneca street. The road along Genesee street consisted of a log causeway barely wide enough for teams to pass one another, with a ditch on either side. Stores extended from the river up Genesee street to what was to become Broad street, up Whitesboro street as far as Hotel, and a little way along Main street. Beyond these limits, shops and stores were sparingly interspersed with private residences and beyond were farms, where wheat, potatoes and other produce were cultivated.

The original village charter was a limited one and the citizens petitioned for greater powers. On April 5, 1805, the Legislature extended the village boundaries. The freeholders were empowered to raise taxes, not exceeding one thousand dollars per year. On May 5, 1805, the residents met in the school house on Main street and elected five trustees, Jeremiah Van Rensselaer, Jr., Nathan Williams, Francis A. Bloodgood, Jerathmel Ballou and Erastus Clark, with Van Rensselaer as village president.

Although the petition to the Legislature in 1805 mentioned the need for a better regulated police force and an expanded fire company, there is little evidence that there existed a police force as we understand the term. Dr. Bagg mentions a constable and tax collector by the name of John Pierce, a son of Captain John Pierce who settled here by the year 1794 and had a farm near the corner of Whitesboro and Broadway. His duty apparently was to serve legal papers and collect the taxes. What was termed "police" must have referred to a "night watch" to warn of fire.

The fire of 1804 which destroyed John Post's store demonstrated the inadequacy of the village's fire protection. The only fire engine was a small one, carried by two or three men, called a "goose neck". It was so called because the pipe on the top could be moved in a circle and the water issued from the top of a condensing case or air chamber, about four feet high. It was not constructed to suck water, but had to be filled with buckets of water from the river or the town pump. By moving the handles, called "brakes" up and down, the water could be forced from the chamber upon the fire. There were few inhabitants who knew how to operate it or had knowledge of how a fire should be handled.

At the second meeting of the trustees, twenty-five able bodied men were appointed as volunteer firemen, with power to choose their own captain "who was to manage their affairs, and to exercise the men on the last Saturday of every month, and also to select five men who were to control the ladders and fire hooks." The newly appointed firemen met at Bagg's Tavern on May 13, 1805 and elected Gurdon Burchard as their Captain. The position of fireman in these days exempted the holder from military service. There was also a social aspect of membership and the first recorded banquet of the fire company was held in March 1808 at Tisdale's (Bagg's) tavern. The bill submitted by him amounted to 10 pounds, 17 shillings, and included, in addition to the suppers furnished, 1 gallon of beer, 3 pints of gin, 3 pints of brandy, 13 bottles of wine, and 100 "segars."

On December 10, 1805, ninety-eight citizens signed a petition pledging to act during the ensuing winter as a night watch to guard against the danger of fire. They were distributed into squads of five or six and took turns in patrolling the village streets from end to end each evening. Their instructions were detailed by the trustees:

> "In the event of an alarm of fire, you will first proceed to cry 'fire' and the place of its discovery. Next instantly, crying 'fire' as you go, knock at the door of each trustee, McComber, the man who rings the bell, the Captain of the Fire Company, Mr. Paine and the other foremen, and then to continue to alarm the inhabitants generally, never forgetting in every instance to direct them to carry their buckets."

The inhabitants were directed to keep leather fire buckets, proportionate to the number of stoves and fireplaces in the house, but not more than six and on the outbreak of fire, to come with their buckets to the scene of the fire, under penalty of 25¢ for each offense. Another ordinance required that every householder place a lighted candle in the front window or door and keep it burning until the fire was extinguished.

The bell ringer, whom the watchmen were to arouse in case of fire resided at the time at the lower end of Genesee street below Whitesboro and the bell he was to ring hung in the Presbyterian meeting house on the corner of Liberty and Washington street. The bell was to be rung three times daily, and in case of fire continuously until the fire was out.

In March 1810, Morris S. Miller, under authorization from the Bleecker heirs donated a piece of land on First street, immediately in the rear of Trinity Episcopal Church as a proper building to house the "fire engine, hearse, etc." Utica Fire Company No. 1, later known as "Clinton Fire Company" was stationed there until 1817.

The usual place for holding the drills of the firemen at their monthly meeting was either at the river or the town pump on the Square. This pump was important and it was looked upon as a very serious matter when it was discovered that somebody had taken away the bolt from the pump on the evening of July 3rd, 1807. The trustees voted a reward of five dollars to be given to anyone who would report the person responsible, so that the offender might be punished. There is no record that the person who committed this nefarious crime was ever apprehended.

In 1817, a third charter was granted the village of Utica which provided for the election of six trustees but their president was to be appointed by the Governor. The village was made a town separate from Whitestown and its boundaries were extended to Turner street on the east, Schuyler street on the west, and Rebecca (now South street) on the south. Nathan Williams was appointed the village president. The first directory of the village was published, listing 2,861 inhabitants. The stores were chiefly on Genesee street below Catharine. Most of the residences were on Whitesboro street between Hotel and Varick streets; on Hotel, Seneca and Washington streets between Whitesboro and Liberty streets; and on Main and Broad streets as far as Third Avenue. The streets leading from Genesee westward were Water, Whitesboro and Liberty streets, while from the east went Water, Main, Broad and Catharine streets.

At a very early period in the history of the village, the subject of procuring a wholesome supply of pure water was considered. In April 1802, the Legislature created a corporation, under the name of the "Utica Aqueduct Company." Samuel Bardwell and Oliver Bull secured possession of the springs at the foot of the sand bank which stretched across what is now Court street, east of State. Where Spring and Cooper streets were laid out, until obliterated by urban renewal in recent years, there was a series of springs of the most delicious water. An aqueduct of hollow logs was built from this source down through the pasture lots to the corner of Genesee and Liberty streets and thence down Genesee street to the "square". This was the first waterworks in the village.

In order to provide more water, the village trustees ordered that three wells be dug and fitted with pumps. The one on the square was located about on a line with the northerly side of Whitesboro street and about in the middle of the Square. Its trough, where the horses drank, was crude, but it was serviceable and there was a constant file of pail-bearing boys and girls who came to turn the crooked handle and get water. The second "well" was placed in front of "the Hotel" at the intersection of Whitesboro and Hotel streets and the third at the corner of Genesee and Liberty streets.

The construction of the Erie Canal in 1817 severed the old aqueduct and the supply of pure water to lower Genesee street was cut off. From 1824 until 1834 the inhabitants had to depend upon the wells for water. In 1834 pipes were laid from the Spring street source through Cornelia, Fayette and Genesee street to Catharine street to supply the upper village. In 1850, the Utica Waterworks was organized.

As early as 1797 the little hamlet began to bury its dead on land owned by Stephen Potter, along the road to Whitesboro. In April 1790, two or three families had arrived here from Connecticut, led by Captain Stephen Potter. He settled on great lot No. 97, a little west of that of John Bellinger. There he engaged in farming until his death in 1810. It was not until 1806 that the village obtained a deed to part of the premises from Potter. The deed, in consideration of the sum of $100 conveyed

> "all that certain parcel of land situate in said village now known by the name of the burying ground . . . containing one acre of land, reserving nevertheless to the said Stephen Potter the right of pasturing sheep and calves and removing the fence now there and the fruit trees on the same premises and further that the said trustees shall keep the same in fence."

Until the opening of Forest Hill cemetery in 1850, "Potter's Field" constituted the principal place of interment for early Uticans and the pioneers. Like the subjects of Gray's elegy, "Each in his narrow cell forever laid / The rude forefathers of the hamlet sleep." There were buried all the prominent citizens. Ezra Cozier, an early village president and the first city treasurer in 1832, who fell a victim to the cholera epidemic of that year was buried there. Just beyond was the grave of Major John Bellinger and across the lane the family of Colonel Nicholas Smith, Bellinger's nephew who died in 1865. Next to the Smith lot was that of Bildad Merrell, another Revolutionary soldier. Talcott Camp, the first village president, James S. Kip, Gurdon and Gideon Burchard, the Devlins, the village's first iron workers, Dr. Solomon Wolcott and many others prominent in Utica's infancy were also buried there.

The burying grounds were, when additional land was added, divided into three portions. The portion on the south side of Water street was known as the "private grounds", purchased by relatives and friends from the Potter heirs. Directly opposite on the north side of Water street was the "old burial ground" which contained about ten private lots, all the rest devoted to the public. West of the railroad tracks was a third cemetery known as the "new burial ground". A roadway ran through the center from north to south, dividing it into two almost equal parts. The portion west of the roadway was owned by private persons, with the exception of a plot in the northwest corner which was public. The portion east of the roadway was also public.

Since the only record of interments known to exist began on March 11, 1841, there is no way of ascertaining how many or where any particular person was buried. When the old burial ground was filled to capacity, the Forest Hill cemetery was opened in 1850 and from that day until the beginning of the twentieth century, except for charity burials, Potter Cemetery gradually became abandoned. By 1871, the Utica, Binghamton Railroad Company purchased a tract through the center of it and built its tracks there.

Agitation began to have the city do something about the old ground which became overgrown with brush and debris. In 1902, about 40 bodies of soldiers and sailors were removed and re-interred elsewhere and in 1909, the State Legislature authorized the city to purchase the land from private owners, re-inter the bodies and use the ground for school purposes. In 1916, the city took over the balance of the cemetery for park purposes. In that year, the bodies of Major Bellinger, his wife, who was the daughter of Nicholas

Weaver of Deerfield, Dr. Solomon Wolcott, Benjamin Ballou, James S. Kip, and others were recovered.

Previous to 1830, there was no Catholic cemetery in Utica, and Catholics for the most part were buried in Potter and other secular grounds. In that year a piece of property on upper Steuben street was donated by John C. Devereux to St. John's Church. He reserved one corner of the ground for himself but none of the Devereux family were ever buried there. The "Utica Observer" of July 27, 1881 gave a description of the old Catholic burial ground:

"The first President of the cemetery was the father of John Magee. Mr. Magee lived near the old cemetery. In 1831 the plot of land was surrounded by a substantial fence, the work being accomplished by various members of the church, there being no sexton at that time. The fence remained standing for nearly 25 years, when a new one was built by direction of Rev. Father McFarland, then pastor of St. John's. The first remains interred were those of Mr. Magee's brother, who died in 1827 and whose body had been buried in Potter's Field in the absence of a Catholic cemetery. John Magee remembers well the first funeral to the Corn Hill cemetery. In 1832 the great cholera year, these funerals multiplied in number and arrived at all hours of the day and night. Mr. Magee Sr. kept the necessary graveyard tools at his house and the friends of the dead were in the habit of borrowing them to dig the graves with their own hands. During the prevalence of the fearful epidemic, the calls at the Magee house for shovels, etc. became very frequent, and the elder Magee became alarmed, got his team ready, put in about six weeks provisions, shut up the house and drove over the other side of Steele's hill, where the family took possession of a deserted log house. They remained there for five weeks, or until the last vestige of the plague had disappeared from Utica. The graveyard tools had, however, been left at a convenient spot near the cemetery. The corduroy road leading to the old cemetery was built over swamps and mudholes, and was generally in an almost impassable condition in those early years. At the time, too, a dense forest was located on the east side of upper Steuben street, which abounded in game."

With the growth of the city, a larger Catholic cemetery was required and between 1841 and 1845 a plot of ground on Mohawk street was purchased by St. John's Church and St. Agnes Cemetery organized and the old cemetery abandoned. In 1896, the city decided to lay out a new street,

Addington Place, running directly through the old cemetery. In the summer of 1903, all the bodies in the old cemetery were removed and re-interred in St. Agnes with a plaque erected:

"in memory of 600 pioneers of the faith in these parts who were buried in the first Catholic cemetery in this city between the years 1830 and 1845, and whose remains were reinterred here with a solemn Mass of Requiem in the open air, September 7, 1903. Requiescat in Pace."

THE EARLY NEWSPAPER PUBLISHERS OF UTICA

S PEAKING at the sémi-centennial of the city of Utica in 1882, DeWitt C. Grove said:

"The early publishers of Utica were printers, moved by their own enterprise and encouraged by local public spirit, to establish newspapers in new settlements, where readers were few and advertisers far between. They struggled for existence as best they could, their main purpose being to make an honest living. To a great degree, they were their own editors, set their own type, mailed their own papers, and collected their own accounts. If a more promising field opened to them, they removed without hesitation and with little trouble. Many of their papers had but a short lease on life."

The first newspaper printed west of Albany was issued on July 11, 1793 in the village of New Hartford, then a part of the town of Whitestown. It was called the "Whitestown Gazette" and its proprietors were Jedediah Sanger, Samuel Wells and Elijah Risley, with Richard Vosburg as the printer. The venture was not successful and the publication lapsed during the winter of that year. In January 1794, a second paper was started at Whitesboro, named the "Western Centinel" with Oliver P. Eaton as the printer. This paper continued for about six years.

Samuel Wells resumed the "Whitestown Gazette" with William McLean as the printer. McLean was born in Hartford, Connecticut on December 2, 1774. A short time after he began to work for the paper, he purchased the business and finding New Hartford less promising than the growing village of Utica, he removed his printing plant to the west side of Genesee street, a few doors south of Whitesboro street. There he began publishing Utica's first newspaper, the "Whitestown Gazette & Cato's Patrol". In 1803, McLean sold his paper to Ira Merrell and Asahel Seward, two young men to whom he had taught the printer's trade. McLean died on March 12, 1848 at Cherry Valley, New York, where he published the famous "Cherry Valley Gazette".

Another early printer was Thomas Walker, who was born in Rehoboth, Massachusetts on November 18, 1777. Learning the printer's trade, he came to Rome and with Ebenezer Eaton, his brother-in-law, began on August 17, 1799, the publication of the "Columbian Patriotic Gazette." Finding the possibilities at Utica more promising, he removed his paper here and on March 21, 1803 began publication of the "Columbian Gazette". Dr. Bagg in his "Pioneers of Utica" described this paper:

> "Its dimensions were ten and a half by twelve inches, and the paper was coarse and dingy. The second page and about half of the third, was devoted to foreign news, editorials and communications; the remainder was filled with advertisements. The office was located near 44 Genesee street. Its sign was a large square one, containing a portrait of Benjamin Franklin — the familiar one, which represents him with his chin resting on his hand, and his spectacles pushed back upon his forehead."

For twenty-two years, Walker published the "Gazette" and finally sold it to Samuel D. Dakin and William J. Bacon, the owners of the rival "Utica Sentinel". At the age of 86, Walker died on June 13, 1863.

When Ira Merrell and Asahel Seward purchased and began publishing the "Whitestown Gazette & Cato's Patrol", they brought in as editor John H. Lothrop, the son-in-law of Rev. Samuel Kirkland. Lothrop was born in New Haven, Connecticut on May 1, 1769 and was educated at Yale. He was a writer of fluent and graceful English and possessed culture and a lively wit. A short time later, he became the paper's publisher and to distinguish it from the rival "Columbian Gazette", he renamed the paper from the "Whitestown Gazette" to the "Utica Patriot". He was very successful and sold the paper in 1811 to William H. Maynard. Lothrop retired to New Hartford, but later came back to Utica as the cashier of the Ontario Branch Bank. He died June 15, 1829. William Hale Maynard was born in Conway, Massachusetts and moved to New Hartford where he studied law with General Joseph Kirkland. He succeeded Lathrop as editor of "The Utica Patriot" in 1811.

Merrell and Seward were the printers of Lothrop's paper for some years. William Williams, the famous Utica printer was born in Framingham, Massachusetts and came to New Hartford with his father, Deacon Thomas Williams. He learned the printer's trade from Asahel Seward and became a partner in 1808. Ira Merrell's eyesight began to fail and he moved to Geneva. Until 1821, Seward and Williams printed the "Patriot". Seward & Williams commenced printing "The Patrol" on January 1, 1815 and continued until January 2, 1816, when it was merged with the "Patriot" under the name of the "Utica Patriot & Patrol". It was issued semi-weekly, Tuesdays and Fridays, for about a year, then weekly on Tuesdays until 1821.

Alexander Seward in his paper, "The Genealogy of a Utica Newspaper" delivered before the Oneida Historical Society in 1878, said:

> "The 'Utica Sentinel' appeared in the place of the 'Patriot and Patrol' March 13, 1821. The cause of this change of name was somewhat peculiar. The 'Patriot and Patrol' was Clintonian in its politics, representing the sentiments of the large majority of voters in this district. The politics of the editor changed and the tone of the paper also. An alarming loss of patronage naturally followed. The arrangement being practicable between the parties in interest, the 'Patriot and Patrol' was dropped by its publisher, under the advice of prominent Clintonian lawyers and the 'Utica Sentinel,' printed by Ira Merrell for William Williams, editor and proprietor appeared in its stead."

The "Utica Sentinel" was sold to Samuel D. Dakin and William J. Bacon. Samuel Dana Dakin was born in Jeffrey, New Hampshire on July 16, 1802 and came with his parents in 1815 to New Hartford. In 1821 he graduated from Hamilton College and in 1823 entered the law office of Joseph Kirkland. William J. Bacon was born in Williamstown, Massachusetts on February 18, 1803. He came to Utica with his family in 1815 and graduated from Hamilton College in 1822, at the age of 19. Immediately thereafter he entered the law office of General Kirkland. It was while the two men were still law students that they purchased the "Sentinel" and united it with the old "Columbian Gazette." On May 6, 1825 they issued the "Utica Sentinel & Gazette", Northway & Bennett printed the paper until April 1, 1828 when Northway and Porter took over as printers. Rufus Northway had learned the printer's trade from Ira Merrell and completed his apprenticeship in 1825. In 1829, Northway & Porter purchased the paper.

The "Utica Intelligencer" was commenced February 2, 1826, with William Tracy as editor and proprietor, and was printed for one year by Ira Merrell, and thereafter by Joseph Colwell. The "Mechanic's Press" was commenced in 1829 by J. M. Todd and W. Schram and shortly thereafter the two papers were merged and published as the "Utica Intelligencer & Mechanic's Press" by Joseph Colwell, proprietor.

"The Elucidator", the organ of the anti-Masonic party, was commenced January 1, 1829 by Beriah B. Hotchkin, as editor and proprietor, and was published from January 1, 1830 by William Williams as editor and publisher. The first number of the "American Citizen" appeared June 8, 1830, with George S. Wilson as editor and proprietor. In January 1831, the "American Citizen", and August 7, 1832, the "Utica Intelligencer" were united with the "Sentinel & Gazette". Finally, the "Elucidator" also merged with the "Sentinel" and the combined paper was issued May 20, 1834 under the name of the "Oneida Whig", Rufus Northway, printer and publisher.

The only rival weekly paper in 1832 was the "Utica Observer". Eliasaph Dorchester was born in 1780, a son of Stephen Dorchester, the Utica hatter, a native of Farmington, Connecticut. In 1808, when his father died, Eliasaph Dorchester was teaching a grammar school in the Welsh church on Hotel street. A short time later, he joined Thomas Walker in the management of the "Columbian Gazette". In 1816, he established the "Utica Observer". Ere long he transferred the paper to Rome, but in the latter part of 1819 or early 1820, he brought it back to Utica and continued to publish it for a time. He served as county clerk from 1821 to 1823 and then returned to teaching. He died in July 1864, at the age of 84 years.

Augustine G. Dauby, in 1823, a printer in the Observer office became editor and publisher. He took as a partner in 1826 Eli Maynard. Maynard became the sole proprietor when Mr. Dauby was made postmaster of Utica by President Jackson and served in that position from May 1829 until May 1849.

THE EARLY SCHOOLS OF UTICA

IN pioneer days, education was not given a very high priority. It was largely a private matter, sponsored usually by religious groups. The teacher was generally the minister of a church and not infrequently the school was conducted by the sexton. The annual term was short; girls were not admitted, and the salary of the teacher was from fifty cents to $1.50 per week and board. The first known school house in the village was located on the south side of Main street, and in 1797 Joseph Dana, an excellent teacher and disciplinarian was the instructor. Blandina Dudley Miller in the "Utica Observer" of December 21, 1900 gave a description of the building:

"It was never painted by man and the clouds of many years had poured rain upon it and stained it with a dark hue. Here and there, the nails were starting from their fastenings and fellow clapboards were becoming less closely intimate. There were six windows with fractures, patches and seams here and there. The shutters were of board. The wood burned in the long, low, flat stove was piled in the yard. Within were the backless benches on which the smaller scholars sat. The two oldest males in the school occupied a special seat and had a writing bench. There was a spelling or reading parade and the desk or pulpit, a plain slab or shelf, was at the eastern extremity. The seats were in part actual slabs of rough boards without backs resting upon legs inserted in auger holes. The room was imperfectly warmed by the box stove. The teacher who presided on week days esconced himself on the left of the entrance. There were two terms of school in the year — one in winter under a master and one in summer ruled by a mistress. This building was used as a place of worship until the completion of Trinity Church in 1806. As a school house and a place for town meetings, it held out a little longer, but after the stove had been sold at auction in 1808, its usefulness departed."

In 1807, Jonathan Child kept a school in the Welsh church on the corner of Washington and Whitesboro streets, but he didn't remain very long. He was succeeded in 1808 by Eliasaph Dorchester, who combined his teaching activities with the founding in 1816 of the weekly newspaper, the "Observer". Just above Elizabeth street on the east side where Grace Church now stands was the two-story "Dixon School House", presided over by Rev. David R. Dixon. Dixon's school was "Federal" in politics in contrast with that of Dorchester, whose pupils were from the "Democratic" families of the village. Mr. Dixon left the area in 1813.

About 1808, a building was designed and erected as a school house on the east side of Genesee street, south of Catharine street. This was used for a time as a place of worship by the Methodists. In 1812, Professor P. H. Ingraham was teaching school in the Welsh church on the corner of Washington and Whitesboro streets. Thomas Jones, the blacksmith, was a trustee of the church and it was his duty to give Professor Ingraham receipts for the tuition he collected. When these were presented to Jones for signature, the latter was asked to sign them at the bottom of the sheet, which he did. Apparently the teacher's moral qualities were not as high as his intellectual capabilities, and he proceeded to write above Jones' signature, promissory notes. Professor Andrew McMillan in his sketch of the early schools of Utica wrote:

"For this offense he was tried and sentenced to State prison for a term of seven years and two days, but he was pardoned before the expiration of the sentence. He then emigrated to Texas, and in the course of time was elected to the Legislature, and became Speaker of the House. This incident is mentioned rather as illustrating the mutability of human affairs, than as an incentive to 'go and do likewise!' "

About 1812, Miss Rebecca Dickens came to Utica to live with her aunt, Miss Mary Flagg and soon after opened a select school in her home on Whitesboro street. The school was very popular, Whitesboro street being then a leading residential street in the village. The building was not a large one. The two women used the back part for living quarters, and a part of the front was a parlor. The rest was a school room. It was small and very plainly furnished, but a great many scholars were crowded into it. Plain wooden benches served for seating and a plain table ran along one side of the room. In winter, the school room was warmed by a box stove, in which hemlock was used as fuel.

Miss Dickens taught school the year round. There were five holidays — New Years', General Training (for the militia), the Fourth of July, Thanksgiving and Christmas. School began at 9 o'clock and continued until noon; business was resumed at 1 and closed at 4, with no recess. Also, school was kept half a day on Saturday morning during the early years. The terms were twelve weeks, and the charge was a shilling a week for each pupil.

Miss Dickens was rather a short woman, inclined to stoutness. She generally stood or sat near the door of the room during school hours, and her glasses and cap left an impression. She invariably did knitting or needle work when hearing lessons, and she knew the books so well that she did not keep them open before her. She would give out word after word from the spelling book in the order in which they occurred, to the wonder of her pupils. She grounded her scholars well in spelling, arithmetic, reading, geography and English history. In the matter of discipline, she was an expert. At her sewing she wore a thimble and for all the minor offenses, a few raps of this upon the cranium were sufficient. For the more serious offenses, a short ruler was employed. She taught school there for some forty years and died in Brooklyn about 1865. The old building was razed in 1885 to make way for a two story store and residence.

In 1813, a private school was in operation, conducted on the third story of a building on the north corner of Broad and Genesee streets. It was known as the Juvenile Academy and consisted of a large hall, designed for a Masonic lodge, and two small rooms in the rear. The first teacher was Henry White and instruction was given to both male and female students in all the branches of a classical education.

In 1813, nineteen citizens of Utica petitioned the Regents of the State for permission to incorporate an Academy in the village. A charter was granted on March 28, 1814 and subscriptions were taken to build the Academy on the west side of Chancellor Square (now Academy Street). It was to serve three purposes — a school, a town hall and a court house. It was a brick two-story building, fifty by sixty feet with a wide hall; one large room on the north and two smaller on the south side of the first floor; and the whole upper floor was the court room which also served as a town hall.

The school was a private high school under a board of trustees and the pupils paid tuition which varied from three to five dollars per quarter. It opened in 1818 with the Rev. Samuel T. Mills as "preceptor" at a salary of $800. In 1868, J. Watson Williams lectured on the history of the old academy and said:

> "it was never commodious for its purpose, and was ill calculated to serve the double purpose it was destined to. Constables were required to stand guard during play hours to stifle urchin's shouts, while the sacred silence of study hours was interrupted by the tread and turmoil of throngs of jurymen, witnesses, attorneys and judges; to say nothing of the pleasant grievances of being routed out of this or that recitation room to make way for the jurymen about to cast lots or toss coppers for verdicts."

In 1853, the control of the school passed to the school commissioners and the high school became part of a free public school system.

The first free school was established when the Legislature in April 1817 passed an Act that all school moneys for the education of poor children must be used for such purpose. The trustees of the village were authorized to raise a sum not to exceed $100 per year in support of such free schools. In the same year, a school building was erected on the south side of Catharine street, nearly opposite Franklin street, and Ignatius Thompson was selected as teacher. Two years later, the Lancaster system, developed by Joseph Lancaster in England, which allowed the older children to teach the younger, was instituted. Andrew l'Amoureux became the teacher. He was followed by Roswell Holcomb in 1824 and in 1828 by Rev. Joseph Carter, when the school had 150 pupils in attendance. Then Eliasaph Dorchester took over as teacher.

In 1824, a private school was established on the northwest corner of John and Catharine streets, conducted by Rev. William Woodbridge, a very successful teacher from Connecticut. In 1826, Mr. and Mrs. Everts Seminary for Young Ladies was established on the southern side of Whitesboro street in one of the houses of the Culver block. Across the street were the hospitable and gracious houses of Judge Nathan Williams and Henry Seymour, whose large families made their houses a gathering place for young people, including the Everts' students. The large parlors were used for rehearsals of music for the concerts which formed an important part of the course of studies in the school.

A private school for boys, known as the Utica High School, later as the "Utica Gymnasium", was founded by Charles Bartlett and flourished about eight years. Mr. Bartlett leased for his purpose the house and farm at the lower end of Broad street which had belonged to Doctor Solomon Wolcott and was then owned by Samuel Stocking. The house was a large wooden building, three quarters of a mile from Genesee street, standing back from the line of Broad street on an elevation which commanded a fine view of the Mohawk valley. The farm which was attached to the house reached a little beyond the present Kossuth avenue and southward some distance toward Albany street and contained 60 to 80 acres, having a large garden and orchard. Joseph Bartlett, the brother of Charles, was in charge of the farm.

The school opened in the autumn of 1827, with an annual attendance at the school of upwards of forty. The annual tuition was $200, which later was reduced to $150. Bartlett was a good teacher, although not a profound one and he was a strict disciplinarian. The school gave instruction in English, Latin and Greek, lectures in chemistry, botany, mineralogy and other sciences. Gymnastic, horseback riding, swimming and gardening were also part of the curriculum. The pupils were required to attend church every Sunday and were instructed in the Bible on Sunday evening.

A new school house was erected on the further side of the playground, three stories in height, with entrances on each side to the lower rooms and stairways leading to those above. The second story contained a school room and four recitation rooms, while the third floor was one large dormitory. A later built school house was still more unique in character and stood farther eastward than the former ones. It was of brick, two stories high, but with only one room and semi-circular in form, with its flat side and entrances toward the street. Around the inside of the whole half circle were ranged two series of stalls, one above the other, and wide enough for a single desk in each. Thus each pupil was unable to communicate with his neighbor and was in plain view of his teacher who sat opposite in the center of the circle. A fire in the year 1835 destroyed the second of the school houses and so disrupted the establishment that Bartlett abandoned it and moved to Poughkeepsie where he conducted a successful school until his death.

There were a number of other private schools. In 1829, Mrs. Adams' and Chamberlain's school was on Whitesboro street, west of Washington; Miss Jones' school was on Hotel street; Miss Stevens' school on Whitesboro, west of Division.

In 1830, an act of the Legislature was passed empowering the village trustees to establish schools at their pleasure and distribute the public money as they deemed best. The next year it was decided to sell the free school on Catharine street and purchase another elsewhere. For a time after this, the school was held in the Session room of the Second Presbyterian Church, at the corner of Elizabeth and Charlotte street. In the same school year, a school district was established in the eastern part of the village and a school opened at the corner of Minden turnpike and East street. At this time, Utica had a population of 8,500 and the number of private schools was over thirty in number.

EARLY BANKING AND CURRENCY

PRIOR to the year 1810, the money in circulation as the medium of exchange locally was silver, mostly Spanish milled coinage. The paper money in circulation consisted of banknotes issued by various State banks in various denominations. These were promissory notes, payable on demand at the issuing bank in coinage. The acceptance of these banknotes depended upon the reputation of the issuing bank, since many were issued by "wildcat" banks which could not be located for payment. In this area, bank bills were few and consisted of the notes of eastern banks. For loans, Utica business men had to depend upon Albany banks.

The beginning of banking operations in Utica dates from the arrival here in 1809 of Montgomery Hunt. He was sent to the little village to organize a branch of the Manhattan Bank of New York. He opened an office in a small building that stood back from the west line of Hotel street, a little south of Whitesboro street. In July 1809, the lot on the corner of these streets was purchased and a brick building was erected thereon as a bank. In those days banks were constructed along the lines of a private home. The Manhattan Branch Bank continued in existence until 1818 when the development of local banks removed the incentive for the branch bank. The old building was then used as a private residence and in 1827 Colonel John E. Hinman, a veteran of the War of 1812 occupied the house and made it his home for about forty years. He was sheriff from 1821 to 1831 and Mayor of Utica from 1850 to 1853. The "Saturday Globe" once described him:

> "With his title he acquired a military bearing, with which he was wont to impress people. He permitted his hair to grow long and topped his tall frame with a rusty plug hat, as was the style in the old days. He also clung to a large military cloak, which, with his title, served to remind people of his war service."

In February 1811, influential citizens were invited to attend a meeting for the purpose of organizing a local bank. The Bank of Utica was incorporated on June 1st, 1812 and began business on December 8th, with Montgomery Hunt as cashier. He soon became known as an able and skillful financier. During the War of 1812, the Bank of Utica advanced large sums of money to the federal government and was well rewarded for its financial support. The signature of Montgomery Hunt was accepted throughout the country as a pledge of financial security.

In 1813, a double-winged brick structure was erected on the north side of Whitesboro street next easterly to the York Hotel. The bank was located there until 1854 when it was moved to the southeast corner of Genesee and Catharine streets. In 1865 it became a national bank, under the name of First National Bank. Hunt's family dwelt originally in the old bank building during the early years and here were spent the boyhood years of his son, Ward Hunt, who later was to serve on the New York Court of Appeals and as an Associate Justice of the United States Supreme Court.

Following the removal of the Bank to Genesee street, the

old bank building became the property of John Butterfield. He remodeled the building, altered the interior; added the wings and built a cupola. The Butterfield family occupied the house for some years. The "Utica Saturday Globe" in 1897 wrote:

> "A feature of the old bank building which clings to the memory of many Uticans were the great stone dollars which surmounted the building. These were carved representations obverse and reverse of the $10 gold piece of 1812. When the building was remodeled by Mr. Butterfield these disappeared. Thirty years later they reappeared in a spot where hundreds of Uticans have since seen them. They now decorate the cashier's room of the First National Bank. Cashier John A. Goodale told a "Globe" reporter yesterday the story of their disappearance and resurrection. When Mr. Butterfield remodeled the old building the carved stone was thrown into a heap of rubbish. Subsequently when that distinguished Utican built the hostelry which bears his name — the Butterfield House — this rubbish was carted up there to use in filling. When the load was dumped into a ditch, Mr. Butterfield saw the stone and recognized its historic value, gave it to John G. Brown, who was a director of the Bank of Utica. Mr. Brown had it removed to the rear of his store, Warnick & Brown's in Burchard Lane, where it remained until 1884. At that time an addition was made to the First National Bank Building and upon Mr. Brown's suggestion the stone was built into the walls of the cashier's room."

The third early banking institution in Utica was the Ontario Branch Bank, associated with a Canandaigua Bank of the same name. It began business here in December 1815, erecting a building on the west side of Genesee street where the Commercial Travelers Mutual Accident Association now stands. The facade of brick and brown stone was regarded as one of the most ornamental in the village and was considered the handsomest structure in Utica. Four stone Ionic columns supported the pediment which was crowned with three gracefully draped urns. The face was further enriched by festooned panels.

A history of this bank would be incomplete without reference to its dominant figure, Alexander B. Johnson, the leading capitalist in the village before the War of 1812. He was born in Gosport, England in 1786, a son of the famous merchant, Bryan Johnson. He came here in 1801 to keep his father's books. In 1812, he wrote a treatise on finance which attracted considerable attention in the business world and labeled him as a skillful financier.

During the legislative session of 1815-16, he succeeded in having the State incorporate the Utica Insurance Company which proceeded to erect a building on the corner of Division and Whitesboro streets. The charter seemed to convey permission only to insure property, but was so skillfully drafted that in reality, it granted banking privileges as well, to the chagrin of the existing banks who would have opposed the granting of a new bank charter. There ensued a war of the financiers. Both the Bank of Utica and the Ontario Bank endeavored in every way possible to embarrass the new company. The Legislature finally passed a law prohibiting companies who were carrying on other businesses from engaging in banking. On July 6th, 1819 the Utica Insurance Company was dissolved, the outstanding policies of insurance being transferred to a New York insurance company. All debts were liquidated with only trifling loss to the stockholders.

In June 1819, Alexander Johnson became a director of the Ontario Branch Bank and in September its president. In 1855, the bank severed its connection with the Canandaigua Bank and became the Ontario Bank. For 38 years Johnson successfully managed the bank but the financial panic of 1857 forced the bank to close. Johnson died in 1867. Upon the closing of the bank the building was idle for four years, three of which represented the time during which F. A. Wetmore as receiver was winding up the affairs of the bank. The steps were removed and the floor lowered to the level of the street and the building was converted into a store. In 1861, it was taken over by William S. Taylor who continued a clothing manufacturing business there until 1892. The building was then occupied by the Oneida County Bank. In 1900 it was vacated by the bank which consolidated with the First National Bank and the building was fitted out as the home of the Commercial Travelers Association.

EARLY MANUFACTURING IN UTICA

AT the end of the Colonial period, manufacturing in America was of little importance as agriculture was the dominant enterprise in the new nation. The word "manufacture" means literally "made by hand". Machine production scarcely existed before 1790. In that year spinning machinery was set up in Rhode Island and when Whitney invented the cotton gin in 1794, a supply of raw material for cotton manufacture was assured. It was not until 1810 that machinery was generally introduced there for textile manufacture. New England's rivers furnished the water power for the operation of the machinery, and in this respect Utica was sorely deficient. Sauquoit Creek furnished the power for the textile plants which grew up along its banks in New Hartford and Whitestown. The Mohawk river, until the building of the Erie Canal was the main artery of travel and without the erection of dams could not be used for power. There was Nail Creek in West Utica but it was a small stream and Ballou Creek in East Utica, also without sufficient volume of water. The early manufacturing in Utica was thus limited to the hand trades, such as blacksmithing, tinsmithing, and harness and carriage making, in which little, if any power machinery was used.

Nail Creek which has disappeared underground as part of Utica's sewage system was called by the Germans who settled there "Nagel Creek." The origin of the name is uncertain but William Smith commonly known as "Nailer Smith" manufactured nails of wrought iron on the bank of the creek, which flowed through what is now the south side of Varick street. About 1813, Joseph Masseth established on its banks a factory for making wrought iron nails. His bellows were operated by two dogs, who in turn ran along a treadmill. The newspapers of the time carried stories of the "dog nail factory", as it was called. Masseth did well financially from his operation and retired to East Utica, where he died June 11, 1852 at the age of 59 years.

In the spring of 1803, David P. Hoyt migrated to Utica from Danbury, Connecticut. By trade he was a tanner and currier and shoemaker. He opened a store on the west side of Genesee road, above Whitesboro street, where in later years was located the Roberts Hardware store. There he carried on an extensive business in shoes and leather. He built a tannery on Whitesboro street beyond Broadway and adjoining the lane which was to become Hoyt Street. He lived at the northeast corner of Whitesboro and Hoyt Lane and owned most of the land in the area bounded by Genesee, Liberty and Whitesboro streets. On Hoyt street he built a number of vats and a windmill to grind the bark used in the tanning process. The "Utica Directory" of 1828 contains the following description:

> "D. P. Hoyt's Tannery, has 110 vats, covered with buildings. Annual amount of manufactures, 6000 sides sole leather; 2500 calf skins; and a proportionate number of sheep and other skins. Employs 16 men, and $30,000 capital. A wind-mill invented by Mullinix, of Long Island, is attached to this tannery. It consists of perpendicular wings, of wood, describing a circle whose diameter is 82 feet. This, with a fair wind, grinds 6 cords of bark a day."

This old landmark was the subject of an article in the "Utica Saturday Globe" of December 29, 1888:

> "Thousands of Uticans have gazed curiously on the circular building now used as a tenement, marveled at its structure and wondered as to why it was ever built. It is perfectly round and the clapboards on the exterior are each bent a little to conform to the surface of the structure. The building is part of the old Hoyt estate and has a history of its own. It was built in the year 1824 for the purpose of grinding bark for David P. Hoyt's tannery, at that time the largest in the State and running 237 vats of the tannery proper. Nothing remains but a small stone part where the leech was. In the upper part of the 'round house' was the bark mill and the power was furnished by an immense windmill. This windmill was the most expensive structure of the kind in this country and probably Europe never had one its equal. The lower part of the building was used for storing the ground bark as it fell from the mill above. The tannery was run in connection with Mr. Hoyt's leather store at that time where the John E. Roberts & Co. are now, and Mr. Hoyt had branch stores in Buffalo and Sackett's Harbor. Edward Curran was the superintendent of the tannery and used to tell wonderful stories of what the old and tireless windmill could do. About 30 years ago the tannery was abandoned, and now nothing remains but the 'round house' and the stone structure referred to."

In 1912, this remnant of the old windmill was razed.

William Inman was born in Somerset, England and came to this country in June 1792 as the agent of Patrick Colquhoun, the High Sheriff of London, for whom he purchased a large tract of land in Lewis county. Impressed with the little hamlet of old Fort Schuyler he leased in 1793 fifty-three acres of land from Rutger Bleecker, consisting of a farm lying halfway between the ruins of the old fort and Whitesboro. He first lived in a house on the north side of the Whitesboro road, opposite the spot where the Halfway Bridge over the Erie canal was later to be constructed. "Disgusted with the 'Yankee dust' which reached him from the highway," he built a larger house which stood quite back from the road on the south side and which was known as Champlin house.

In 1804, he erected the first brewery in Utica on the northwest corner of Broadway and Whitesboro streets, where he brewed English ale. He then built a house for his own use on the east side of Broadway, just above the corner of Whitesboro street. He moved to New York city about 1813. For a few years afterward, the old brewery was not in use, except for a short time, during which it was used as a theater for the presentation of "morality plays" by a man from Albany. In 1817 it was taken over by William Harden as the "Utica Brewery" and "Harden Brewery." On February 20th, 1827, the brewery owned by Mr. John Harden, situate at the corner of Broadway and Whitesboro street, was discovered on fire, and was burnt, together with his dwelling house adjoining, to the ground. ("Sentinel & Gazette", Feb. 23, 1827).

Sometime prior to 1827, Matthew Codd operated a brewery at the old basin in East Utica, called the "Gulf Brewery" where he produced and sold "new beer of fine flavor and strength" and also Irish whiskey. The brewery was later taken over by John C. Devereux who then sold it to Michael McQuade, who conducted the business for half a century.

On the banks of Starch Factory Creek, in East Utica in 1807, John Gilbert began to make starch, being joined in 1812 by his brother Edward. The story of the old starch factory was related in the "Saturday Globe" in 1904:

> "Three quarters of a century ago, Edward Gilbert, an English gentleman of the old school, whose heart was as warm as his head was cool, built a starch factory on his vast property near the Herkimer county line. His lands extended from Broad street to a point considerably south of Bleecker street, covering several hundred

acres. He was prominent in the Broad Street Baptist church, and in this relation, as well as in matters of business, was esteemed an upright man. His residence was a two story brick building, of unpretentious design, but delightfully situated amid huge trees and surrounded by a well kept lawn. Hospitality reigned and the neighbors ever found a welcome at the Gilbert home.

"The Starch Factory was a low wooden building which stood east of the dwelling. Some of the foundation stones can still be seen. Power was supplied to it from dams situated on the south side of the Erie Canal, and water came through a pipe under the canal. Those pipes were found a few years ago when the canal was enlarged, and remains of the dam can still be seen near the addition to the Utica Pipe Foundry. The process of making starch was crude, and weeks were required where days now suffice. The starch was extracted from corn, wheat, potatoes and other vegetables, and its separation from the other elements was secured by mashers and a series of troughs running from the top to the bottom of the building settling in the troughs and drying there. It was then put up in the boxes as at the present time and shipped to all parts of the country. About 40 men were employed.

"The starch industry in Utica at one time was the largest in the State. With the discovery of new processes by Kingsford and the establishment of the Oswego Mills, the Gilbert factory began to decline and closed before the Civil War. Mr. Gilbert lived in comfort the rest of his life. His son went to Little Falls and descendants are still living there, prominent in business and socially. The property was gradually divided and sold and today, a once flourishing industry is only a memory."

In tracking the development of the industrial occupations that have found a place in Utica's history, we discover that the pottery industry was established here early in the nineteenth century. The exact date is unknown, but it is said that as early as 1819, a man named Nash had two small clay potteries on Whitesboro street. A few years later, between 1820 and 1828, Samuel Addington commenced the manufacture of stoneware upon or near the extensive works of Messrs. N. A. White & Sons, a well-known pottery establishment.

Noah White was a native of Bradford, Vermont and lived in Vernon for some years with his family. At the age of 35 he moved to Utica to work for Mr. Addington. A few years later,

White conducted the business with Addington furnishing the buildings and machinery. Soon, Noah White purchased the business outright and in 1840 took his son, Nicholas as a partner. The building was quite small at first, but soon building after building was added until it occupied an area of 400 feet frontage on Whitesboro street, extending back to the Erie Canal. The goods manufactured in 1840 were common stoneware; then firebrick was added and later sewer pipe.

When Noah White died in 1866, Nicholas White became the head of the firm. He was alderman and supervisor of the old Sixth Ward and he took as his partner his son, William N. White under the name of N. A. White & Sons. Nicholas A. White died in 1886 and William White took his son, Charles, into the firm and made him the head. Just prior to the death of the senior White, extensive alterations were made. The old fashioned method of forming the different shapes of stoneware by turning the same on a table with foot power was discarded and new machinery enabled them to produce equally fine goods with less skilled labor. Four great kilns belched forth volumes of flame and smoke, while their interiors contained thousands of pieces of stoneware undergoing the process of baking.

Stone beer mugs were almost an exclusive product of Germany and as a consequence of their cost, were not in general use in this country. The production of beer by the German brewers of West Utica created a demand and White produced these mugs about 1888 and they were not only fully equal in all respects to the best of the imported ones, but also in many respects superior. In color they were bluish gray, with deep indigo blue decorations. Since most potteries were unable to obtain a suitable coloring and produced plain mugs, White developed a secret process of coloring composition, which made them distinctive. Up to 1889, firebrick and the coarser grade of stoneware were produced, but thereafter the manufacture of fine Flemish ware was taken up and it was the only plant in the United States which produced this grade of goods.

White's Pottery was the last stoneware plant in the State of New York to yield to the changes of time. The cost of material proved to be excessive. In 1906, the firebrick machinery in the old plant was shipped to Hayes, Pennsylvania, where the Hayes Firebrick Company utilized it in their business. The property in West Utica was sold to the Capron Knitting Company which remodelled it and used it for a bleachery, dye house and similar purposes.

Examples of White pottery are considered to be greatly desired items for collectors because of the artistry of design. Birds, flowers and animals were commonly found on the stoneware. W. C. Ketchum, Jr. in 1970 in his "Early Potters and Potteries" wrote:

> "Many of the most luxuriantly decorated crocks and jugs were made here, including some which bore astonishing cobalt peacocks, the largest of which were over two feet high. The traditional flower patterns from Utica also often had a vigor lacking in their counterparts from the more eastern potteries."

Alfred Munson was born in Barhamstead, Connecticut in 1793. He came to the village of Utica and in 1823 opened a shop in the basement of the Kirkland block on the corner of Hotel and Liberty streets, where he began the manufacture of burr-stones, millstones cut from siliceous rock. The business became successful and he soon removed to Washington street at the Erie Canal and about 1855 to the west side of Broadway at the canal and in 1868 to the east side of Broadway. His daughter, Helen E. Munson married J. Watson Williams. Mr. Munson was a most charitable man and gave at least one-tenth of his estate to various charities and to Grace Church. He died May 6, 1854.

From the earliest days when the settlers here had to carry their grain to a grist mill at Canajoharie, there had been agitation for the erection of a similar mill in the village. Such a mill required water power for its operation and the only available supply was the Mohawk River. Dr. Bagg writes:

> "Despite all opposition an act was obtained from the legislature in 1823, a dam was thrown across the river in September two or three rods below the bridge, and a mill erected for the grinding of flour with three runs of stone. The dam was erected by William Alverson for the proprietors, Messrs. Parker & Seymour. The first miller employed not succeeding to the satisfaction of the owners, Ira D. Hopkins was at the end of three months engaged to run the mill, and he continued to do so while it was in operation. But ere long parties owning property on the river some miles above complained that their land was flooded by the setting back of the water to a height, as they alleged, of four feet. A suit was brought against the mill owners, and although it proved unsuccessful it impaired the popularity and custom of the mill so that when a second suit was afterwards begun they anticipated its verdict by giving up their enterprise. This was about 1829."

Dr. Bagg also wrote that the mill was destroyed by fire on November 18, 1834 and that "the dam below which it was located and which had been the cause of much litigation was soon broken up and was never rebuilt."

In 1828, Ballou Creek drained into the Mohawk river through a culvert which ran under the Erie Canal. This was stopped up and "Miller's Basin" was created by allowing the water of the canal to back up the creek. The "Utica Sentinel & Gazette" of February 14, 1832 contains the following advertisement:

> "Extensive Flouring Mill. An extensive mill establishment has just been completed in this town by J. E. Bloomfield, Esq. It is located near the Great Basin, and the machinery is propelled by the surplus water of the Erie Canal, at that point. The building is very large and substantially built, the timber being the best we ever saw; and it is constructed for carrying four runs of stone. When the establishment shall get in full operation, which we understand will be shortly, the benefits will be extensively felt both in town and country; and the public will feel under many obligations to Mr. Bloomfield, to whose enterprize, sagacity and persevering energy, we are chiefly indebted for so valuable an improvement."

The Utica City Flour Mill continued in operation until shortly after midnight on April 19, 1870 when it burned to the ground. The massive brick chimney, 165 feet in height, withstood the ravages of the fire. The constant flow of the mill steam over the water-wheel and flume, and adjacent areas, saved these. A few blackened, crumbling walls and casements were all that remained of the once prosperous flour milling industry in Utica.

The making of soap and candles had its origin in 1812, in the old market house near Bagg's Square. In compliance with an ordinance of the village board declaring that the market place was unfit for such an industry, it was removed in 1814 to the north side of Water street near Division. In this building the manufacture of soap and candles was begun in 1830 by two men named Boyd and Chamberlain. Mr. Chamberlain died in 1832 and the rights of the surviving partner were purchased by John and Stephen Thorn, who were not related. John Thorn, who had learned the business in England had been an employee of the old firm, and Stephen Thorn conducted the business until 1835, when he sold out his interest. The business had meanwhile been removed to the south side of Water street.

56

In 1837, John Thorn took as a partner, Isaac Maynard, his brother-in-law. John had married Mary Maynard in 1833. The business grew to large proportions and gave them a profitable return. In the year 1840, they purchased the wool and pelt business of James DeLong, then located at Whitesboro and Water street, which they continued until 1870.

In 1839, Benjamin Cahoon began the manufacture of soap and candles at Nail creek, on the south side of Whitesboro street, near Wiley. James S. Kirk was born in Glasgow, Scotland of Scottish parentage in 1818 and came with them to Canada when he was a year old. There he grew up and married Nancy Dunning and the couple came to Utica in 1839 seeking to find employment here. He found this employment with Benjamin Cahoon and worked for him until this business was taken over by Thorn & Maynard. Accumulating sufficient funds, he went into partnership with Thorn & Maynard.

In 1860, Thorn & Maynard viewed Chicago as a favorable place to establish a soap and candle business and James S. Kirk went there and opened a small plant. He was successful until the great fire of 1872 destroyed the plant. Thorn & Maynard desired to withdraw from J. S. Kirk & Co., and sold their interest to Kirk in 1876 who built a new plant. In Utica only soap and candles were manufactured. In Chicago, Kirk added a full line of toilet soaps and perfume and the business grew to large proportions and became one of the largest and most successful in the world. When he died on June 16, 1886 in Chicago, he was a millionaire. He had seven sons and a daughter. His eldest son, James Alexander Kirk was born in Utica in December 1839 and was the head of the firm after his father's death until his own death in Wisconsin on February 22, 1907. John B. Kirk was born in Utica in November 1842 and was vice president of the firm at the time of his death on November 1, 1904.

William Heath was born in Corsham, England in 1818 and came to Utica in the spring of 1845 and was employed by the Kirk firm until 1849. He went to Oswego and returned four years later, forming a partnership with Isaac Maynard under the firm name of Maynard, Heath & Co. which continued until 1857. In that year Mr. Heath left the firm and joined the partnership of J. Tavender and Co. as Heath & Tavender. In 1866, they acquired possession of the West Utica plant of Thorn & Maynard and there they continued the soap and candle business until 1885 when Mr. Heath retired.

The old plant became vacant and the "Utica Herald-Dispatch" on January 4, 1902 reported that E. F. Downer & Sons had purchased the "old soap factory" from the Tavender estate and was demolishing it to erect a two-story retail lumber yard and salesroom.

John Reed was born in Wales and came to this country in 1801. He was a carpenter and knowing that carpenter's planes were mostly imported and costly, he decided to make his own. In 1826 the first plane ever made here and among the first manufactured in the United States, was fashioned in the low ceiling kitchen of an old house standing at 46 Elizabeth street. He continued the business in his kitchen, each plane being fashioned by hand. Later he built a shop in the rear of the house and sharpened his knives on a huge grindstone. In this plant, twelve journeymen and two apprentices were kept busy. Dana & Co., the hardware dealers on Genesee street sold all the planes Reed could make. The old weather-beaten shop was remodelled into a livery stable about 1895.

Iron manufacture in Utica, which was later to become an important part of local industry, developed slowly. Machinery of improved types were introduced in the 1810s and 1820s but the greater part of the work was carried on in a primitive fashion, until the 1850s when anthracite began to be substituted for charcoal in smelting. Thereafter the increase in production was rapid.

Seth Peckham of Troy, settled in Westmoreland in 1817 and in 1819 moved to No. 22 Catharine street in Utica where he began the manufacture of ploughs and other implements of iron. In 1827 he sold his factory to his nephew, John S. Peckham and afterwards engaged in the business of making vinegar on Lafayette street. John was joined some years after by his half-brother, Merritt and the firm of J. S. & M. Peckham continued to the time of the death of the senior partner in 1879. Up to 1835, the business made ploughs and cradles, but with the advent of steam power, added stoves. In 1857, the factory occupied the entire block bounded by Broad street, Catharine and Third streets to the Canal.

Another leading iron foundry was started in 1822 by Ephraim Hart, who took as his partner Andrew S. Pond. The factory was located on lower Cornelia street near the canal and by 1828 was manufacturing iron plough points, iron kettles, sleigh and cutter shoes and simple wood-burning stoves. John Dagwell was born January 28, 1808 in Hampshire, England. In 1831 he came to Utica and built the old City Flour Mill for J. E. Bloomfield. It was in 1836 that he became connected with Ephraim Hart in the foundry business. He began as superintendent of the foundry and six years later became a partner. The firm of Dagwell & Hart continued from 1842 to 1865, when Dagwell went to Ilion to become superintendent of the Remington Arms plant there. This firm was the predecessor of Hart & Crouse.

In 1828, Philo Curtis opened a machine shop on the west side of lower Cornelia street, opposite Hart's foundry. He was a skilled mechanic and built the first steam engines made in Utica. In 1831, he erected a stone building, three stories in height and in the same year took out a patent for an apparatus for heating the supply of water of boilers after the water had passed the pump and was under boiler pressure. This patent was universally used in this country. In 1832, of the 21 steam engines in use in the county, eighteen were made by Curtis and ten of these were in the city of Utica. The location of Mr. Curtis' factory was then a suburb of Utica, known as Washingtonville. The city line extended west to the center line of Schuyler street. Farms intervened between the machine shop and Genesee street and a dirt road led to the city. Mr. Curtis encountered financial difficulties about 1835 and he retired, leaving the business to Andrew S. Pond. The firm secured a contract with the Utica & Schenectady Railroad to furnish cars and keep them in repair for a charge of one cent per mile for each mile run by the cars. They also made all the rails and switches, etc.

In 1847, the firm was known as the "Vulcan Works" owned by Messrs. Higham & Co., employing about 80 workmen. In that year, the firm made the powerful steam engine used by the Utica Steam Cotton Company in Utica and was working on one for the Globe Woolen Mill, then under construction. Later the property passed to Truman K. Butler and Washingtonville became known as "Butlerville".

Philo S. Curtis, the son of Philo C. Curtis attained his majority and induced his father, who was conducting a small machine shop on Pine street to rent the old original building from Butler. The elder Curtis and the Remington family of Ilion had always been good friends. At the beginning of the Civil War, the Remington firm secured large contracts for arms and sub-contracted much of the work to Curtis. This rush of business made Curtis financially secure. In 1896, the firm was incorporated as the Utica Steam Engine & Boiler Works.

The Eagle Foundry or "Eagle Furnace" as it was commonly known, was established in 1837 by Chester Dexter. It was located on the corner of Cornelia and Columbia streets and remained there until 1897. Joel C. Bailey purchased the Eagle Foundry in 1842. Russell Wheeler entered the firm as a clerk, married Mr. Bailey's daughter and became a member of Bailey, Wheeler & Co. In 1856, Mr. Bailey retired and Russell Wheeler continued the business. When he died in 1894, his son, Frank E. Wheeler continued the business. The firm was incorporated as the International Heater Company in 1898 and Mr. Wheeler was the president of the corporation until 1931.

John Carton, born in Dublin in 1815, became apprenticed to Owen O'Neil in 1828 to learn the tin and coppersmith business. At the age of 21, he finished his apprenticeship and remained with O'Neil until 1842, when he gained an interest in the business. In 1845, he established his own shop at 133 Genesee street. Later he moved to the east side of Genesee street just south of the Busy corner and during the 43 years he conducted his own business, became financially well-to-do. He had an inventive mind and among his ideas were a steam vat for the manufacture of dairy cheese and the first locomotive headlight to burn kerosene oil. He patented the "Carton Hot Air Furnace". He died in 1881. In later years, his furnace was taken over and improved upon by the International Heater Company.

About 1832, a man named J. D. Edwards began the manufacture of oil cloth in Utica. He borrowed money from Dr. Theodore Pomeroy and Thomas P. Walker. When he was unable to repay the loans, Doctor Pomeroy found himself operating an oil cloth factory. The factory was located along Cornelia street from Columbia to Cooper and fronting on Columbia. It was a wooden building, one hundred feet in width and during its hey day produced the finest oil cloth in America. Burlap was used as the base of the oil cloth. After it was sized, it was sandpapered and color blocks were imprinted upon it. After being dried for a week, it was varnished in order to give it the necessary gloss and then it was scraped and smoothed. During the scraping process, friction from the knives generated electric sparks which often set fire to the building. One day it was discovered that metallic wires attached to the knives and grounded would prevent the sparks. This was considered the greatest forward step in making oil cloth.

Doctor Theodore Pomeroy was born in Southampton, Massachusetts on March 14, 1785 and died on June 26, 1860. His son, Theodore Pomeroy, Jr. was born in Utica on January 14, 1820. Educated in the public schools and Columbia College, the young man studied law in the office of Beardsley & Crafts and was admitted to practice in 1845, but instead took over his father's oil cloth business. He later took his own son, George Dutton Pomeroy into the firm as Pomeroy & Son. George Dutton Pomeroy was born in Utica in 1847. His education was in the public schools and at Princeton. At the age 20, he began to work in his father's factory. He modernized the business and substituted machinery for the handwork. He died in February 1895 and his father lost interest in the business and soon wound up its affairs. He died July 4, 1897 and the old factory and office were torn down and every trace of what was once one of Utica's leading industries disappeared. It was later the site of the Cox Furniture Store and in recent years, E. Tudor Williams Company.

THE COMPLETION OF THE ERIE CANAL
1825

AS early as 1810, the Legislature adopted a resolution appointing a committee to study the possibility of building a canal from the Hudson to Lake Erie. On July 4, 1817, the project which was to be so important to the State and to the villages along its course, was begun at Rome, a few rods west of the United States arsenal there. The eastern portion of the middle section between Rome and Utica was completed by the fall of 1819 and that channel was filled with water from Oriskany creek.

On the morning of October 23rd, 1819, Governor DeWitt Clinton and about seventy invited guests proceeded in carriages from Bagg's Hotel a short distance west of the village of Utica to the eastern extremity of the completed section. There they boarded a boat, sixty-one feet long, eight feet wide and a depth of four feet, containing two cabins. This boat, "Chief Engineer of Rome" was built there by Messrs. Miller, Chapin and Brainard, contractors. It was drawn by a single horse, by means of a rope 80 feet long, of which one end was connected with the whippletree, and the other with a hook secured to the bow of the boat on the towing side.

The trip began at a quarter to nine in the morning and proceeded to Whitesboro for a brief stop to take on passengers, amidst the ringing of Whitesboro bells and an artillery salute. The westward passage was resumed to the end of the channel, a few rods southwest of the hotel in Rome. The stop at Rome was forty-eight minutes with appropriate salutes and refreshments. The return trip ended at ten minutes before eight o'clock the same evening. The actual travel time for the approximately thirty miles was eight hours and twenty minutes. Everybody was surprised that a single horse could draw a boat with 70 to 100 passengers at the rate of four miles per hour. A new era was about to begin for the residents of Utica.

The statement that the Irish built the Erie Canal has historical foundation. A man named Canvass White went to England in 1817-18 to inspect the canals being built there. He learned that the English had found that the Irish laborers were the best workers on canals. He became acquainted with the engineer, J. J. McShane, a native of Tipperary, Ireland and White persuaded McShane and his crew to come to America to take on the job of turning "Clinton's Folly" into the "Grand Western Canal" which was to open up the west.

In 1818 hundreds of young Irishmen were encouraged to come to America and hiring agents waited for them at the docks in New York city. The pay was fifty cents a day but that was more than they could earn in Ireland. Over 3000 Irishmen were working on the canal that year. The canal was finally completed from Buffalo to the Hudson in 1825 and the first boat, the "Seneca Chief" left Buffalo for New York city on October 26th, 1825. The "Utica Sentinel & Gazette" of November 8, 1825 described the celebration in Utica:

> "On Wednesday, October 26th, soon after the signal cannon which announced the departure of the first boat from Lake Erie to the Atlantic Ocean, were heard reverberating along the banks of the canal, a large party of ladies and gentlemen took an excursion on the canal as

far as Whitesboro, in several packet boats. In the evening, most of the stores in Genesee street, and many buildings in the neighborhood of the canal and the canal bridge in Genesee street, were brilliantly illuminated, and the concourse of citizens was immense to witness the display of fireworks and interchange mutual congratulations. At seven o'clock, an illuminated boat, having on board the music, passed up the canal from one extremity of the village to the other, moving in the finest style, the band playing their liveliest airs. After this ceremony had been conducted, a numerous party of ladies and gentlemen assembled in Washington Hall and attended a concert, succeeded by one of the most splendid and delightful balls ever given in the village.

"The assembly room was tastefully decorated with evergreens and a small beautiful boat, emblematic of the occasion of rejoicings, and elegantly painted, was suspended from the centre of the arch, surrounded with a wreath of evergreens and lighted up in the most imposing style. The paintings, illustrative of the event, executed tastily for the occasion and designed by J. H. Lothrop, Esq., were placed at each end of the hall. We particularly admired the significance of the pieces, in which the union and strength, that will be produced among the states by the great system of internal improvement, is represented by a column which occupies the foreground and which is surrounded by twenty-four arrow-shafts designating the several states, and bound together by a hand attached to boats in the canal which washes its base. The ball was honoured by the presence of beauty and fashion, and 'all went merry as a marriage bell.' We would also add that the refreshments, which were provided by Mr. James Hinman, were got up in his usual style. Thus ended this happy part of the ceremonies."

It was not until Sunday, October 30th, that the "Seneca Chief" reached Utica, with Governor Clinton aboard. The distinguished party was conducted to Bagg's Hotel for luncheon and then at 2 p.m. to the Presbyterian meeting house for public worship. On Monday morning a public meeting was held in the Academy where speeches were delivered. The procession then returned to the boat and the trip was resumed to Albany. The effect of the canal upon the village of Utica was reported in the "Utica Sentinel & Gazette" on May 23, 1826:

"Several new docks and warehouses have been built on the canal, and a dry dock for the repairing of boats, situated a little below the village, have been constructed. This town is becoming every day more generally a place of deposit for the neighboring counties at the north and south; and those sections of the country are the sources of a great share of its business. This business will doubtless gradually increase without any extraordinary effort, but cannot some measures be taken not only to hasten that increase, but also infinitely to multiply other sources of trade? One of the two things, we think, would affect this object — the improvement of the navigation of the Mohawk, or the construction of a railroad from this place, to connect with that now making from Schenectady to Albany. By either of these means, Utica would become the depot for the merchandise and produce of an immense tract of country, and the center of its trade and intercourse."

Although the canal was not built especially for passenger traffic, a number of Uticans had incorporated on May 17, 1823, the Utica & Schenectady Packet Boat Company. The corporation had a capital stock of $12,000, divided into 48 shares of $250.00 each. Among the subscribers were Jason Parker & Co., Abram Varick, James Lynch, Joseph Kirkland, Montgomery Hunt, Benjamin Ballou, Eziekel Bacon, E. B. Shearman, John H. Lothrop, A. B. Johnson, John Williams, Theodore S. Gold, James H. Hackett, Samuel Stocking, David P. Hoyt, John E. Hinman, Ephraim Hart, Moses Bagg, William Williams, John McElwaine, P. J. Thurber, S. Stafford, Jr., S. Stafford Sr., Alexander Seymour, William Ganier, Theodore Pomeroy, Seth Gridley, Henry Seymour, John C. Devereux, Nicholas Devereux, Levi Cossens, and DeGraff, Walton & Co. This company continued in business for eighteen years and by its careful management returned dividends in the amount of $206,620 to its investors.

A typical packet boat was sixty to seventy feet long, a large part of which was devoted to the dining room, where two rows of tables were set. At night, mattresses were spread on the seats and on each side and another row above them on cots suspended from the roof. The ladies were accommodated with berths in the cabin, which was usually carpeted and hung with curtains. The kitchen and bar were conveniently situated; the bar was always well stocked and the tables were spread with an abundance of food and often a delicacy. The packet boats carried no horses on board and operated on the same principle as the stage coaches, with changes of horses arranged at convenient points along the route. Utica to Schenectady was an 18 hour journey which cost $1.75 if meals were served on board and $1.25 if the traveller brought his own lunch.

A ride on a packet boat was described in the "Utica Morning Herald" in 1869 by an old-time resident:

"From the days of my boyhood, I have heard much about the old Erie Canal Packet Boat Company and of the marvelous results of that wonderful enterprise. I can well recollect my joy in treading the deck, and, in eating and sleeping in the 'grand salon' of one of those floating palaces, called a packet boat. How many a man have I heard congratulating his neighbor upon the great improvement of the age, in being carried to Syracuse or Schenectady at the rate of four miles an hour, so safely and so quickly, compared with the dangers and discomforts of the old-fashioned stages, especially in the wet and muddy seasons of the year. To be sure there were a few drawbacks to the perfect luxury of a ride on the grand 'raging canawl' such as a cabin, crowded with passengers, used both for eating and sleeping purposes, and as a common sitting room. Children would cry, and sleepers would snore, and the boat running against a lock or another boat, would shake the sleeper, and sometimes pitch him out of his narrow berth, but in spite of all these things, the packet boat was considered one of the greatest improvements of the age to the travelling community and a marked advance in the progress of the country."

In Utica, the packet boat dock was located on the southeast side of the Genesee street bridge, where the Exchange building (later the Foster Building and the Boston store) was constructed. The heyday of the packet boat on the canal was short, giving way to the railroad after 1836. The Utica & Schenectady Packet Boat Company ceased operations in 1841.

During the days of the Canal, all the grain that came to Utica arrived on the canal and the grain and feed stores on the south side of Liberty street abutted on the towpath. When a boat load of corn or grain tied up at the rear of one of the stores, a gang of men would go aboard and shovel the cargo into buckets to be hoisted out. A tired old horse, a long rope and a pulley block on the upper floor constituted the equipment for conveying the grain to the store. When the bucket was filled, a shout to the horse would start it east on the towpath; the rope would tighten and the bucket swing clear. When it reached the upper door opening, the driver would shout "whoa" and the horse would stop while the bucket was emptied. Then the bucket would be pushed out the door and the horse, feeling the weight, would then back up to the place of starting. This process was repeated until the boat was unloaded.

The boatyards for repairing the canal boats were located in both East Utica and West Utica and they did a thriving business. Orville Olcott commenced business in West Utica in 1837 and when he sold out in 1850 to Linus Dean and John N. Penfield, he had turned out over 60 packet boats and line boats, besides doing a very extensive business in repairs.

One interesting business was explained in the "Utica Directory" of 1828:

> "A Screw-Dock, for raising boats out of the water to repair them, erected in 1827. It occupies sufficient width in the canal to admit boats and the power is located in four perpendicular iron screws. Four men can raise an empty boat, and eight men a boat of the largest size with full freight. Invented here in 1825. S. Doolittle, patentee and proprietor."

Until 1882, when tolls were abolished, the State collected revenue for the use of the waterway, based on the kind and quantity of the freight carried. In 1829, the Utica "weighlock" was completed on the south side of the canal just west of John street. It was a small one story structure, built along Greek Revival lines and here the boats were weighed.

Every boatman was required either to enter his boat at every such weighlock or show clearance papers from the weighlock last passed to prove that the toll had been paid. A stone pier in the middle of the canal carried the roof of the building and such mechanism as made up the working part of the scales. Gates were built from the central pier and an iron lever protruding above the stone work operated the opening and closing of these gates, which were buried deep in the masonry. When a boat entered the lock and the gates were closed, an assistant walked across a foot bridge to the pier and turned a lever and the water in the lock would gradually disappear. It emptied itself into a sewer six or eight feet in diameter which extended down John street and was discharged into the Mohawk river just north of the old American Hotel on the west side of Bagg's Square. The boat then rested on a cradle connected with the weighing apparatus inside the building.

The work of computing and recording the weight of the

cargo was done by clerks inside the building. The weight of the empty boat was a matter of record and this was subtracted from the total weight shown on the scales to determine the amount of the toll. When this calculation was completed, the lock was refilled with water, the gates would be opened and the boat floated on its way.

The young lads of the town enjoyed watching the process at the weighlock and a favorite sport was to slip aboard a boat and ride west to the guard lock at Schuyler street, where they would get off and catch another boat moving east to take them back to the place of starting. After 1882, when the tolls were abolished and the weighlock was no longer used for weighing the boats, other machinery was introduced to furnish water power for lifting the John street and the Hotel street lift bridges (constructed in 1873 and 1888 respectively). The Utica newspaper described the old abandoned weighlock in 1921 just before it was demolished:

> "Perhaps like a haunted house, its walls still echo to the tread of unseen feet and some eyes might see through the ancient casements the flitting shadows of the dead."

NEW HOTELS AND TAVERNS
1820-1840

THE construction of the Erie Canal turned the attention of tavern owners southward along Genesee street. Several new taverns were erected in the vicinity of the packet dock, where the Boston Store now stands. One of the most famous was the "National Hotel" (originally called the "Mansion House"), opened by Amos Gay. It was a brick structure of four stories, built in 1823, on the east side of Genesee Street and extending in the back to the Erie Canal.

Standing close to Genesee street, it had no porch or veranda. It possessed an archway entrance in the front, through which the stages of the old Butterfield Line, after stopping at the hotel, the place of arrival and departure, passed to the barns, which were located in the rear. The old National Hotel was conducted by successive landlords and was a popular temperance hotel. It was purchased by Charles Millar in 1864 and in May 1867, the work of demolishing the old hotel was begun. On its site was erected a new four-story "National Building" which then served as the hardware and plumbing supply store of Charles Millar & Son until 1914, when Millar built a new building on Main street. It was then taken over by the "Utica Sunday Tribune" and the "Utica Herald-Dispatch" for their newspaper offices.

Sometime in the 1820s, the exact date being unknown, there was built on the south side of Catharine street on the west brink of the old Livingston warehouse canal dock, a small hotel which for three score years was known as the "Catharine Street House". Long a favorite spot for the farmers who drove into the city, it was sold in February 1883 to the shoe manufacturing firm of H. J. Holbrook and was converted into a shoe factory. The increase of railroad facilities had decreased the demand for accommodation of farmers and their teams. They could come to Utica on the morning trains to do their shopping, and return the same evening. On the morning of March 2, 1884, a fire occurred in the basement of the shoe factory, which developed into the worst fire in Utica's history subsequent to the famous fire of 1837. Before it ended, practically an entire business block was burned to the ground.

Another of the early taverns was the "Bull's Head" at the northeast corner of Genesee and Elizabeth street, kept for a time by Levi Thomas. Following Thomas came Joab Taylor and Lorenzo Taylor, who kept the tavern from 1829 to 1835. In 1840-41, John Westlake changed the name to the "Farmer's Tavern" and it was demolished in 1841-42 to make way for a new hotel called the "Central".

On the other corner of Elizabeth street stood the "Eagle Tavern", a brick structure erected in 1824 by John Bocock. It was a popular stopping place for travellers along the Genesee road. This structure was torn down in 1857 and was replaced by the beautiful Grace Episcopal Church.

In 1827, the old Presbyterian Church on Hotel street was removed to make way for a new edifice. Dr. Bagg writes:

> "The old church was neither torn down nor burned up;
> it was dismembered. The larger part of it went over the
> canal and rested at the corner of Fayette and

Washington street, where it was thereafter known for
many years as the 'Mansion House'."

The early history of the Mansion House is very obscure,
but it is known that Captain John Luddington, of
Stonington, Connecticut was its first landlord. After a series
of proprietors, it came into the ownership of Pliny F. Martin
(1859-1883). The hotel was a popular place for politicians,
the supervisors and grand jurors making it their headquarters. In 1915, Lester J. Sheridan became the proprietor and
renamed it the "Montclair". This he operated until his death
in recent years.

In 1828, Amos Gay built a large brick building on the
southwest corner of Genesee and Pearl Streets as a theater,
but it enjoyed only limited success and was soon converted
into a hotel, taken over by Abraham Shepard, who gave up
Bagg's and named the new hotel "The United States Hotel".
It was not successful as a hotel and was occupied by the Utica
Female Academy for a time and again as a hotel by Hazael
Dunham (1845-47) and William Ives (1848). It was torn
down to provide the site for the Utica City Hall in the early
1850s.

On the east side of Genesee street, just above the canal,
where the Arcade Building was later built, there was the
"Franklin House." The "Mechanic's Press" of May 29, 1830
announced that R. Sanger had taken possession. In
November 1872, the old hotel was taken over and demolished as the site for what was termed "a novel project" —
the Arcade Building.

In the 1830s, there was erected on the southwest corner of
Broad and John streets, where the Federal Building is now
located, a building, popularly known as the "Broad Street
House". It went through a series of proprietors and name
changes, the "Columbian Hotel" (1843-55), the "Sherwood
House" (1856-68) and finally as "Kelley's Hotel" (1869-70).
An important adjunct to the Sherwood House was Concert
Hall, built in 1850 by Samuel Stocking, and leased to William
B. Smith, the famous dancing teacher. It was the largest hall
west of New York city and all of the fashionable balls were
held there and on its stage dramatic and minstrel companies
displayed their talents. In the early 1870s, it was taken over
as a furniture store and warehouse for Lord & Co. It became
finally the site of the Post Office.

Arnold Mason erected a hotel on the northeast corner of
Genesee and Carnahan (now Blandina) street in 1832. It was

four stories in height, of wood. This area was known at the time as "Genesee Hill". Harvey Mason, Arnold's brother became its first proprietor and conducted the hotel until 1837 and a succession of landlords followed. In 1864, Mrs. Cornelia Green, from the old National Hotel on Genesee street, purchased the building and in 1866 renovated it into the "Clarendon Boarding House". The "Utica Morning Herald" reported:

> "An important and new feature for Utica hotel or board-
> ing house accommodations will be an 'elevator' — an
> article of carpentry much used in large cities, and ex-
> tremely convenient since by it, one's effects, as indeed
> one's self, can be taken, from the lower to the upper
> story and vice versa."

THE EARLY HOMES OF UTICA

THE first architects of Utica were carpenters and masons with some experience in draftsmanship. It was not until later that any particular style of architecture took form here. Samuel Hooker, of Albany came to Utica to build the York Hotel, the first brick building in Utica and with his son John constructed old Trinity Church. Another early builder was Robert McBride who came to Utica in 1807 and erected the first brick residence here as well as the Whitestown Court House and the new brick Bagg's Hotel.

Colonel Benjamin Walker, an Englishman by birth and educated in France, had been appointed during the Revolution by General Washington as aide to Baron VonSteuben at Valley Forge. The old drillmaster of the Revolutionary troops had difficulty in making them understand his commands in German. This was overcome by the Baron giving his commands in French, which Walker translated into English. As a result, a deep friendship existed between the two men and the old general made Walker his agent for the land in Oneida County which was given to the old soldier. He also made Walker his heir. To superintend the Steuben lands and as agent for Lady Bath who owned land in western New York, Walker came to Utica. At the eastern end of Broad street he laid out beautiful grounds and built an ample wooden house.

The property embraced about fifteen acres between Broad street and Albany street. The mansion house stood at the end of a spacious lawn, some 250 feet in length, and was approached from Broad street by avenues of beautiful trees. When Catharine street was extended eastward many years later, the Walker homestead was actually on Catharine street. The residence consisted of a main building and two wings on the sides and in its day was perhaps the finest residence anywhere. Behind and at the side was a grove of forest trees, all of which were planted by the Colonel himself. West of the house was an office, in which he transacted the extensive business which he had as agent for both the Baron and Lady Bath. The easterly side of the property was lined by an extensive range of outbuildings. Westward of the grove and lawn was the garden, containing an acre of ground, on which he raised fruit and especially strawberries.

Here Colonel Walker lived in state and elegance with his three slaves as house servants. His coach is said to have been the first ever seen in Utica. He died on January 13, 1818. The house then passed to Peter Bours, who married Mary Robinson, a niece of Walker's wife. Bours, who came to Utica in 1807 and opened a grocery and dry goods store, occupied the house for a very brief time and it was then used as a school by Madame Despard. Later occupants were Asahel Seward, David Wager and Abram Culver (1856-1885).

Peter Smith, the fur trader had built a house on the south side of Main street, between Second and Third. In 1804 he leased the residence to Morris S. Miller, who came here as the agent for his father-in-law, Rutger Bleecker. The house was a cheerful, unpretentious wooden structure with a long piazza. There were two gardens with fine fruits, vegetables and flowering shrubs brought from Albany.

James S. Kip, son of a Dutch gentleman, whose valuable farm on Kip's Bay in New York yielded a family fortune came to old Fort Schuyler in 1794 and bought from the Bradstreet heirs 400 acres of great lot No. 96 of Cosby's Manor. The purchase price was 627 pounds, four shillings. It was a choice piece of land, extending in width from a few feet

71

east of Broadway, to a little west of the line of Cornelia street and stretching south from the river some three miles. He didn't settle there but leased a farm of 366 acres in great lot No. 93, which included the site of the old fort. He constructed a small log cabin as a store near the eastern end of Main street and constructed a landing at the mouth of Ballou Creek, striving thus to divert business from John Post and the others west of him.

His first house was a handsome one at the corner of Main and Third street, which became subsequently the residence of Judge Morris S. Miller. About 1809, Kip built on a portion of his original purchase in West Utica, what was the finest mansion in the village at the time. It was built of cut stone and stood on the westerly side of Broadway near where the Erie Canal was later dug. It was surrounded by spacious grounds on the south side which he used for military purposes. He was the inspector of militia and was made sheriff in 1804.

When plans for the Canal were announced, he had sufficient political influence to induce the canal commissioners to run the line where it was eventually dug instead of south of his house as planned. The result was that the channel was so close to the rear of the house that water seeped from the canal into his cellar. He moved to Connecticut in 1825 but returned in 1830 and died at the house of his son-in-law on Chancellor Square in August 1831, at the age of sixty-four.

Apollos Cooper came to old Fort Schuyler in 1790 and on April 11, 1795 purchased from Kip one hundred and seventy acres of great lot No. 96 of Cosby's Manor. This land constituted a narrow strip, extending from the river southerly nearly to the intersection of Genesee and State streets. He built his home on Whitesboro street near its junction with Liberty, and as the village grew, his property increased in value and he sold parcels of it to newcomers. He was a county judge and sheriff and died on March 2, 1839, at the age of 72.

Nathan Williams, the first president of the village was born in Williamstown, Massachusetts on December 19, 1773. He studied law in Troy and arrived in Utica in 1797. He was also the first district attorney and first Congressman from Oneida County. His original house was on Main street and although it was one of the best at the time, it was a crude story and a half residence.

In 1798, he purchased a lot on what is now the northeast

corner of Whitesboro and Seneca street and built a frame building. In this dwelling, two years later, his sister Parmella married General Jacob Brown, afterwards famous as the Commander of the American forces on Lake Erie in the War of 1812 and subsequently general-in-chief of the Army of the United States. In 1809, the frame house was demolished and in its place was erected the brick structure which for almost one hundred years was a landmark.

It was a gracious dwelling with a beautiful garden extending to Water street and in the first year, Judge Williams tendered a reception to his close friend, Alexander B. Johnson, when the latter brought his charming bride, the granddaughter of President Adams, to Utica. It is said that Aaron Burr visited Judge Williams on several occasions when he was in Utica to argue cases before the Supreme Court of Judicature, held annually at the old Academy.

In 1810 occurred the birth of James Watson Williams, son of Nathan Williams. Two years later, Mary was born, whose marriage in 1840 to the brilliant young lawyer, David Wager, was one of the notable events which occurred in the old house. Judge Williams was appointed Circuit Judge in 1823 and served until his resignation in 1833 to become clerk of the Supreme Court. He moved to Geneva. His death occurred September 25, 1835 and his body was brought to Utica for interment in Potter cemetery.

The old homestead was purchased in 1854 by David Wager. Senator Wager's daughter, Mary Williams Wager, was married to Alexander T. Goodwin, Recorder of Utica, State Senator, and Mayor, and most of their married life was spent in the Williams homestead. The Williams home was demolished in 1911 to make way for a warehouse.

Next to Judge Williams' house was a double brick house built by David W. Childs in 1810 or 1812. Mr. Childs was director and attorney for the Bank of Utica. This house was afterwards purchased by Henry Seymour in 1820. Henry Seymour moved to Utica in 1819 as canal commissioner. He later was a State Senator and Mayor of Utica. His son, Horatio Seymour, born in Pompey, New York on May 31, 1810 was destined to be the Governor of New York during the Civil War years and the Democratic candidate for President of the United States in 1868 against General Grant. Blandina Dudley Miller in 1900 wrote about the Seymour House:

"Here, as in many other houses of the time, we shall find the delightful fireplaces and Dutch ovens, and a large, cheerful, basement kitchen whose windows open on the attractive garden. The comfort and cheerfulness of this large house was much increased by the beautiful garden which joined that of Judge Williams, with only a hedge between. All the family were strongly attached to the house and carried its ruling ideas into their own widely scattered homes as much as possible. Governor Seymour spent many of his happiest days in this house. Although the last years of his life were spent in Deerfield on his farm, he seldom let a day pass without spending many hours in the old home."

The Seymour House still stands, one of the few remaining landmarks of early Utica.

Around 1800, Watts Sherman, a pioneer merchant, built a wooden house on the west side of Genesee street, south of Court street. This house originally consisted of a main house, two stories high and a south wing. This house was bought in 1813 by General Joseph Kirkland and was occupied after his death by Judge Philo Gridley. During these years, the house was enlarged by the addition of a third story to the main part and a north wing to balance that on the south side. These exterior details were added, it is believed, about 1840. In 1882 Dr. Willis Ford purchased the property and removed the north wing and attached it to a stable in the rear yard. The site is occupied today by the County Federal Savings & Loan Association.

In 1809, John H. Lothrop built a handsome mansion on the east side of Genesee street, the present location of the Savings Bank of Utica. Lothrop occupied the house until 1811. The widow of George Clinton, afterwards Mrs. Abram Varick, lived in it for a few years to 1814, when it passed into the hands of Alexander B. Johnson. In 1895 Blandina Dudley Miller described the Johnson home:

"Surrounded by its beautiful garden with its famous pink thorn trees, rare roses and flowering shrubs of all descriptions, the house is still one of the most striking of our old residences. It stands well up from the street on a terrace, its deep stone steps guarded by two frowning lions, which were always objects of terror to youthful minds. Mr. Johnson was known all through the State as an able banker and a man of rare intellectual gifts and attainments. His marriage with the daughter of Charles Adams and the granddaughter of President John Adams brought a delightful circle of friends into his home life, while his high standing as a banker and financier brought him into close intercourse with the leading men of the time."

The old mansion was sold to the Savings Bank in 1897 to be replaced by the present "Gold Dome" bank building.

Egbert Bagg wrote in the "Observer-Dispatch" of March 6, 1932:

"Eighteen hundred twenty to eighteen hundred thirty, or a little later, seems to have produced the best domestic architecture in Utica. By this time the merchants and tradesmen had acquired enough worldly goods to want more pretentious homes. Better communications, more leisure and culture had brought a desire for greater comfort and luxury. Most of these houses were built of brick, close to the street with a straight front, decorated entrance and rather high stone steps with wrought iron railings on either side. The hallways were made running through to the rear and the garden was always a feature. The stairways were wide and decorative, usually with mahogany rails. The ceilings were high and all the principal rooms, including the bedrooms had fireplaces. The mantles of the period with their wide openings, pilasters, engaged columns, moulded shelves and carved decorations are too well known to require description. Most of them were of wood, but in the more costly houses they were of marble. Many of them were removed either when the original owners left or later and now adorn the living rooms of modern homes. Most of the houses of this type built in Utica were on Broad and Whitesboro streets, and were erected before the building of the Erie Canal. Shortly afterwards similar houses somewhat less pretentious were built along Lafayette street. Typical houses of the type were then erected on Broad street by Moses Bagg in 1824, on a site later occupied by the mill and office of the Frisbee Stanfield company and that erected about 1830 on the corner of Broad and First streets by Samuel Stocking, and later occupied for many years by Mr. Louis Tourtellot, the basement walls of which are still in use as a garage."

The village life was centered in Bagg's Square and the boys who attended the old school house on Main street, waded and caught trout in a brook which flowed diagonally across what was to become Broad street between John and First streets. Broad street originally extended from John street east to the basin and was not continued through to Genesee street until 1808. Homes had been built on Broad street east of John before that time and Trinity Church was built in 1806. The street was a departure from the other roads, being one hundred feet wide instead of the usual four rods. Between 1815 and 1850 as the village grew, Broad street became an avenue of fashionable homes. Here were the dwelling places of the old families, where gentility and influence abided in quiet elegance. The family coach and the retinue of servants were a part of the domestic life of the street. These old houses had beautiful gardens and garden parties where the guests walked amid roses and lilacs, and were features of the social life of the crinoline period of Utica's history. The names of the residents of Broad street are written in bold letters in the industrial, political and social history of the time — John C. Devereux, Samuel Stocking, Judge Hiram Denio, the Peckhams, the Manns, the Ballous, and many others. The encroachment of commercialism changed the atmosphere of the old street and by 1910 most of the old mansions had given way to knitting mills and business houses.

Samuel Stocking was born in Ashfield, Massachusetts on June 10, 1777 and learned the hatter's trade. He came to Utica in 1803 and opened a little hat shop on the north side of Whitesboro street near Seneca. He was a successful merchant until his death on March 1, 1858. By careful purchases he acquired a large real estate holding here.

His house was one of the more beautiful specimens of the early domestic architecture in the village. The magnificent hall, adorned with old English paintings, was a feature. A brick wall ran along the garden on the First street side up to a brick barn. It was a high wall, so high that not even the tallest passerby could glimpse the ladies and gentlemen who gathered in the garden for afternoon tea. Postern doors in the wall admitted the guests.

In 1839, Judge Hiram Denio purchased the Stocking House. Oneida County produced few jurists who ranked higher than Hiram Denio. He was born in Rome in 1799 and moved to Utica in 1826. A successful lawyer, he was appointed a circuit judge in 1834. From 1853 to 1866, he was a judge of the New York Court of Appeals and was considered among the best that ever sat upon that bench. He died in the Broad street residence on November 5, 1871, at the age of seventy-two.

The judge's daughter, Elizabeth, married Doctor Louis A. Tourtellot and they and their children, Louis, Frank, Miss Annie and Miss Violet lived there for many years. After the

76

death of Doctor Tourtellot, the family continued to live there until Mrs. Tourtellot's death. For nearly one hundred years, until it was torn down in 1924 and its bricks used to construct a modern garage, the "Tourtellot house" stood as one of the most attractive and prominent residences of Utica.

Theodore P. Ballou, son of Jerathmel Ballou, and grandson of Joseph Ballou, who came to Utica in 1792 from Rhode Island, had extensive real estate holdings, including blocks of property in Utica and 23,000 acres of Adirondack forestlands. For nearly one hundred years until the death of his son, Henry Clay Ballou on February 13, 1927, the Ballou descendants lived in a house on the southwest corner of Broad and First streets. The "Utica Daily Press" of July 15, 1927 thus described the house:

> "High steps lead to its front entrance, and there is a brick barn in the rear and an old fashioned garden concealed from public view by high brick walls. A polished door plate displaying the name of Theodore P. Ballou may still be seen on the front door of the house. There is a large old fashioned hall, as one enters the building, with a formal parlor in the front, a library or living room next to it, and a small room in the rear which was used by Henry C. Ballou as his office. The rooms are all upon the east side of the building. There is a large porch extending across the whole back of the house in the rear, and steps lead on the west to the old fashioned garden. The garden itself covers a large area, and lies in the rear and to the west side of the house. It is still kept up and contains a variety of rose bushes, shrubs and old fashioned flowers."

In 1929, the property was purchased by the Crane Plumbing Company. After razing the structure, a modern brick building was erected as a warehouse and showroom.

Another of the streets of Utica which had beautiful mansions prior to the Civil War was Lafayette Street, originally known as Fayette street. It was along this old road from Whitesboro that the Marquis de LaFayette entered Utica on June 9, 1825 during his triumphant tour through New York State. He was taken to Bagg's Hotel (then known as Shepard's) for luncheon, where he had strawberries taken from the old garden of Colonel Walker. In the afternoon, he paid a visit to Mrs. Alexander B. Johnson, the niece of President Adams, at her home on Genesee street, before continuing his journey to Albany.

None of the houses on Broad or Whitesboro streets surpassed in thoroughness of construction, commodiousness and elegance of furnishing, the brick building on the northeast corner of Fayette and Cornelia street, erected in 1829, by Ephraim Hart at a cost of $14,000 which was an enormous sum in those days. It was one of the oldest houses in that vicinity, though an old brick tavern on the southeast corner antedated it. The rooms were large and conveniently arranged, and the mural decorations were among the best in Utica.

Ephraim Hart was born in Farmington, Connecticut on December 27, 1774 and in his youth located with his family in Clinton. Succeeding his father in business in 1810, he was a trustee of Hamilton College. He moved to Utica in 1815 and engaged in iron manufacture. He was a State Senator from 1816 to 1822, an ardent friend and supporter of Governor Clinton, and a staunch advocate for building the Erie Canal.

When he decided to build his house, it was natural that he would supervise its construction. He had the cellar walls made a foot and a half thick, and a framework of iron bracing constructed to hold the walls together. Sometime after his death in 1839, the house was occupied by David Prentiss, who kept a boarding school in the house and in the rear conducted a day school. This was about 1850. After Prentiss, the old mansion was occupied by William Churchill, an agent for the Globe Woolen Mills and when he vacated it in 1863, Dr. William Russell purchased it and used it as a residence until 1880 when he moved to a house he had erected on Genesee street opposite South street.

In the latter year, Joseph Kleespies, a jovial host who was an accomplished musician, purchased the house and made a hotel of it, giving it the name of the "Germania". Thousands enjoyed his hospitality and listened to the strains of the zither which he fingered with skill. Others followed Kleespies as proprietors. In 1902, the building came into the possession of Hart & Crouse, who constructed a three story building in the rear. In recent years the building was demolished and the site is now used for parking.

In 1897, the Utica Masonic Association purchased the Beardsley residence at 251 Genesee street, upon which it proceeded to erect the present Masonic Temple. This resulted in the demolition of one of Utica's early homesteads. The old landmark was erected by Kellogg Hurlburt about 1830, the exact date is unknown. Utica had not yet been

78

incorporated as a city and the village had not spread further south than Columbia street. Beyond that point were a few scattered houses. In 1839, Samuel Beardsley purchased the Hurlburt house and thereafter made it his home. Samuel A. Beardsley was born in Rensselaer county in 1790 and came to Utica in 1823 where he held the office of district attorney and from 1823 to 1830 was the United States Attorney for the Northern District of New York. In the latter year he was elected to Congress and served until 1836, becoming a leader of the Democratic party. He resigned to become Attorney General of New York. In that position, he succeeded Greene C. Bronson, a former Utican, who had in turn succeeded another Utican, Samuel Talcott. In 1842 Beardsley was re-elected to Congress and in 1844 was appointed a justice of the old Supreme Court of New York. In 1847 he became Chief Justice, continuing until its dissolution. Subsequently he practiced law in New York City and Utica and remained a prominent leader in Democratic state politics. He was a friend and adviser of Andrew Jackson and is credited with having brought about the nomination of James Buchanan for President. Samuel Beardsley died on May 6th, 1860.

Of the old mansions of Utica still standing, none is of more historic interest than the Conkling-Kernan residence on Rutger Park opposite the head of John street. It was originally known as "Miller's Seat" and no house had as guests more of the great and distinguished personages of the era.

The farm on which it was located was owned by Rutger Bleecker, of Albany. At the beginning of the 19th century, he divided his property in Utica among his four children. He planned to have them all live close together and each was to have a residence fronting on Rutger street, on the ridge of what is called Corn Hill, with farms to the south extending to Steele's Hill. Mrs. Brinckerhoff was to have the lot on the corner of West street (so called because it was the western line of the Bleecker property); Mrs. Morris S. Miller, the one at the head of John street, which had a frontage of 666 feet; Mrs. Dudley, the one at the head of First street; and John R. Bleecker the one at the head of Second street. The building of the Erie Canal was thought to detract from the beauty of the view and the children, with the exception of Mrs. Miller, decided to stay in Albany.

Maria Miller had married Judge Morris S. Miller, who came to Utica in 1806 to manage the Bleecker property. He first occupied a house at the lower end of Main street and supervised the Bleecker property, then estimated to be worth $400,000. He planned carefully to build his home at Rutger Park, but died before doing so on November 19, 1824. He had had a distinguished career, being president of the village in 1808 and county judge until his death. He was also a trustee of Hamilton College and a Member of Congress from 1813 to 1815.

His son, Rutger B. Miller, finally built the mansion in 1830 and lived there until 1841 or 1842 when he moved to Alder Creek. His mother continued to reside there with her family until her death in 1850, when Rutger inherited the property. This was the only house on the Bleecker plot. The nearest house on the west was at the corner of West street, later the site of the Park Baptist Church. Northward along John street, the nearest house was at the corner of Park Avenue, the Buckingham house, which was occupied by a man named Whitely, who made flutes. Howard avenue and Miller street had not yet been laid out, but between West street and Howard avenue was pasture land. A stone retaining wall with wide coping was built along the entire front, and back of this was a row of white and colored lilacs. To the west of the mansion was a small building which Mr. Miller used as an office. Back of this was a house occupied by the coachman and gardener, and still further in the rear of a long greenhouse filled with grapes, probably the first hothouse grapes ever grown in this city. East of the house was a tool house and back of it the woodshed, stables and carriage house. There was a large circular driveway in front of the house and another in the rear. To the south was a large orchard.

Rutger Miller's wife was the eldest daughter of Henry Seymour and a sister of Horatio Seymour. She entertained many famous people with graciousness at the house. A list of these visitors, including Governors and Generals and statesmen appeared in the Daily Press on November 25, 1893.

On August 10, 1850, Miller sold four lots from his 666 foot plot of ground. The one nearest to Howard Avenue was sold to Mrs. John Munn, whose husband built the stately stone mansion, later occupied by Samuel Remington, John C. Devereux and Walter Jerome Green.

The lot adjoining on the east was sold to J. Wyman Jones. He built a house thereon which was later occupied by Rev. R. H. Fowler and later by Charles A. Butler.

To the east of the Miller residence, he sold a lot to Egbert

Bagg, who built thereon. Later occupants were James Bailey and John H. Howard. The final lot to the east was sold to George B. Dana. This lot remained vacant for some years and was finally sold to Thomas E. Kinney, who built the residence now occupied by the Teamsters Union.

In 1852, Mr. Miller sold the old mansion to J. Wyman Jones and he in turn sold it in 1853 to Mrs. Breese, mother-in-law of Thomas R. Walker. Walker had attended Hamilton College but did not graduate and the rumor was that it had something to do with the firing of a cannon in one of the college halls. He then studied law and was admitted to practice, first with his brother-in-law, John H. Ostrom, and later with Roscoe Conkling.

Walker was quite an art connoisseur and he became acquainted with the leading writers and artists of the period, whom he entertained at the mansion. One of these was E. D. Palmer, a carpenter by trade, who was working at the time as a pattern maker for J. S. & M. Peckham in their foundry. Palmer also developed a skill in cutting cameos. This young man became one of the most famous sculptors in America and afterward moved to Albany.

The house was then sold in 1868 to Roscoe Conkling, as Mr. Walker moved to New York city. Roscoe Conkling was born in Albany on October 3, 1829, the youngest son of Alfred Conkling, United States District Judge for the Northern District of New York from 1825 to 1852. Young Roscoe Conkling came to Utica in 1846 to study under the tutelage of one of the most renowned law firms in the State, Spencer & Kernan. Admitted to the bar, he was almost immediately appointed by Governor Hamilton Fish to fill a vacancy in the office of District Attorney of Oneida County. Although he failed to be elected at the next election, in the spring of 1858, he was elected Mayor of Utica and in 1859 was elected to Congress. In 1867, he was chosen United States Senator from New York and was re-elected in 1873 and again in 1879. He was a trusted political adviser to President Grant who offered him the chief justiceship of the Supreme Court, which he declined. Later, President Arthur actually appointed him as an associate justice of that court, but he again declined. His wife was the youngest sister of Horatio Seymour and the couple entertained many famous personages during their occupancy of the old mansion. Conkling died in New York City on April 18, 1888.

81

THE EARLY MARKETS OF UTICA

THE old homes of Utica were substantially constructed and furnished elegantly, but they were rarely warm except immediately in front of the fireplaces, which were a feature of all of the rooms of the house. The woodshed, with its supply of maple, birch and beech wood, occupied a prominent spot in the yard. In the rear was the barn for the storage of the carriages and housing of the horses. Until John Carton invented an efficient furnace for central heating, the owners were dependent upon wood burning kitchen stoves. Fuel and hay were furnished by the farmers of the surrounding countryside, for those who did not provide their own. Meat, eggs and produce were also brought in from the country to the village.

John Post recognized the need for a market place and as shown on a map of his property on file in the County Clerk's office, he set aside a portion of his property at Bagg's Square as a public market. In 1805 a protest was filed by those residing in the vicinity of the square to the effect that it was a private enterprise with the village receiving no revenue; that it encroached upon the too narrow streets of the village; and that instead of answering the purposes of a regular market it was "being converted into an aleshop and a rendezvous for the idle, the noisy and the tippler." Since all the village records, save this protest, were destroyed in a later fire, we have no knowledge of whether this protest was acted upon by the trustees.

In 1812, it was voted by the trustees to build a public market house on the square between Bagg's Tavern and the store of John C. Devereux at a cost of $300. By the provisions of the ordinance, butchers and victualers, licensed by the payment of six shillings, were the only persons allowed to sell meat in quantities smaller than the quarter of the animal, and this only in the stalls of the market, at least during market hours. Butchers refusing for six days to supply their stalls with good meat were subject to penalties, and they were required to pay the village clerk a tax of ten cents for every cow or ox and two cents for every sheep and lamb sold. Other provisions excluded standing carts, live animals, undressed carcasses, hides, and unwholesome meat, and required rigid attention to cleanliness.

The market was still a bone of contention and in the fall of 1814, the corner of Division and Water streets was designated as the location of the market, and seventy-five dollars were appropriated for its removal there. Marketing in the future was made free to everybody, and at all times and places.

The Hay Market was also located in Bagg's Square, with the Wood Market adjoining it. Loads of hay and wood were brought into these markets from the countryside, and the contents weighed on the village scales located there. There was a city weighmaster or wagon master to attend to the accurate weighing of wood and hay so that the public would know how much they were getting for their money. These two markets were in existence until the time of the Civil War, although they were moved up John street near the canal at Catharine street.

When the Erie Canal was completed in 1825 and the center of business activity began to move up Genesee street, the demand for a new and improved public market increased. The residents of the square area attempted to keep the market there, which prompted "Senex" to write in the "Utica Sentinel & Gazette" of July 19, 1825:

"The earlier settlers feel a particular attachment to that spot; there they held their first political meetings — it was the place where the militia mustered — it was resorted to on public occasions. Its great convenience was lately most strikingly tested, for at that place General Lafayette received the welcome and congratulations of a happy, free and grateful people. Would it not be profanation to have that square disgraced by butcher's shambles and a Gothic barbarism, to have the finest approach to the village, disfigured by meat stalls and its breezes tainted by all kinds of putrid exhalations. And let it be remembered, that in our climate, fuel is nearly as necessary as food; the former articles come to use principally from the north and east. The area alluded to has been found of the utmost importance as a stand for the wood and hay wagons, and prevented the blocking up of our streets. . . . Let us extend our view to the future. Utica cannot be extended north. Her growth must be, nay now is, to the south and west. Markets more central for her population must be erected there; having more custom they will be better supplied, and will become the general resort. That on the northern line will be abandoned, soon abated as a nuisance, or remain a monument to the folly of those who built it, and of the want of foresight in those who permitted the erection. There is one consideration more, on which I will touch but lightly. The western or Genesee road was made before Utica had a name."

In 1827, a petition was signed by about two-thirds of the freeholders of the village and a committee was appointed to select a suitable piece of ground. A lot was selected and purchased from John R. Bleecker on the corner of Bleecker and Back (renamed Market) street at a cost of $1000. On January 25, 1828, the committee was instructed to receive bids for the construction of a market building two stories high. It was known as the Bleecker Street Market, but was generally called the "Old Clinton Market".

The main floor of the market was devoted to the sale of meats and poultry and game of all sorts. Each butcher had a stall in the room, with racks on which were hung the beef and mutton for sale. Around the building were a number of "lean-to" sheds where produce was displayed for sale. The market was opened usually at 4 o'clock in the morning, and before breakfast the housewives arrived to buy the day's provisions of meat and incidentally to get the gossip and news. At 1 o'clock the market was closed for the day.

The upper story of the building was used as the municipal court room after the Recorder's Court was established in 1844. The basement was used as a lockup and police watch-house. It contained two or three cells. It was a foul, ill-smelling place, four or five steps underground. It was often quite filled with drunks and unfortunates, especially on the arrival of the canal packet boats, since whiskey was only 25 cents a gallon at the time. The basement was often damp and filled with water because of seepage from the canal in the rear. The public insisted that it be changed and for some years thereafter, the watch-house was moved to the second floor, from which prisoners often escaped through the rear windows, jumping down on the sheds below and running along the towpath to parts unknown. The hey day of the Clinton Market was between 1828 and 1850. Later, the old market was demolished and the State took over the site for an armory.

OLD WASHINGTON HALL
1822

THE first building in the village designed for offices was Washington Hall, the venerable landmark on the northeast corner of Broad and John streets, which recently fell victim to progress. It was a three story brick structure built in 1822 by Abram Varick. Abram Varick, Jr. came to Utica in 1804 from New York City, as an agent for the sale of lands owned by the Holland Land Company. He became so impressed with the possibilities of the village that he purchased farm land in West Utica which he laid out into building lots. He opened a number of streets in that area and gave his name to what was long the principal thoroughfare in West Utica. The building was designed to house offices on the first two floors with a large public hall on the third.

Many notables had their offices in this venerable building; Ward Hunt, Abram Varick, Alexander Johnson, Charles Doolittle, John F. Seymour and most notable of all, Horatio Seymour, once Governor of New York. In 1837 James Watson Williams, agent for the Aetna Insurance Company advertised that "persons wishing to be insured apply at Washington Hall." The third floor was the public hall which was often used for dances, concerts and entertainments. The "Saturday Globe" of January 26, 1901 described the social usage of the hall:

> "While the lower floors were thus devoted to the serious and perplexing affairs of life, terpsichore reigned above. About 1850, a somewhat celebrated dancing master named Cobleigh opened an academy there and the leading men of the town sent their sons and daughters to receive instructions from him. He was succeeded by William B. Smith, another adept in the terpsichorean art, who is well remembered by many Uticans and whose death occurred a few years ago in Rome. Next Charles L. Dobson, who died last week, took charge of the dancing school and many merry hours were spent under his tutelage by people who still recall with pleasure the time when he guided them through the mazes of quadrille and lanciers, and taught them the graceful glide of the waltz. The old hall continued to be one of the principal

dancing places of the city up to 30 years ago. Since then the upper floors have been occupied as living quarters."

In 1853, Mr. Varick moved to New York city and he sold the building to David and Thomas Owens, who moved their bakery from Main street to the new location. There they conducted their business and also dispensed ice cream. This era was graphically captured by Penelope Conkling in an article in the "Way to Wealth" published by the Savings Bank (Vol. 7 No. 30):

" 'I'll take vanilla, thank you, Mr. Owens — and some ladyfingers, please, Ma-ma.' Such polite and wheedling requests were familiar to the ears of David Owens, the rather bald and very kindly little man, whose 'fine Ice Cream Room', connected with his large wholesale and retail bakery then located in Washington Hall, was a fashionable place of refreshment back in the 1860s and thereabouts. Outside, summer insects would be droning in the tall elm trees, horses and carriages would be clattering over the cobbles of Broad and John streets, and perhaps the distant whistle of a packet boat on the canal would be wafted into the cool, shaded Ice Cream Room, where hoopskirted ladies and prim little girls and boys, remarkable for their endurance of the tortures of heavily starched collars and dresses, partook of Owens' delicious refreshments.

"That was an age when drug stores dealt strictly in drugs and the soda fountain with its fancy concoctions was yet undreamed of. David Owens' ice cream was truly 'homemade', being prepared and frozen by old fashioned methods somewhere in the mysterious regions downstairs, whence came the tempting odors of hot spice and molasses, of browning loaves and baking crackers. For the establishment of David Owens & Son was famous for big, scallop-edged molasses cookies — thick and soft and lusciously flavored; also for Boston crackers of sauce-plate size which were favorites on many Utica breakfast tables seventy years ago. Delicious they were, split and toasted and spread with fresh butter.

"Those were the days when the cracker barrel — open and inviting — stood in every corner grocery and cross-roads general store. David Owens & Son carried on a wholesale cracker business. The big ovens where thousands of barrels of crackers were baked were down in the great cavernous cellar of the interesting building. Today remnents of those ovens may be seen, useless now, and partially filled with loose bricks and debris. In the deep, cool recesses of this cellar were stored great hogsheads of molasses for use in the famous cookies.

"The Ice Cream Room and bakery salesroom were on the first floor. That part of the old establishment is now occupied by McQuade Brothers, owners of the building for over sixty years. Here may be seen the deep cookie bins, drawers and counters which were part of the erstwhile bakery equipment. The quaint bow window that juts over the sidewalk at the upper end of the building facing Broad street was used in the long ago for the tempting display of Owens' cakes and candies. A large, lyre-shaped sign bearing the legend, 'David Owens & Son, Wholesale and Retail Bakers', was fastened to the large girthed elm that stood on the corner. This tree was a familiar landmark until recent years. It was the last of the beautiful arching avenue of elms which lined old Broad street when it was the residential district of the 'best people' of the city.

"The old time builders cared more for ample proportions and substantial workmanship than architectural display and Washington Hall is an arresting specimen of such ideals. A generously planned, three-storied structure, it was designed from the start to serve in a combination of private and public uses. Time has subdued the red of the brick walls, and twisted the four tall chimneys somewhat askew. The oval of the inset bricks, high up in the John street wall, sadly attests that some practical owner called in a mason instead of a glazier when the oriel attic window was in need of putty and new diamond-shaped panes.

"The simplicity of the recessed doorway that gives entrance to the upper floors, offers a striking contrast to the fluted and carved pilasters that ornament the wall on the main corner of the building. Weatherbeaten into insignificance now, they must have been of great beauty, freshly painted white against the background of new brick. That was long ago; beyond the memory of anyone now living.

"The arrangement of the stairways and rooms on the second and third floors has undergone no change. The second floor rooms open off a wide central hallway. In a past era these spacious rooms, each having a generous fireplace and large, many-paned windows, were occupied as private living quarters. David Gaffin, afterward Mayor of Utica, brought his young bride to live in the comfortable, socially correct atmosphere of a Washington Hall apartment. At a later period this floor was also occupied as offices. A. J. Lathrop, a leading architect of the city and northern New York, conducted a class of young men in architectural drawing in one of those second story rooms for a number of years after the Civil War.

"On the top floor is the unchanged shell of the old ballroom. Two noble fireplaces face each other across the long expanse of the wide plank flooring. But the feature of the room is the vaulted ceiling. Although the plaster is cracked and dingy with age, and ugly remnants of gymnasium equipment dangle from its lofty curves, yet one is immediately charmed into a glamorous past by the overhead beauty of this forgotten ballroom."

EARLY AMUSEMENTS IN THE VILLAGE OF UTICA

THE development of entertainment in Utica was outlined by Carroll T. Waldron in an article in the "Utica Sunday Journal" in 1906, a typescript of which is in the Oneida Historical Society files, entitled, "A Hundred Years of Amusement in Utica":

"There were a few shops and more than a few taverns, perhaps the most popular of the latter being the inn of George Tisdale at a location near the present site of Bagg's Hotel. In the yard of this house, a century ago, was witnessed the first performance of which authentic records exist. The attraction was heralded as a 'caravan' or 'menagerie' but its sole object seems to have been an elephant. And this the quaint advertisement that startled our quiet little hamlet into a knowledge of the prodigious event: 'A Live Elephant. The elephant not only being the largest but the most sagacious animal in the world but the peculiar manner in which it takes food and drink of every kind with its trunk, is acknowledged to be the greatest natural curiosity ever offered to the public. She will draw the cork from a bottle and with her trunk will manage it in such a manner as to drink its contents to the astonishment of the spectators'.

"So that none should catch a free glimpse of the marvel, it came to town before daybreak, lumbering in from the southward over the old Genesee Road — now Genesee street. But to look upon its thrilling performance at the tavern cost only 'twenty-five cents, children half price' and it is safe to assume that all paths led to Tisdale's during the exciting three-day engagement of our first entertainment in that autumn of long ago.

"After the sojourn of the elephant not again was the village visited by amusement devices until early in 1809, when Potter & Bishop called attention to their 'New Museum of Wax Works' to be shown at 'the hotel'. The building referred to, situated on the north side of Whitesboro street, directly opposite Hotel street, was the first brick structure erected in Utica. Among the features of this large and elegant collection of wax figures together with music on an elegant organ 'were likenesses of' Columbus, the first Discoverer of America in princely robes; the late General George Washington; Thomas Jefferson, President of the United States, etc. etc. Also a representation of Stephen Arnold, a schoolmaster, whipping a little girl six years of age in such a barbarous manner as occasioned her death. For ten days the wax people held forth at the hotel and then, crowded aboard a river boat, were paddled to Rome.

"Two years later (1811) came the first circus. Truly a 'one horse show', it comprised but three performers, one of whom was the proprietor, Mr. Stewart. Tents had not yet come into general use but the showman advertised that he 'had been at considerable expense in erecting a circus at the lower end of Broad street.' Mr. Franklin, equestrian extraordinary, was billed to perform 'a number of new and surprising feats of agility on the horse. Also will toss the oranges and will ride with his toe in his mouth while the horse is in full speed.' This highly-diverting accomplishment, and a riding act by Mrs. Stewart, together with her husband's 'many astonishing feats of buffoonery in the character of the clown, afforded the spectators their whole half-dollar's worth of excitement.

"Eratus Row, proprietor of the Utica Coffee House, is credited with having made the first effort to establish a permanent place of amusement. Gathering together a small collection of second-hand wax figures and curiosities, he set them up in a room of the house and in May 1812 threw open the door of Utica's pioneer museum. Not only did he bid for patronage but announced that he would be at all times ready to accept

89

gifts of rarities, especially such curiosities as might be picked up by travelers in the 'western country.' But to no purpose. The time was not ripe for such an enterprise. Row received little of the encouragement for which he had hoped and within a few weeks his show room had grown dusty with neglect.

"At this time, and for some years subsequent, the village possessed an accomplished choirmaster and all-around musician in the person of Mr. Curphew. Upon him the community seems to have wholly depended for such entertainment as might be had between visits of professional talent. More rare than angels' visits were the latter and the choirmaster, with his amateurs, were given many opportunities to shine. Promoted by Curphew and managed by Curphew and played by Curphew's band, these musicales consisted largely of selections composed by Curphew under the personal direction of none other than Curphew. But that all-pervading personage seems to have been a versatile genius and his efforts were well rewarded. Not to attend, and afterwards discuss, Curphew's concerts, was to argue oneself below par socially and musically.

"Next are noted two museums; one conducted by Henry Ennalls and the other by Stowell & Bishop. The latter opened at a location in Main street and later on is found at 'Briggs Tavern, near the canal.' Ennalls' Utica Museum was on the east side of Genesee street midway between Broad and Main streets. It was in existence as early as 1820 and the discordant, day-long droning of its organ continued a familiar sound in the village for fully ten years. Both of these enterprises were of the wax-work variety and, although of little importance in themselves, they prepared the way for the more ambitious Peale's Museum, which entered upon a long career in 1828."

In all probability, the first theatre in Utica, designed for the specific purpose of entertainment, was the old "Amphitheatre" on Culver street, on the south bank of the Erie Canal, east of Welles Canal Coffee Shop at the packet dock and just north of Bleecker street. This old wooden building was destroyed by fire in 1854. The site was later taken by the Shuberts for the erection of the "Shubert Theater", subsequently known as the "Colonial". The old wooden building was erected in 1823 by Samuel Stocking and others as a circus building. It was first occupied by Mr. Parsons, who brought an excellent company of equestrians to the village.

The far-famed horse, "White Surrey", ridden by West and afterwards by Master Burton, was a great favorite.

During the years 1825 to 1828, the opening of the Erie Canal brought travelling dramatic groups to Utica and they generally played in the Amphitheatre. On the night of May 25, 1825, the drama had its inauguration in Utica. The advertisement reads that

> "Mr. H. A. Williams, late stage manager of the Chatham Garden Theater, New York, most respectfully informs the ladies and gentlemen of Utica and its vicinity that he has altered the circus in the rear of John Wells' Canal Coffee House, and will fit it up as a theater for a short season with new and splendid scenery, dresses, and decorations."

The first offering was "Tobin's celebrated comedy called the Honeymoon and the farce Lovers' Quarrells."

In December of 1825 the public was informed that for a limited engagement a company will present "Timour the Tartar", "Grand Romantic Drama of the Forty Thieves" in which the whole stud of beautiful horses will be introduced, and finally, "The Grand Melo-Dramatic Equestrian Spectacle of the Secret Mine". On January 17, 1826, it was advertised that

> "The Wonderful Leaping Horse White Surrey will go through his astonishing leaps, at the conclusion of which he will leap over a horse sixteen hands high with Master Burton on his back."

It was in 1826 that the Drake family began coming to Utica. They were English and travelled and slept in their covered wagon, on top of which was carried a limited wardrobe and scanty scenery. They presented such plays as "Macbeth", "Damon and Pythias" and "Love's Sacrifice."

Utica's first contribution to the stage may well have been James Henry Hackett, who as a lad of twenty, came to Utica and opened a small grocery business, to which he added a stock of earthenware. This adjunct to his grocery business proved so profitable that he soon became a wholesaler. Having accumulated a fortune of $18,000, he went back to New York city in March 1825, invested his money in a business venture and promptly went broke. As related by Waldron he

> "had been a shop keeper here in the town's pioneer days. A born mimic and comedian, his impromptu entertainments were a delight to the little coterie of village wits that nightly made his grocery their gossip exchange.

His business prospered and, in fact, it was perhaps with an over-flush of success that he took leave of the village to seek greater conquests in New York. Disaster met his embarkation there and the year 1825 saw him penniless. In his hour of need it was but natural that he should follow his bent and seek a living upon the stage. He made his debut at the old Park Theater and gained a name in a single night. In after years Hackett won success in imitations of great players, his impersonations of Kean bringing unusual encomiums. In his day he was a famous Falstaff and he assumed other Shakespearean roles most creditably. His achievements were ever a source of pride to his village associates and his appearance here in 1826 was as the triumphant return of an artist to a people who had seen his merit in the rough."

The Amphitheatre was not destined to last very long because of the antagonism of the spiritual leaders of the village. Waldron wrote:

"Such antagonism as had been given it aroused a spirit of antagonism among the ultra spiritual and there followed an era of bitterness between church and stage fully as keen as had been experienced in larger communities at earlier times. Guileless as must have been the plays in the shack back of the old coffee-house, they were a sufficient thorn in the side of the prejudiced to furnish theme for many a soul-harrowing Sunday morning sermon from the pulpits of the village. And that these attacks proved a set back to the local popularization of the drama, there can be little doubt.

"During 1826 was published a series of sermons on 'Theatrical Exhibitions' by the Rev. Samuel A. Aiken of the Presbyterian Church, a man of intellect and a powerful preacher, locally perhaps the ablest writer of his time. The following paragraphs, one of many equally fervid ones in Dr. Aiken's denouncement, furnished a good idea of the sentiment then prevailing against the stage: 'There is a charm in the dazzling vanities which binds their deluded votaries as with a chain of iron. One indulgence only sharpens the appetite for another and creates a thirst that is never quenched, so long as there is the possibility of obtaining more. How many youth, once the highest hopes of their country, by entering upon this highway to ruin, have travelled on until they finally ended their career in the prison or upon the gallows.'

"And the editor of the paper sealed the argument with an accompanying editorial, in part as follows: 'We believe that the great mass of inhabitants in this portion of the country are convinced that any theater, whether situate in a city or village, is, in every moral point of view, to be considered as a perfect nuisance. Now what we ask is consistency. Let no motives of curiosity, amusement or popularity prevail upon them to do violence to their consciences. Let them not for a single instance, permit their example to be recorded among those who deliberately prefer present gratification to the best interests of society and to the great cause of morality and religion.' In the face of such tirades, few had the temerity to visit Satan's own recruiting station and the venture languished into oblivion. The structure was soon occupied for commercial purposes."

Amos Gay, a native of Connecticut came to Utica about 1813 and operated various hotels with such financial success that he built in 1827 a spacious three-story brick structure for a theater on the southwest corner of Genesee and Pearl Streets, later the site of the City Hall. It enjoyed only one short season, as recounted by Waldron:

"Headed by a Mr. and Mrs. Barnes and directed by one Roberts, the troupe produced a series of pieces on the order of 'The Heir at Law', 'Isabella', 'Midnight Hour', and 'Devil's Brigade'. But public sentiment continued strongly puritanical and the rows of hungry seats that nightly confronted showman Gay speedily brought him to a realization of his folly. The short life of this playhouse however, was not without its one 'big night'. The occasion was the appearance of Edwin Forest, then a very young man but already a great favorite in the cities. Supported by the troupe attached to the theater, he gave a presentation of Virginius and although the night was an insufferably hot one in August, standing room was at a premium and the famous player was applauded to the echo."

On July 22, 1828, the "Utica Intelligencer" announced:

"United States Hotel. The subscriber has taken the above establishment at the corner of Genesee and Pearl streets. The building which has been occupied for a theatre, is very large and spacious, and has been fitted up at great expense. E. Cary."

Colonel Comfort Butler provided Uticans with amusement for a longer period than any other one individual. A soldier in the War of 1812, he returned to Utica and opened a saddlery shop. He erected a four story brick structure in 1827 on the east side of Genesee street just south of the Erie

Canal. On May 13, 1828, Rubens Peale announced in the "Utica Intelligencer" that he had taken the Butler building, and

> "through the urgent solicitations of some of its inhabitants he has been induced to establish a Museum of Natural History and Miscellaneous Curiosities in this village, which will be conducted on liberal and correct principles; it will form a moral and interesting resort of every thinking mind, and people of every religious denomination. It will be under the superintendence or management of his brother, Mr. Linneaus Peale, of Philadelphia."

It was scheduled to open on May 21, 1828 and on the day previous, the "Utica Sentinel & Gazette" reported:

> "The Museum is situated on the most pleasant part of Genesee street, a few doors above the canal, in that splendid building lately erected expressly for the museum by Colonel Comfort Butler of this place. The Utica Band attached to the 8th Regiment of Artillery have politely volunteered their services to celebrate the opening."

Colonel Butler took over the museum shortly thereafter and his contribution to entertainment in the village was described by Waldron:

> "Butler proved a most tactful manager. The good villagers were made to understand that if the dictates of strict Christianity forbade indulgence in entertainment, all the more reason had they for flocking to so moral and instructive an exhibition as that at the Museum. Its three hundred live and stuffed birds and animals constituted in themselves a lesson in natural history, to say nothing of the innumerable wax figures, pictures, Indian relics et cetera — all for twenty-five cents. And the place had another feature, a phase of summer amusement that nowadays is accepted as typical of the up-to-the minute smartness of blase New York — the roof garden. Yes, the old museum had a roof garden, set out with ferns and hung with lights upon occasion, where sauntered and chatted our forebears with the muffled music of the village band coming up to them from the show room below. Indeed the roof promenade was a point of pride with Butler and he advertised that 'it afforded a magnificent view of the surrounding country, showing the winding of the Canal.'
>
> "At intervals special attractions were secured by Butler — giants, magicians, ventriloquists, albinos, fire-eaters,

jugglers and once a 'real mermaid.' Here also were shown the famous Siamese Twins and tiny Tom Thumb. In one way and another interest in the museum was deftly kept alive and when an announcement appeared that another part of the building had been fitted with stage and seats for a 'saloon' for the giving of dialogues, concerts and lectures, the same people who would have denounced Butler had the word 'theater' been used in connection with his new department, took kindly to the innovation. The Museum and saloon became the chief resort of the period and dialogues and concerts soon gave way to quiet little temperance plays, in which the chief character was usually the 'horrible example', more drunk and disorderly than any intoxicated Hooligan that now staggers about the stage for the admiring gallery gods. From temperance plays the step to undistinguished drama was an easy one and gradually the greater part of our people were weaned from their unwarranted prejudice against the stage. Colonel Butler guided the destinies of Utica's big little playhouse until the autumn of 1850 when he sold out to one Roth and took reluctant leave of Utica for a new home in Brooklyn."

In addition to Washington Hall, there were several other halls which were occasionally utilized for theatrical presentations. On the corner of Genesee and Whitesboro street was "Hooker Hall" and at No. 6 Catharine street was "Knickerbocker Hall."

In the pioneer days of the village, there was little need for public parks since a few minutes walk would bring one into the countryside. Lacking the modern convenience of bathrooms, bathing was a problem since swimming in the river or the Erie Canal could be hazardous unless one was an accomplished swimmer. To provide bathing facilities, James Hinman in 1825 became the owner of property on the south side of Whitesboro street which had been the Bryan Johnson homestead. The "Utica Sentinel & Gazette" on June 13, 1826 announced the opening of the Utica Bath and Garden:

"We are happy to announce the completion of this elegant establishment, which has been lately erected by Mr. James Hinman of this village, that an establishment so extensive and costly has been undertaken here. Mr. Hinman has spared no pains or expense to fit up his bath and garden in the most commodious and elegant style and to render it a delightful resort during the hot months. The baths are provided with every convenience

95

and comfort and will be a great luxury not only to our own citizens, but also to the numerous travellers who pass through this place and will find the bath very refreshing after suffering from fatigue and dust and heat during the day. The garden is tastefully laid out and suitably provided with arbors, retreats and places of refreshments, and nearly in its centre, is a pretty jet d'eau which serves to cool the air."

Hot, cold and tepid shower baths could be had from 6 a.m. to 10 p.m. for a modest fee. Along the sides of the grounds stood summer houses where refreshments were served when desired, and the open space between was crossed by winding paths, bordered with shrubbery and flowers. Later promenade concerts were made a special feature of the garden and local and instrumental attractions were presented.

The game of bowling, then called "ten pins" was a popular sport and alleys were built there. The Fourth of July celebrations were held in the garden for many years, the first being held on July 4, 1826.

The great fire of 1837 which levelled much of lower Genesee street, destroyed all of the buildings at the Garden, with the exception of the bathing houses. Peter Palmer was the proprietor at the time and he set about restoring the "garden". The "Utica Democrat" of June 6, 1837 reported:

"When we lately saw the 'great fire' at work in the City Garden, crackling among the latticed arbours, withering and crisping the shrubbery, and wrapping itself about the cleat board orchestra, we had many pleasant reflections. We thought of the ice cream we had eaten, and concluded we should never eat any more there — we thought of the fireworks we had seen there, and concluded we were witnessing the last — we thought of the flowers that used to load the air with perfume, and concluded we should never nose them again — we thought of Peter Palmer, the proprietor, and concluded that Peter was a ruined man. Man's wisdom is a small light; nature has been at work, and so has Peter — the flowers are up, and so are the fences, the arbours rebuilt, the ice cream ready, the fireworks all cocked and primed, and everything is to 'go off' tonight if the weather is pleasant; and if not the next fair night — Sundays excepted."

In the middle 1840s, Dr. John Marchisi was the proprietor and he connected the grounds with Genesee street by an alleyway. In 1846 it was called the "Columbian Garden" with

William D. Smith, proprietor; in 1847, it was renamed "City Garden" by Volney Smith, proprietor. In 1849, Livermore, Cole & Co. became the owners and advertised that there were four bowling alleys in one large room, with a large eating house and kitchen.

In 1851, William H. Green became the proprietor and renamed it the "Magnolia Garden". In 1855, Perry Bradley and H. C. Porter took over and renamed it again the "City Garden". Bradley ran the place alone in 1856-58 and in 1859 took J. P. Dorr as partner. In 1860, G. A. Allen owned the garden, followed by Peter Agne (1861-66).

With the development of the waterworks, the popular bath was transferred to private dwellings and hotels and the only attractive feature left was the bowling alley. As baseball grew in favor, bowling lost caste and the garden was closed about 1866 and the buildings were thereafter used as a repair shop and storage for the horsecars of the street railway. The bowling alley was torn down on February 4, 1870 and another old landmark was gone.

Probably the first bowling alley in Utica was constructed by William McIncrow at Military Hall on Catharine and John streets sometime in the 1840s. In an article on bowling in Utica contained in the "Utica Sunday Journal" of October 18, 1896, we note the following:

"In 1855 to be exact, a bowling alley was started in the old City Garden. The City Garden was the only resort the Uticans had at the time and they made the most of it. Great bowling matches were rolled on this alley in a widely different manner from the present time. The alleys were constructed differently then. The rolling space was but thirty-six inches wide, where it is now forty and forty-two inches and the balls were much different. A set of balls in those days cost $100 and were made without places for the fingers. The balls were perfect spheres and only the good bowler could use a large one.

"There were about ten alleys in the town about that time and a great bowling club used to play all over the State. In 1872, a fine alley was started in Deerfield a short way over the bridge, and the foundation still remains. The foundation of an old alley is still noticeable at Sedgwick's on Genesee street. The largest ball then was much larger than the largest ball used now. Of old, the large ball was thirteen inches in diameter, and now the principal ball is about nine inches in diameter.

"The best known alleys at that time were the Dillon alley on Columbia street, the Hulser alley on Liberty street,

97

the Deerfield alley just across the bridge and the old City Garden alley. Bowling lost favor, when the pool table came in. This was a game that all could play and they did. After that bowling fell steadily."

THE DOCTORS AND DRUGGISTS OF EARLY UTICA

DOCTOR Francis Guiteau, a descendant of one of the Huguenot exiles from France who came to Massachusetts, settled in Deerfield in 1792 and moved to Utica in 1801. He was a genial and pleasant man who administered to the medical needs of the little village. On April 4, 1803, he formed a partnership for the practice of medicine and as a druggist with Doctor Solomon Wolcott.

Doctor Wolcott was born in Colchester, Connecticut in 1769 and was persuaded to come to Utica by his old friend Nathan Williams in 1803. The two doctors formed their partnership that same year and each built a house on Whitesboro street near the old York House. Their first office and drug store was on Whitesboro street near what was later to be Burchard Lane. This partnership was dissolved in January 1807 and Dr. Guiteau devoted himself to his private practice until his death about 1823.

Doctor Wolcott moved to the east side of Genesee street, a few doors above the corner of the Square. His store and office was distinguishable by the sign, "The Sign of the Good Samaritan." Two years later, he moved to the corner of Whitesboro street on the west side of Bagg's Square. For the next hundred years until 1911, this store was operated as a drug store by various proprietors. A feature of the old store was a carved figure of trade and commerce just within the entrance. All that was known about the curiosity was that it was part of the drug store from 1803 and tradition was that it had been purchased in New York City about 1801.

During the War of 1812, Doctor Wolcott was appointed garrison surgeon in charge of the hospital established to take care of the sick and injured soldiers. In 1804, he bought a farm east of Matthew Hubbell in East Utica beyond the "gulf" and built a large wooden house, later occupied by the Utica Gymnasium school. Toward the close of the war, he became interested with a William Gaylord in dealing in crockery. The venture was ill-timed, for money was scarce and Gaylord disappeared, leaving Doctor Wolcott with a debt of $16,500 to the Bank of Utica. Crushed by the debt and seized with an acute illness, he died October 30, 1818 at the age of forty-nine.

Doctor Alexander Coventry was born in Scotland in 1766 and after studying medicine at Glasgow and at Edinburgh, sailed in July 1785 for America and settled in Hudson. He came to Utica in 1796 and opened an office on the west side of Genesee street, about two doors south of the corner of Whitesboro street. About 1804, he took as his partner Doctor David Hasbrouck. Doctor Hasbrouck was a native of Ulster county and came to Utica in 1804. Doctor Hasbrouck left Utica about 1815 and died in October 1823 at Schenectady.

Doctor Coventry then formed a partnership with Dr. John McCall in 1817 and their office was on the northwest corner of Broad and John Streets. Doctor McCall was born in Hebron, Washington county, New York on Christmas Day 1787 and studied medicine at Columbia College. He was appointed an assistant surgeon in the army during the War of 1812 and in September of that year marched through Utica with the 13th Infantry Regiment. He was so impressed by the little village that he settled in Deerfield in 1815 and joined Doctor Coventry in the practice of medicine.

Doctor Coventry was a leading family physician and obstetrician and was twice elected president of the Medical Society of the State. While attending a case of sickness in the Nicholas Devereux family, Doctor Coventry fell a victim to an influenza epidemic and died December 9, 1831.

When Doctor Wolcott relinquished his drug store at the Square, selling out his share to his brother Waitstill, a partnership was formed between the latter and a man named Williams, and this continued until 1817. Jared E. Warner, a druggist clerk, together with Sylvanus Harvey took over the store and the two men continued the business until 1829. The firm then became known as Warner & Southmayd and erected a new building on the same site in 1833. From 1835 to 1842, Mr. Warner conducted the drug store alone. Benjamin F. Ray was a clerk in the store and in 1842, the firm became Warner & Ray. In 1867, Mr. Warner retired and in 1887 Franklin F. Ray & Company took over the store, followed in 1897 by Arthur S. Evans & Company. In 1911, the construction of the overhead crossing began to change the character of Bagg's Square, the drug firm moved to the new Mann Block on the northeast corner of Genesee and Broad streets. Its former location, known as the "Miller Block" was purchased for the wholesale grocery firm of Thomas G. McMahon.

John Baptiste Marchisi, Utica's pioneer of Italian descent, was born in Carmagnola, Piedmont, Italy in the year 1789. He early showed a natural taste for chemistry, and started out as a physician. He studied for seven years in a doctor's office and five years in a pharmacy. About that time Napoleon made his march into Italy and conscripted young Marchisi. An expert penman, he was placed in the quartermaster's office. Crossing the famous St. Bernard's Pass with Napoleon's army, he was one of the few who lived to tell about the experience. Later he and others fell into the hands of British near Gibraltar. Taken a prisoner of war, he was brought to Canada.

When the British learned of Marchisi's position with the French, they offered to release him if he would agree to enter upon the same service with the British. He was finally persuaded to do so, and became a clerk in the adjutant's office in Kingston and eventually a paymaster. During his stay in Kingston, he wooed and married a young lady of German parentage. He then determined to escape to America and eventually to return to his native Italy. He managed to escape with her to Cape Vincent and came by stage to Utica. Mrs. Marchisi had relatives named Forbes living near Utica, and he was persuaded to postpone his return to Italy. During this delay, he made the acquaintance of Doctor Hull, who prevailed upon him to practice with him.

Marchisi also worked for Warner in his drug store on the square and later he conducted the "Drug Exchange" in the old Devereux block and also the Utica Bath and Garden for some years in the forties. Then he opened his famous drug store on Genesee street underneath the Utica Museum. The father of twelve children, he outlived all but three, dying at the home of his son Henry in February 1885, in his 95th year.

THE EARLY IRISH SETTLERS OF UTICA

ALTHOUGH the great wave of Irish immigration to America did not occur until the potato famine of the late 1840s, there was a considerable number of Irishmen in the village until the time of its incorporation as a city. The chief Irishman here was John C. Devereux, the successful merchant who until the time of his death in 1848 was grand marshal of the St. Patrick's Day parade each year, wearing a green sash and sporting a genuine shamrock from the "ould sod" in his button hole.

There were also James Delvin (nailmaker), Robert McBride (builder), John Queal (shoemaker), Matthew Codd, the husband of Martha Bradstreet, Owen O'Neil (coppersmith), and Michael McQuade and his brother Thomas (brewers and coopers).

The small Irish population, augmented by the Irishmen who came to work on the canal, formed the Utica Hibernian Benevolent Association in 1822. These benevolent societies were a feature of every ethnic group which settled in any numbers in Utica. Each member of the Hibernian Benevolent Society paid one dollar at the time of his initiation, and a dollar yearly while he continued to be a member. After one year's membership, he became entitled in case of illness to medical aid and in addition a sum of money which ranged from fifty cents to two dollars per week. On the death of a member, the society attended the funeral and paid the funeral expenses.

St. Patrick's Day has always been significant to those of Irish birth or extraction and John C. Devereux arranged for the first banquet in Utica on St. Patrick's Day in 1824. It was held in Bagg's Tavern and among those attending in addition to Devereux, were Moses Bagg, Owen O'Neil, Rutger S. Miller, Charles C. Broadhead, David P. Hoyt, Charles E. Hardy, Thomas Williams, Herman Pease, George Martell, Johnny Quail, Squire E. S. Crozier, Squire Ezra S. Barnum, Dr. Alexander Coventry, Walter Fleming, and Matthew Codd ("Utica Observer" 1879).

Owen O'Neil came from Wexford, Ireland in 1816 and learned the trade of tin and coppersmith from James Delvin. He then conducted a copper and tin and general hardware

101

store on lower Genesee street until his death July 29, 1875. One of O'Neil's apprentices was John Carton, born in Ireland in 1815. John came to Utica about 1828 as a penniless boy and walking down Genesee street saw the store of O'Neil and applied for work. In later years, he was to become one of the leading merchants in Utica. He died on September 9, 1881. Upon the death of the last of his children, Matthew Carton, the Carton estate was given to charity.

Michael McQuade was born in Ireland in 1801 and came to Utica in 1823 to join his brother Thomas (1791-1865). Both were coopers by trade and established a lumber and cooperage business on Catharine street. He then purchased the old Gulf Brewery which he operated for forty years. He died April 5th, 1879, survived by a number of children, one of whom was General James McQuade, who distinguished himself by his service in the Civil War.

The potato famine in Ireland in the 1840s brought many Irish immigrants to Utica. Most of them settled in the old First and Fifth Wards in East Utica and immediately applied for citizenship. When they became citizens, they faithfully voted at each election. On the eastern end of the "Gulf" stood the blacksmith shop of Michael O'Rourke, the oracle of the Fifth Ward and the dean of the Board of Elections there. No election was considered legal unless Mike presided at the ballot box to insure an honest election.

Patrick Killigrew was born in County Waterford, Ireland in 1826 and came to Utica about 1849, living on lower Park avenue. He voted regularly at every election until his death in 1906. The story is told that one day when he came to register to vote in the fall election, a young poll clerk, asked in a flippant way how he spelled his name. To be asked by a whipper-snapper of a boy how he spelled his name was enough to raise his blood pressure. He drew himself up, threw out his chest and said, "Kill-hurrah-double-ou", Write that down if you can."

General McQuade, who was elected Mayor of Utica in 1870, once alluded to the fact that the majority of the early Irish were poor and lacking in influence and were sometimes the objects of prejudice, and then said:

> "It must not be forgotten, however, that no other place, perhaps, has been so free from it as Utica. We must not forget that the first Mayor of Utica, elected by the people, was that good citizen and courtly Irish gentleman, John C. Devereux, whose name will ever hold the first place among Irishmen."

102

Prior to the year 1840, the Mayor of Utica was chosen by a vote of the members of the Common Council. In that year, the charter was changed and John C. Devereux was chosen by the citizens of Utica.

Utica was first lighted with street lamps on December 29, 1827. These lamps burned whale oil or kerosene and were lighted each night by a lamplighter. Eventually these lamps numbered 55 and extended from the foot of Genesee street to the intersection of Court street and at the corners of other streets. When Utica became a city in 1832, the Mayor, Joseph Kirkland, lived on Genesee street just south of the intersection of Court. On April 9th, 1832 at one of its initial meetings, the Common Council took the following action:

> "On motion it was resolved that the committee on lighting streets be instructed to erect a lamp-post and lamp, in front of the Mayor's residence on Genesee street, and to furnish the same with light, at the expense of the corporation."

Each ward of the city had its own appointed lamplighter to walk around each sunset and light the lamps and at sunrise, extinguish them. On December 28, 1878, James Crumley, the veteran lamplighter of the First Ward died. Born in County Tyrone, Ireland in 1790, he was one of the early settlers in Utica in the old First Ward, then the enclave of the Irish here. He was not rich or distinguished, nor one about whom newspaper editors would be expected to write any extended obituary. Nevertheless, James Crumley was accorded a fitting tribute of which the following are excerpts:

> "Probably few of our readers who have reached middle age were unacquainted with James Crumley, the veteran lamplighter of the First Ward, who, after having walked his lengthy round, light in hand and light in heart, sank beneath the weight of eighty-eight years and on Saturday last, quit this earth for the land where the lamps need no replenishing, but forever brightly shine.

> "When James Crumley commenced his duties as lamplighter, there was no gas in Utica and the faint glimmer of unfrequent whaleoil lamps were like dull spangles on the dusky robe of night. Nevertheless, Jimmy served them with unvarying punctuality, and faithfully developed all the light they were capable of displaying.

> "It was before Faxton and Butterfield had given up stage-coaching to build a telegraph line; and while there was still a vigorous competition between the swift pack-

ets of Captain Greenman and the dangerous Schenectady railroad recently built. Jimmy Crumley lived to see all these changed; he saw the growing dissatisfaction with the dim light of his lamp, the introduction of lard oil, which, by the aid of some patent process, burned brighter than sperm; then gas and kerosene and all the other modern improvements, which were bad for the eyes — and for the ancient lamplighter. Thus he witnessed the light of other days fading from the streets which he had traversed for forty years, and while he was able to resist all the efforts of ambitious men to displace him, he was forced at length to yield to gas. Jimmy went out with the rusty oil lamps." ("Utica Observer")

"For over forty years James Crumley was the faithful lamplighter of the First ward, commencing when the feeble oil lamps of the olden time lost their rays in the short tunnels which they bored through the darkness; and serving continuously, through all political fluctuations and changes of control — a lamplighting Vicar of Bray — until, at length the faint gleam of the oil lamp was swallowed up in the superior brilliancy of gas.

"Many of the changes in Utica since the light-compelling Crumley first took his nightly rounds, with perforated tin lantern and short ladder, to make darkness visible for the early retiring inhabitants of the first ward . . .

"Times change, but not Crumley. Except for the hoary incrustations of successive years, there was nothing to distinguish the veteran who lighted the few vestiges of the expiring era of oil, from the strong and vigorous lamplighter of other days, who was once the sole public illuminator of the old first ward. And it was only when there were left but few oil lamps to light, and when age and infirmity pressed him down so that even these were beyond his reach, that he extinguished his lantern and retired to the shade of private life. Saturday night, after fluttering intermittently for some time, his own light went out."

THE CITY OF UTICA
1832

IN 1831 the village of Utica had a population of 8,393 persons. The assessor's rolls for that year showed a total of real and personal property of $2,672,575. In November, a meeting was held for the purpose of petitioning the Legislature to grant a city charter to the village. There were then only five cities in the State — New York, Albany, Troy, Hudson and Schenectady. As a result, Utica was granted a charter on February 13, 1832. The new city boundaries extended from the Mohawk river on the north to about Oneida Square on the south and from Third avenue on the east to the Utica State Hospital grounds on the west. The city was divided into four wards by a line drawn north and south along the middle of Genesee street and by a line drawn east and west along the channel of the Erie Canal. The First Ward was designated as the northeast quadrant; the Second, northwest; the Third, southwest; and the Fourth southeast. Each ward was entitled to elect three aldermen.

The first election was held on March 6, 1832 and the following aldermen were chosen: First Ward: John Williams, Charles A. Mann, and Harvey Barnard. Second Ward: Rudolph Snyder, John Ostrom, and Ezra S. Barnum. Third Ward: Ephraim Hart, Augustus Hurlburt and Chauncey Rowe. Fourth Ward: Robert McBride, Rutger B. Miller and John A. Ross. The Common Council held its meetings on the second floor of the Clinton Market on Bleecker street and Hon. Joseph Kirkland was chosen by the Council as Mayor. Thomas Colling was appointed city clerk and Ezra S. Cozier, treasurer.

On April 27th, laws and ordinances were adopted and published as a supplement to the "Utica Sentinel & Gazette" on May 22nd. The ordinances covered a great many subjects and included a ban on swimming or bathing in the Erie Canal within the city limits, or between the hours of five o'clock in the morning and eight o'clock in the evening

> "in the Mohawk river, between the brick store house at the foot of Division street and the line of Second street; and any person violating either of the provisions con-

105

tained in this section, shall for each offense, forfeit and pay a penalty of two dollars."

There was no particular court established by the city charter and criminal cases were to be disposed of in the same manner as in the towns. The Mayor possessed the powers of a justice of the peace, and the Common Council designated Ezra S. Cozier as the police magistrate and his office was on Whitesboro street next to Burchard's Inn. There were only two police constables, Samuel Hall and Thomas E. Parmalee. In addition, there was a Night Watch, whose chief function was to watch out for fire in the night time and alert the volunteer firemen.

The fire department, commanded by the Chief Engineer, John H. Ostrom, consisted of six volunteer fire companies and a Hook & Ladder Company. The fire equipment in those days was very primitive by modern standards. The engines were pulled by ropes and consisted of a condensing case or air chamber about four feet high placed over the hind wheels of the vehicle. The early engines were not constructed to suck the water which was pumped from it. The tank had to be filled with buckets of water, obtained from wells, the Mohawk river or the canal. The water was forced on the fire by pump handles, called "brakes" operated up and down by the firemen, sending the water from a pipe on the top which could be turned in a circle. They were thus nicknamed "Goosenecks". Later, the engines were constructed with a suction pipe which could be dropped into a well or cistern and the contents forced on the fire. Later, the "Coffee Mill" engine was acquired, the pump being operated by cranks on each side of the machine. The fire companies in 1832 were:

Clinton Fire Company No. 1 (organized May 15, 1805) and named for Governor DeWitt Clinton. In 1832 it was located on the south side of Catharine street.

Hardenbroke Fire Company No. 2 (organized September 29, 1817) named for Alderman Hardenbroke, of New York city, who was the head of that city's fire department committee. In 1832, this company was stationed at the corner of Washington and Liberty streets.

Hook & Ladder Company No. 1 was organized in 1819, by taking members of the two fire companies then in existence. It was their task to carry the ladders to the scene of a fire. In 1832, it was located in a building on Franklin street, between Catharine street and the Erie Canal.

On January 27, 1831, fire broke out in the harness shop

attached to Jason Parker's stage coach barn on Water street, which destroyed the stables and resulted in a demand for additional fire protection.

Fulton Fire Company No. 3 was organized soon thereafter and was named for Robert Fulton, the inventor, and in 1832 was located at the corner of Fayette street and Broadway.

Lafayette Fire Company No. 4 was organized on June 8, 1831 and named in honor of the Marquis de Lafayette. In 1832 it was stationed at the corner of Elizabeth and Charlotte streets.

Neptune Fire Company No. 5 was organized July 6, 1831. In 1832 it was located on the east side of Division street, between Whitesboro and Water street.

Mechanics Fire Company No. 6 was composed of mechanics employed in the iron foundries and was organized December 28, 1831 and was stationed in Hotel street.

There were thirty-three schools in Utica in 1832, but most were private schools. Public school education was not established until long after Utica became a city. After 1817, the village had been authorized to support a free school for the education of such poor children as were entitled to a gratuitous education. The two-story "Lancaster School" on the south side of Catharine street nearly opposite Franklin street was the public school. Eliasaph Dorchester was principal in 1832 and those who could pay were assessed fifty cents to a dollar per quarter.

Uticans were foremost in the movement to improve the lot of the common schools and the Utica Lyceum was formed November 27, 1823 to encourage the study and dissemination of knowledge of natural history and other useful sciences.

Two other schools of a public nature were in existence. The Infant School Society of Utica was formed in April 1828 and conducted a school in Bleecker street at the foot of Burnet street. In May 1832, an infant school for the citizens of West Utica was established on Lafayette street, between Varick and Whitesboro streets.

The Utica Academy on Chancellor Square received trifling assistance from public funds and was largely dependent upon the tuition it received. David Prentice was the principal in 1832 and school was conducted forty-eight weeks a year with instruction in English, Latin, Greek and French as well as science and mathematics.

The city built a two-story structure of brick at the corner of Bleecker and Park Avenue, then known as Bridge street in 1834. This was known as the old "Fourth Ward Free School". Children in those days had to carry tickets signed by a school trustee before they could be admitted. Geography, arithmetic, reading, spelling and writing were the limits of educational advantage.

The City directory of 1832 lists "The Catholic School" in John street above Bleecker in charge of Patrick Finnegan with "Upwards of 80 scholars, many of whom are sustained by private subscription; about 40 of them enjoying the munificence of an individual". This building was torn down in 1913 and the "Saturday Globe" of September 13th, 1913 gives this information:

> "Another old landmark in Utica is in the process of demolition. A gang of wreckers is engaged in tearing down the ancient frame building at 86 John street between St. John's Church and Elizabeth street, so long in use as a carpenter shop and in a few days one of the oldest buildings in the city will have disappeared.
>
> "The long, one-story building was erected in 1805. After its completion the little building housed a school, known as St. John's parochial school, and its principal Brother Finnegan, lived in rooms in the rear. Brother Finnegan was a schoolmaster of the old type, inflexible and strict in his rulings and many a boy whose children long since passed away as gray beards owed something of his sterling manhood to the teaching and discipline received under Brother Finnegan.
>
> "After the building ceased to be used for school purposes John Russ occupied it as a carpenter shop and the droning and whispering and shuffling of schoolboys gave way to the sounds of the saw and hammer.
>
> "As the old structure is being torn down the carpenters and builders who halt to watch the progress comment on the material of which it is composed. Where, for example, in these days, could a builder find such boards — 20 inches wide — as compose the siding."

After its use as a school, the building was used by Mr. Russ until the time of his death. Then as a carpenter shop by Edmund Richards, and by Owen Williams. About 1903, it was used as a paint shop by Thomas J. Finn.

There were three banking institutions — the Bank of Utica, the Ontario Branch Bank and the United States Branch Bank, with John C. Devereux, as president. This was located at 123 Genesee street, just below Bleecker. It was a branch of the United States Bank, chartered by the government, which owned one share of each twenty shares of stock. President Andrew Jackson opposed the continuance of this United States Bank and shortly after his re-election in 1832, withdrew all government funds which were deposited only with its branches. Shortly afterwards, the bank closed. Banks were open for business every day, except Sunday from 9 a.m. to 1 p.m. and from 2 p.m. to 4 p.m. Bank notes of other banks were discounted on Tuesdays and Fridays.

There were no daily newspapers in 1832 but eight weekly newspapers: "Utica Sentinel & Gazette", "Utica Observer", "Utica Intelligencer", "The Elucidator", "The Lever", the "Western Recorder", the "New York Baptist Register", and the "Evangelical Magazine & Gospel Advocate", issued a total of 17,852 copies per week.

There were no railroads at the time and travel was by stage coach, 91 arrivals each week. The mails were delivered by stage coach to the postoffice on the east side of Genesee street below Catharine street. James G. Lundgreen, the city letter carrier, distributed letters from this office immediately after the arrival of the morning mails. Postage for a single letter was six cents for up to 30 miles, etc. up to a maximum of 25 cents for over 400 miles.

The stores usually specialized in a particular line of goods, the largest groups being: Dry goods 44, groceries 63, hardware 10, boots and shoes 17, millinery and dress shops 19, saddles and harness 6, watches and jewelry 6, drug stores 6. In industry, there were 4 brass foundries, 2 breweries, 8 cabinet makers, 16 carpenter shops, 2 candle factories, 3 coach makers, 5 copper and tin manufacturers, 5 cut stone yards, 1 distillery, 3 drydocks, 2 flour mills, 3 iron foundries, 5 lumber merchants, 2 machine shops, 2 morocco manufacturers, 1 plough manufacturer, a rope maker, 3 sawmills, 1 starch factory, 1 steam engine factory, 3 stoneware potteries, 4 wagon maker shops.

THE CHOLERA EPIDEMIC OF 1832

IN the middle of June 1832, Asiatic cholera first appeared at Quebec and Montreal and shortly thereafter at Prescott, Kingston and York, Canada. Since many visitors passed through Utica either by stage coach or on the canal packets, the Common Council on June 16th, 1832 passed a resolution establishing a Board of Health and authorized the Board to adopt such regulations as they deemed expedient to prevent the introduction and spread of disease in the city. The Board of Health consisted of Aldermen Mann and Ostrom and Doctors Goodsell, McCall, Coventry, Peckham and McCraith. Doctor McCall was appointed Health Officer. A resolution was passed directing that a temporary hospital be erected at some point east of Miller's Basin and near the old weighlock on Broad street, to receive such sick persons as the Board should direct be placed therein. Fifty bushels of lime were purchased for the use of the poor. General Ostrom and Dr. McCraith were designated as a committee to designate a proper place where boats might perform quarantine and where they might be cleansed and purified.

When cholera broke out in New York city and Albany in the beginning of July, the Board of Health adopted a series of resolutions:

1. That the owner or occupant of every house, store, shop, stable, outhouse, tenement or lot in the city shall forthwith cause the same to be thoroughly cleansed and purified and to be put in a healthy and pure state, by removing every impure or unwholesome substance or water, calculated to engender disease.

2. Every owner or occupant of any house, store, shop or tenement in the city shall place and deposit when there directed as required by the Board of Health or any member thereof or by their agent, in his or her cellar, sewer, gutter, drain or vault, lime or chloride of lime, in sufficient quantities to purify the same.

3. Every owner or occupant of any house, building, tenement or vacant lot in the city, shall forthwith sprinkle or deposit in the gutter of the street in front of the same house, lot or tenement, lime or chloride of lime in sufficient quantities to purify the same.

On August 3rd, five fatal cases were discovered among the Oneida Indians at Lenox, Madison county. The first victim was employed by the captain of a boat on the canal to bury a person who had died of cholera on board. The circle of danger was closing and the disease was expected in Utica at any moment.

On August 13th, the Board of Health reported:

> "The Board of Health have the melancholy duty of announcing to their fellow citizens that the malignant cholera has at length appeared in our city. For the past twenty four hours there have been four cases, all of which proved fatal. Physicians are ordered to report all cases at or before noon of each day."

The first person who fell victim to the disease was Philo Rockwell, who lived on Washington street in the house of County Clerk John Ostrom. His case was fatal as it was to two others in the house. Hospitals were established above Mr. Plant's house on Genesee street at Oneida Square and at the corner of Columbia and State streets. Opposition to these locations arose and the Academy-Court House at Chancellor Park was taken over for that purpose. A reign of terror commenced as described by Dr. Bagg in his "Memorial History of Utica":

> "The alarm felt by the community and with which it was seized upon the first appearance of the disease had become extreme, and large numbers fled from the city. It was estimated that 3,000 persons had departed to various parts of the surrounding country in search of a securer refuge from the mysterious scourge. All business was suspended. Schools and churches were closed; the silence of death reigned in the streets; few other vehicles were seen but hearses for the dead and carriages for the sick, or in provision for their needs; ministrants in like services were the only persons on foot that ventured abroad."

Fifteen years after the epidemic, the "Utica Daily Gazette" wrote:

> "The bolts of death fell thick and fast. The dead were hurried to their graves as soon as the breath left the body, unaccompanied by friends and without any of the usual formal ceremony. It was difficult to procure sufficient attendants to carry the bier. For a week the disease accelerated daily in violence. Four more fell victims to it on Washington street on the 14th, 15th and 16th. It prevailed next on Whitesboro street, and isolated cases

appeared in different parts of the city. On Thursday, 16th, ten new cases were reported and six deaths. Among these lost are the names of Mr. Gurdon Burchard and a daughter, Ezra S. Cozier, Esq., and Miss Olive White.

"Sunday the 19th was remarkable for an uncommon storm of rain which began on Saturday night and continued uninterruptedly until Sunday evening. The Mohawk at once overflowed its banks, and the canal gave way at Nail Creek. On account of the cholera, the number who had left town and the storm, the churches, so well filled the previous Sunday, were mostly closed. The paper of Tuesday, 21st bears other indications, than the tenor of its contents, of the condition of things in Utica at that time. Its columns are eked out by the use of the largest type, the scantiness of matter is accounted for by the 'flight of workmen', and the usual editorial articles, particularly political ones, are omitted on account of the tone of feeling which prevails.' All business in the town is said to be suspended, most of the mechanics to have left, and at least 3000 of the inhabitants.

"There was a marked abatement in the violence of the disease immediately after the heavy rain of Sunday, which seemed to have cleansed the atmosphere of the pestilential ingredients. The report of the Board of Health for Sunday and Monday together, mentioned 33 new cases and six deaths. Tuesday the twenty-first, there were only 13 new cases; Wednesday 11, Thursday 6, Friday 11, Saturday 6, and Sunday and Monday 7. The deaths of cholera during the first week were 38, in the second 18. In the third week, ending Monday noon, there were 20 cases and 10 deaths, and in the ensuing week 14 cases and 4 deaths."

On September 11th, the hospital at the Academy was discontinued by the Board of Health and it was announced that there was no danger to persons returning to the city, if reasonable precautions were taken. On September 25th, the Board of Health reported that there were no new cases and that the health of the city was now good. The final report indicated a total of 206 cases and 65 deaths during the epidemic.

UTICA ORPHAN ASYLUM
1834

THE Utica Orphan Asylum had its inception in the Female Society of Industry, which was established in Utica in October 1826. It had 70 members who paid $5 annually, either in cash or needle work, and in January 1828 they began to raise funds for the founding of an orphan asylum. Thomas Arthur and his wife died, leaving three children, John, Jane and James. The Society of Industry determined to maintain these orphans and placed them in the care of a competent woman.

On January 7, 1830, there was held in old Washington Hall a public meeting for the purpose of forming an orphan asylum society. On April 18th, the Orphan Asylum in the Village of Utica was incorporated. Housekeeping was begun in November in a building on the northeast corner of John and Catharine streets. In May 1833, the family was moved to a location near the southeast corner of Chancellor Square. In 1836, the name was changed to the Utica Orphan Asylum.

The financial panic of 1837 and the resulting depression almost forced the society to close. The charter of the society was broadened to accept half orphans. The asylum was reopened in May 1845 on the east side of Broadway, a few doors above the canal. In 1846 the lot at No. 312 Genesee street was purchased from the proceeds of two fairs conducted for that purpose. A commodious structure was completed in May 1848, at a cost of $5,500. On this site was later built the Thomas R. Proctor residence. The society received some money from the State of New York and various legacies and donations. Utica's Fulton Fire Co. sold a fire engine for the sum of $485 and contributed that to the society. The will of Alfred Munson provided for the sum of $34,000 conditioned upon Uticans contributing $10,000, to be given to the society for the purchase of suitable grounds, within five years of his death. Benjamin F. Jewett gave the society three acres of land on the northwest corner of Genesee and Pleasant street. The cornerstone was laid on May 30, 1860 and the building was completed in the summer of 1861, at a cost of $25,600.

ST. JOHN'S ORPHAN ASYLUM
1834

IN the year 1834, John C. Devereux and his brother requested the Sisters of Charity to conduct a Catholic orphanage and day school in Utica. As a result, three Sisters were sent from the Mother House at Emmitsburg, Maryland. Tradition has it that they arrived, with their scant belongings, by canal boat on May 1st, 1834. The Sisters were lodged in Devereux's home on Broad street until the first building could be completed for their use. Each of the Devereux brothers contributed $5,000 and they opened the first orphanage in a small frame dwelling house in the center of the lot just south of St. John's Church on John street. In December of that year three children were received in the small story and a half house, which number soon increased to eight. Sister Angela, who was also a sister of Archbishop Hughes, was made Mother Superior. John C. Devereux, a kindhearted man, a lover of little children although he had none of his own, visited the orphanage daily. The institution was incorporated in 1848. A day school, the predecessor of Utica Catholic Academy, was opened a short time later in an adjoining building on Burnet street.

As the city grew in population, the number of orphan children increased and by 1853, there were sixty children in the orphanage and 250 students in the day school. The old building was enlarged to three stories, with a front of 52 feet and a depth of 36 feet. In addition, a brick wing was added to the main building, occupying a frontage of 30 feet and running back 53 feet. This was done in the fall of 1853.

The enlarged orphanage was again quickly crowded. The "Utica Observer" of November 30, 1858 reported:

> "The Catholic Orphan Asylum, on John street has recently been materially enlarged by the addition of a new building at the northern end. The asylum, by this and former additions, has grown from the size of an ordinary dwelling house to an establishment of formidable dimensions. The whole building is now 110 feet front on John street by 36 feet in depth, and three stories in height, besides a high basement and well-lighted attic."

Entrances to Some of Utica's Old Mansions

62 Broad Street

Nicholas Devereux Home
Elizabeth & First Streets

Hinman Home
Whitesboro & Hotel Streets

Stocking-Denio Home
Broad & First street   1825-1924

Old Utica Mansions

Henry Seymour Home
Whitesboro street   c.1812

Alexander Johnson Home
Genesee street   1809-1897

Theodore S. Faxton Home
Lafayette street   c. 1830-1907

The social life of Utica was centered in these old mansions. Garden parties were held which attracted persons prominent in the business, political and social life of the state. It is said that the plans for the establishment of the telegraph and Associated Press were made in Faxton's residence and in his library, Judge Demo wrote legal opinions which became the law of the state.

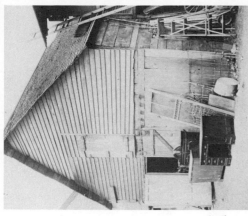

Joseph Kirkland
c. 1802

Early
Homes
of
Utica

Bellinger House
1st Frame House in Utica

Gerrit Smith Birthplace c. 1798-1920

Benjamin Walker House c. 1800-1920s

*Broad street scene shows the Dutch Reformed Church on corner of John street;
millinery shops and the Sherman House.*

Early Rutger street with the home of George Young; white house on the right.

Aristocratic streets in the 19th Century

Morris Miller Home
1830

Morris Miller who was married to Maria Bleecker designed Rutger Park for the use of the Bleecker children who were to locate in Utica. Five lots were surveyed, but only Morris Miller's family built the historical house in the center. The other four lots were sold to others during the century.

J. Wyman Jones Home
c. 1848

Munn Residence 1854

FRANCIS KERNAN (1816-1892)
United States Senator from New York 1875-1881

WARD HUNT (1810-1886)
Associate Justice, United States Supreme Court
1873-1879

ROSCOE CONKLING (1829-1888)
United States Senator from New York 1867-1881

JAMES S. SHERMAN (1855-1912)
Vice President of the United States
1908-1912

HORATIO SEYMOUR, 1810-1886,
Governor

JOHN C. BUTTERFIELD, 1801-1869
Founder American Express

JOHN C. DEVEREUX, 1774-1848,
Mayor

THEODORE S. FAXTON, 1794-1881
Founder of Telegraph

Original Stage Coach Overland Mail

Tally-Ho — Re-furbished old coach

The Overland Mail

The original stage coach used on the Overland Mail, and as restored and rented for private parties.

19th Century Church buildings
designed by Edward Crane
1821–1826

Bleecker Street Baptist Church, 1826–1886

Saint John's Church, 1821–1836

Saint John's Church moved to the northwest corner of Bleecker & John street. Long used as a public hall, Father Mathew Hall and for commercial purposes. It still remains although remodeled for other purposes. Bleecker Street Baptist Church built for the Second Presbyterian Church society. This was the scene of the Abolition Convention in 1835. Taken over in 1845 by the Bleecker Street Baptist Church Society. Sold to the Y.M.C.A. in 1886 and demolished.

First (Welsh) Baptist Church, Broadway, 1806–1904

Bleecker Street M.E. Church
1826–1866, Bleecker Street

19th Century Churches

Hope Chapel — Elizabeth Street, 1864–1916

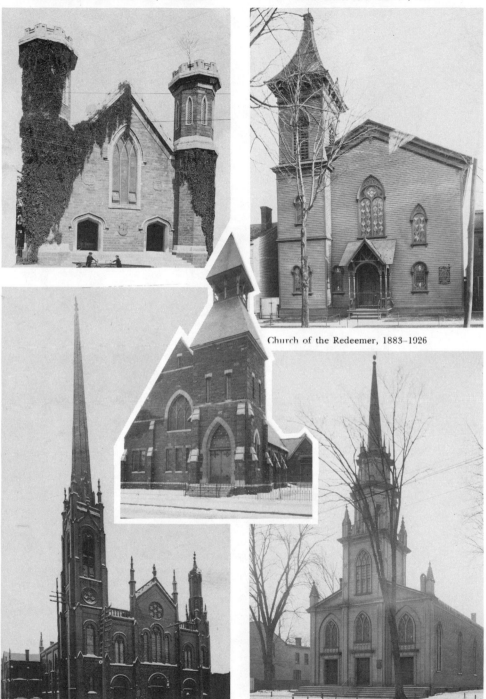

Church of the Reconciliation, 1851–1914

South Street M.E. Church, 1853

Church of the Redeemer, 1883–1926

First Presbyterian Church, 1851–1919

Trinity Episcopal Church, 1810–1922

19th Century Churches

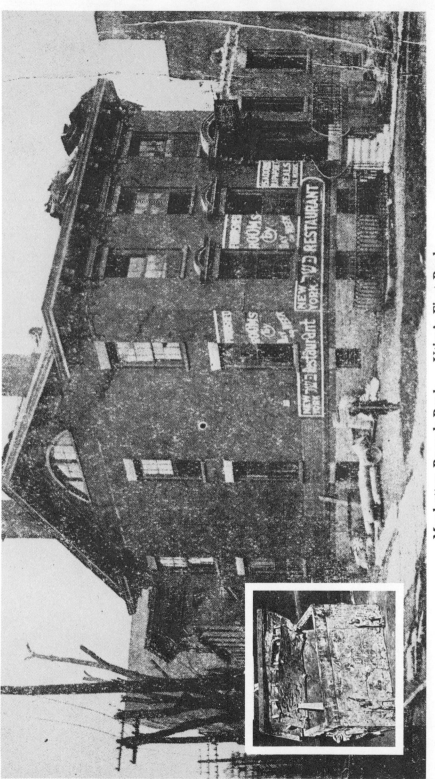

Manhattan Branch Bank — Utica's First Bank

This brick building was erected about 1810 on the southwest corner of Whitesboro and Hotel streets for the Manhattan Branch Bank which occupied it until the bank ceased business in 1818. Thereafter it was the residence of Colonel John E. Hinman, who was Mayor in 1851. After his death, the property was occupied by different persons. It was demolished in 1917 and the bank's strong box was discovered in the walls of the building.

Kirk Soap Company
Whitesboro Street 1839

Manufacturing in Utica

Hoyt's Windmill
*Used to grind bark for use
in his tannery on Hoyt Street
demolished in 1912.*

Remington Automobile
*Manufactured in its plant at
Broad, Niagara and Ontario streets
1901-1904.*

First Railroad Depot — American Express Office

Second Railroad Depot   1865-1914

Bagg's Hotel   1866

The Butterfield House
1869-1910

Famous Hotels of the 19th Century

Both Bagg's Hotel and the Butterfield House were favorite stopping places for kings, Presidents, Governors and persons prominent in the arts and literature. The taking of the picture of Bagg's Hotel is described in detail on page 290.

The Erie Canal view easterly from Washington street. Note footbridge at Seneca and liftbridge at Hotel street.

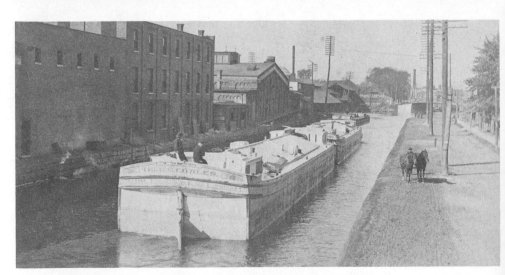

Erie Canal view westerly from Cornelia street to the bridge at Whitesboro street. The building at the left is the Carton Foundry.

THE ABOLITION CONVENTION OF 1835

THE years 1833 to 1860 were characterized by a great debate throughout the country on the question of the abolition of slavery. While slavery was early abolished in this State, slave owners in other states where slavery was an established institution could recover runaway slaves who escaped to free states under what was known as the "Fugitive Slave Act". Since a slave was considered an item of property instead of a human being, the owner could present proof of ownership to a local magistrate, who was required to issue an order for the slave's arrest and return to the owner.

Certain citizens of Oneida County and particularly Utica played significant roles in promoting the abolition of slavery as an institution throughout the country. The American Colonization Society was organized for the purpose of purchasing the freedom of the slaves and returning them to Africa. The Rev. Beriah Green (1795-1874), the head of the Oneida Institute of Whitesboro, was an outspoken foe of slavery on moral grounds and was opposed to the colonization idea as the alternative to abolition.

It is difficult today to appreciate the deep division and strong feelings which existed in Utica during those years between those who promoted the abolition of the institution of slavery and those who, although they personally despised the subjugation of slaves, feared that the abolitionists would destroy the Union. On the second floor of Green's school building in Whitesboro, was a printing office. In this printing office, was published, "The Friend of Man", a red hot abolitionist paper, which a majority of the citizens of Utica and the county considered a seditious and dangerous publication.

In 1832 there moved to Utica Alvan Stewart, a lawyer, who became the president of the Utica Anti-Slavery Society. He issued a call for a State Convention to be held in Utica on October 21, 1835, for the purpose of forming a State anti-slavery society. It was proposed to hold the meeting in the courtroom on the second floor of the old Academy at Chancellor Square, but a large group of citizens held a meeting and declared that the hall of justice should not be desecrated by such a radical meeting. As a result, the Common Council rescinded its permission and arrangements were made to hold the convention at the Second Presbyterian Church (later the Bleecker Street Baptist Church) on the corner of Bleecker and Charlotte streets on October 21, 1835 at 10 a.m., and among those invited to attend was Gerrit Smith.

Gerrit Smith, son of Peter Smith, was born in Utica on March 6, 1797 and his childhood was spent in the Smith house on Broad street between Mohawk and Hubbell. Peter Smith moved to Peterboro, in Madison county in 1806 and his son Gerrit became heir to the vast holdings and fortune of his father. He contributed money and tracts of land for humane causes, and in 1825 joined the Colonization Society and contributed money for the relocation of the slaves in Africa. He came to the convention merely as a spectator, but his experience here was to change him from a passive to a militant abolitionist, one of the greatest in the country.

On the morning of the convention, a large group of citizens gathered at the Utica Academy, and under the chairmanship of Chester Hayden, appointed a committee to go before the convention, report the resolutions adopted by the group and respectfully urge that the convention adjourn and the delegates leave the city forthwith. In his "Memorial History of Utica" Doctor Bagg wrote that,

"there were undoubtedly some lively scenes inside the church. The appearance of the committee was an incentive to whatever rowdy element was present in the church, as well as on the outside, to create a disturbance; there was much noise, some threats of violence, hymn books and other missiles were tossed about, and some personal attacks, in one of which Spencer Kellogg's coat was torn from his back. Meanwhile an immense crowd gathered in the streets. While the committee was still in the church a sudden disturbance occurred on the borders of this crowd, and there was a swaying of the multitude toward Genesee street. This was caused by a lot of roughs who broke through the crowd with the ladder of one of the hook and ladder companies. The ladder was raised against the church and two men sprang up it. Then some one started hurriedly into the church, crowding his way as best he could, and informed the assemblage of the impending danger, and soon Charles A. Mann, then agent of Charles E. Dudley, of Albany, the owner of the building, came upon the porch of the church and asked the crowd to disperse, telling them that the building was private property. He begged them to respect it and protect it from violence. The men on the ladder then came down. The excitement was intense and it was remarkable that a destructive riot did not follow."

Gerrit Smith was so moved by the actions of the mob, that he invited the delegates to assemble at his mansion at Peterboro and continue the proceedings.

The Convention re-assembled at the Presbyterian Church in Peterboro and Gerrit Smith was selected as chairman. In his speech to the delegates, he said:

> "My hatred to slavery always existed and always will. We have and hold probably between five and six million slaves in the United States. I will fight the institution that makes this thing possible as long as I am able and when I can no longer fight, I will bequeath the contest to my children. I don't expect to live to see slavery abolished, but the wicked institution will and must go. Slavery and liberty cannot exist side by side; one of the two must surrender."

Gerrit Smith did live to see slavery abolished. Professor Ralph Harlow in his book, "Gerrit Smith, Philanthropist and Reformer" (1938) wrote:

> "For some reason Central New York was one of the most important areas in which this complex movement (abolition) went on. And in so many ways the most conspicuous leader in the central region was Gerrit Smith. Other enthusiasts were equally generous of time and effort, but he, almost alone in the group, was in a position to supplement his zeal with substantial sums of money. The story of his life is in itself a history of the reform movement."

Smith took an interest in the movement by John Brown to make Kansas a free state and contributed financial support to that cause. He was a peaceful man and always maintained that his help was for a peaceful solution to the problem of slavery. John Brown, however, used some of these funds to finance his ill-fated raid on the United States arsenal at Harpers Ferry. Gerrit Smith became so disturbed at the resulting bloodshed that he suffered a nervous and mental breakdown which lasted several months.

During the Civil War, he financially contributed to the Union cause and at the conclusion, he was one of the bondsmen for the release of Jefferson Davis, the Confederate president, who was arrested for treason. Smith died at Peterboro in 1874.

THE UNDERGROUND RAILROAD IN UTICA

THE "underground railway" of pre-Civil War days was neither "underground" nor a "railroad" as such. It was the name given to a clandestine operation established by the abolitionists whereby runaway slaves from the South would be secretly hidden and passed on from person to person until they reached a place of safety, usually in Canada. It was a dangerous matter for a person to harbor such a runaway or help him to escape from his master. The penalty was $1000 fine and three years' imprisonment. Despite that fact, Utica was one of the way stations in this operation.

The free blacks of Utica lived by themselves in a settlement at the eastern end of Broad street, known as "Hayti". Fugitive slaves from the South naturally sought refuge at Hayti but were warned off as the local authorities would normally seek them there. They would be advised to go to the home of James B. DeLong on upper John street. James B. DeLong was born in Dutchess county, New York on July 4, 1790. He came to Utica in January 1813. He was a morocco dresser and after coming here formed a partnership with William Clark to conduct a tanning business. He lived for many years on Main street and conducted his factory on land later covered by the "gulf" basin. He then moved his tannery to Water street and lived on Whitesboro street. This he sold later to Thorn & Maynard and was in retirement for the last forty years of his life. He had two great aims in life, devotion to his church and the abolition of slavery. He was one of the early members of the Main Street Methodist chapel and contributed to the erection of the new Bleecker Street Methodist Church in the early 1820s. He also was a delegate to the abolition convention in 1835 and became an active "conductor" on the underground railroad, and pressed his family into the service. His home on upper John street was one of the "stations" and he often secreted runaway slaves in the church building on Bleecker street.

An old tale exists that early in the nineteenth century, two parties of surveyors were engaged to survey the land which is presently Roscoe Conkling Park. One party was working south and another party north. They did not finish their work at the same time. Their lines did not meet and the result was a "gore" or strip of land, which in its widest part was about 500 feet and then ran out to a point. Land was not very valuable at the time and rather than make a new survey, the engineers concluded to let it go on that, and so the "gore" belonged to no one, or was claimed by none. At any rate the belief seems to have been that a fugitive slave was safe as long as he was on the "gore".

Joshua Howe lived on this "gore" with his family in the 1830s and his cabin was one of the most important "stations on the underground railroad." Much of the "gore" occupied a high plateau between the Mohawk and Sauquoit valleys, and was not badly located as a lookout on both.

"Josh" Howe was a free man whose early life is the subject of several versions. One is that he was a slave of Colonel Benjamin Walker, the pioneer Utica resident who gave him his freedom and told him to go and live on the gore as he would not be molested there. Another story is that he purchased his freedom from a New Hartford man named Norton. The final story is that he was owned by a Revolutionary officer named Howe and fought with him in the War of 1812 and was given his freedom as a result.

The cabin of "Josh" on the "gore" not far from Third street, offered a secluded retreat and one where fugitive slaves could rest and recuperate before continuing their journey to Canada.

Uncle "Josh" was dead for a half century and buried in old cemetery No. 4 in the eastern part of New Hartford, when Thomas R. Proctor in 1915 decided that a suitable memorial should be placed in the park to commemorate "Josh's" contribution to the cause of freedom from slavery. A big boulder was placed near the flagstaff on the south side of the South Woods in the park. (Sunday Tribune, April 4, 1915).

THE COMING OF THE IRON HORSE
1836

PRIOR to 1826, there was not a single railroad in America. In that year, the Mohawk and Hudson River railroad was chartered to build a road from Albany to Schenectady. This was completed in October 1831, the roadbed being constructed mainly of solid stone. A wood-burning engine was ordered from the West Point Foundry and was completed in June 1831. This was shipped by boat up the Hudson to Albany. The engine was ten to twelve feet in length and was named the "DeWitt Clinton". Its principal features were large wheels, a long boiler, lofty smokestack and a central dome. A large flat car was attached to the rear of the locomotive and on this stood two large water barrels. These were connected to the boiler with a leather hose to create the steam and a pile of cut wood for fuel was carried. The engineer stood in the rear of the engine without any covering to shield him from the sparks and weather.

Uticans played a prominent part in securing a charter in 1833 to build a railroad from Utica to Schenectady called the "Utica & Schenectady Railroad." On July 11, 1834, the Common Council granted the new railroad permission to lay tracks in Main, or Water, or Jay or John street, "provided that no steam be used in propelling cars after they pass Third street." On October 30, 1835, the Council granted permission to the railroad to erect such wooden buildings as were deemed necessary on the south side of Water street provided no such wooden building shall be erected within one hundred feet of Genesee street.

The road was completed in the summer of 1836 and a trial run was made from Schenectady on July 22nd. The citizens of Utica were thrilled as the DeWitt Clinton puffed into sight with its three passenger coaches and five or six flat cars coupled to each other and the engine with wrought iron chains. The tracks ended at the rear of Bagg's Hotel and for the return trip, the locomotive and cars were run into a large flat circle and it took a dozen men to turn them around, one at a time and re-couple them. The return trip took six hours and a half for the seventy-eight miles. Stops had to be made at wood sheds along the way to take on a fresh supply of fuel and water. The official opening for passengers occurred on August 2nd.

The "Oneida Whig" of August 9th editorialized the event:

> "For three or four years, at least, this city must be the termination of this great railroad, and the point farthest west that has direct communication with tidewater. Hence, for some time, this point will possess peculiar facilities and advantages. We feel confident that in a short time this city will be a favorite residence for families of wealth and intelligence from the large cities and neighboring country. We think also that the various kinds of artisans and manufacturers will find this city a good place for carrying on their business. It is probable, also, that when the Chenango canal is under operation, coal can be delivered here so cheap as to give us the use of steam power on such terms as to be quite as good as water power, and at all events to be a great help to the branches of industry to which we have alluded."

The Syracuse and Utica Railroad Company was chartered May 11, 1836 to build 53 miles of road to connect Syracuse and Utica. The road was completed in June 1839, at a cost of $700,000. The new railroad was to end at Bagg's Square, requiring passengers to change to the Utica & Schenectady railroad to complete the trip east. One drawback to this route was that it passed through the swampy ground west of Bagg's Square. As a result, the new railroad was built for some distance upon piles, a system invented by E. P. Williams, of Utica.

On June 27, 1839, the first train left Utica and arrived in Rome 45 minutes later and then continued to Syracuse. Regular service began on July 3rd. One writer said, "The road being elevated on piles the excursionists were able to fancy they were sailing through the air." The new railroad created such national interest that Henry Clay came from his Kentucky home for a ride and President Van Buren did the same on September 10th.

To supply the coaches for the new railroad, the firm of Lyons & Williams of Utica obtained the contract. These were constructed in a red brick building on the south side of Elizabeth street, now the Oneida County parking lot. This building was demolished about 1893 and its history was given in the "Daily Press" of February 20, 1893:

> "The little place was built and was used as a car shop, for the erection of passenger coaches for the New York

121

Central & Hudson River road by the firm of Lyons & Williams, wagon and carriage makers, who at the time of its erection, 56 years ago, conducted a large shop at the corner of Burnet and Bleecker streets. David A. Lyons, with Mr. Williams, comprised the firm. Both are now deceased. Early in the days of the Central's advent through this section they obtained a contract to build passenger coaches for the new road. Their carriage shop was running to its full capacity, so for the accommodation of their new business, they purchased the corner from James Van Rensselaer, who owned a big strip of land on Elizabeth street and erected the shop. Shortly afterward the alley was cut through Mr. Van Rensselaer's garden. The cars used in that time were not so large by half as the present coaches, consequently the distance they had to be conveyed to the railroad was not considered a great inconvenience. Two coaches were made at a time within this small building. The work was done by a few men and was by hand under the direction of the junior member of the firm. The place was so constructed that on pleasant days the coaches were run out on a large platform on the east side to dry the paint and varnish. When the cars were completed they were run onto a low truck, a number of horses attached and the journey to the road commenced down John street, the high bridge over the Erie being the most difficult thing in the way of transportation. For about five years the business of making coaches was continued in this building until the road erected shops of its own at eastern points. Then, of course, the firm of Lyons & Williams manufactured no more cars."

It was not long after the railroad line to Schenectady and the one to Syracuse, that the railroad built its first depot in Utica. When it grew too small for the volume of traffic, a new railroad station was built east of the old one and the old depot was taken over as the main office of the American Express Company. It was finally demolished in 1910 and the "Utica Sunday Tribune" of October 9th noted its passing:

"The two-story frame structure now used by the American Express Company at the foot of Bagg's Square, next to Bagg's Hotel, was the first station erected by the Hudson Valley Railway Company in this city. At that time the station was the center of one of the main sections of the city. Passengers, after leaving the trains found a handy stopping place at Bagg's Hotel, from which the old stage line coaches departed for various sections of the State. In case the stage coach routes were

122

not desired, packet boats left on the Erie Canal, a form of travel much in vogue in the earlier days. Two and sometimes three trains a day arrived and left between Utica and Schenectady, and two trains each way daily between Utica and Syracuse after the line was extended that far west. The old station was the central point of interest in the city, for the railroad trains were ever objects of interest to the adults and amazement to the younger folk, with their huge smokestacks and the volume of smoke which rolled from the old wood-burning locomotives. It was with such early scenes that the old building was associated and with its removal will go the last vestige of the old days on what is now the Central."

To eliminate the inconvenience of changing trains in Utica, the New York Central Railroad was formed in 1853 and combined the old Utica & Schenectady and Utica & Syracuse roads. In 1869, the Central merged with the Hudson River Railroad from New York to Albany and the new railroad was known as the New York Central & Hudson River Railroad.

Between 1865 and 1869 a new railroad station was built in Utica. It was not constructed in a single year but, like Topsy, just grew. It was opened officially on January 29, 1869. It was a two-story brick structure with a wing containing the ticket office and ladies' and gentlemen's waiting rooms. The first floor of the main structure fronting on the river was used as an eating house which was opened on March 2, 1869 by Delos M. Johnson, formerly steward of the Manhattan Club in New York City. Thus began what was to be Utica's oldest continuing restaurant. It was open day and night and in its early days, one of the employees met all trains, beating a brass drum with a big drumstick. No hungry traveler could resist this invitation.

LOCOMOTIVE HEADLIGHTS

I N the early days of the railroads, the problem of providing light for night travel became important. Crude attempts to furnish light were not successful and it remained for a Utican to solve the problem by his inventive genius.

In 1800, Levi Williams, a native of Connecticut, came to Oneida county and settled at Manchester, near Kirkland but later moved to Coleman's Mills. He was a direct descendant of Roger Williams, the founder of Rhode Island. His son, Abijah Williams was born in Coleman's Mills in 1805. He came to Utica in 1841 and established a business on Church Lane which ran between Devereux and Blandina streets. He made and improved harness, reels, shuttles, spools and bobbins.

His son, Irvin A. Williams was born in Oriskany on June 9, 1829 and came to Utica with his parents in 1841. He studied in W. W. Williams' private school on Devereux street. At the age of 18 he learned the trade of woodturning and afterwards that of machinist in his father's shop. The lanterns then being used on the railroads furnished feeble light. Being of an inventive nature, Irvin Williams experimented in 1851 with various types of illumination. It is believed that he made the first practical locomotive headlight and secured patents in 1854 and 1857 and a third in 1862. This last was for a circular hollow wick burner to burn coal oil or kerosene. The contrivance worked well in the shop but Williams was not certain how well it would work on a swaying locomotive at night. Paul C. Willard., described the testing of the new device in the "Daily Press" of March 30, 1962:

> "So Williams asked and received permission to ride from Utica to Rome on the cowcatcher of the locomotive with his contraption. One important and ominous string was attached — he was to go at his own risk. The night rides of Irvin Williams will never outshine the exploits of Paul Revere, but, if ever a hall of fame for inventors is established, the young Utican deserves a niche. By day he labored over his invention. When night came, he risked everything, even his life, on the railroad.
>
> "There were mishaps and failures enough to dishearten

a less tenacious man. Sometimes the light went out before the train left the Utica yard. Often the sensitive flame died under the terrific lashing of wind that beat on the locomotive. Day after day Williams made changes and improvements and night after night he was rewarded by seeing the light beams lengthen on the silvery rails. At long last came a night when Williams felt satisfied that his headlight was finished, a reliable piece of equipment ready to shed its rays on the nation's path of progress. With blackened hands, he unleashed the lamp from the smokestack for the last time, shook the cinders from his clothing and returned home. His lonely, dangerous task was ended, but in a sense he did not ride alone. Unknown to him Fortune rode with him."

His burner was placed in a copper, silver-plated reflector about two feet in diameter and the whole was enclosed in a sheet metal case with a round, glass-covered window in front. He began the manufacture of locomotive headlights in Utica and the expanding railroads in the country bought this headlight as fast as he could make them. In 1881, he took Charles I. Williams as a partner in the I. A. Williams & Co. Rival companies sprang up and a memorable lawsuit followed. William and Nicholas Kernan, among the most eminent lawyers in the State, were successful in upholding Williams' patents and the railroads agreed to buy their headlights from Williams.

In 1889 he built a five story brick building on the north side of Blandina street (now the site of the State Office Building) and in 1892, his youngest son, Aras J. Williams, joined the firm. In 1894, the six leading headlight manufacturers in the country decided to amalgamate and the United States Headlight Company was incorporated with Williams as a director. The company continued to manufacture headlights in Utica until 1899 when the plant was moved to Buffalo.

Mr. Williams amassed a fortune and in 1871 purchased the Charles A. Yates house at 307 Genesee street, now the home of the Knights of Columbus. Oil headlights were used until about 1900 when electric lights made their appearance. Irvin A. Williams died in Greenwich, Connecticut on February 29, 1912.

SWIMMING IN THE OLD CHENANGO CANAL

THE Chenango Canal was built between the years 1834-1836 to connect the Erie Canal with the Susquehanna River at Binghamton. The purpose was to provide a means of transporting coal from the Pennsylvania coal region to supply the infant industries in Central New York. The legislative act provided that the comissioners construct a canal from Binghamton to the Erie canal and in determining the route and where it should join the Erie, they should be influenced by a regard for the local economy "and the amount of gifts, grants and donations". Several cities sought to have the junction with the Erie at their city, but Uticans voted to impose a tax on property owners who would benefit by its location here . . . This was successful. The work on the canal began in July 1834.

When it was completed in October 1836, it was 97 miles long, 40 feet wide at the surface with a depth of four feet. To carry the canal over the deep divide separating the waters of the Mohawk from those of the Susquehanna, 116 locks were constructed of rubble stone, each being 20 feet long by 15 feet in width. The first lock was located on Columbia street, near State, where in later years the Utica Steam Cotton Mills were built. After passing through this lock northward, boats had access directly to the Erie canal at Whitesboro street. Southward were a series of locks in West Utica. The fifth lock was located near Mandeville street and the sixth lock near Sunset avenue. The present Lincoln avenue ran almost parallel to the canal and was originally known as Chenango avenue. The ninth lock, near the present Burrstone road was located near a grove in the woods. That section of the towpath extending from Lincoln avenue to the Ontario & Western railroad tracks was for the most part lined with a dense growth of forest. Here clambakes and picnics were often held.

For some years, the canal was of great importance and the cost of coal for Utica's industries and home consumption was materially reduced. Large quantities of coal were received here by barge and to handle the business numerous coal yards were established near the canal. The remains of some can still be seen. But with the building of the railroads whose companies secured control of the coal fields, the Chenango canal became of little value and by the late 1870s was gradually abandoned, passing into history, its banks filled in and its course obliterated. Building lots were then surveyed and sold to West Uticans.

The boys of West Utica in the middle of the nineteenth century found the old Chenango Canal ideal for swimming and a reporter for the "Utica Daily Press" recalled those days in that newspaper on June 2nd, 1888:

"No doubt it will never fade from the recollection of those who were boys early in the 60s. The boys of the Second Ward had the Mohawk, or that portion of it known as the 'Butter Bowl' and the 'Button Ball', as a bathing place. Schwab's boat yard and Broad street basin on the Erie served a like purpose for the boys of the First and Fifth Wards — the Fifth comprising what is now the Fifth and Eighth Wards. The boys of the other portions of the city — Cornhill, Frog Hollow, and West Utica — used the Chenango canal for bathing purposes, the West Utica boys occupying the sixth lock, and the others the seventh, which is just over the line in the town of New Hartford.

"There was always a feud or strife between the boys of West and East Utica, the cause of which was never definitely known. The tradition was that the East Utica boys had been in the habit of using the fifth lock, and that when the advance of civilization and the constables drove them away, they sought to take the sixth lock from the West Utica boys, who rebelled and refused to go further south. On the contrary, they compelled the East Utica boys to go to the seventh lock, which was outside the corporation and fully a mile from the inhabited portions of the city. This tradition like many others, was probably not founded on fact, but under it, many of the boys of West Utica, of whom I am proud to be one, fought and suffered, for the feud often took the form of personal encounters. A West Utica boy who ventured into East Utica was sure to receive a thumping; and the East Utican who came into our territory was lucky if he escaped with his life, though sometimes Frog Hollow rallied in force and drove us into our dooryards and houses. The boys of both sides fought for home rule, and though the fight may not have been for that principle, each side was very much in earnest although very much mistaken. Sometimes this happens to older people.

"What a refreshing pastime and luxury 'goin' in swim-min' was to the boys, especially during the dog days of a summer vacation. The salutation and inquiry among boys on the street was abbreviated to 'Goin' In?' and when parents were near, it was expressed by holding up two fingers with a nod or shake of the head. Parents then were watchful and as we thought unreasonable, and insisted that 'goin' in' once a day, in the evening, was enough for the health and cleanliness of any youth. But we were wiser than stern fathers and anxious mothers, and concluded that three times a day was about the proper caper, and on this conclusion we acted, although we knew and often felt the 'penalty' for disobedience to be 'strap oil'. The afternoon pilgrimages to the water were therefore cautiously made, generally by way of any street except the one we lived on. The boys met, how-ever, near 'Redner's', just above the point where McCormack's coal yard now is. Thence we proceeded by easy stages to the lock above, sometimes riding on a boat, sometime wading in the bed of Nail Creek to gather mint or blueflag lilies which rivaled Solomon's robes in the gorgeousness of their apparel. Sometimes we caught crabs for their 'eye stones' or leeches to be sold. Some-times we paused at the Burned Bridge, to annoy the old Dutchman who patiently bobbed for eels at that point, by throwing stones into the water. Sometimes we chased the yellow butterflies which flitted and flocked around the muddy pools, or stoned the yellow birds which swung in time to their own music on the ripening thistle heads. In late summer we caught bumble bees in the pods of the milk weed. It was the waywardness and wantonness of youth. Under the ban of disobedience we felt we 'might as well be killed for a sheep as a lamb' and the spirit of mischief was uppermost and strong.

"Arrived at the lock the process of disrobing was short and simple. The 'cornplanter's' hat, once white, was thrown off with one hand, the thumb of the other un-shipped the single suspender, and the pantaloons drop-ped off while the cotton shirt was being pulled over the head. It was literally undressing one, two, three order, as jackets, collars, neckties, shoes, stockings and under-clothing were not generally worn. They were regarded as fashionable follies affected by the big feeling Corn-hillers, who bathed in the seventh lock, and whom we regarded with increased contempt for such affectation. Once undressed, the custom of wetting the leg to pre-vent cramps was religiously observed, and then we plunged into the canal head-foremost to reappear in a moment on the opposite side and announce with a shout that the water was 'just bully' as regards temperature. Everybody could swim, of course, for the art was soon learned. The boy who for months patronized the 'baby hole' where the water was so shallow that he could not wade beyond his depth, was coaxed or dared into coming upon the bank near the lock, where the depth was about eight feet. One of the big boys would then seize the struggling youngster, throw him in, and as he appeared above the surface, the crowd would shout 'Paddle or drown, you sucker'. 'Go it dog fashion'. The youngster found that opening his mouth to yell only filled it with water, and his sole salvation was in paddling. In a minute or two, which seemed ages, he would reach the shore more dead than alive. Everybody then assured him that he could swim like a duck. Hesitation and caution were regarded with contempt, and so the youngster was induced to repeat the experiment, and learned to swim before he knew it. The rise of ground at the jaws of the lock was quite rapid, the vertical walls being capped with large stones. He who could dive off the 'first stone', which was about a foot out of water, was not satisfied till he tried the second, which was higher. Soon he took the highest degree by diving from the plank which crossed the lock, about ten feet above the water, and thereafter he was regarded as fit to associate with the big boys.

"Playing tag was a favorite game, especially when the lock was full, as one had only to dive across. The water was clear and everybody was willing to dive for white shells, pieces of soap, and sometimes, though rarely, for pennies which were thrown in. To know a boy thoroughly you must see him undressed. We could always tell the boys of Catholic faith by the scapulars which they wore about their necks. Some wore a strip of eel skin about the ankle as a charm to ward off cramps. The boy who was built like a living skeleton, with skin as white as a corpse, but covered with goose pimples, like a nutmeg grater, could not remain in the water long before his eyes were watery, his lips blue, and his teeth chattered, but he was only an indifferent swimmer. Such boys were few, yet they were almost invariably well dressed and wore shoes and stockings, and had money. When dressed they were envied, but in the water they were despised. The boy who was brown as a berry, and built like a young Hercules, swam everywhere with ease and grace. The sun did not blister his back nor the water fatigue him, and he would take a dare from no one, yet when he came to dress, his clothes consisted of a pile of rags.

"Shortly after supper we were ready to join the army of men and boys who had worked in the woolen and cotton factories all day and return to the lock for another swim. There was no fear of parents now, for we had their permission, nor of the East Utica enemy, for we were out in force. The water below the lock was fairly alive with shouting, sputtering bathers, and we could hardly jump in without getting astride of some one. The boys pelted each other with wads of wet eel grass, and summary punishment was inflicted on the youngster who cracked stones together under water, as it is supposed to make the swimmers deaf. There was always a similar swarm Sunday afternoons, and those who had had enough of swimming would go to the hill west of the lock, where there was a group of beeches, on whose smooth bark we would carve our initials. Under the spreading branches many were initiated into the mysteries of card playing, and the place was known as 'Eucher Hill' in consequence. Here, too, the boy who had been bold enough to 'swipe' a clay pipe from his 'old man' would take his first lessons in smoking. 'Rough and Ready' was the motto of the fire company in our ward, and we tried to live up to it.

"Just above the lock was a waste weir, the water from which formed a large pool before it joined Nail Creek. Here we took our first lessons in angling, quarrelling among ourselves for favorite spots along the shore. The catch, a few shiners, horned dace or bullheads, were carried home proudly as trophies of our skill and provender for the cat. There was a wild, hilarious joy about swimming, but the quiet though eager expectancy of fishing gave us greater pleasure. The hook was a bent pin, the sinker a shingle nail, the line a cord and the float a flat piece of wood, but we watched the float eagerly while the bubbles floated lazily by it, looking ever so longingly for little waves in circles which should mark the first nibble. Swimming makes a boy hungry, but in fishing supper is forgotten. The sun sank unobserved behind the western hill, and soon we were surprised by seeing stars reflected on the bottom of the pool. But the string of fish grew, and the little brook sang a quiet song of tuneful rest to the sleeping flowers and we were happy. Hark! What is that? From the western hills where a broad band of dim light marks the place where the sun went down an hour ago, comes the chime of bells in the neighboring village of New York Mills, tolling the hour of nine. It is taken up and repeated by the bell on the Steam Woolen Mill in West Utica. They were the boys' curfew bells and seemed to repeat as plainly as talking, what our mothers had often told us they said 'Bed-time'. 'Bed-time'. Bed-time'. Hastily gathering up our trophies, we scampered home through the wet grass, past the sleeping cows lazily chewing their cuds and flocks of white geese quartered for the night on the common.

"I walked over the sixth lock the other day. Only newly leveled earth remains to tell where the canal, and the lock were. The burned bridge is gone, the beeches and the single pine on Eucher Hill have long since been cut down. The boys of those days are scattered far and wide. Nail Creek is the only landmark left, and here it is laughing gaily in the sunlight, and at night mirroring the silent stars and crooning to itself sweetly as of yore. 'Men may come and men may go, but I flow on forever.' "

THE ONEIDA NATIONAL BANK
1836

WITH the expiration of the charter of the United States Bank and the withdrawal from circulation of its bank notes, there was a necessity for additional banking capital for Utica merchants and industry. The Oneida Bank was incorporated May 13, 1836 and took over the premises on Genesee street previously occupied by the U.S. Branch Bank. This is the present location of the downtown branch of the Oneida National Bank & Trust Company, which became a national bank after the Civil War.

The bank was scheduled to open for business on November 21st and subscriptions to its capital stock were collected. On the preceding Saturday, in preparation for the opening, the proceeds of the sale of the stock amounting to

$108,000 consisting of silver and bank bills of various banks were placed in the vault of the old Branch Bank. This old vault had a door which was secured by a lock. In addition, a big iron bar could be let down from the room above the office by means of a pulley and it descended into a socket in the floor below the vault door. When it was in place, an iron collar or yoke was affixed over the top of the bar in the upper room, and this was secured by two heavy padlocks. Cox, the porter of the new bank, was hired to remain on guard in the bank over the weekend. He remained on duty until about sunrise of Monday morning when he decided to go home for breakfast. An hour or two later, the teller of the bank arrived and found the door to the bank locked and apparently all was in order, However, when he went upstairs to raise the bar to the vault below, he found that the two padlocks on the yoke had been removed, one of them being broken and the collar itself lying on the floor. When he raised the bar and hurried downstairs to open the vault, he found that the entire cash capital of the bank was missing. The burglars, however, had been careful not to take any of the brand new, crisp Oneida Bank bills, which would be worthless and could easily lead to detection.

Although the Oneida Bank could not open on schedule because of a lack of cash, this proved no problem and in a short time new capital was raised and the bank has been in continuous business since that time. No trace of the burglars could be found until the summer of 1837 when the Bank of Rome, New York, reported that it had received for redemption its own bank bills. This parcel had been forwarded by a Rochester Bank, and consisted of $2,500 in $20 denomination notes. A check disclosed they were part of the proceeds of the burglary and were checked as coming from a bank in Canada. They were eventually traced to a George Harvey who was arrested in Canada and extradited to this country. He was returned to Utica to face trial. He decided to cooperate and surrendered his portion of the loot which amounted in all to $44,000.

Harvey's confession to the crime was given in detail in the "Utica Observer" of December 26, 1837. He said that he had come to Utica without any intention of committing the crime. On the sidewalk, he met a William Morgan, a noted robber and after some discussion, they planned to rob a bank. Observing that the old U. S. Branch Bank was being remodelled for use by the new bank, they entered the building

132

one night and in an old desk, they found keys to the vault and to the padlocks which fastened the bolt. They took these and Morgan, a locksmith made wax impressions and returned them to the bank. From these, he fashioned keys and also made a key for the front door.

After the building had been remodelled, they entered and tried the keys. Finding that there was not money enough there at the time (about $20,000), they concluded to wait until the weekend before the bank was to open. They arrived at the bank about daylight on November 21st, 1836 and saw Cox, the porter leave the bank for breakfast. After they were satisfied that he had reached home, Harvey's accomplice entered the bank, with a carpet bag under his cloak, while he remained outside to give an alarm, should it be necessary. The vault was opened with the keys, except one padlock, which was wrenched off, the key to that one not having been completed, and the money deposited in a carpet bag. They left on a canal boat, throwing their carpet bag among the baggage on top of the boat as though containing nothing of value.

Harvey was sentenced to State Prison, but Morgan, although traced to England, was never apprehended. The old indictment against him is still on file.

THE EARLY PARKS OF UTICA

NO map in the County Clerk's office is so much consulted as that filed in 1811 by Charles C. Brodhead covering the property of the Bleecker family. There was set out an area of three and four-tenths acres as a public common or park, known as Chancellor Square and this included the original site of the Academy and Courthouse. The lots on the east and west ends originally fronted on the square itself and could only be approached through it. Eventually Bleecker street wormed its way on the north side and Elizabeth on the south.

As the city grew, Chancellor Park became a sort of gateway between the business section to the northwest and the residential portion to the southeast. The residents enjoyed the cool shade of the trees for picnics and celebrations. To keep the rummaging hogs and stupid ducks of the townspeople from invading its sacred precincts, the city fathers erected a wooden fence around the park. Streets were laid out on the east and west sides, and by ordinance of the Common Council of April 7, 1837, the street on the east side of the park between Bleecker and Elizabeth was named Kent Street and that on the west side Academy. Both Chancellor Park and Kent Street were named for the same person, James Kent, the distinguished jurist and chancellor of the State.

We read in the "Daily Gazette" of June 28, 1845:

> "The workmen have commenced tearing away the unsightly old fence around this beautiful piece of ground and are rapidly replacing it with a new one. The interior of the Square has also undergone many improvements. Tastefully planned walks, in all more than a mile in extent, have been laid out and a number of new trees planted."

Steuben Square was laid out in 1827. It stood well out of town at the time and Charlotte street which terminates at its northern side contained only a few residences. It was named for Baron Wilhelm von Steuben, the Prussian nobleman who fought in the Revolution. Our first Mayor, Joseph Kirkland, ordered a fence erected around it and laid out gravel walks. On July 13, 1832, the Common Council decreed that that part of Bridge street (Park Avenue) extending across Steuben Square be discontinued and the street altered to run on the northwesterly side; that it be enclosed with a fence and walks made around and diagonally and transversely across said square. On June 13, 1834, the name was changed from Steuben Square to Steuben Park. In 1841, William Begg was appointed park keeper; followed in 1857 by John B. Marchisi; and in 1866 by Bernard Malloy, a landscape gardener. Later the old picket fence was removed.

The third of the early parks was Johnson Park at the intersection of Square and West Streets. It was deeded to the city by Alexander B. Johnson on October 27th, 1849. The deed recites that,

> "A. B. Johnson has resided in the said Utica for the last forty-nine years and feels toward the inhabitants thereof much good will; that his parents resided therein and are

there buried, and that his father, Bryan Johnson, as early as the year 1799 gave Utica its first commercial impulse by the purchase of country produce for the New York market, and by the sale of foreign merchandise on an enlarged scale and at low prices."

When Charles W. Hutchinson became Mayor of Utica in 1875, he determined to add handsome fountains in Utica's parks. The one at Steuben Park was purchased from J. L. Mott, of New York city. It was made of iron with the figures of zinc. It was 18 feet high, constructed in the Renaissance style, surmounted by a large and graceful figure of Canova's Hebe, the goddess of youth, holding a pitcher in her right hand above her head from which she poured water into the bowl held in her left hand. The figure was semi-nude and very graceful and beautiful. Around the base were the figures of four boys in different attitudes of bathing, and two swans. Two of the boys were seated and in the act of undressing. Of the other two, one had his hands folded as if to dive into the water, while the second was taking off his last garment. The swans were on the east and west sides, and had their wings extended heads down, and bills open as if enraged. The fountain had two pans. On the first pan were four Triton boys, and a jet of water leaped from the shells held in the mouths of each. The second pan was six feet in diameter, and around the sides were four ornamental jets. But time took its toll on the fountain and we read in the "Saturday Globe" of October 6, 1906:

"Perhaps it is the effect of a change from Graeffenburg to Adirondack water; it may be that she has grown weary of standing there on a pedestal beckoning lovers to commune under her protection; or possibly the influence of the melancholy days is upon her and she cannot resist an inclination to self-destruction. Whatever it be that ails her, Miss Steuben, the creature of art who has posed for a generation in the park whose name she bears, has acted in a manner alarming to her friends. Through the summer she showed no disposition to deviate from her staid habits, but early this week it was noticed that she was growing dizzy and was inclined to tip her head toward the west. For years she has flirted with old Sol, as he sent his evening good-by glances down Park avenue. Now she seems to be bending toward him, as imploring an embrace. Slowly but steadily she leaned over. Passersby looked at her and smiled, but like those hard-hearted folks who permitted the victim of the robbers on the road to Jericho to lie uncared for in his wretchedness they went their way. Mention of her condition was made in the daily papers, however. By this time, the lady of the fountain had turned over and stood upon her head on the edge of the basin. A standpipe through which she had sucked water these many years refused to desert her and clung to her skirts so tenaciously that she was prevented from self-destruction which would have ensued had she plunged into the water basin which surrounds her pedestal."

The city fathers came to her rescue and in June 1907, she was removed and J. L. Mott constructed a new one. The basin was ten and one half feet in diameter and together with the statue was 12 feet high. The figure of a boy holding high in one hand an electric globe was selected and from the globe the electric radiance spread over the park. The jets of water came from the base of the statue of the boy and fell into an octagon basin.

The 1875 fountain placed in Chancellor Park was made of zinc, covered with bronze and represented Neptune riding in a shell chariot upon two dolphins. He grasped the traditional trident, which he pointed at the head of one of the dolphins. From the nostrils of the dolphins, two jets of water were thrown to a height of twenty-five or thirty feet, while from their mouths were jets fan shaped letting the water fall into the basin. On the back of the chariot were numberless small spray jets. The fountain was eight and one-half feet high and rested on a stone base about five feet square. The basin was fifty feet in diameter.

MECHANIC'S HALL
1837

ONE of the few remaining landmarks of early Utica is Mechanic's Hall on the northwest corner of Liberty and Hotel streets. It was erected by the Utica Mechanic's Association in 1837. The initial steps toward organizing the association of Utica's mechanics were taken at a meeting in John King's Tavern on the corner of Washington and Liberty streets on May 19, 1827 and it was finally incorporated March 30, 1833. The association maintained a reading room and library on the third floor of the Law Building on Genesee street. In August 1836, a building known as the "Clinton House" was demolished to clear the site at Hotel and Liberty streets. The new building was designed by a Mr. Bourn of Utica and the builders were James McGregor and Abraham Culver. The ground floor was of cut stone and was intended to be rented for stores. The upper floors were constructed of brick, with pilasters of the Tuscan order extending to the cornice. The second floor contained a reading room and library. The whole of the third floor consisted of a hall, forty feet by sixty seven feet six inches, with a lofty ceiling. It was adapted for musical performances, lectures and public meetings.

From time to time, extensive alterations were made. In 1851, a gallery to seat three hundred persons was erected in the third floor hall. It was six feet wide and ten feet on the southern side facing the stage. The gallery was supported by a wrought iron bar, resting on iron brackets fastened firmly on the south side. The front of the gallery had an iron balustrade, all the work of Messrs. Dana & Lynch of Utica. In 1854, a lot on the north side of the building was purchased and the building enlarged and improved. In 1866, the small stage was enlarged.

For a long time the Association conducted annual fairs of manufactured products and conducted courses of lectures in the winter. The fairs were finally abandoned but the lectures continued until about 1880. The hall was also the scene of many political gatherings and conventions. The post office was located in Mechanic's Hall for many years prior to the erection of the Post Office on Broad street in the 80s.

By 1870, Mechanic's Hall had outlived its usefulness as the city grew. As operatic and dramatic productions became more elaborate, the demand for a first class theater with an auditorium large enough for political conventions and mass meetings became so urgent that the public spirited citizens came to the aid of the Association and money was raised to build an "Opera House" on the north side of Lafayette street, between Hotel and Washington streets.

In 1899, Mr. E. L. Wells reminisced:

> "Away back in the days of the Civil War the best hall of amusement Utica could grieve over was old Mechanic's Hall in Hotel street. It was about big enough to hold a fair-sized prayer meeting in, shaped like a dry goods box with narrow galleries hanging to three of its sides, a level floor, a diminutive stage without scenery, on which about the only interesting performances were furnished once a year by the Academy boys and girls, who paralyzed the natives with second-hand reproductions of the oratory of Webster, or Paine, Patrick Henry or Wendell Phillips or tortured the ghost of Hamlet with the immortal question 'to be or not to be', while the leading lady in the cast, clad in a robe of spotless white, advancing to the footlights with timorous step announced in a scarcely audible whisper, but with conscious pride in her new gown, 'I'm to be queen of the May' and for their herculean efforts to please were showered by a worshipping audience with garlands in which the classic laurel was replaced by the modern burdock or thistle."

When the new Opera House was opened on Lafayette street, the Mechanic's Association then sold the old hall in 1871 to Harrison Gilmore, who owned it for a number of years prior to its purchase by the Herald-Dispatch Company for its newspaper production. In the 1920s it was purchased by Thomas J. Griffith's & Sons, publishers of 29 periodicals and newspapers, including "Y Drych", the national Welsh language weekly. In December 1924, fire completely destroyed the upper part of the building with an estimated damage of upwards of $100,000. It was thereafter repaired.

UTICA FEMALE SEMINARY
1837

THE citizens of Utica for some time were of the opinion that a place for the training of their daughters comparable to the Academy for their sons would do away with the necessity of sending them away to be educated. The Utica Female Academy, a private institution, was chartered April 28, 1837. Until the proposed building for the use of the Seminary should be erected, the building on the corner of Genesee and Pearl streets which had been originally built as a theater and then converted to the United States Hotel was utilized. Under Miss Sheldon, English, Latin, French, Chemistry, Drawing, Painting and Music were taught.

In June 1838, the cornerstone of a new building was laid on a plot at the head of Washington street, near its junction with Genesee street. The building was designed by Robert Higham, an architect, and was 150 feet long, by fifty wide and three and a half stories. Constructed of brick, its estimated cost was $20,000.

On March 27, 1865, fire broke out at four o'clock in the morning in a wooden building adjoining the rear of the building and used as a woodhouse. It spread to the main building and in two or three hours consumed the entire building. Mr. William Metcalf of the firm of Metcalf & Dering designed a new building, one of the finest in the State.

The building contained a gymnasium and recitation rooms and in each of the second and third stories were 21 bed apartments of various sizes. The old school continued to educate women during the last half of the nineteenth century. In 1908, the building was sold to the YMCA and is today the location of the new and modern building.

UTICA CITIZEN'S CORPS
1837

IN 1837, Captain E. K. Barnum, U.S. Army was stationed in Utica with a small detachment of regular Army soldiers. He was a veteran of the Seminole Wars in Florida and proposed that the younger people of Utica should form an independent military company and offered his services as drillmaster. Some 36 members signed up from the prominent and influential families of the city. Their first armory was in the Miller block on the west corner of Bagg's Square, over the Ray Drug Store. The City Council purchased 50 stand of rifles and the first public parade of the new company was held on December 20, 1837. Thus began the existence of Utica's most famous military organization. For more than a century its members, whose motto was "We Lead", fought in the wars and performed public services.

At the outbreak of the Civil War, its three officers and 74 men, under Captain James McQuade, immediately volunteered and became Company A, 14th New York. Two of its members, McQuade and Daniel Butterfield came out of that war as Major Generals. After the War, the Corps occupied quarters in Chubbuck Hall on Hotel street, adjoining old Mechanics Hall, and later moved to the old Armory on Bleecker street. In 1887, the Corps joined the National Guard and was mustered in as the 44th Separate Company.

In 1898, President McKinley called for volunteers and the company left on May 2 and was sent to the Hawaiian Islands as Company E of the First New York Volunteers.

In 1917, it was sent to guard the aqueducts conveying New York city's water supply and later in the year, all but seven men, all non-commissioned officers, were distributed to other outfits. The seven men formed the nucleus of Company B, First Pioneer Infantry and went overseas for service, seeing action on the Marne, at Chateau Thierry, and in the Argonne. After its return from that war, it became Company L, 10th Infantry, National Guard, New York.

GRACE EPISCOPAL CHURCH
1838

THE Episcopalians of the city worshipped at old Trinity Church on Broad street. The growing needs of the parish made the establishment of another church necessary. On May 21, 1838, Grace Episcopal Church was incorporated and the new congregation worshipped for a time in a small 20 by 35 foot room on the second floor of No. 215 Genesee street.

During the year 1839, a lot was secured at the corner of Broadway and Columbia street and on it a small frame church was erected. In 1888 on the occasion of the 50th anniversary of the church, the "Utica Observer" described this first church:

> "It was a very unpretentious structure of wood, having sixty pews, a gallery or organ loft at the west end, and what is known as a 'three-decker' arrangement in the chancel, the pulpit overlopping the whole, and being entered from the vestry room through a door in the wall. It also had a steeple, for the erection of which $300 was appropriated by the vestry. This church, which with the steeple cost $1,900, was opened in 1839, and in less than ten years it had to be enlarged at a cost of $1,500, thirty two pews being added for the increasing congregation."

Alfred Munson was interested in the erection of a new church for Grace Episcopal and he secured title to the lot on the southeast corner of Genesee and Elizabeth streets. He procured plans for the new church from the distinguished architect, Richard Upjohn, of New York City. The vestry determined to build on the lots purchased by Mr. Munson, and early in the spring of 1856 commenced to take down the old Eagle Tavern on the site.

The cornerstone was laid on July 10th, 1856. The last service in the old church was on April 15, 1860 and on May 20, 1860, the new church was opened for worship.

141

CIGAR AND TOBACCO MANUFACTURE
1839

THE manufacture of cigars and the processing of tobacco began in Utica about 1835. The first person to undertake this business was a Mr. Tomlinson, first on Pine street and later on Liberty street. His business was sold to Leslie A. Warnick and John Bryan in 1839.

Leslie A. Warnick was born in Downpatrick, Ireland in 1807, and he died at the age of 100 years in 1907. In the later 1830s he came to Utica and opened a cigar shop in Bagg's Hotel. The next year, he moved to Catharine street and took his brother-in-law, John Bryan as a partner. When Warnick & Bryan commenced to operate the Tomlinson business at 26 Liberty street, they produced chewing and smoking tobacco and snuff. In 1845 they moved to lower Genesee street and the "Utica Daily Gazette" of November 11, 1847, thus described their factory:

> "They occupy the old store of John Williams & Co., since occupied by F. Hollister and by Lansing & Miller (on Genesee street). The front part of the building, used as a store, conducts to the factory. One room is used for picking and culling. A machine is in operation constantly cutting the weed, which is dried on scaffolding in the upper rooms, then dropped through a tunnel in the floor into a lower apartment to be put into papers."

The fire of 1848 which originated in O'Neil's hardware store damaged some of its stock, but the building itself was saved. In 1852 Mr. Bryan was succeeded by John Golding Brown as partner. He was born at Danville, Vermont, in 1822 and at an early age came to Utica, where he worked for Frederick Hollister, the merchant. The Warnick & Brown firm continued for over a half century. Mr. Brown died on March 27, 1903 and his son, Leslie W. Brown continued his father's interest as John G. Brown & Son. When Mr. Warnick himself died in 1907, his surviving children included names well known to Uticans, Mrs. William Kernan, Mrs. Francis Kernan, Jr., and Mrs. William S. Doolittle.

MILITARY HALL — JOHN AND CATHARINE STREETS

OLD Military Hall, at the northwest corner of Catharine and John Streets, was demolished late in 1913 to make room for the new Post Office. It is at the present the loading dock for the mail vehicles. When it was being demolished, the "Saturday Globe" of November 29, 1913 reminisced:

"There is an air of romance lingering around the old building, which arises from the fact that history has neglected to record the date of its erection. Tradition has it, however, that it was built in the early '30s and that it received its name from the fact that for many years Utica's leading military organizations were quartered there. For years it divided with the York House, on Whitesboro street, the distinction of being the most popular place of entertainment in the city. The city directory of 1840 contains the following advertisement of Military Hall, then conducted by Daniel Wood.

'This establishment is considered one of the finest edifices, as well as most pleasing situations in the city. It contains two of the most elegant and well furnished ball alleys west of the city of New York which from their location and neatness, furnish a place of resort to those who are fond of this manly and healthful recreation, a place of resort at once agreeable and refreshing. There is also on the second floor a very beautiful and capacious room, fitted up expressly for a lecture room, or for the temporary exhibition of amusements of any kind. The third floor is occupied as the Armory of the Utica Citizen's Corps, where its meetings and drill are regularly held. There is connected with the saloon a bar, well furnished with the choicest fruits and wines. And the proprietor assures the public that no pains will be spared to make this establishment one of the best and most fashionable places of resort in the city.' "

REV. ANDREW WETZEL AND THE GROWTH OF LUTHERANISM

REV. Andrew Wetzel was born in Wurtemberg, Germany on January 27, 1808 and was educated in philosophy and theology at the University of Turebingen. Three years later he graduated and came to America, where he settled in Verona and preached there, at Rome, West Leyden, Constableville and Boonville. It was in the fall of 1832 that Mr. Wetzel preached for the first time in Utica and thereafter services were regularly held in private houses at intervals of four weeks. There were only six families of Protestant Germans in the city, George Neejer and his wife, two families named Schwabe, the Goebel family, the widow Julienne Haeuser and another family whose name is forgotten. Varick street marked the western edge of the city and there were but two houses on the street at the time, Watkin's store and the Goodliffe House, on the bank of Nail creek at the junction of Varick and Court streets. The woolen and cotton factories had not yet been established and Pastor Wetzel's flock were all poor people. In 1834 and 1835 the number of Germans in the city began to increase.

One of the first places where Lutheran services were held was in Masseth's lane, next at the old Fire Engine House No. 7, and in a dwelling on Canal street near Potter's Bridge. A larger place was needed and the society secured the use of an old tumble-down frame school house on the corner of Bleecker street and Park avenue. It was very small and uncomfortable, the ceiling was low and the seats were arranged against the walls; in addition, the entire structure was constantly in danger of falling down. This place was shared with the black population of the city in holding services. These quarters soon became too small, and the society secured the use of the Sunday School room of the Second Presbyterian (later Baptist) Church on Bleecker street.

A year later, when the church was sold, the city fathers granted permission to use the school house on Columbia street, a small one-story structure, whose low seats, designed for children, hardly answered for adults. In 1836 or 1837, the society obtained the use of the small church on Fayette street, originally built by the Methodists, and later occupied by the Episcopalians, and also as the original site of St. Joseph's Roman Catholic church. In the summer of 1838, this church was sold to St. Joseph's congregation.

The society then turned to Henry Huntington, of Rome, who gave them the use of the "old Bethel church", owned by him, rent free. This was located on Fayette street, at the corner of Varick. The lower floor was used for a private school, and the upper floor for church services. The building was afterward converted into a dwelling house, and one half was later removed to make room for the Utica, Clinton & Binghamton Railroad.

On April 5, 1842, a lot was purchased on Columbia street (later the site of St. Patrick's rectory) and a frame building, 55 by 36 feet was built, being completed in 1844. Pastor Wetzel had married in 1832 and lived in Verona, from which he rode on horseback every Sunday to hold services. In May 1845, he moved to Utica and first lived on Whitesboro street just west of Potter's bridge and later on Varick street. In the little white church on Columbia street in 1845, Pastor Wetzel gave Utica its first glimpse of a Christmas tree (a beautiful custom from his Fatherland).

During the incendiary period of Utica's history in 1851, this church was burned to the ground. The society then bought a lot on the corner of Fay and Cooper streets in April 1851 and began the erection of a brick building 70 by 40 feet. While the church was being built, the society held services in Central City Hall, afterward known as "Turn Halle", on the north side of Fayette street, between State and the Chenango Canal.

The church was dedicated December 16, 1851, at a total cost of $5000. In 1853, a division took place among the members, which resulted in the establishment of the Moravian Church.

The first meeting to form the new society was held in 1854 and services were held in the homes of Daniel Hess and Frederick Dauer. In 1855, services were held in the Lutheran church, but by 1856, it was decided to build a separate church building. A lot was purchased for $1600 on Cooper street from Thomas Hopper. The first church building, a frame structure, was consecrated on September 10, 1856. The congregation outgrew the building and in 1891, it was demolished and replaced by a brick building, with a minister's residence in the rear facing Cornelia street.

With the growth of Corn Hill, the formation of a Moravian

Society there was deemed necessary and a mission and Sunday school were held in Mr. Busacker's shop on South street. In 1912, Trinity Moravian Church was organized, with the Rev. George Remmer the first pastor.

There were many Germans in the eastern part of the city and Pastor Wetzel established a mission on Corn Hill in May 1860 from which St. Paul's Evangelical Lutheran Church was created. With the decline in immigration and the desire of the younger children for the English language, it was necessary to conduct two sessions of Sunday school, one in German and the other in English.

This led to a demand that preaching be in English at intervals which caused considerable dissention. The call for the establishment of an English speaking Lutheran congregation was sent out in June 1877 and the first meeting was held at the home of John C. Hieber on June 10th. On July 15th, the English Lutheran Church Association was organized at the home of Henry Martin, and eventually took the name of the Church of the Redeemer. Services were held for several years in the Dryer Methodist Episcopal Church, corner of Court and Stark streets.

In July 1881, the old malt house property on Columbia street near the southeast corner of State was purchased for $6000. The contract for a church, Gothic in style and of handsome bluish-gray Clinton stone, was let in May 1883 and the cornerstone laid July 26th. From April of 1883 to Christmas 1884, services were held on the third floor of the Utica City Hall, which was known then as the City Opera House. The new church seated 500 and a chapel seated 350, both buildings so arranged that they could be thrown open together and used as one structure. The first service was held in the Chapel on Christmas 1884, and the first service in the church itself on May 17, 1885.

The Rev. Arnold F. Keller began his pastorate November 15, 1922 and in January 1923, the congregation decided to relocate the church on the Hieber property on the west side of Genesee street, near the Parkway. The final service in the old Church was August 1, 1926 and the building was taken over as an automobile salesroom.

146

THE VOLUNTEER FIRE COMPANIES
1833-1850

FROM 1832 to 1850, in addition to the six original volunteer fire companies, several new engine and hose companies were organized as the city grew in size: Cataract No. 7 (1834) which was renamed Washington No. 7 (1847); Eagle No. 8 (1840, disbanded 1842), Niagara No. 8 (1847, disbanded 1849) and Osceola No. 9 (1840). In 1833 Stalhan Williams sold a lot on the east side of Hotel street for an engine house and when the building was completed in 1834, the Common Council Chambers occupied the second floor. In 1835 the Council approved a proposal to build an engine house on the west side of Union street.

The great fire of 1837 began on the second story of a frame building owned by Samuel Lightbody on the corner of Genesee and Broad streets and the high wind spread the flames to the wooden buildings in lower Genesee and destroyed practically all the buildings in the vicinity of Bagg's Square, including Broad and Whitesboro streets. (The details of that fire are reported in the "Utica Observer" of April 4, 1837).

One result of the fire was the organization by John S. Peckham of the Utica Fire Bucket Company No. 1, composed of sixty members. It was formally organized July 8, 1839 and continued in service until May 24, 1844 when the development of the suction type fire engine made unnecessary the old bucket brigade. The Osceola Fire Company No. 9 was stationed on the east side of Main street and they acquired the first "piano" type fire engine in the city. This was a large and heavy vehicle and cumbersome to handle, but it could throw three streams of water at the same time and the men were very proud of it. Fulton No. 3 members were equally proud of their machine and this was the beginning of a period of rivalry which was to have tragic results.

On June 12, 1843, the two companies met on the canal near the Broadway bridge, to test the relative merits and prowess of the two companies. A bet of $50 was laid. The test was to try to "wash" the other machine. This consisted of filling the tank of each engine almost to the top, and attaching their hoses to each other. The members would then man the handles and attempt by their pumping up and down, to force more water to the opponent's engine than it would receive from it. The victor would be the one who overflowed the tank of the other and "wash" it by forcing the excess water to flow down the sides. This made a mess and necessitated a cleaning up of their machine by the losers. It was actually a test of strength and endurance. The contest ended in a draw but one of No. 3's men, Daniel Nessle collapsed and died on the spot. The Common Council forbade any such future contests.

One of Utica's famous old volunteer companies was the one in West Utica known as "Washington Engine and Rough & Ready Hose Co. No. 7." West Utica was all that part of the city west of the Chenango Canal to the city limits. In 1842, that area had so increased in population and industry that its residents desired fire protection from the city. The city fathers promised that if the residents would build their own fire house and recruit a volunteer company, the city would provide a new fire engine. The residents built the house and recruited the company with H. C. Pond, as foreman. When all was ready, the Council adopted a resolution, sponsored by Alderman Simeon V. Oley, the chairman of the fire committee:

> "Resolved, that the fire engine known as No. 1, City of Utica, and all the appurtenances thereto belonging be at once sent to the new fire engine house recently built by the West Utica folks, to assist them in extinguishing their big fires in compliance with the City Council to that effect."

In one of the engine houses there stood for years the old condemned fire engine No. 1 — long thrown away as unfit for use. In due course the old engine was hitched to a cart and delivered to West Utica. In 1883, Orville Olcott recalled:

> "The boys all turned out in their new rigs to receive it and if you ever saw a lot of disappointed long-faced men, it was then and there. They looked the aged veteran over, and with all sorts of unfeeling remarks, cusses and threats that Germans can make use of, they concluded at once not to accept the machine. One dark night not long after that an old, dilapidated thrown-away fire engine could have been seen wending its way down the towpath until it arrived at Hotel street; from that point it took a turn to Liberty street, till directly in front of a certain shoe store on the corner of Liberty and Genesee streets; there it was chained to a lamp post, the

boys retiring in good order. Whatever became of the old engine I saith not. We were afterwards given our old faithful No. 7 and peace was fully restored."

The lamppost in question was in front of Alderman Oley's shoe store. The old condemned engine No. 1 was returned to the Hotel street engine house where it was destroyed in the fire of 1848.

On December 7, 1848 at about five o'clock in the morning, flames and smoke were observed coming from a wooden building on Burchard Lane, occupied as a cigar manufactory by Warnick & Bryan and at the same time from Owen O'Neil's hardware store on Genesee street. The wind was blowing strongly at the time and a steady rain was falling.

The efforts of the firemen contained the fire in the front part of O'Neil's store but apparently a separate fire in the center and rear did considerable damage, While the O'Neil fire was burning on Genesee street, the fire on Burchard Lane made considerable headway, consuming the building. The flames then extended to the Hook & Ladder house in the rear of the Common Council building on Hotel street which was soon consumed. The lower part of the building was occupied by Lafayette Engine Co. No. 4 and Niagara No. 8. Old fire engine No. 1, condemned and out of use since it was rejected by West Utica was destroyed. The furniture in the Common Council room upstairs, including a valuable full-length portrait of George Washington, the assessor's maps, one of the portraits of the Mayors and most of the early records of the village and city were consumed.

The rivalry between the various volunteer companies apparently continued because we read in the "Daily Gazette" of May 18, 1850:

"A. Hubbell, Chief Engineer, presented a report to the Common Council: 'It is my unpleasant duty to report to you that at the fire on Washington street, on Monday morning last, engine companies No. 3 (Fulton) and 5 (Neptune) turned their pipes upon each other. I ordered the foremen of both companies, when both together, to order their men to stop working their machines and to stop throwing water on each other. Both foremen said they would do it if the other would. My order was not obeyed for sometime, nor until some one, but I do not know who — it was not done by my order — cut the hose of No. 3.' "

The Council at its next meeting reprimanded the firemen and threatened disbandment if it occurred again.

JOSHUA A. SPENCER AND THE TRIAL OF ALEXANDER McLEOD

1841

U TICA'S renowned criminal lawyer of the early 19th century was Joshua A. Spencer. He was born in Great Barrington, Massachusetts in 1790, the second of four sons. The eldest brother, Ichabod S. Spencer ten year's Joshua's senior, left Great Barrington and settled with his wife at "Quality Hill", a short distance from Canastota. Ichabod read law in 1806 with Joshua Hathaway, Rome's first lawyer and was admitted to the bar in 1808. That same year, Joshua joined his brother at "Quality Hill" and began the study of law, and was admitted to practice in 1814, after service in the War of 1812. In 1828 or 1829, Joshua moved to Utica and formed a partnership with William Maynard. Later he formed a partnership with Francis Kernan. He died in Utica in April 1857 at the age of 67. No lawyer in the State was more well-known than Joshua Spencer and none had greater success with a jury. He was unquestionably the ablest criminal lawyer in the State.

The most spectacular trial in the history of Utica and Oneida county was that of a Canadian citizen, Alexander McLeod, tried in the old Academy before Judge Philo Gridley and a jury in 1841. For a time the outcome of that case threatened war between the United States and Great Britain. The case arose out of a well-organized rebellion in the Province of Ontario (known then as Upper Canada), led by a man named MacKenzie, a journalist. The purpose was to seek independence from the British crown. American citizens, especially in the counties of New York State and Vermont which bordered on Canada were strongly in sympathy with the so-called "patriots" in Canada. They formed what were called "Hunter's Lodges", a secret organization named it is believed after a Vermonter named Hunter. Their purpose was to aid the cause of the Canadian rebels, by seizing arms and cannon from the United States arsenals. An Albany man by the name of Van Rensselaer, who assumed the title of "general" organized a group of Americans and seized and occupied Navy Island in the Niagara River at Buffalo. This island was on the Canadian side of the river and that action, of course, was a violation of American neutrality under international law. An American steamboat called the "Caroline" owned by a Mr. Welles of Buffalo, plied between the port of Schlosser on the American side near Niagara Falls and Navy Island. His purpose was to make money by transporting sightseers to the island, but it seems clear that on at least one occasion he transported a cannon and other stores to the island. The Canadians were determined to stop the practice and dispatched several boatloads of Marines to Schlosser at night. They boarded the "Caroline" tied to the dock at Schlosser, cut the ship loose, set fire to it and then towed it out to midstream where it was swept over the Falls. The next morning, a black man by the name of Amos Durfee was found dead on the dock.

Both sides screamed for war and the British government argued that under international law, they had a right to enter American waters to destroy a vessel hostile to them. The American government was ready to accept the explanation, but desired compensation for the owner of the vessel and perhaps a diplomatic apology. The matter dragged on for several months without resolution, but the issue reached a crisis when a deputy sheriff of Canada by the name of Alexander McLeod began boasting in several taverns along the border that he participated in the attack and had shot a "Yankee". In November 1840, he came to Buffalo on business, and was arrested for the murder of Durfee. Since it seemed impossible to obtain a fair trial in that region, the Supreme Court of New York ordered the trial to be held in Oneida county. Great Britain retained Spencer to defend McLeod and warned that if any harm came to its citizen, serious consequences would follow. The London newspapers reported that the British Mediterranean fleet had been ordered to Gibraltar from Syria, to be ready to sail for Halifax if war should break out. Our Minister to France reported that the feeling in Paris was that if McLeod was executed, war would be declared.

If that was not enough of a problem, rumors were rampant that the Hunter Lodges planned to attack the Whitestown jail, where McLeod was confined and lynch him. Governor Seward ordered Sheriff Moulton to post extra guards around the jail; called out the militia and requested a company of United States troops be sent to Rome. The Governor directed that Moulton see to it that McLeod did not escape if

151

convicted; and to give him safe conduct to the Canadian border if acquitted.

The case was ably defended by Spencer and conducted impartially by Gridley. A reading of the testimony discloses that the prosecution had difficulty placing McLeod at the scene, and the statement of his boastings came from persons obviously sympathetic to the members of, or were themselves members of, the Hunter's Lodges. Several refused to tell whether they were members. In addition, Spencer produced witnesses who placed McLeod some miles away from the scene at the time.

In a masterful charge to the jury, Gridley said:

> "If you believe that this man is guilty of murder then, fearless of the consequences, whatever those consequences may be — through they shall wrap your country in a flame of war — whatever they result, look to the God of Justice and say whether the prisoner be guilty or not!"

In 28 minutes the jury returned with a verdict of not guilty. Although the courtroom was crowded during the trial, there was little interest shown by Uticans generally and the stenographer noted in his minutes that when the prisoner was taken for lunch to a local tavern, probably the Bagg's Hotel, only a handful of children paid any attention. The sheriff was happy to deliver his prisoner safely to Plattsburgh. McLeod received a hero's welcome in Montreal, Spencer received a fee of $10,000 from the British government for his services, and Judge Gridley was loudly praised by the London papers for his integrity and fairness.

DEVELOPMENT OF THE COMMON
SCHOOL SYSTEM
1842

WHEN Utica was incorporated as a city, education was largely confined to private schools. The population was about 8500 and the number of private schools was something over thirty. The Utica Academy was essentially a private school, with tuition. There were but four schools of a public nature: one in the session room of the Second Presbyterian Church, on the corner of Charlotte and Elizabeth streets; one on the corner of Minden turnpike (now Albany street) and East street (now Tilden avenue); a third opened in 1834 with Abraham Yates as principal; and about the same time, a primary and intermediate school was established at the corner of Washington and Whitesboro streets with William Osborne as teacher.

In the year 1840 there were four free schools in the city: the Second Ward Free School at Whitesboro and Washington streets; the Third Ward Free School at No. 63 Columbia street; the Fourth Ward Free School at No. 79 Bleecker street; and the Bleecker Street Infant School at No. 35 Bleecker street.

By an act of the legislature passed April 7, 1842, the schools of Utica were placed under the control of a board of school commissioners. The public schools were in a deplorable condition and the number of pupils was about 1,000. There was also a school for black children, not then in operation, but soon established at No. 11 Union street. The commissioners began immediately to make improvements to the few schoolhouses owned by the city.

In 1844, it was decided that the joint occupancy of the old Academy building at Chancellor Park by both the courts and the private academy was not conducive to the efficient operation of either. The "Daily Gazette" of June 8, 1844 reported:

> "The departments of education and for litigation have been entirely separated from one another, having no longer an entrance hall, or even a street or yard in common. The Academy front continues on John street. The old hall leading through the lower part of the

building has been removed, and nearly the whole of the first story thrown into one large school room for study, sufficient for the accommodation of a hundred scholars. The entrance to the Court room (second floor) is from Academy street, the Court House being considered as fronting on Chancellor Square."

In 1846, John R. Bleecker gave to the city a piece of land on the northwest corner of Charlotte and Elizabeth streets. The conditions of the deed were that the land was to remain in the use of the city as long as it was devoted to educational purposes, but in the event of it being used for other purposes, the title should revert to the heirs of Mr. Bleecker. The "Utica Sunday Tribune" of June 25, 1911 reported:

"The present building with some changes was completed in 1847, and the edifice became a central school to which were transferred pupils from intermediate schools. There they receive a course in common school education and were prepared for entrance to the Utica Free Academy which was then located at the corner of Bleecker street and Chancellor Square Park.

"The original building was of brick and three stories in height. It was designed to accommodate 400 pupils. The school was divided into three departments, with a principal over each with six assistants. The building has been considerably enlarged since its erection.

"The expansion of the Utica Public School system was marked after the building of the Advanced School. In 1851 the Hamilton and Steuben street schools were erected. A year later there were built the schools on Blandina, Aiken and Catharine streets, though these were not occupied until 1856. The Whitesboro street school was erected in 1853; the Albany street and Lansing street schools in 1858; the Court street school in 1860, and the South street and Francis street schools in 1867."

The Faxton Hall building was erected in 1868 on Varick street and was used as a school. In 1869, St. Patrick's parochial school, occupying a brick building on Columbia street was organized as one of the city's public schools. The next year, the commissioners purchased the Welsh Congregational Church on Washington street and remodeled it for school purposes, and in 1870-71, the commissioners built a brick school house on the corner of Miller and Leah streets.

In 1874, the Union street school was erected; the Court street school was enlarged in 1878 to double its former capacity; and in the succeeding year, the Lansing street school was similarly enlarged and improved. In 1881, the brick school house, on the site extending from Blandina to Mary street, near Jefferson avenue, was erected. The Washington street building was sold in 1888, and the proceeds devoted to building a modern school house on Washington street known as No. 18. Number 19 was built in 1892 on the south side of Oak street in west Utica; Number 20 built in 1893 on corner of Brinkerhoff and Arthur streets and Number 21 built in 1896 at corner of Downer and Highland avenues in West Utica.

The increased number of ward schools in the city which kept the pupils through the grammar school grades, caused a gradual decrease in the number of those attending the Advanced School and in 1911, the building on Elizabeth street was given over to vocational training until the Second World War. After the war, the building was demolished and replaced with a parking lot for the office of school administration.

In 1853, the school commissioners were made trustees of the Academy and the school for the first time became the "Utica Free Academy."

On the morning of May 13, 1865, the old Utica Free Academy building was destroyed by fire. By permission of the Board of Supervisors, the school was transferred to the John street Court House until the completion of a new building. This was commenced in 1866 on the site of the former building. It was in the Renaissance style of architecture, built of brick, two stories high, and covered with a Mansard roof. A tower fourteen feet square projected from the east facade and was ninety-eight feet high. There were recitation rooms on the first floor and a huge study hall on the second floor.

The need for a large high school building became apparent in the late 1890s and the property on Kemble street was purchased and a new high school building commenced. In 1897, when almost completed, it was destroyed by fire. The high school building was rebuilt and opened in 1899, with the large addition on Hobart street being added in 1917. The old Academy building at Chancellor Park was renovated, altered and became the Bleecker Street school.

THE ADVENT OF THE DAILY NEWSPAPER
1842

PRIOR to the year 1842, the only newspapers in Utica were published weekly or semi-weekly. Among the most widely read were "The Oneida Whig", "The Utica Observer", and "The Utica Democrat". The "Utica Democrat" was first issued in 1836 and later merged with the "Observer" in 1852.

The first attempt to issue a newspaper on a daily basis was made by Lyon & Arthur in early 1842 under the title of "Utica Morning News". It was not successful and ceased after about three months. On February 3, 1842, "The Daily Gazette" was published from the offices of the "Oneida Whig", with Richard U. Sherman as editor and Rufus Northway as publisher. Richard U. Sherman was born in Vernon, New York in 1819, the son of Willet H. Sherman and Catherine Schoolcraft. After graduation from Utica Academy, Richard developed a taste for newspaper work and politics.

The next daily newspaper was a four-page Whig paper, the "Oneida Morning Herald". It appeared on November 1, 1847 and espoused the cause of anti-slavery. Richard U. Sherman was the editor. In 1850, Mr. Sherman was elected clerk of the New York State Assembly at Albany and the vacant editorial chair fell to Ellis H. Roberts, who, when Mr. Sherman withdrew from the paper the following year, became the proprietor and changed the name to the "Utica Morning Herald." Under his leadership, the newspaper turned to advocacy of the newly formed Republican party.

Ellis H. Roberts was truly one of the great journalists of Utica's history. He purchased the "Utica Daily Gazette" on January 29, 1857 and combined the two newspapers into the "Utica Morning Herald and Daily Gazette", which continued until 1900. He was born in Utica on September 30, 1827. His father, Watkin Roberts, was a stone mason who emigrated from Wales in 1816 to Utica. After attending the public schools of Utica at the age of 9, Ellis went into the printing office of Utica's great printer, William Williams, and learned the printer's trade. He decided to further his education and after finishing at Whitestown Seminary, went to Yale. After being graduated in 1850, he was hired as principal of the Utica Academy and on May 1, 1854 became the editor and publisher of the "Herald". He was instrumental in the formation of the "State Associated Press" in 1851 and served as its Secretary-Treasurer to 1871. As editor and publisher of the newspaper until 1899, he was strongly committed to the principles of the Republican Party and served as Congressman in 1870 and again in 1872. In April 1889, President Benjamin Harrison appointed him Assistant Treasurer of the United States, at New York city. When the Democratic Party came to power, he was replaced and for a time was the President of the Franklin National Bank of New York. On July 1, 1897 he became Treasurer of the United States and served until March 3, 1905. He died in Utica at the age of 90 on January 8, 1918.

The third daily newspaper was the "Utica Daily Observer" which appeared on April 27, 1848. In 1852, under Lyon & Grove, the "Utica Democrat" was united with "The Observer".

On May 1, 1851, the "Utica Evening Telegraph" was commenced by Thomas R. McQuade, with J. F. McQuade as editor. In February 1858, the office was burned. The publication resumed in May and continued until 1866. It was a breezy, folksy paper, written in a humorous style.

The next daily newspaper was the "Utica Daily Republican" (October 22, 1877 to February 4, 1879) published by Dennis T. Kelly. The "Daily Bee", a breezy little publication, made its bow to the reading public in 1870. It was started in offices upstairs on the Busy Corner. Its publisher was a man named Seth Wilbur Payne. He was a brilliant, erratic sort of individual, but his reporting of the Josephine McCarty murder trial was his undoing as a journalist.

Josephine McCarty, claiming she had been wronged by a prominent Utica real estate and insurance man, attempted to shoot him on the horse-car while travelling down Genesee street near Hopper street. Her aim was bad and she killed a fellow passenger, for which she was charged with murder. The "Daily Bee' whipped up public sympathy for the jilted female, and Payne accused the judge of favoring the moneyed interests and not the defendant. The judge laughed it off, but the district attorney thought the majesty of the law ought to be upheld, and Payne went to the Albany penitentiary for thirty days for contempt. The paper folded shortly thereafter.

THE WESLEYAN METHODIST CHURCH CONVENTION
1843

THE issue of slavery created a dissention among the members of the Methodist Church in the United States. About 1841 six hundred members seceded from the Methodist Episcopal Church and had organized themselves into a conference bearing the name "Wesleyan Methodists". About the same time, there was organized in Utica the "Wesleyan Methodist Church" with the Rev. George Pegler as pastor. Its house of worship was on Pearl street at the corner of Broadway.

A Wesleyan Anti-Slavery Convention was held in the Methodist Church in Andover, Massachusetts on February 1, 1843 and at that meeting, a call was issued for a convention to be held in Utica, New York, beginning on May 31st of that year. Its purpose was to consider the ultimate formation of a Wesleyan Methodist Church "free from Episcopacy and Slavery".

The Convention opened in the Wesleyan Church in Utica at the appointed day and the roll call revealed the names of thirty-five ministers and one hundred seventeen laymen from nine states. The Convention continued for eight days, with meetings held in the Broad street Baptist Church and the Bleecker street Baptist Church.

There was organized the "Wesleyan Methodist Connection of America", an association of local churches organized in annual conferences. A "Discipline" was adopted which avoided the episcopacy. Moral and social reform were strongly emphasized, with slaveholding and involvement with intoxicating liquors being prohibited.

Around 1850, the Wesleyan Church in Utica moved to an edifice at No. 6 Washington street. In 1867, the Wesleyan Methodist Church became the Welsh Wesleyan Methodist Church. The crusade against slavery had ended with the Civil War and emancipation and thereafter, many felt there was no reason for the "Connection" as such to continue.

PLANK ROADS AND TOLL GATES
1844-1860

THE early settlers of Oneida county made their way along the primitive roads which were used to transport cannon and military supplies during the Revolutionary days. Between 1797 and 1807, various private turnpike and bridge companies were authorized to build roads. The most famous of these was the Seneca Turnpike from Bagg's Square through New Hartford. For years a toll gate at the Parkway collected tolls for the use of that road.

The old stage coach route from Deerfield Corners to Bagg's Square was the poorest in the state. Heavily loaded wagons and carriages were often stranded in the mud of the flatland flooded by the Mohawk. Abner Churchill, who was the proprietor of Bagg's Hotel in 1839, determined that for the benefit of his establishment and for the good of the city, this mile of road should be put in better condition.

On April 26, 1839, the Legislature authorized Calvin Hall, Aaron Barnes, Frederick G. Weaver, Theodore S. Faxton and John Butterfield as commissioners to cause a Macadam road, so called, to be constructed on the "dyke road", leading from the city of Utica to the river north of the dwelling house of John D. Leland, and on the road leading from Deerfield corners, so called, in front of said Leland's dwelling house to where the Miller turnpike, so called, intersects said river road.

A Scottish engineer, John L. Macadam (1756-1836) had developed a method of road-building using granite broken into small pieces which when traveled over became perfectly compact and smooth. Sufficient funds were not secured until 1844 for the construction of the road. To defray the cost of construction, repair and upkeep, the commissioners were authorized to collect tolls. When the road was completed, a toll house was erected on the road. It is said that this toll house was placed about halfway between the Square and Deerfield Corners, near where the present bridge over the Mohawk river is located. When the county took over the road in 1910, the old toll gate house was removed and is said to have finished its "ignominious old age as somebody's chicken coop."

Plank roads were more easily built and less expensive than Macadam roads, and in 1848 the Legislature passed a general plank road act. Pursuant to this authorization, upwards of a dozen plank road companies were formed in Oneida county. Among these were: Bridgewater and Utica (18 miles); Burlington and Utica (30 miles); Frankfort and Utica (14 miles); Waterville and Utica (18 miles); and Rome and Utica (15 miles).

The Rome and Utica Plank Road Company filed a designation for a road from the south abutment of the canal bridge, known as Potter's bridge, in the city of Utica to the village of Rome. The road was 14 miles long and extended along Whitesboro street in Utica to Yorkville, Whitesboro, Oriskany and Rome. Following the course of the Erie canal in a general fashion, it made use of the area adjacent to the canal towpath in several places. For many years before the road was improved, teamsters and others found that the frozen surface of the canal during the winter months was an even surface upon which to travel to Rome.

The plank road was constructed through the village of Whitesboro as far as the Marcy road by the winter of 1848. The "Utica Daily Gazette" of June 28, 1848 reported:

> "Rome and Utica Plank Road. The building of this road is proceeding with much activity. From this place to Whitestown there is to be a double track of plank. It commences in front of Higham & Co.'s Vulcan Works, and the plank is already laid for some distance."

Toll Gate No. 1 was placed at the easterly terminus of the town of Whitestown, adjacent to the State Hospital grounds and the other about a mile west of Whitesboro village. This second gate was east of the Marcy road intersection. As a result, Marcy residents were required to pay double toll for the distance travelled, one at the first gate and the other at the second. During the winter of 1849-50, citizens began the practice of turning off the road before they reached the gate and getting on the ice of the canal to a point a mile or more east of the gate, where they came back on the plank road. Since the penalty for the evasion was a suit by the company for debt, the juries almost invariably found for the defendant. The companies were never very popular, and several times the gatekeepers were assaulted and their toll houses burned.

The old Minden turnpike which led from Broad street and Bleecker streets over Frankfort Hill was one of the poorest in

160

the county. The Utica and Burlington Plank Road Company was organized and improved the road from the easterly side of the Gulf basin on Bleecker street, over what was to become Albany street to the foot of Frankfort Hill. The "Oneida Morning Herald" of August 30, 1849 reported:

> "The Minden road has hitherto been maintained at the expense of the city; but in consideration of being allowed a gate within the city limits the company have bound themselves to keep it in good order at their own cost including the repair and re-erection of all necessary bridges, culverts, etc. The city treasury is thus relieved of about $200 annual expense, while the tolls collected come almost wholly out of the people of Herkimer county, who supply our inhabitants with wood, coal and building materials.

> "A delightful drive may be had by going down the Minden road from Mohawk street to the old Welsh Bush road, which branches off a few rods this side of Underwood's, and crossing thence to the Mohawk road at Ferguson's, returning by the latter thoroughfare to the city. The whole distance is about six miles, all the way through a highly picturesque and beautiful section of the country; one too which has hitherto been little traversed as a pleasure road."

Unfortunately these plank roads quickly deteriorated and became a danger to horses. The heavy wagons broke up the planking and the boards rotted. The plank road companies seldom earned enough revenue to pay for the necessary repairs. When timber became scarce and expensive and money, after the panic of 1857 was unavailable, the plank road companies started to go out of business, The Rome and Utica Company in 1866 abandoned the road, except for the four miles and forty rods from gate No. 1 to gate No. 2, which portion was eventually sold to the town of Whitestown in 1869.

THE DEVELOPMENT OF MODERN HOTELS
1845

WHILE many of the old taverns continued well into the nineteenth century, the increased travel by railroad and the growing business activity in Utica required a more modern type of hotel. Bagg's Hotel was considerably enlarged and improved. In 1844, Henry Clay came to Utica and stayed at Bagg's. He visited the town of Paris and made a speech, and the old village of Paris Furnace was renamed Clayville in his honor. The "Oneida Whig" of June 10, 1845 reported:

> "The most noted of our hotels is, of course, Churchill's, better known, however, as Bagg's, situated at the foot of Genesee street, and immediately above the depot of the Utica and Schenectady railroad. This establishment now embraces two large hotels, the old Bagg's Tavern and the Bleecker House, erected by Mrs. Brinckerhoff of Albany, and is one of the most extensive in the country. At this time, the store between the two houses is being taken down for the purpose of having it built up uniform with Bagg's, and occupied entirely for hotel purposes. When this alteration is completed the dimensions of the entire establishment will be 165 feet on Genesee street, and 138 feet on Main street, four stories in height throughout. On the first floor in the new part, a spacious ladies parlor is to be fitted up, to take the place of the old room in the corner, familiar to so many travelers but decidedly behind the age. The dining room of the Bleecker House is to be temporarily divided into four apartments, one intended for a ladies' washing room for railroad passengers, another for a nursery, another for a lodging room for invalids, and the fourth for a smoking room. There are in this establishment about 140 lodging rooms, besides parlors, reading and dining room, etc."

Louis Kossuth, the famous Hungarian patriot, came to Utica in 1851. After delivering an oration at the old Museum, he spent the night at Bagg's. In 1860, the Prince of Wales, Albert Edward, the heir apparent to the British throne, passed through Utica and made a brief stay at Bagg's, enjoying the excellence of the cuisine.

In 1841, the American Hotel was built on the west side of Bagg's Square, directly opposite the Utica and Schenectady railroad depot. It was a four story building. In 1851, it was known as the Averill House, but soon reverted to its original name. For many years, it was one of the most popular of hostelries. During the years of the Civil War, it was a favorite gathering place and a number of famous personages enjoyed its hospitality. The hotel was demolished about the year 1884, to give place to the Lackawanna passenger depot.

On the site of the old Bull's Head tavern on the north corner of Genesee and Elizabeth streets, was built the new Central Hotel in 1841-42. It was a four story building with pleasant and spacious rooms, parlors and lounges. Its yard and stabling accommodations were very ample. It was first opened by Charles N. Griffin, and in 1845 it was Alvin White who leased the property. He was one of the most popular landlords and conducted the hotel from 1845 to 1857. Various other landlords succeeded him, but the building was finally sold in 1871 and converted into the Parler Block, the predecessor of the First National Bank Building. The "Utica Observer" in 1871 wrote:

> "Who among those who were boys in those days, will forget the double rows of wagons which were closely packed together along Elizabeth street, on circus days, each wagon bearing on the dashboard the hostler's hieroglyphics, indicating the number of the harness and the horses which belonged to them? The circus horses, too, were always stabled in the Central barns, and many a boy that we know of could not resist the temptation to play 'hookey' as he passed along Elizabeth street to the Advanced School, and saw the horses and the golden chariot and other gaudy paraphernalia of the circus man's profession."

When the fire of 1837 destroyed the old Burchard tavern, "The Sign of the Buck" on Whitesboro street, the site remained unoccupied until 1842, when James McGregor, the mason builder, who built the old Dutch Reformed Church on Broad street, decided to build a new hotel nearby, two or three rods west of the site of the old Burchard tavern. The "Utica Daily Gazette" of October 30, 1843 reported:

> "The house is situated on Whitesboro street, near its junction with Genesee street and within a few steps of the railroad depot and the stage offices. The building itself is 65 feet front by 55 in depth; is four stories high, exclusive of the basement, with a large yard, sheds, etc.

It is entered by handsome granite steps and portico, has two ranges of rooms on the right and one on the left to the fourth story. Among them on the lower floor, is a handsome dining room, with receiving rooms, parlors, etc."

The new hotel was operated by James McGregor until 1852; from 1852 to 1860 by Isaac Fisk. It then became the Dudley House, which was a favorite spot for the prominent Uticans of those days. Roscoe Conkling lived there prior to his marriage. In 1905, the Dudley House was remodeled and expanded as the Yates Hotel, recently demolished.

THEODORE S. FAXTON
1794-1881

THEODORE S. Faxton, one of Utica's great benefactors, was born in Conway, Massachusetts on January 10, 1794. He was a penniless lad when he came to Utica and broke stone on the Miller turnpike leading to the village. He became a resident in 1812 and was employed by Jason Parker as a stage driver on the line running between Albany and Buffalo. He was such a good employee that he was made superintendent of the lines. He made frequent trips, inspecting the drivers and equipment. If he found incompetence, he would dismiss the driver on the spot, take his seat on the box and finish the run himself.

In 1822 he was offered an interest in the business, with the privilege of paying for it out of his profits, as they accrued. The same opportunity was given to Silas D. Childs, who came from Conway in 1816 as a penniless boy but later married Mr. Parker's daughter.

It was some time about the winter of 1822-23 that Faxton performed a feat which gave much notoriety to Parker & Co. He held the reins over a four-in-hand turn-out belonging to the company which carried James Platt, Richard R. Lansing,

John H. Ostrom, Charles P. Kirkland, Joseph S. Porter and William Williams from Utica to Albany and back in eighteen hours. They started at midnight, had relays of horses, reached Albany before the opening of the morning session of the Legislature, rested an hour, returned to Utica, pushed on to New Hartford and returned to make the distance 200 miles and left the stage in Utica by early bedtime.

After the death of Parker in 1830, Faxton & Childs carried on the business until the railroad drove the stage lines off the road east of Utica. The stage company gradually closed its business, and the following advertisement appeared in the "Oneida Whig" of July 9th, 1839:

> "The subscribers having been served with a supersedeas by the travelling community, through the agency of steam, offer for sale their entire stage stock, in such lots as to suit customers — consisting of a large number of horses (upwards of 100), coaches, sleighs, harness, wagons, wheels, etc. The variety being so great and the determination to sell so fixed that we confidently say the purchaser will be accommodated unless he is disposed to be more nice than wise. The stock can be seen at our stables in Water street. Parker & Co. Utica. July 8th, 1839."

Faxton thereafter engaged in other business enterprises and made great contributions to the growth of the city.

When Faxton married in 1826 (the daughter of William Alverson, brewer and grocer) he went to live at what was 24 Seneca street. In connection with John Butterfield, Hiram Greenman and others he was involved in the operation of the packet boats on the canal. Captain Greenman then owned a fine residence and property on the northwest corner of Lafayette street and Broadway, the house having been built in the early years of the century. In 1837, Mr. Faxton and Captain Greenman exchanged properties, and Faxton took up his residence on Lafayette street, where he resided until his death, November 30, 1881. During Mr. Faxton's occupancy, an east wing was added to the house, but otherwise its general appearance remained the same. Miss Mary F. Powell, a niece of Mrs. Faxton continued to occupy the old mansion until 1907, having lived there continuously for 61 years. It was then taken over by the Utica & Mohawk Valley Street Railway Company for use in connection with its rapidly growing express business. A car barn was then erected on the site, which still exists, although used for other purposes. The "Utica Saturday Globe" of March 9, 1907 said:

"Could the walls of the old house speak, they would tell of the not inconspicious part they have played in the development of our city. For within its spacious corridors and rooms were first discussed many plans whose fruition added much to the prosperity and growth of Utica. In its comfortable rooms in the early days of the city's history, Faxton and other commercial giants of his day gathered to discuss ways and means for the successful inception of the great mills and other mammoth manufacturing plants which have made Utica what it is today.

"It was in this noted house that first was discussed the advisability of telegraphic communication between New York and Buffalo, for Theodore Faxton was the first big man in the Empire State to recognize the wonderful commercial possibilities of that invention which revolutionized the business interest of the world. Indeed, the house is like a great book which contains chapter after chapter of the most interesting history of our beautiful city.

"There is another side to the story of this old mansion — the history of its social triumphs. In the generation past the Faxton home was one of the show places of the city. For years the imposing residence was pointed out with pride by Uticans as the home of one of the city's greatest benefactors. Here in the first half of the last century came the dainty belles of those days in their crinoline and picturesque bonnets and their old world mannerisms. What delightful pictures must the walls of the old mansion be able to conjure up; pictures of the old time balls and parties, when the wealth and fashion of old Utica gathered under Faxton's handsome rooftree."

JOHN BUTTERFIELD
1801-1869

JOHN Butterfield was born at Berne, in the Helderberg mountain, near Albany on November 18, 1801. As most young lads, he was fond of horses and dreamed of being a stage coach driver. At the age of 16, he went to Albany to drive for Thorpe & Sprague where he gained a reputation as one of the most capable and dependable of drivers in that city. In February 1822, he married Melinda Harriett Baker.

Theodore S. Faxton, the superintendent of Parker & Company went to Albany in search of a person suitable for the needs of that firm. He induced Butterfield to come to Utica to undertake the duty of frequenting taverns and the canal boat docks to solicit passengers for Parker's stage lines. He proved equal to the task and thoroughly identified himself with the success of the firm.

After some time at the task, Butterfield dreamed of establishing his own business. One day, he met a traveler at the Canal Coffee House, who in need of funds, offered to sell his horse and wagon to Butterfield. Butterfield purchased the horse and wagon and from this small beginning eventually grew the American Express Company. His first stable was in the rear of the Coffee House on Culver street. As his means allowed, he added to his equipment. In this venture, he was materially aided by his wife who kept a boarding house. He purchased from Parker & Company four or five teams which they had used on the Utica & Oxford road. In association with Parker, Butterfield operated stage coaches from Utica to Cooperstown and from Utica to Easton, Pennsylvania. He carried the mail every Monday, Wednesday and Friday to Cooperstown; and every Tuesday, Thursday and Saturday to Easton, Pennsylvania. Later he added a stage line to Sackett's Harbor and Watertown.

At the height of his stage coach career, until the railroads supplied the demand, he had forty lines running from Utica north and south. In the course of time, his stables were removed to Catharine street behind the old National Hotel. He also had a stable on the north side of Main street to the east of Bagg's Hotel, where John C. Hieber later erected his building to house his wholesale drygoods business. On June 9, 1851, Butterfield moved that stable to the south side of Main street. The first floor was devoted to a blacksmith shop, while the stables were in the rear. To the east at No. 16 was a wooden building occupied as a bakery by Owen Owens prior to 1855, when it passed to Mr. Butterfield and became part of the livery stable. In 1904, the "Utica Daily Press" decided to replace its old plant at 17 Main street and purchased the entire old Butterfield stable property for a new and modern newspaper plant. All the old buildings were razed.

In the 1840s, Lafayette street was a fashionable residential area. On the northwest corner of Lafayette and Washington streets, where later the Avon and Lumberg theaters were built stood a stately house. Butterfield did not build the house but he owned it from early in the 40s to about the close of the Civil War. The "Utica Daily Press' of April 4, 1914 wrote:

> "On the corner of Broadway stood a large poplar tree, which the boys of the street used to climb and get material for making whistles. It was in front of a wooden building which was used as an office for Downer's lumber yard. In time, Mr. Butterfield bought this corner and added it to his grounds. A low wall of stone was put around the property on Lafayette and Broadway, and this wall was surmounted with a brown stone coping, matching the house. In this wall was an iron picket fence, of ornamental design. The whole space west of the house was a flower garden, one of the most attractive in the city. The flower beds were edged with box borders, and in the center of the plot was a fountain in which the water spashed all day and birds bathed. The earliest spring flowers were found in this garden, and children stopped on their way to school to admire it. Just across Broadway was the residence of Theodore S. Faxton, whose garden was the spot now occupied by the Electric Express buildings. In this garden was a tall trellis overgrown with Michigan roses which bloomed profusely. The two houses and their grounds formed the most attractive part of the street given up wholly to the residence of Utica's leading business men."

Butterfield purchased the property at the old State Fair grounds on Genesee street just south of the Parkway, just beyond the old toll gate on the New Hartford road. The "Morning Herald" of May 24, 1866 wrote:

"Immediately beyond the roll gate, upon the left, John Butterfield has nearly completed a tasteful edifice which he contemplates himself occupying. The main building is 47 × 50, with an addition in the rear 32 × 40, Mr. Butterfield has chosen the American style of architecture for his new residence, the outline being bold, with very little copying about it. From the observatory, one can overlook the three hundred acres which belong to and surround the dwelling."

But Butterfield was not to enjoy this new home very long. In October 1867 he was stricken with paralysis and died in Utica on November 14, 1869, a shell of his former physique. The property was then subdivided into lots with streets laid out. In addition to the name Butterfield, others were named for his daughters, Mrs. James B. VanVorst, Mrs. Alexander Holland, and Mrs. William M. Storrs.

THE DEVELOPMENT OF THE TELEGRAPH
1845

SAMUEL Winchester Chubbuck was born in Winchester, Vermont on December 25, 1799 and at an early age moved to Eaton, Madison county, New York, and when he reached manhood engaged in the jewelry business in Morrisville. He became well known as a goldsmith and designer in precious metals. He was a splendid mathematician and applied his talents to the use of his inventive powers. When Professor Samuel F. B. Morse was working on his idea of an electric magneto to transmit messages, he learned that Chubbuck was working on the same idea. The two men corresponded and engaged in mutual study and research. Professor Henry of the Smithsonian Institute was also working on the problem and he joined the other two men. It is said that Chubbuck's inventive genius made possible the practical development of the telegraph.

Sometime before 1840, Chubbuck manufactured the first telegraph instrument and it was through his accomplishment that Congress was brought to realize that the telegraph was a feasible project and appropriated money for the erection of an experimental telegraph line from Washington to Baltimore in 1844. On May 24, 1844, the first message, "What hath God wrought?" was sent from the old Supreme Court room in the Capitol to Baltimore.

Mr. Chubbuck had moved from Eaton to Utica in 1842 for the purpose of manufacturing the appliances for use on telegraph lines which he envisioned would be built. He put his telegraph in operation in a small workshop in the Ballou Block, facing Bagg's Square. He lectured and illustrated his lectures with his invention in order to interest local capitalists in promoting his project. It was a combination of his inventive genius and the financial acumen of Theodore S. Faxton, John Butterfield and others that made possible the commercial development of the telegraph.

The first instruments manufactured by Professor Chubbuck and put into operation weighed from 400 to 500 pounds, but he later succeeded in reducing the size down so fine that a complete instrument could be carried in a person's pocket. Through the efforts of Butterfield, Faxton and others, the State Fair was to be held in Utica in 1845 and they decided to demonstrate the device at the Fair which was held on the outskirts of the city at Oneida Square. The "Oneida Whig" of September 16, 1845 reported:

> "Genesee street was alive with curiosity on Friday (12th) at the operation of extending the wire for the Electro-Magnetic Telegraph from the railroad to the grounds of the Fair, a distance of about one mile. The wires were carried over the tops of the stores on the west side of Genesee street as far as Fayette street, where they cross to the Museum and thence pass along over the houses on that side of the street. They are supported by an occasional twist round a chimney. Our own smoker is thus honored, and we contemplate constructing a branch up our stove-pipe in order to get the earliest intelligence from the Fair by tapping. The wires are of copper, and wound with twine, and well tarred. This is as near 'greased lightning' as anything we have seen."

On September 16th, 1845, the editor of the "Utica Daily Gazette" made use of the line. What transpired was reported the next day.

" 'The editor of the Gazette wishes to know whether the books with the list of articles entered are on the ground, or still at Bagg's?' Immediately word returned, 'I'll see'. 'Do'. After a lapse of a minute and a half, the concluding answer was reeled off. 'They are here.' The whole transaction occupied six minutes."

The New York, Albany and Buffalo Telegraph Company commenced the construction of a line along the route from Utica toward Albany and plans were made for an early start westward from Utica, Utica being midway between Springfield, Massachusetts and Buffalo. The Springfield connection was later abandoned and the line was extended to New York. Twenty-eight poles to the mile were placed and two copper wires were strung between them for a metallic circuit. The insulation was a glass knob on a wooden pin. The first wire used was copper, costing about $60 per mile. Professor Morse believed that iron would rust and could not be used unless insulated. Mr. Faxton's attention was directed to the wire fence which had been in use twenty-five years at Colonel Walker's house on Broad street. He concluded that if iron wire was good for fences for such a length of time, it would also do for telegraph wire. The copper wires were taken down and sold for enough money to put up two iron wires, the latter costing only $18 per mile.

The telegraph line between Utica and Albany was completed on January 31, 1846. The "Utica Daily Gazette" on February 2nd reported:

"The Electric-Magnetic Telegraph between Albany and Utica was put in operation Saturday forenoon, and worked all day to a charm. Various items of news from Albany and New York were transmitted, the proceedings of the legislature as they transpired, and innumerable messages between individuals. The greatest excitement prevailed along the street for the whole day, and the operations of the wonderful instrument were witnessed in silent astonishment by a continually changing crowd at the telegraph office. The telegraph office is in the second story of Dudley's Triangle and the room is open from about 8:30 o'clock a.m. till dark. The machine is situated upon a platform, and its operation may be seen from any part of the room. The operators are however necessarily protected from being crowded at their work by a rail inside of which spectators are not allowed."

On the 4th of July 1846, the line was completed to Buffalo

and the first commercial telegraph line was in complete operation. The "Utica Daily Gazette" on July 4th reported:

> "The Hudson Talking to Lake Erie. The lightning flashed from Albany to Buffalo, 325 miles by railroad, this morning at 8:30 o'clock. The Telegraph now spans the Empire State. The events transpiring at the Capitol, at one end, are made known at the other extremity in less than no time. This is the longest line of telegraph in the world. The swift messengers upon whose wings messages are sent along the copper track, are bred in a large galvanic battery in the Dudley's Triangle in this city. The fluid there generated makes a circuit of 650 miles. The only object it has in view is to get from one end of the battery into the other, like a carrier dove returning to the spot where it was trained. This fiery steed, whose speed surpasses the imaginings of tales of the Genii; this mighty agent, whose sports are the volcano and tornado; this weapon of the ancient king of heaven, forged in the infernal regions; the utilitarian of our day approaches and says 'I'll trouble you with a line.' "

The telegraph line was constructed from Albany to New York. It crossed the Harlem River on a drawbridge at Third avenue, and whenever the bridge was opened for the passage of vessels, the wires had to be disconnected. Occasionally this interruption occurred during the time that should have been devoted to newspaper service. Consequently the newspapers received abridged reports or none at all. Frequently, the upstate papers printed: "By Telegraph. No report today. Bridge Open."

THE DEVEREUX BLOCK
1845

THE Devereux Building, occupying the triangle between the old Erie Canal, Genesee and Hotel streets, is one of the survivors of the early days of Utica. It was erected sometime in the year 1845, as we read in the "Utica Daily Gazette" of March 21, 1844 that,

> "In the way of important improvements, we understand that Nicholas Devereux, Esq., is about to erect an elegant and substantial four-story block of stores on the triangle between Genesee and Hotel streets and the Erie Canal. This will complete the renovation of the four corners in the centre of the city, occupied half a dozen years ago by the shabbiest looking tenements on the street, the two-story yellow wooden building, between the National and the canal, the huge and fire dreaded Kirkland building on the other side of the street, and the old Coffee House, where now the Exchange Block stands. It is but justice to the remaining block, now about to meet its doom, to say that it was the most respectable of the four.

> "We notice that an application is pending before the Common Council for an exchange between the city and Mr. Devereux, of small strips of ground, in order to enable him to make his new block of a better shape and a handsome appearance. He proposes to throw about fourteen feet of the point of his ground into Franklin Square, so as to have a square front to his building of about sixteen feet, instead of a sharp edge as at present, and to have the city grant him in exchange a strip off Hotel street of about five feet in width at one end and ten at the other."

Apparently some of the citizens objected and started a lawsuit to prevent this exchange for we read in the "Gazette" of August 19, 1844 that Nicholas Devereux proposed to put a cupola and a clock on his new building on condition that certain lawsuits by individuals to part of the ground be discontinued. The Council replied that it had no control over what individuals did. The town clock continued to be the one on the Bleecker Street Baptist Church until the City Hall was built later.

The big four-story building was unique. Its unusual triangular shape known as Utica's "Flatiron Building", with 100 feet on Genesee street, 100 feet on Hotel street and 60 feet on the south side of the Canal made it an outstanding business block. Until later in the century, it had a very decorative iron balcony along the second floor on the Genesee street side, a favorite spot for viewing parades.

The block was visited by fire three times during the century. The first was in 1852, the second a little later, and the third, and most serious, on February 22, 1871. Just after midnight, fire broke out in the upper story. It was a remarkably cold night and the water froze as it cascaded down the roof. The morning sun disclosed, "myriads of beautiful ice formation, in the most fantastic shapes, shining in the sun like crystals, which covered the block from the roof to the sidewalk."

The Devereux building was then completely renovated. The "Utica Observer" of August 8, 1871 described some of the changes:

> "The whole of the interior of the building, above the ground floor, has been entirely remodeled. The old staircase in the south end of the block was taken down, and the space occupied by it added to the Down Brothers' cozy little cigar store. The bewildering iron staircase on the north corner of the building has been untwisted and straightened out, now forming an easy and comfortable means of ascending to the second story on the outside of the building, and leading to another convenient outside staircase which leads to the comfortable and roomy offices in the third story. In the rear of the building on the south end, a handsome iron outside staircase has been erected which communicates by wide and easy flights of stairs in the interior of the building to the attic."

From 1845 to the present, the Devereux block has been a center of trade, law and industry. With the retirement of John C. Devereux, his brother Nicholas continued their business there with Horace Butler, James McDonough and VanVechten Livingston as partners at various times.

Francis Kernan was born of Irish parents on a farm in Schuyler County, New York on January 14, 1816. He entered Georgetown University and graduated in 1836. In 1839, he came to Utica and completed his law studies with Joshua Spencer. His acceptance of a partnership with Spencer laid the foundation for the Kernan law firm, which has since held a foremost position in legal circles. Mr. Kernan married Miss Hannah Devereux, daughter of Nicholas Devereux on May 23rd, 1843. It was in the Devereux Block that he established his office. What more natural than that the Kernans and the Devereux block should be identified in business, inasmuch as the families were closely identified by marriage.

In 1872 he was the Democratic candidate for Governor but the popularity of General Grant who was running for President caused his defeat. In 1874 when the Democratic party controlled the State Legislature, he was elected United States Senator and served for six years. Utica enjoyed the unusual distinction of having both Senators from New York as residents. The other was Roscoe Conkling. Mr. Kernan died in Utica on September 8, 1892.

THE BEGINNING OF THE ASSOCIATED PRESS
1846

THE Associated Press, the great news-gathering newspaper organization, was the result of the foresight of Theodore S. Faxton. On July 3rd, 1846, on the day prior to the opening of the telegraph line to Buffalo, Faxton invited all the editors of newspapers in the State to be on hand the next day at the various telegraph stations. They were to agree upon the time and place of a proposed meeting to form a press association to utilize the telegraph and share the expense of collecting and transmitting the news.

On August 18th, 1846, an association of 19 newspapers in upper New York State was formed and Mr. Snow of the "New York Tribune" was employed to transmit news by telegraph to the subscribing newspapers. (See, Oneida Historical Society MMS 1-NYN 1)

Not all the newspapers were satisfied with the arrangement and on September 19th, the "Syracuse Star" complained that the telegraph agent at Oswego was furnishing the reports to the Oswego papers. On the 22nd, it complained that "Snow's reports are so jumbled together that it needs a full blooded Irishman to unravel them." The first daily reports to the press were concluded with "30", the now well known numerical signal signifying the "end of report". The origin of this final signal was based upon the fact that thirty minutes were devoted to this work, to free the telegraph line for commercial messages.

In May of 1848, six New York City newspapers set up the "Association Press in New York City" which later became the "Associated Press."

THE BEGINNING OF TEXTILE MANUFACTURING
1846

THE early settlers of Whitestown were in need of clothing and since the Sauquoit Creek was the only available source of waterpower, it was not surprising that early textile factories were established along that stream. The first cotton mill in the State of New York, as well as the first woolen mill, so far as known, was in the town of Whitestown. Dr. Seth Capron and Benjamin S. Walcott began spinning cotton yarn in 1809 at the lower mill in Yorkville. In 1810 the New Hartford Manufacturing Company was organized and erected a cotton factory there about 1815 or 1816. In 1812 a company of Quakers spun cotton yarn by hand at Sauquoit and let it out to private families to weave into satinets. These factories produced cotton and woolen goods for many years.

During the summer of 1845, the "Utica Daily Gazette" began an editorial campaign suggesting that the interest of business men in Utica should turn from banking and commerce to manufacturing.

"There is a waterpower of some extent at the locks of the Chenango Canal, and at the City Mill. They may be of no little value, with the aid of steam in carrying machinery for manufacturing purposes".

In October 1845, it urged that

"steamboats, railroads and canals will, to a great extent, give to the great West the supply of our food, and we in self-defense, to preserve our relative standing, must, in connection with New England, supply them with clothing."

After much thought and study of the operation of the textile industry in New England, the public-spirited business men of Utica decided to build a woolen mill. This was in the spring of 1846 and in the fall of that year the Utica Steam Woolen Mill was in full operation, with Andrew S. Pond as president. The site of the factory was an old mill pond at the corner of Columbia and Schuyler streets, formed by damming Nail Creek, which was then quite a pretentious stream, and which was on property owned by Nicholas Devereux. The water power here developed was used to operate the machinery in a little wooden structure, which had been built for a flour mill, and was later used as a silk manufactory. This building was burned sometime later. Besides forming a place for the development of power, the old mill served another purpose. It was the boys' favorite swimming hole in that section.

Ground was broken for building the new factory on April 15, 1846. It was four stories high plus an attic. Weaving was commenced January 11th, 1847. The first invoice of finished goods was completed March 10th, a little less than a year from breaking ground. The machinery was driven by a steam engine of from 70 to 75 horsepower, made at the Vulcan Works of Higham & Co. Forty-one broad looms, made by A. J. Williams of Utica were on the second floor. 160 employees worked 1100 pounds of wool and made 450 yards of broadcloth per day.

In April 1847, ground was broken for a second steam factory, the Utica Globe Mill. This building was erected on the south side of Court street, where Nail Creek then crossed the street. It began operations toward the close of the year 1847. Its first eight years of operation were not successful and a new company, the Utica Woolen Mills took over on August 1, 1855, with Theodore S. Faxton as President. Its name was changed to the Globe Woolen Mills and at the

177

height of its success, a disastrous fire in September 1871 laid the old mill in ashes. New buildings, covering nine acres on the corner of Stark and Court street were completed in 1873, with a worsted mill added in 1886.

The Utica Steam Cotton Mills was organized in 1848 by Alfred Munson, Theodore S. Faxton, Andrew S. Pond, Silas D. Childs, Charles A. Mann, Horatio Seymour and Edmund A. Graham, with Mr. Munson as President. The first building, 302 feet long by 65 feet wide, and three stories in height above the basement, with two wings of two stories was erected on the banks of the Chenango Canal in the oblong block bounded by State, Columbia and Court streets. It started in operation in 1850 with a work force of 165. The business proved successful and in 1867 it was decided to add to the factory. Cooper street which ran through the site was partially closed, resulting in a Cooper street and a West Cooper street.

The "Utica Observer" of October 18, 1867 reported:

> "In May, the Utica Steam Cotton Mills Company commenced excavations on the corner of Columbia and State streets. On this site, adjoining as it does the present buildings of the company, they proposed to erect a new mill. The new mill occupies a space (including Cooper street) of 800 feet on State street and about 150 feet on Columbia street. The dimensions of the main structure will be 247 × 72 feet. Two wings, one on the rear corner next to the Chenango Canal and the other on the front corner towards State street, will be attached. The dimensions of the first will be 60 × 60 feet; of the second 30 × 40 feet. The structure, which is to be built of brick, will be three stories in height."

By the close of the Civil War, Utica came to be known as a "mill town" and West Utica began to develop residentially. In 1881, an addition was built to the Cotton Mill, and designated as No. 3. With No. 2 and No. 3 being separated, manufacturing was handicapped and ten years later these separate units were united by the erection of Mill No. 4.

Realizing that waste from the mills could be made into by-products, a new plant was erected in 1902 on the east side of State street, between Spring and Cooper. Seven years later, a wing was built along Court street, and in 1913, the extension to the old Mill No. 4 westerly toward Fay street. In 1923, a modern storehouse was erected on the Fay street side of the mills.

The popularity of the products of the textile mills of Utica prompted the formation on February 19, 1880 of the Mohawk Valley Cotton Mill and the Broad street mill was erected in 1882, with additions made in 1894, 1899 and 1916. On August 27, 1901, the two companies were consolidated into the Utica Steam and Mohawk Valley Cotton Mills.

WEST UTICA WAS ONCE KNOWN AS WASHINGTONVILLE

WASHINGTONVILLE in the 1830s, 40s and even into the fifties, was that portion of West Utica west of the Chenango Canal. Originally there were a few scattered houses west of Schuyler street, and all that portion south of Court street was pasture land, owned by William and George Tracy, prominent lawyers. The main industries in that area were the potteries and the foundry at the junction of Whitesboro and Lafayette streets, which became the Utica Steam Engine and Boiler Works. A village hall and tavern completed the scene. The coming of the textile mills began to change the area. The "Utica Daily Gazette" of November 22, 1847 noted:

> "No part of our city feels the effects of impulse more than West Utica. It has always been creeping along slowly, often nearly discouraged as to making any progress whatever. But since the building of the factories, it has begun to pick up. Property has increased very considerably in value, and the increase of business holds out inducements for all classes to locate there. We notice several new houses that have been lately erected and many more will be built before the expiration of a year. Nothing, however, has so much changed the appearance of things, as the opening of the several streets, and the grading in the vicinity of the Globe Mills. For pure air, pleasant location and fine prospects, these streets are not surpassed by any in the city. All that is wanted now

to complete the improvements is the starting of the factory operations. This will be done in a few weeks, and we anticipate rapid growth of the city west of Nail creek. Within a year, the late pasture ground will be the residence of gentlemen of the cloth."

The mill workers worked long hours, being obliged to labor from 5:30 in the morning until 7:30 at night. They would go to their work without breakfast and leave at 7 for something to eat. Returning at 7:30, they would work until noon, when half an hour was taken up with dinner. After the second meal, they worked until 7:30 at night. The pay of the majority of the help was small, receiving about "five and six pence" a day (69¢). From this, because of the few amusements of the day, the frugal were able to save enough to purchase houses costing $500, and many of the families had this ambition. The table fare was not epicurean, but was sufficient. It was the custom to lay in a barrel of pork in the winter, together with a stock of potatoes; and this, with milk and bread and butter, constituted the every day repast. Carpets in the houses of the mill workers were an almost undreamed of luxury, and the only heating to be had was the stove that was used to cook meals for the table. Scraps of wood gathered at nearby lumber yards furnished the fuel. Nearly every family could boast possession of a cow, and in addition, some had hens, ducks and geese. These were allowed to roam about as they pleased, and the streets seemed their favorite place.

The "Oneida Morning Herald" of May 1, 1848 wrote:

"The prospects in West Utica are certainly very flattering. The Utica Cotton Factory, which lies alongside the Chenango Canal, and when finished will be the largest factory in the State, is to be put up the present season. The foundation of the building is already laid, and we understand that workmen will commence next week laying into the walls, the large piles of brick that now are heaped around the spot on which the building is to be erected.

"The termination of the Waterville, Clinton and Utica Plank Road, in Court street near the Chenango Canal, and the Rome and Utica Plank Road, which will probably enter the city on Whitesboro street, will have a tendency to build up that part of the city still more rapidly. Already we are reaping the benefits of manufacturing aside from the direct profits of the business, according to the proficiency of our enterprising citizens."

The growth of West Utica was enhanced in a large measure by the arrival of German immigrants who settled there and found employment not only in the textile mills, but as tradesmen, cigarmakers, brewery workers, and shoemakers. In 1839 there were only about eight or nine German families in Utica. On July 8, 1839, the few German residents formed the German Mutual Aid Society of Utica. The revolutionary struggles in the Fatherland in the late 1840s brought increasing numbers of Germans to the city. They formed on October 29, 1848 the German-American Workmen's Society. In January 1856, the name was changed to the Utica Deutsche Lese Verein, the oldest continuing literary society in Utica. Its library in 1906 contained 3000 volumes of the best German literature.

Among its founders were John M. Hahn and John B. Wasmer, who were dominant figures in business and politics. Mr. Wasmer was a carpenter and builder and many of the new homes in West Utica were erected by him. He lived on Columbia street and owned considerable land in the neighborhood of the Cotton Mills. A street in that area was named after him. Five times he was elected alderman of the Sixth Ward.

John M. Hahn was a grocery and provisions dealer on Whitesboro street. Like Mr. Wasmer he was often elected alderman and supervisor of the ward. He was three times alderman and twice supervisor. These two men were typical of the industrious, honest and patriotic German residents of the city.

To take care of the spiritual needs of the Catholic Germans in West Utica, St. Joseph's Roman Catholic Church was organized in 1842. The first house of worship was the frame building on Fayette street, which was purchased from the Methodists. The congregation grew rapidly and in 1855, a two story building was erected and used as a parochial school.

In 1874, the old frame church on Fayette street was torn down. It was no longer needed because the handsome new brick church had been built on Columbia street by the Franciscan Fathers who took care of the congregation in 1858. In 1878, a rectory was built on the east side of the church and in 1885, a spacious brick school house was erected on Varick street, with eight school rooms. In 1892, the Convent of St. Clara for the nuns teaching at the school was erected in the rear of the church on Fayette street. These buildings are still standing.

THE ONEIDA STREET ROPE WALK
1848

JOHN Adams was born at Shouldham, near Lynn, Norfolk, England on January 16, 1820. His father was a rope maker and he learned the trade from him and worked at it until 1844. That year he came to America and located at Troy where his brother Newton was engaged in the same business. Mr. Adams worked for his brother for three and a half years, and in 1848 came to Utica with his brother William and established the unique business of rope-making in Utica. They made the first rope out of doors, spinning it along a fence to an oak tree in a pasture which extended on the west side of Oneida street from Charles Dobson's store to Walker street.

Finding a ready market for their rope, the Adams brothers built the first rope-walk, as the factory was called, further south on the east side of Oneida street, later designated as 1501. It was a one-story building made with railroad ties as posts and supporting a roof made of slabs. Later a floor was laid, especially for the track on which the small hand-driven machine ran. On the lot north of the rope-walk, a tan-bark walk, out of doors, with only a shed at the end to cover the spinning wheel, extended parallel to the rope-walk itself.

Jute from the East Indies, hemp from Russia and Italy and flax from Europe as well as America were used. Three men abreast spun the rope from masses of fiber wound around their waists. These fibers were continually being twisted by the action of the spinning wheel which was turned by hand at the Oneida street end. At the Kemble street end, two horses attached to a machine furnished the power that turned spindles by which the yarns, spun by the men, were twisted into strands. Later these strands were made into rope. Since the ropes were dripped with sizing, made in huge cauldrons, the workmen wore leather aprons.

Like most old landmarks, it gave way to a modern apartment complex, appropriately named, "The Rope-Walk".

THE DEVELOPMENT OF THE JEWISH COMMUNITY

1848

DRIFTING through Utica in 1830 came the vanguard of the Hebrew peddlers, selling their wares and in many cases buying furs, which were still plentiful in the area. They were a hardy group, familiar with the perils of travel and packing their merchandise on their backs or in wagons. As peddlers they stopped a little while in Utica and then went westward and never returned here.

Rabbi S. Joshua Kohn, who served the Congregation Temple Beth El in Utica from 1930 to 1946 traced the history of the Jewish community in his book, "The Jewish Community of Utica, New York 1847-1948" published in 1959. From the scant records available, he determined that Abraham Cohen was the first Jew to settle permanently in Utica. Cohen opened a savings account in the Savings Bank of Utica on October 15, 1847. Most of the new arrivals about the same time came from Poland, although there were some from Germany.

Because the Jewish people and their religion are inseparable, the first Hebrew congregation appeared soon after the arrival of these early settlers. "Beth Israel" was established on the 1st of October, 1848 and included about twenty families. Its trustees were Harris A. Hershfield, Max Levy and Eleazer Hart. They fitted up and occupied a small wooden house of worship, near the corner of Hotel and Whitesboro streets. These services apparently did not continue long, as the records show that from 1855 to 1870, the congregation had no place of worship.

By 1850, the Jewish population in Utica numbered 140. The small community did not have a cemetery of its own and the early burials were in Potter Cemetery on Water street. Later the remains were re-interred in the Jewish cemetery on Watson Place (originally called Jewett street) near the intersection of Lincoln avenue. This plot of ground was purchased for $100 from Charles and Emma Mann by Abraham Cohen and other trustees as "A free burial ground for all the Israelites" on September 26, 1857. During the late 1860s, a large Jewish immigration to America brought an enlarged Utica Jewish community.

On October 16, 1870 the Congregation House of Jacob was organized with thirty-six charter members. At first the congregation worshipped in a house at No. 117 Whitesboro street which was later purchased (1876). In 1882, the congregation sold the building at No. 117 Whitesboro street to Solomon Griffiths, who established a residence there. The congregation then purchased the old Welsh Calvinistic Methodist Church at No. 11 Seneca street the same year. The Welsh church had decided to build a new church, Moriah, at the corner of Park Avenue and Dakin street. The congregation made alterations to the old church. On the southside of the building, the stone inscription of the Welsh church was removed from the front and a marble slab inserted. On the slab was placed in Hebrew characters: "This is the Gate of the Lord, in which the Righteous Shall Enter."

On December 7, 1888, Levi Lyons, Elias Marwilsky and David Rothstein purchased from the city of Utica a schoolhouse at the corner of Whitesboro and Washington streets. This building had been the Welsh Congregational Church until about 1870. The Congregation House of Israel was organized on January 5, 1889 and the building was repaired and renovated to seat about 375 persons.

In 1904 another synagogue was organized by a group of people who originally came from Poland. They organized Congregation House of David and took over the former First (Welsh) Baptist Church on the west side of Broadway when that church ceased to exist about 1900. This congregation continued until 1950 when it was amalgamated with a new synagogue, Tifereth Zvi which purchased the old James Street theater and remodelled it.

In 1909, Louis Abelson and others began to hold Conservative Jewish services in the New Century auditorium. This was a second attempt to form a Reform synagogue. The first attempt in 1903 was not successful. The second attempt, too, was not successful, but a few years later, in September of 1918, Julius Rothstein and Jacob A. Goldstone took up the proposal. As a result, eighty people on June 11, 1919 organized a Conservative synagogue which they named Temple Beth El. They purchased the old Welsh church, Coke Memorial, on the corner of Hopper and Union streets for services. In 1926, the congregation decided to build a new temple on the corner of Genesee and Scott streets which was dedicated on May 2, 1927.

In 1943, the Congregation House of Jacob decided to move uptown to be closer to its members. It renovated a large mansion on Clinton Place, conducted religious services there and started a religious school. In late years, the House of Jacob merged with Tifereth Zvi to form the Congregation Zvi-Jacob, at its new synagogue on the Memorial Parkway.

The education of the young is always uppermost in the minds of Jewish religious and lay leaders and as early as 1850, there was a Hebrew School in Utica. When the Jewish community grew in size, and became conscious of its educational responsibilities, the Talmud Torah was formed (Hebrew Free School). This was located in a house on Washington street in 1903.

In 1912, a group of people, who formed the Conservative Beth El in 1909 were instrumental in organizing a "Modern Hebrew School" at 207 Whitesboro street. This was in response to a growing demand particularly among the younger people that Jewish religion, history and literature be taught in English.

Rabbi Kohn summarized the development of the Jewish community in the fields of business, political life, and in the professions:

> "Most Jews who came to Utica between 1847 and 1871 were peddlers, approximately 155 out of the 225. The others were trades men, manual workers and a few were farmers. Some went into the jewelry and drygoods business; others into the grocery business and quite a few were cigar makers or cigar manufacturers. There was an influx of Jewish workers in the cap manufacturing industry, furriers' and tailors' trade in the first decade of the twentieth century. In the same decade a number of the Utica Jews entered into the wholesale business of dry goods and knit goods and many others in the scrap iron and waste products industry."

UTICA WATER WORKS COMPANY
1848-1849

WHEN Utica was incorporated in 1832, springs and wells supplied most of the inhabitants with water. The Utica Water Works Association which was formed at that time did not construct their works until 1834. It connected together two or three of the old springs at Spring street and from there laid small pipes through part of the city. This system supplied water until 1850.

On March 1, 1848, the Utica Water Works Company was incorporated. The stock was to be not less than $30,000 nor more than $100,000. Thomas Hopper was the moving force in its creation and development and he, together with James Watson Williams, Nicholas Devereux, Alfred Munson, Andrew S. Pond, Charles A. Mann, Horatio Seymour, Silas W. Childs, and Willard Crafts were the trustees of the company. A contract was entered into April 21, 1849 to build the works. The source of water was located on Graeffenburg Hill, in the town of Frankfort, where a well-patronized "water cure" was conducted prior to that time. The company constructed a collecting basin on the site and the water was conveyed in a brick aqueduct to the city's first distribution reservoir. This reservoir was dug between High Street (now Summit Place) and Chatham street (now Linwood Place) about in the center of the block between Park avenue and Eagle street. A map and survey of the aqueduct prepared by S. Whipple, engineer, on October 4, 1849 (Oneida County Book of Maps, No. 21, page 36) shows the location. The only streets laid out at that time in Corn Hill were Steuben, West and Miller street and the aqueduct ran from the source along what was to become Pleasant street, then north (Brinckerhoff), then east (Arthur) and northwest along Chatham to the reservoir. The "Utica Daily Gazette" of May 25, 1848 gave the details of the project:

> "The water is to be brought from the springs, 3¼ miles from the city in a brick aqueduct to a reservoir 200 by 240 feet located in the southerly part of the city, between Chatham and High Streets, nearly in the rear of the brick house of Mr. S. Whipple.

"The reservoir is to be made by excavating and banking, having a depth of 10 feet, the bottom being of hard pan, which has two or three feet below the surface in that region, and the sides of puddled clay. It will be enclosed with a high fence. The reservoir will be capable of containing over 3,000,000 gallons, more than a month's supply, but as the aqueduct will be continued through it and connect with pipe supplying the city, the water used will be that coming directly from the springs. This is an improvement on the Croton works, and it has been ascertained that water thus taken is fifteen percent cooler than when drawn from the reservoir. An iron pipe of 10 inches diameter is to bring the water through Dakin street into Genesee street, and then it is to be conveyed down in two pipes, one on each side of the street, other pipes branching off at the intersections of the several streets. Another main pipe will probably be laid through Bridge street (Park Avenue).

"The company brings the water in front of a man's door, whence he is permitted to conduct it for a yearly payment of from $5 to $7 for ordinary family uses. Public house, manufacturing establishments and other businesses requiring a larger supply of water will pay from $10 to $100 or more, the city some $500, and the two railroads probably as much more."

By 1854, the supply of water, about 800,000 gallons, was found to be inadequate and forty acres of land for a storage reservoir on Graeffenburg Hill were purchased. In 1858, the company purchased the lot on the corner of South and Steuben streets and began drilling for water. Back in 1828 and again in 1836, boring for coal had produced no results. The water company erected a derrick over the old shaft and began digging for a water supply. Only oil and gas but no water was struck. The gas burned brightly for a time and the oil was not sufficient for commercial use. The project was abandoned and for some years, the old derrick stood on the site.

The High Street reservoir was maintained for some years, but was drained, abandoned and filled and the site sold for building lots in 1868.

UTICA GAS LIGHT COMPANY
1849

IN the group which organized the Utica Gas Light Company in 1845 were men whose names are prominent in the history of the city. They were Nicholas Devereux, Silas D. Childs, George S. Dana, Hamilton Spencer, Thomas P. Walker, James Watson Williams, John F. Seymour, John Lee and Lemuel H. Davis. It took time and effort to convince Uticans that gas light was superior to oil or candle illumination. The gas works were built on the north side of Water street, between the foot of Washington and Seneca streets. The "Utica Observer" of July 20, 1849 reported:

"We understand the Gas Company has already laid down two miles in length of pipe — all it is intended to put down at present and contractors expect to be ready to light up by the middle of September. The buildings for the manufacture of the gas, near the Syracuse and Utica freight depot, are nearly completed. The gasometer, a singularly constructed thing, and which is really nothing but a store house for gas, draws many visitors, and excites considerable curiosity."

The newly constructed buildings were described in the "Utica Daily Gazette" of August 30, 1849:

"The centre building is the Retort House. On the north side are four furnaces, over each of which are three retorts, making twelve retorts in all. Into these retorts, which during the process of generating the gas, are kept at a cherry red heat, are placed bituminous coal, and sometimes when it is necessary to make gas rapidly, a little rosin. From the retorts the gas passes to connecting pipes from each of them into the main pipe, which runs along over the furnaces, and conducts the gas into condensing pipes which are laid in serpentine form in the earth. It passes through these into the washer, an upright iron cylinder at the east end of the Retort House. This vessel is partly filled with water, through which the gas entering it at the bottom, passes into the upper part, where it is further washed by means of a jet of water, constantly playing on the cylinder. The effect of the condensing and washing is to separate the ammonia and other impurities from the gas, and condense them into coal tar. A chimney about 60 feet in height, completes the appurtenances of the Retort House.

"The purifying house is the eastern building. On reaching it the gas is received into purifying boxes, and undergoes another cleansing process. Each of the boxes contain layers of lime. In passing through these boxes the lime absorbs the sulphurated hydrogen, and renders the gas free of this offensive odor. The gas is now made, and it leaves the boxes, passing through the Station Meter, a most ingenious and interesting contrivance, by which the gas is correctly measured and then conveyed by an underground pipe, situated in the rear of the lot, to the Gasometer.

"The Gasometer, or store-house of the establishment, is an iron vessel 60 feet in diameter, 16 or 17 feet high, cylindrical in form, and air tight. It will hold 40,000 cubic feet. It sets into a brick cistern or tank filled with water. The gasometer rises and falls as the gas enters or flows out. It is guided by a center post or mast. From the gasometer, the gas, as it is required, passes back into the purifying house, and comes under the control of a simple machine called the 'Governor', by which all the mains in the city are controlled. A turn of a screw in this machine shuts off all the gas at once, and can extinguish every burner in the city. The coal shed, the only remaining building is in the rear of the office. It is built of brick, and will hold 500 or 600 tons of coal."

On September 19, 1849, the "Utica Observer" reported:

"The Gas Works are now in successful operation, and the clear, powerful light afforded, gives great satisfaction to those using it."

The "Oneida Morning Herald" of October 6, 1849 wrote:

"Our city has enjoyed the luxury of gas lights nearly a month. The works operate to the entire satisfaction of both the Gas Company and their patrons. The light for steadiness and brilliancy is equal to any we ever saw, and is superior to the gas light of most cities. There has been no defect or failure since the works started. The improvement in the appearance of Genesee street since the introduction of the light has been very striking. Most of the stores have already introduced the gas, and the plumbers have engagements ahead for supplying others. Many dwellings are also preparing for its introduction. Among other noticeable improvements consequent upon the establishment of gas lights, are the two street lamps in front of the Central Hotel, which illumine the whole neighborhood. We hope the enterprise of Captain White will stimulate others. The Common Council have offered to light lamps erected by the citizens in place of any of the old lamps, or in neighborhoods where they are needed. As the lamps if left to be erected by the city authorities will have to be paid for by local assessment, they will be no gainers by waiting. Hotel keepers or merchants who desire light in front of their places of business by putting up their lamps now will save the cost of assessment. The offer of the city authorities is a fair one, and we hope it may be generally accepted by the residents of those streets in which pipes are laid."

In a few years, more and more gas lamps appeared on the streets of the city; public buildings and private homes were furnished with elaborate gas fixtures. For thirty six years, as the city grew, the gas light company prospered. When upper Genesee street became a popular residential area, the company built a gasometer on the southwest corner of Tracy and Francis streets, to store and supply gas to the homes in South Utica. In later years, this was abandoned and became commonly known as the "Round House Garage".

WELSH METHODIST EPISCOPAL CHURCH
1848

THE Welsh Methodist Episcopal Church (known as Coke Memorial) was organized in July 1849 with 27 members. A room was rented at the old Cambrian Hall, near Mechanic's Hall, for worship. On May 1, 1850, the society purchased a building on Washington street known as the Commercial Lyceum and fitted it up at a cost of $2,000. The story of this old church was related in the "Utica Weekly Herald" of April 20, 1886:

"The little one story brick church is a familiar object to all, and has considerable interest as a relic of old time

Utica. It was built in 1819 for a school, and was long used as a private school for boys. Under its roof many of Utica's old citizens received their early education. The school was conducted for a long time by Lewis Bailey, and also by the late Silas Kingsley, a son-in-law of Levi Cozzens. John C. Hoyt was a student under Mr. Kingsley, and also William Smith, now president of the Herkimer Bank."

The cornerstone of the new church on the northwest corner of Hopper and Union streets, was laid in August structed of brick, with trimmings of Trenton limestone, and the stone wall above grade was finished with Higginsville blue stone. The roof was of slate, supported by three trusses. The church had a handsome tower at the corner, the spire of which rose to a height of 70 feet. The main entrance was on Hopper street from a wooden porch. On the end of the building facing Hopper street was a large rose window under which was a triplet window and at one side a large circle-beaded window. On the Union street side was a rose window, all of stained glass. The auditorium seated 225. The predominant feature of the architecture was Queen Anne, and the structure cost about $14,000.

In 1919, this church was purchased by Temple Beth-El and was used by that congregation until its new temple on Genesee street was built.

THE INCENDIARY TIME IN UTICA
1850-1851

I N the history of Utica, the years 1850 and 1851 are known as "The Incendiary Time" when fires broke out in churches, barns and woodsheds with such regularity as to indicate they were incendiary in origin.

On January 13, 1851, fire broke out at 1 o'clock in the morning in the upper part of the First Presbyterian Church on Washington street below the canal. The flames raged with such fierceness that the steeple and belfry were immediately enveloped. In half an hour the swaying of the tower imperiled the neighboring buildings and the spectators, but though it broke with a terrific crash it fell so perpendicularly that there were no injuries resulting to persons or property.

During the next two months, a number of spectacular fires occurred, all of which were deemed incendiary in origin. These included the drug store of Foster & Dickinson on Genesee street on February 15th, 1851, in the barn of James Sayre on Sayre Alley on February 26th, the Sixth Ward Bowling Alley and the German Lutheran Church on Columbia street on February 27th, and on March 4th in the stable of John Butterfield on Main street.

On April 3rd, 1851, John Butterfield's two barns and sheds on Catharine street in the rear of the National Hotel burned. Eleven horses, a cow and calf, 150 to 200 bushels of oats and a large quantity of hay were destroyed. This fire was to be the undoing of the incendiaries.

The city fathers had recruited a secret force of detectives to frequent saloons and follow any suspects. One of these detectives was Miles G. Barber. Just before the fire, Barber observed James J. Orcutt, a young man coming out of the City Garden on Genesee street and followed him to several drinking places and then observed him walking down Genesee street to Catharine, and disappear out of sight. Barber followed and taking off his boots, crawled along the canal slip by the Catharine street House. He saw someone go toward the Butterfield barn and disappear around a corner. Later, he heard a barn door open and soon smelled wet straw burning. Running to the barn, he found it full of smoke and sounded the alarm.

As the firemen worked on the blaze, Barber observed Orcutt assisting them with the hose. He went up to Orcutt, arrested him and on searching found a book of matches and some paper in his pockets. Further investigation disclosed that a man by the name of Horace B. Conklin, a house painter, and a Henry Newell were also implicated in the whole series of fires. Indictments were returned by the Grand Jury. Arson was a capital crime, requiring the death penalty, if the fire was set in a building where persons normally lived. Most of the fires were in churches and barns, where no one resided. However, in the case of Butterfield's barn, drivers occasionally slept there; in the case of Sayre's barn, it was so attached to the dwelling house by a single

192

board nailed to both, that it was considered in law to be part of a dwelling house.

Orcutt was tried first for the Butterfield barn fire and was promptly convicted and sentenced to be hanged. He was ably defended by Joshua Spencer who told the jury that no one was in the barn at the time; that the barn was not a dwelling house in the popular sense of the term; and that there was no intention to endanger life.

Conklin was next tried for the fire at Sayre's barn. The co-defendant Newell was a prosecution witness and placed Conklin at the scene of the fire. Spencer also defended Conklin, saying to the jury:

> "The question of life and death is too grave to hang upon a mere brace. This brace was simply placed by Mr. Sayre to support the wall of the woodhouse from giving away to the pressure of a pile of wood. One end of this brace touched the wall of the house, and the other that of the woodhouse."

The jury ignored the plea and found Conklin guilty and the sentence was death.

The youth of Orcutt drew sympathy and the Governor commuted his sentence to life imprisonment. He refused to commute the sentence of Conklin and he was hanged on a gallows erected in the jail yard at Whitestown on the morning of November 21st, 1851.

THE AMERICAN EXPRESS COMPANY
1850

THE American Express Company, which for over a century played a prominent part in the industrial and commercial development of the United States, was the creation of John Butterfield. He was the first to appreciate the commercial value of an express company to collect and deliver freight to and from the railroad depot in Utica. His business grew and prospered with the result that express companies were organized in other cities of the State. C & B Wasson & Company in Albany handled freight in that city and sometime in the 1840s, Butterfield joined with Wasson to form Butterfield, Wasson & Company to conduct the freight business between Albany and Utica.

The "Utica Daily Gazette" informed its readers on April 4, 1850:

> "The express lines of Wells & Co. and Butterfield, Wasson & Co. have been consolidated into the American Express Company. The direction of the company is vested in seven directors, and the principle of individual liability is incorporated in the articles of association. Henry Wells, of New York, has been chosen President; John Butterfield, of Utica, Vice President and W. G. Fargo, of Buffalo, Secretary."

The new company was in a position to handle freight on the railroads from New York city to Buffalo and both the company and the railroads experienced a considerable increase in business and profits. When the original railroad depot in Utica was replaced a few years later by a new structure, the American Express Company occupied the old depot at Bagg's Square as its headquarters. This old depot was scheduled for demolition in 1910 and the finding of the old records of the company prompted the "Utica Sunday Tribune" of October 9, 1910 to report:

> "Like the telegraph lines, the express companies were born and nurtured in this city, and the same man whose idea of the usefulness of the telegraph was laughed at was the one to see the commercial value of the express delivery system. That man was John Butterfield, and his express company business grew and grew with the result that others saw the possibilities of the scheme. In the early days of the American Express Company Utica was its headquarters. In this city were the main offices, and Utica was the central point from which express was sent East and West. The auditing force and clerical staff of the company was located at Bagg's Square, and the other offices, including that in New York, were subsidiary to the local one.
>
> "Those interested in the first company were Mr. Wells, whose name is perpetuated in the Wells-Fargo company, and Mr. Butterfield, and the organization was known as Wells, Butterfield & Co. This company owned the American Express Company as well as the New York,

Albany & Buffalo Telegraph Company, over the lines of which were flashed the first message of a commercial nature forwarded in the world.

"Later the Wells Butterfield Company took over the Merchants' Union Express Exchange, which operated in the northern part of New York State though in a very small manner and at infrequent times.

"In 1868 the farthest that the company had extended its service was to St. Paul in the Northwest and to St. Joseph, Missouri in the West. This service was gradually extended and the present system which spans the country either way was due to the business acumen and foresights of Mr. Butterfield and Mr. Wells who with his partner saw the possibilities of such a system.

"In Utica in 1860 the Company employed three men and had six horses. In 1875 the Company had nine men. This year (1910) there are employed (in Utica) 53 men and 20 horses are required for deliveries and collections.

UTICA FIRE BRIGADE
1851-1857

ALTHOUGH there was no evidence that the volunteer firemen were responsible for the incendiary fires of 1850 and 1851, the Common Council voted to disband the volunteer fire companies in the spring of 1851 and to organize in their place a police and fire brigade. On April 16, 1851, a brigade of 120 members was authorized to consist of the following: No. 4 Engine and Hose, on Seneca street; No. 5 Engine and Hose, on Union street; No. 7 Engine and Hose, on Fayette and Whitesboro streets; No. 9 Engine and Hose, on John street, opposite St. John's church; Central City Hose Company No. 2 on State street, opposite the cotton factory; Columbian Hose No. 9 at Thorn & Maynard's lot on Whitesboro street; and Hook & Ladder No. 1 at Fayette and Seneca streets. On June 18, No. 4 Engine was removed to John street.

On October 23rd, the Mayor recommended that the firemen be paid. The Council agreed and in December authorized four engine companies of 25 men each; eight hose companies of 10 men each; a hook & ladder company of 20 men and a fire-police company of 20 men. The city was to own the apparatus. Each engine company was to receive $300 per year, to be equally divided among the men. The members were to report from their regular places of employment on an alarm of fire.

The new firemen had little or no experience with fighting fires and the small pay did not inspire any kind of company spirit. In addition, there was widespread resentment among the old volunteers at the disbanding of their companies because it reflected upon the character of the many fine men who had given honorable service in past years. The citizens generally agreed with the volunteers and when a fire occurred, they would gather to deride the new men, laugh at their efforts, step on the hose and otherwise hinder their efforts. The Mayor, John Hinman, was unable to forget his military experience and often supervised the fire brigade astride his horse, to the amusement of the spectators.

THE ORDER OF GOOD TEMPLARS
1851

THE Washingtonian movement, dedicated to the cause of temperance, was started in Baltimore in 1840. Soon numerous meetings were held in Utica and newspapers espousing the cause of temperance were published. "The Central New York Washingtonian" was published in Utica and Rome in 1842; the "Washingtonian" in 1843 by J. C. Donaldson; the "Washington News" in 1845 by Matteson Baker. In 1849, Wesley Bailey commenced the "Utica Teetotaler", which in 1856 was united with the "Ilion Independent", taking the name of the "Central Independent".

Rev. James E. N. Backus was born near St. Johnsville in 1835, the son of a Methodist minister. He came to Utica at the age of seven; attended the Advanced School and at the age of 12, learned the printer's trade. Two fellow apprentices were E. Prentiss Bailey, who in later years was the owner of the "Observer", and Thomas L. James, afterwards Postmaster General of the United States. Mr. Bailey's father, Wesley Bailey, at that time published the "Liberty Press" at 42-44 Genesee street, a name later changed to the "Teetotaler". Mr. Backus joined the Cadets of Temperance at the age of 12, along with Bailey and James.

It was on a night in July 1851, that Backus and some 15 or 20 printers in Utica gathered in the temperance hall on Franklin Square and organized a new society, the Good Templars. In addition to advocating the prohibition of alcohol, the new order favored equal rights for women. The little society of Uticans grew rapidly and spread to other cities. About a year after its founding in Utica, a convention was held in Syracuse and the Grand Lodge of the Good Templars was organized. Mr. Backus entered the ministry and devoted his life to organizing lodges of the order throughout the country. He died in February 1899 at Lincklaen Center.

WHEN JENNY LIND SANG IN UTICA
1851

A memorable event in the year 1851 was the appearance in Utica of the Swedish "nightingale", Jenny Lind. Volkert W. Roth, the proprietor of the Utica Museum, induced the singer to come to Utica provided he could arrange for a suitable auditorium seating 1000 people. The only available location was the Bleecker Street Baptist Church. The price of admission was to be $3 or $4 according to the location of the seats. On July 14th, the day previous to the concert, tickets were being sold at inflated prices of from

$5 to $8. Captain Green who owned the Bleecker Street House adjoining the church took advantage of the affair to place seats in his back yard, which he sold for $1 each. Some sharp promoters obtained entrance tickets from the surplus stock of her concert held in Albany and sold them to unsuspecting Uticans.

On the night of the concert, crowds of people surrounded the church hoping to see and perhaps hear her. Her carriage was driven up to the side windows of the church on Charlotte street and she alighted on a platform and passed through the flowered entrance. The number of tickets sold was 1,033 and the church was filled to capacity. About 2000 people stood or sat outside the church. A reporter for the "Daily Gazette" acknowledged,

> "We don't know sostenuto from appoggiatura, but we would stand another half hour in such a crowd as that whose elbows ruined our constitution last Saturday in order to catch one note of her voice. We concede the infinite superiority of the Swedish nightingale."

The music critic of the "Oneida Morning Herald" wrote:

> "Her personal appearance, to which no portrait we ever saw does anything like justice, is exceedingly striking. The chief impression is that of intellect, deeply engrossed in a single idea. She speaks English with a little foreign accentuation; yet so little as to add to rather than to mar the beauty of her singing."

CHURCH OF THE RECONCILIATION
1851

NOTHING was done to revive the old Universalist society whose church on Devereux street was sold to satisfy the creditors in 1844, until the late 1840s when regular services began again at Mechanic's Hall. The Church of the Reconciliation was erected on the west side of Seneca street just below the corner of Columbia in the summer of

1851 and was dedicated in July 1852. The architect was C. C. Sargent, of Chelsea, Massachusetts.

The church was located on what was later to become the site of the Homestead Aid Association, with the Citizen's Trust Company on the corner and the store long occupied by C. H. Bremer & Company on the north. It was an impressive looking building. An observer, standing at the point which forms the junction of Seneca and Genesee streets, facing the church saw at each side of the front two massive octagonal towers. A curiosity in the downtown section of Utica in the late 1890s was a tree growing on top of the north octagonal tower. The tree, a mountain ash, had grown to a height of about eight feet when the church was demolished in 1907. It was thought that it grew from a seed blown there by the wind or carried to it by a bird and became lodged in the dirt which had accumulated there through the years. In any event, it was not disturbed and was often photographed and illustrated in national magazines.

In 1907, the church society purchased the old Comstock residence at Genesee and Tracy streets and converted it into a church. The Seneca street property was purchased by the Citizens Trust Company and in 1914, the old church and the buildings on the corner were demolished for a new bank building.

THE METROPOLITAN THEATER
1851-1859

T HE Metropolitan Theater was built in 1851 by General Volkert W. Roth in the rear of the Utica Museum on Genesee street, just above Bleecker. Built at a cost of $16,000, it was then the prettiest little theater in the State outside of New York city. It was 115 feet long by 38 feet wide and 28 feet high. The stage, 36 feet square, was furnished with an abundance of splendid scenery, painted by Oscar F. Almy, from New York, scenic artist of distinction. The drop curtain was splendid and represented the ruins of Carthage. Machinery for regulating the scenery was provided in order to eliminate the awkward scene-shifting usually found in the theaters of the city. In the rear of the stage were dressing rooms.

Entered from the second floor of the old Museum building, were the pit and parquette. The seats had a gradual ascent, so that those at the greatest distance were twelve feet higher than those nearest the stage. From what was formerly the saloon, on the third floor of the old building, but what had been made into an elegant parlor, one could enter the gallery and boxes. The gallery like the pit and parquette had a gradual elevation. Twelve hundred persons could be comfortably seated in the several parts.

Red and white, with a profusion of gold, were the prevailing colors. At the right of the stage was a splendid organ manufactured for the Museum by A. Andrews, of Waterville, at a cost of $1,500. In addition to the organ, a full orchestra was provided for. The whole building was lighted by a great number of gas burners, shaded by ground glass to soften the light.

Nelson Roth conducted the theater for some years and presented many fine artists for the entertainment of Uticans. John Roth then became the owner, but found that it was not a very profitable investment as the years went on. The theater was destroyed by fire on January 27, 1859.

THE ORGAN BUILDERS OF UTICA

ALVINZA Andrews & Son began the building of organs in Waterville in 1834, and among the fine organs built by him was the one which was installed in the Metropolitan Theater in 1851, at a cost of $1,500. In 1852, he removed to Utica, as reported in the "Daily Gazette" of August 18th:

"Mr. Andrews has taken possession of the rooms built for him in the new block of Messrs. Faxton & Childs, in the rear of the Exchange buildings. He occupies the second and third stories over two of the stores. In front, on Charlotte street, is an exhibition room, for putting up and displaying organs, fifty feet long and thirty high, occupying both stores. This will accommodate an organ of the greatest dimensions and is as fine a showroom as is possessed by any organ factory in the country. An organ of eighteen stops, price $1,000, is now being put up in this room. It was made at Waterville, from which place Mr. Andrews has not yet removed his workmen. The case of the organ is butternut wood, which makes a very handsome exterior. The rear part of the building is conveniently divided into workshops and store rooms. The rooms were built expressly for Mr. Andrew's use and afford every facility for his business."

John Gale Marklove was born in Berkley, Gloucestershire, England on March 12, 1827. When only six years old he became a member of the boy choir in the church at Berkley. As a young man, he served an apprenticeship for five years with Gray & Davison, organ builders in London. He then established himself in the organ business at Cheltenham, England. In 1851, his physician advised him to take a sea voyage. He came to New York city where he found employment for three years with Hall & Lapaugh, organ builders. He came to Utica in 1854 and was employed by Alvinza Andrews to voice his instruments. Andrews suggested a partnership with him but the plan did not materialize and Andrews and his son, George, carried on their business in a factory on Seymour avenue in later years.

SQUIRE WHIPPLE: THE FATHER OF AMERICAN BRIDGE BUILDING

SQUIRE Whipple was not a rural justice of the peace; he was given the name of "Squire" at birth. He was born in Hardwick, Massachusetts on March 24, 1804 and when he died on March 15, 1888 at Albany, New York, he was considered one of the country's great iron bridge builders of the nineteenth century. After his graduation from Union College in 1830, he was engaged in canal and railway surveying. He settled in Utica and the city directory of 1840 lists him as a civil engineer, boarding at the Bleecker Street House. Afterwards until 1851 he lived on Steuben street above Rutger.

Bridges had been made of wood in the early days. Whipple studied and analyzed the stresses in the truss design of bridge-building, observing among other things, that cast iron had about the same tensil strength as wood formerly used in bridge-building. He put his theory into practice and began to build in 1840 an experimental iron bridge of seventy-two feet span over the Erie Canal at Newville, near Rome, which proved perfectly satisfactory. His initial form of bridge was the "bowstring truss", originally developed in France a few years before. The following item appeared in the "Utica Observer" of March 9th, 1841:

> "I have been shown within a few days past, a structure erected in our city. It is the frame work of a bridge made of cast and wrought iron. The inventor is Mr. Whipple, civil engineer of this city. The erection is merely a single frame, of a size adapted to that of the new bridges, over the enlarged Erie Canal, for the purpose of illustrating the plan of Mr. Whipple, to cover all spans, from a single canal crossing to the largest railway aqueducts. It stands opposite to Bushnell's shop in Seneca street, immediately below the corner of Fayette street, where any one may have an opportunity of visiting it, and examining its merits."

The "Whipple Iron Trussed Bridge" was patented in 1841 and secured a contract to erect a new bridge, to replace the old wooden one at the Genesee street crossing of the Erie Canal. We read in the "Utica Daily Gazette" of July 8, 1851:

"Yesterday morning the first blow was struck in the demolition of this time honored structure. The crooked arches of evergreens that crowned it on the Fourth, were, it appears, sacrificial garlands. Having served as triumphal emblem three days, and as cypress, the fourth, the bridge was stripped of them and attacked by workmen with crowbars and axes. By noon the west end was rendered unsafe for any but teetotallers and before this reaches the reader's eye, little but a skeleton will remain of this long familiar object. It is to be replaced by an iron bridge of the same width."

The Genesee street width was erected by Squire Whipple and his nephew, J. M. Whipple. The wrought iron needed for its construction was made by Shipman Brothers, at Springfield Center, Otsego county, New York. There were no rolling mills or similar establishments in those days and what wrought iron was required was made in blacksmith shops. The bridge was built to sustain a uniform weight over its surface of 100 pounds to the square foot, but not intended to carry a greater weight concentrated at one part of the bridge. Despite that fact, soon after it was built, the Utica and Binghamton railroad company began to haul loaded freight cars across the bridge, some weighing twenty tons. The result was the overstraining of one beam, but not injuring the trusses or main support of the bridge. Later, the railroad secured another entrance to the city and ceased drawing its cars over the bridge.

Squire Whipple designed a type of bridge known as the "Whipple Trapezoidal Type". In 1872, Whipple secured a patent on his design for a lift bridge, to be raised and lowered to allow the passage of bigger boats. He persuaded the State to build such a bridge at the Hotel street crossing of the Erie Canal. The plans were drawn by Chubbuck & Whipple, of Utica and construction began in 1874. The parts were molded and hand forged in their foundry which was then on upper Whitesboro street. The total cost of the bridge was $10,000.

The bridge rested on four pillars of iron, two on each side of the canal. On each side of the bridge platform, iron rods rose perpendicularly and terminated in cables. On the inside of the lateral section of the superstructure ran shafts. On these shafts were pulleys, each pulley being directly above the iron rods extending from the platform below. In the center of the superstructure and extending across it above, was another shaft, which was surrounded by a drum, which connected with the two lateral shafts by means of cog wheels. Each cable of the platform rods passed over the pulleys on the lateral shafts. To the drum on the transverse shaft was attached a cable which passed down over the pulleys to the towpath and terminated in a weight. The bridge platform was counter-balanced so that it could be raised or lowered by the weights.

The process of raising and lowering the lift-bridge was described in the "Utica Sunday Tribune" on October 1, 1911:

"The treadmill on the bridge is out of sight, and the passerby would not realize that such an appliance is in existence on the bridge, but all the doubting person has to do is climb the stairs, and if he thinks the task of lifting the starting weights is a sinecure, all he has to do is help as a worker on the circular platform. The treadmill is ten feet in diameter and in winding the cables around the drums 360 steps are required. The cables are 83 feet long and do not work with any too great ease.

"The bridge is so delicately balanced that changes are necessary to the weights in rainy and stormy weather. The pieces of pig iron in the boxes which extend lengthwise on the bridge are supposed to exactly counterbalance the weight of the bridge. In rainy weather the weight of the water which is absorbed by the wooden driveway is often so great that it is necessary to add some pieces of iron. In extremely hot weather it is necessary to remove some of the iron. To do away with these changes, the bridge tenders in summer may frequently be seen throwing pails of water on the driveway. The passerby often might think that this was being done to lay the dust, but the purpose of this action is to put sufficient water on the bridge to make it balance exactly.

"The platform, or crossing of the bridge, is supposed to be exactly balanced by the counterweights on the overhead part of the bridge. The cross or jack shaft has two loose bevel gears that engage by means of springs to operate the bridge. One loose gear is attached to the starting weight of 300 pounds. When the 'dog' is thrown into the loose gear, this becomes a part of the jack shaft and when released the weight starts to pull and the bridge begins to rise. The other loose gear on the same jack shaft after the bridge has been raised is then engaged by the 'dogs' to the shaft and the loose gear that was engaged to raise the bridge is then released, and the second gear that is attached to another weight of 390 pounds by means of a cable is started and the bridge lowers to the roadway. The raising and lowering weights have to be raised in position by means of the circular threadmill platform."

In 1888, a lift bridge was erected over the canal at John street. It was 96 feet in length with a roadway 24 feet wide, on each side of which were two sidewalks, one above the other. The upper sidewalks were designed for use when the bridge was raised to allow boats to pass. On the top of the bridge, nearly in the center was a small house, from which the bridge-tender could raise and lower the bridge, which was operated from water power obtained from the canal. Gates were placed at each end of the bridge to prevent the possibility of teams or pedestrians falling into the canal when the bridge structure was elevated.

In 1901, a lift bridge was erected at Washington street, constructed by the Havana Bridge Works of Montour Falls, New York. Unlike the Hotel street and Genesee street bridges, which used water or weights to force the bridge upward, the natural tendency of the Washington street bridge was to be up. This was caused by massive counterweights which exceeded the weight of the bridge itself. To lower the structure it was only necessary to overcome this surplus weight by forcing city water into a four-inch pipe which increased the pressure upon the cylinder at each end of the bridge. The bridge tender could lower or raise the bridge in 15 seconds and could stop it at any point.

A reporter for the "Sunday Journal" decided to study human nature and visited the bridge tenders and reported his findings in the issue of November 8, 1896. He stopped at John street and interviewed Elijah Evans, in the little box on top of that structure. Evans said,

> "Do I see many strange things? Once in a while a horse, or a child or a man falls overboard, or a bicyclist runs into the guards, or a canal man bumps his head and leaves a dent in the beams, or a woman tries to get on when the span's rising, or the blamed thing gets stuck and everyone swears."

Just then a temporary diversion was occasioned by an obstinate horse belonging to Mr. Lux backing into the water, wagon and all.

Next he visited Billy Cudd at the Genesee street bridge who reported that he had to raise and lower the lifts about fifty times a day.

"Here Mr. Cudd pressed a button and the bell did the rest. Then a turn of a lever let the compressed air into the chambers and the bridge rose high enough to allow two canal greyhounds to sail majestically in their course. A reversal of the lever enabled the impatient throngs to save themselves the trouble of walking up and down two short flights of steps. 'Queer how people, even in a hurry, will wait for the bridge to come down rather than cross by the upper footway.

"Nearly halfway between Heaven and Hotel street is perched Johnny Gorman, who for the past two years has operated the apparatus which raises the grade of the thoroughfare in the interest of commerce. This mechanism is of the treadmill variety. Mr. Gorman is a good talker. 'The women are much quicker than the men. When the bell rings nine out of ten men will stop and say bad words about canal boats and cuss till they can get across. But the women. No matter how much time they have, the moment the bell rings, they gather up their skirts and make a dash for their lives.' If you want a good day's fun go sit a few hours with the busy bridgemen."

THE OLD COURT HOUSE ON JOHN STREET

1852

WHEN Utica was incorporated as a city in 1832, there was a growing need for a Court House devoted exclusively to the business of administering justice. The old Academy, facing Chancellor Park where the Bleecker street school now stands, had served as a joint court house and school, but with separate entrances in later years. The County determined to build both a new jail and a new court house in Utica. The "Utica Daily Gazette" of May 6, 1852 reported:

"Work has been resumed on the new Court House. It is expected that the building will be completed this season. The foundations only are now built. This edifice, situated in front of the old Academy on John street, is to be sixty feet in width and ninety in length. On the first floor will be several apartments, for the accommodation of juries, officers, etc., besides a large room for holding such courts as are thinly attended. The court room, on the second floor, will be seventy-three feet long and fifty-eight wide, with height to correspond. It will be provided with ventilators at the floor and in the ceiling. The exterior of the building is to be plain with the exception of four Corinthian pillars on the front and a cupola."

In 1875, the building was completely remodeled. On entering the building, there was a small lawyer's room, from which a private stairway led to the lawyer's room on the second floor. The grand jury room and the District Attorney's office were on the first floor. At the eastern end of the building were two large cells for prisoners. Each cell could accommodate half a dozen prisoners or more. The cell doors were iron gratings, with a lock placed so as to be out of reach of the prisoners. At the east end was a wide stairway, of ash trimmed with black walnut. The railings and posts were of walnut, trimmed with ash, and very ornamental. There was a window at the first landing, to light the hall. From this landing there were stairways to the right and left leading to the court room.

The court room on the second floor was wainscoted with ash, trimmed with black walnut. The large windows were furnished with inside blinds of ash. Four large chandeliers hung from the ceiling. Two double doors led into the court room. The space allotted to the members of the Bar was enclosed by a black walnut railing and was covered with Brussels carpet. The judge's bench was large and wide, made of black walnut, trimmed with ash, the panels being of French walnut. A large portrait of Joshua Spencer hung in the rear of the room, while portraits of Judges Doolittle and Beardsley were placed back of the judge's bench. Back of the bench were three rooms, the one on the north for the petit jury, the center one for the judge and the one on the south side for lawyers.

For more than half a century, this building served as the court house of the County in Utica. Through its portals passed the distinguished members of the Bench and Bar of the State — profound judges of the law, eloquent advocates who swayed juries with their logic and impassioned pleas, and men prominent and powerful in the political affairs of the State and Nation — Roscoe Conkling, Francis Kernan, Horatio Seymour and others.

When the 20th century arrived, the need for a larger court house became evident and the new Court House at Charlotte, Elizabeth and Mary streets was opened in 1909. The old edifice was sold at auction and was opened as the Jacobus Dancing Academy.

THE OLD COUNTY JAIL ON MOHAWK STREET
1853-1883

ONE of the most picturesque buildings in Utica in the middle of the 19th century was the old County Jail on Mohawk street built in 1853. For years the old jail in Whitesboro was inadequate for holding prisoners either awaiting trial or serving time for minor criminal offenses. The County appointed a committee to superintend the building of a new jail and court house in Utica. On May 30, 1851, one and one-half acres of land on upper Mohawk street near Eagle street and the old "gulf" were sold to the county and the building of a jail was begun.

Its two tall towers suggested an ancient castle and stronghold. The house was made of plain red brick, while the jail portion was of sandstone, which was dug from nearby quarries. There were twenty cells with iron doors. These were located on the first and second floors of the jail. An iron railing was built on the second floor, and about five or six feet back of this, the cells were placed.

The jail had been opened but a short time before its inhabitants learned that it required but very little effort to break out. The bars of the iron doors to the twenty cells were made of soft iron instead of steel and many prisoners sawed their way out. In addition, the bars on the cell doors were not close together and prisoners could reach out and pick the padlocks. The outer walls were constructed of small stone and the mortar used in the construction crumbled easily with the result that a piece of hard wood was sufficient to remove the stones and allow the prisoner to escape. Scarcely a week passed without some prisoner escaping. On May 10, 1853, the "Utica Daily Gazette" published an editorial from the "Albany Argus":

> "The people of Oneida County have found out a new method of dealing with criminals. They have a jail constructed on the principle of a cullender or sieve, in which the criminals are put, and the idea is that the finer ones will fall through and the grosser be retained. It is not however the smallness of the offense or the offender that ensures an outlet. The filtering process is adapted to the mental grossness of the prisoners. An acute rogue is sure to go through, those of obtuser built are retained, and thus the villains of the former class leave the county, which is good riddance, and the dull rascals are punished, as stupid people deserve to be. But are not our neighbors likely to overshoot themselves by this ingenious process? Is it not good presumptive evidence that a prisoner who does not escape from this looped and airy habitation is non compos mentis."

William Perkins and his brothers, Porter and Sebry, of West Utica were known as the "Peculating Perkinses" who committed in all about fifty burglaries in the 1870s. They played hide and seek with the Sheriff so often that one Utica newspaper termed the jail, the "Paste Board" jail.

Porter Perkins was finally convicted of burglary, sentenced to seven years and lodged in the Mohawk street jail pending transfer to State prison. He wanted no part of that and at night, sawed off the bolt from his cell door, released two other prisoners and with the aid of a bar slipped in by outside friends, the three men cut a hole through the outer wall and escaped.

Four months after the escape of Porter, his brother Sebry was arrested for robbing a woman of $60 and a watch. Young Perkins was confined in a cell on the upper tier. At odd times when not observed, he succeeded in making three saws out of knives. With the saws, he managed to sever the bolt on his cell and with a piece of wire taken from a soup pail, succeeded like his brother in raising the severed bolt. In his cell was a two-inch plank, supported on three two-inch legs. He removed the legs. Out of one he made a chisel; out of the other a wedge. About two o'clock in the morning, he crept from his cell and with the tools he had fashioned and the third leg of the stool as a hammer, he commenced work on the outer wall of the cell. However, his fond hopes were not to be realized.

Captain Berry for some time suspected something of the kind, although he was unable to discover any traces. On February 13, 1874, Captain Berry heard some noise and rushed to Sebry's cell. He found him on his cot in the cell, but in his haste he left the tools where he had dropped them at the outer wall. Although he at first professed ignorance of the whole affair, family pride compelled him later to acknowledge that he had made the attempt.

Porter Perkins was not apprehended until 1880 and the Court, distrustful of the security of the old jail, ordered that he be forthwith conveyed to Auburn prison to serve the original sentence. The Perkins brothers performed at least one public service. They were in large measure responsible for the decision to build a new jail in 1882-1883 on Bleecker street, at the junction of Albany street.

CORN HILL WAS ONCE KNOWN AS "FROG HOLLOW"

UTICANS are familiar with the area known as "Corn Hill", a term applied to the entire area south of Rutger street to Steele Hill and from Elm street to Mohawk street on the east. The name derives from an immense field of corn which grew along South street easterly of Steuben street. Less familiar is the term, "Frog Hollow" which referred to an original frog pond between Elm and Steuben street, south of Leah street.

Utica was not without other frog ponds in its early days

because we read in the "Oneida Whig" of May 17, 1836 a letter to the editor from a citizen:

> "I will at once announce the extraordinary circumstance to which I refer. It is no less than a nightly concert of frogs, on the corner of Bleecker and John streets. Here, at twilight, as one passes along, his ears are assaulted by sounds which, if they do not charm, will at least penetrate. No one even of the most insensible nature, can help being affected if not overcome by this twilight serenade. I really hope that this curiosity will not pass without due honor by those who are bound to point out to world the 'rural sights and sounds' of Utica."

Lorenzo M. Taylor, a civil engineer, who made many of the early surveys and maps and was city engineer from 1838 to 1850, began to transform this wilderness into habitable areas. He laid out building lots and streets, giving them names of the various members of the Bleecker family. His own name was later given to Taylor Avenue.

The main street of Corn Hill in the middle of the 19th century was South street. Originally that part of the street west of Steuben to Bridge street (now Park avenue) was known as George street, and the portion from Bridge to Genesee, as Rebecca. It is not known when South street was opened, but Rebecca is mentioned in the records as early as 1816, when there were only two houses fronting on it and it was the only street south of Elizabeth.

Of South street, the "Utica Saturday Globe" wrote on April 12, 1902:

> "We might also recall the days before the Civil War when the boys and girls would dance in the evenings on the plank driveway which extended through the middle of South street from Steuben to Albany. The corner of South and West streets was a favorite place for these little informal terpsichorean gatherings. Light was furnished by the old-fashioned kerosene street lamps, and Joe Parker played the fiddle.
>
> "Perhaps some of the same old people saw George and Thomas Hopper when they bored 500 or 600 feet into the earth in the lot at the southeast corner of South and Steuben streets in an attempt to strike oil. Many people of only middle age recall the derrick, which stood for years after being erected over the unprofitable hole.
>
> "Shortly before this event the first brick block in the locality was built on the northeast corner of South and West streets by Daniel Morgan. It was known as Mor-

gan's Hall, for the upper story was used for public gatherings, entertainments, and amusements. In 1865, the block was partially destroyed by fire, but was repaired and is about the same today as when built. After a time the space devoted to hall purposes was changed to living apartments and James Wood then permitted the upper portion of his business block to be used for amusements. At church socials and amateur entertainments, Wood's orchestra furnished the music. The elder Mr. Wood was the first violin and leader, and members of his immediate family played the other instruments. Diagonally across the street from the Morgan Block and in front of the present Howarth brick block, the old hay scale was located. To this the farmers would come to have their loads of produce weighed. The scale was put in service in the early '60s, and was not removed until 1885, some time after the street railway was built.

"Many will recall excursions to Hugh McGee's orchard, now occupied by the brick block at the northeast corner of South and Steuben streets, where they procured apples as only boys know how to do. Then again they may remember some of their ball games which in those days were never complete unless a few fights were interspersed. If a row could not be started between the opposing teams, the two clubs would unite and thrash the umpire. It was their special delight to catch a fellow from some other part of the city coming into their district with one of the Corn Hill girls. If he escaped a drubbing when he tried to make his return, he was either a remarkably fleet sprinter or as elusive as a Boer general. When they were not purloining McGee's fruit, camping in a vacant lot, playing ball, or fighting, they were making bonfires of all the moveable property they could get hold of on Corn Hill. Many of the boys at different periods of their lives belonged to the Osceola Engine Company No. 4, or the Protection Hose Company No. 4, which flourished in the late '50s and early '60s and which were quartered on the site now occupied as stores at 60 and 62, on the south side of South street, a few doors west from the corner of West street."

In Corn Hill there was a "commons", a strip of woods and pastures which extended from Oneida street on the west to Third avenue on the east and from Arthur street on the north to Pleasant street on the south. In part of the "commons" there was no woodland, and the residents who owned cows pastured them there. The city had an ordinance which prohibited cattle from wandering on to the streets. A "poundmaster" was appointed by the Common Council to enforce the ordinance. If he found an unattended cow wandering from the "commons" he could seize the animal and take it to the "pound" where he could keep it until ransomed by the owner at $2 per animal. During the Civil War years, the "pound" was located during the summer at Alexander Robinson's circus barn at the corner of Seymour avenue, Neilson and Eagle streets. This barn, 80 by 125 feet, had a circus ring for practice and Robinson's equipment and vehicles were quartered there during the winter season.

The owners of the cattle hired young lads — "the cowpunchers of Corn Hill" — to drive the cows from their barns up either Steuben or Elm street to the "commons" and keep them from falling into the hands of the poundmaster. The lads worked from 8 o'clock in the morning until 5 o'clock at night, for twenty-five cents per head. If they allowed the poundmaster to catch an unattended cow, the boys had to pay the poundmaster his two dollar fee. To avoid that liability, a continuing feud resulted and the lads were not above resorting to violence to rescue an animal. If a cow got off the grass and the boys saw the poundmaster coming, they would do their best to get the cow back on the "commons" before that official could get his hands on the animal. Even when the latter had seized the animal and was taking him to the pound, they would pitch into him and rescue the animal, and in a few minutes the animal was back in the fold. The boys were not above breaking into the pound to rescue their animals while the poundmaster was elsewhere.

On one occasion the poundmaster was seen coming down Steuben street one day driving three cows which had strayed from the pastures. He chanced to meet a boy and asked him if he wanted to make 25 cents by driving the three cows to the pound, as he had two more cows to get over on Elm street. The boy accepted the money and drove the cows over Eagle street to Miller street to Arthur street, into a barn where two of the cows belonged. ("Sunday Tribune" November 11, 1906).

UTICA'S CITY HALL
1853

A FTER the fire of 1848 which destroyed the Council chamber on Hotel street, rooms for the meetings were taken in Mechanic's Hall. In 1850 the question of building a City Hall was taken up. Two sites were considered, one on the south corner of Genesee and Pearl, the location of the old United States Hotel — Female Seminary; the other the Thorn & Maynard lot on the east side of Genesee street. A special election was held on October 2, 1851 when 417 votes were cast for the Pearl street site and 173 for the other. The city purchased the site for $6,500. To defray the total cost of the building of $66,000, the United States Congress appropriated $12,000 for a perpetual lease of one floor to house the United States Courts. This lease was abrogated when the Federal Building was built on Broad street in the 1870s.

In 1852, Richard Upjohn, New York City, was commissioned to design a suitable structure. Generally regarded as one of the foremost architects in the country, he had designed the new Grace Church in Utica. He chose an Italian style, characterized by arched openings, low-hipped roof and vertically proportioned windows. At the corner, a tall campanile was placed, with small arched windows, and near the top of the tower were located four glass clock faces, surmounted with triple arched arcades, opening to the belfry. Cells were built in the basement of the tower for the detention of prisoners arrested by the constables. The first two floors were devoted to offices but the entire third floor was a large hall for public meetings, dances, receptions and church festivals. The cornerstone was laid September 27th, 1853.

The builder was William Jones, born in Carnarvonshire, Wales on January 17, 1810. When he was eight years old, he went to work carrying mortar for his father who was a stone mason. There he learned the trade and came to America as a deckhand on a vessel from Liverpool to Philadelphia. He came to Utica in 1837 and after working at his trade for a few years, he went into business for himself in 1840. He constructed 120 of the stone and brick buildings in Utica during his career. In addition to the City Hall, he built Cotton Mills

Nos. 1 and 2 on State street, the Utica Female Seminary, the Bradish and Tibbitts blocks, the Butterfield Flats on Lafayette street, as well as six churches — Reconciliation, St. Luke's, First Methodist, Bethesda on Washington street, Grace and Calvary Episcopal. The city hall was ready for partial occupancy in 1854.

The original city clock was located in 1834 in the Bleecker street Baptist Church on the corner of Charlotte street. The official clock was partially illuminated on June 8, 1855. For more than a hundred years, this clock was a familiar landmark and its bell not only announced peace and war, the passing of distinguished citizens, but until the telegraph alarm system was installed, announced the location of fires. The custodian would strike the bell the number of times which corresponded with the ward where the fire had occurred, to the total originally of seven. The bell was installed in 1854 and was cast by Jones & Hitchcock of Troy and weighed 4000 pounds. It cost $1,400. During the Civil War, a crack developed in the bell and it had to be replaced. On May 15, 1862, a new bell was made by the same firm and installed and observers said that it had the weight and tone of the old bell.

The bell was on the top floor of the tower and was supported by a framework of heavy beams. Originally it had three strikers, one of which was for fires (later electrified). In later years the other two strikers only were used. One was a great sledge hammer which rose automatically from the framework outside the bell and struck the hours resoundingly if not always accurately. The other was a tongue inside the bell which was operated by a pumping handle three floors below. This was used to inform the citizens of important events. Two or three men were required to operate it if the tolling continued any length of time.

According to a plate attached to it, the clock was made by Lefevre & Bear, locksmiths, New York City. It was hand wound; the jeweler in charge being obliged to visit the tower once a week to wind it. The winding was a 15 minute job, requiring no little strength on the part of the winder who had, by turning a crank, to lift two weights of about 500 pounds each, which furnished the power for the mechanism. One of the weights operated the striker, the other the clock itself. The pendulum was about four feet long and the ball at the bottom about a foot in diameter. The clock had two jewels, both of which were on the pallets, the parts of the clock subject to the most wear.

Space on the four floors of the tower was necessary for the operation of the clock. On the second floor were the main works, four feet high but simple in construction. Two cables passed from each side up thru holes in the floor above, where, in the center of the room, a small box set on a standard regulated the hands on all four sides. Each face had a box of its own connected by a wooden bar with the center box. The faces of the clock were made of ground glass painted with Roman numerals and were about six feet each in height. Later, at night, four electric lights illuminated the face.

PHILO BALLOU'S "Crystal Saloon"
1853

A favorite eating place during the heyday of the Metropolitan Theater was Philo Ballou's "Crystal Saloon" located on the west side of Genesee street, just south of the corner of Fayette and opposite the theater. The "Daily Gazette" of June 2, 1853 contained the following announcement:

> "P.C. Ballou, well-known to the public, as an obliging caterer to all who enjoy the good things of life, opens his new saloon, directly opposite the Museum, tomorrow morning. He has been at considerable expense in fitting up and arranging it for the convenience of patrons which renders it as elegant and tasteful a saloon as can be found in the city. Game, fruit, and all delicacies will be served in good season and style."

Philo Ballou was a man of ample proportions, with a beaming countenance and a noticeable hesitancy in his speech, as the "Saturday Globe" once recounted. The bar, which catered to the thirsty part of the citizenry was located in the rear of the first floor and was an unpretentious affair. The rest of the room was given over to stalls, which occupied each

216

side. These booths had entrances in front which could be closed by curtains, which secured privacy for its occupants. Each booth had a table and chairs. On each table was a castor, containing salt, pepper and pepper sauce. A stall would accommodate four people, and the place was the favorite gathering place for the actors and playgoers at the Metropolitan Theater across the street. The kitchen was in the rear, with an entrance on Fayette street. There was a second floor, which was more private and here, according to the "Globe",

> "Utica's upper crust repaired to feast on the toothsome viands served by the corpulent host. Oysters were to that generation what lobsters are to this and for a fellow to treat his best girl to a feast of raw oysters and other toothsome food in a private dining room at the the Coffee House was considered quite the proper thing."

John R. Scott, the great tragedian actor was one of the stars who often appeared at the Metropolitan. In the "Utica Observer" of January 19, 1901, Blandina Dudley Miller related a story about him:

> "A laughable little incident is told of Scott during one of his engagements here. The gentleman who relates the story does not remember what the play was, but it was a tragedy and Scott was in fine form to give a vigorous performance. The play called for a clash at swords between Scott and the leading man. Scott was a capital swordsman and the leading man of the company prided himself that he too was some pumpkins, when it came to fencing; so when the two met in combat that night the leading man thought that he would teach Scott a thing or two about the art. Scott, all wrapped up in the performance, went at the leading man as though to put him out in one round, but the leading man was game and parried the thrusts so skillfully that Scott was surprised at first and then angry. 'Quit, you fool,' he hissed and as he did he gave the leading man a prod that made him grunt. The audience was in ecstacy over the excellence of the battle, and it applauded when the leading man gave Scott a return thrust that made him wince. Scott was furious. He fell upon his adversary and threw science to the wind. He closed with him and walloped him over the head with the weapon as if it was a sand bag. The leading man saw that Scott was in earnest and instead of dying, as all well-regulated stage villians should, he turned tail and ran. Over the footlights he jumped with the infuriated tragedian in hot pursuit and

his sword in the air. The audience was so dumbfounded that no one moved. Down the stairs he went three at a time, and into the street. Across the street was Philo Ballou's Crystal Saloon, and into this ran the leading man, followed by Scott, who had not ceased to bellow imprecations from the moment that he jumped over the footlights. The occupants of the saloon thought that a volume of Chaucer or Shakespeare had come to life and they scattered in all directions. Scott finally cornered him and there would have been bloodshed if someone with more temerity than the rest had not interferred. Scott was finally calmed and they went back to the theater and resumed the play where they had left off — or as near to it as they could conveniently."

FISHER'S STEAM CARRIAGE
1853

In 1853, J. K. Fisher of New York City came to Utica to develop a steam carriage for use on the roads. The "Utica Morning Herald" of June 23, 1853 reported:

"Some time since, our readers will remember we mentioned the fact that J. K. Fisher, in this city, at the Vulcan Works was constructing a steam carriage for common roads. We have since had the pleasure of examining the drawings and a part of the machinery for the vehicle. We will now attempt a description. Suffice it to say, that the boiler is to be at the rear of the carriage, a small engine on each side near the back part, and the machinery will all be visible. The steering apparatus is connected with the forward wheels, and is operated by a lever reaching to the seat of the conductor. The furnace is surmounted by a sort of hopper, which will contain and furnish to the fire as needed, fuel sufficient for about ten miles. Mr. Fisher is now constructing a carriage to seat comfortably six persons, and expects to have it completed in three weeks or a month. He also has

218

drawings for omnibuses, in which the machinery will be covered from dust. He expects to be able to attain a speed of fifteen to twenty miles an hour on good roads. When the carriage is completed, we shall give it the attention it deserves."

Mr. Fisher completed his steam carriage and took it to New York City in 1854 to display it at the New York Crystal Palace. It created a great deal of interest and the "New York Evening Post" gave a detailed description of the machine, which was reprinted in the "Utica Morning Herald" on January 13, 1854:

"There is on exhibition in the machine department of the Crystal Palace, a vehicle intended to be propelled by steam power on common roads. It is the invention of Mr. J. K. Fisher, of this city, and is worthy of an examination by all persons interested in improvements of this description. The carriage occupies a space of thirteen feet from the fore to the hind wheels. It is calculated to carry four persons and is of four horse power. The steering wheels are directed by a lever in front of the carriage, and one can move it with a slight effort. The boiler is fixed at the end of the vehicle, outside of the axle.

"This carriage differs from most of the English (models) in the mode of connection between the engine and the wheels. Theirs had what are called inside connections, which required the body of the vehicle to be placed nearly a foot above the axle; this has outside connections, which allow the body to be within a foot of the ground.

"Mr. Fisher also claims to have improved the means of steering and turning corners, which he has done by taking away the apparatus for attaching and detaching the driving wheels, so that either one could be made to turn upon the axle.

"The English carriages usually require three men, none less than two, to work them. Mr. Fisher has applied a hopper to feed the fire, and devised a self-gauging pump to feed the boiler, so that, having avoided the necessity of a man to disconnect the wheels, he is confident that one man can manage a carriage of the largest size.

"The carriage is not yet covered, being only so far done as to enable it to run experimentally. Its general appearance is simple and compact. The boiler is composed of fourteen upright tubes, connected by annuler chambers at top and bottom. The tubes are 2¾ inches in diameter, so small that they are not likely to burst; and, as the water is inside of them, and there is no large chamber, not much damage could be done in case of their bursting.

"Mr. Fisher proposes, as soon as funds are advanced, to build a dray, or drawing carriage, of the most economical size for passenger service; and to draw after it several passenger carriages — probably four or five — when the roads are good; and one or two when they are bad.

"The speed that he has attained, in a trial, on soft ground, has been about seven miles an hour. On a good road he has no doubt that the speed will more than double."

For some unexplained reason, Mr. Fisher's invention never progressed beyond this single steam wagon.

THE ASSUMPTION ACADEMY
1854-1932

UTICA had many fine educational institutions of which she had reason to be proud. In addition to the Utica Academy established in 1818 near Chancellor Park, another which sent into the world men who made enviable names for themselves in the various walks of life, was the old Assumption Academy on the northeast corner of John and Elizabeth streets, now a vacant lot. Its graduates clung to their memories of the old school and their teachers and were fiercely loyal to their alma mater.

The Catholics of Utica who attended St. John's Church determined to provide the religious training for the boys of the parish, the girls being educated by the Daughters of Charity next to the church on John street.

The building was erected in 1854 on what was prior to that time a cow pasture, covered with berry bushes. The foundation stones were very large and were drawn from the Trenton quarry. The Christian Brothers staffed the school, under Brother Habakkuk, who came here from Montreal. Among the first students was Thomas A. Burke, later the Bishop of Albany. Among others were Brother John the Evangelist (Walsh), the first alumnus of Assumption to join the Christian Brothers and who was principal from 1887 to 1889; Rev. Brother Azarias, a distinguished Catholic writer and his brother, Reverend John F. Mullaney.

During the directorship of Brother Justin (1859-1866), the need for some sort of an institution for Catholic orphan boys, similar to the one for the girls, conducted by the Sisters of Charity, became apparent. The Brothers turned over a part of the building to the housing and feeding of the orphan boys and to educating them along with the day students. The orphan boys lived in the attic. On October 23rd, 1866, a fire occurred in the large cupola and completely demolished the roof and damaged the building. Many old citizens attested to a peculiar incident during the progress of the fire. Around the burning cupola there suddenly appeared a white dove, which flew around the tower in all directions. The 275 boys found shelter in St. John's church, the Court House nearby and in many private residences. Repairs were quickly made and the building was again occupied.

Along in the 1860's, the school became so crowded that it was decided to build a new home for the orphan boys. A site on the corner of Third Avenue and South street was donated by John Butterfield and St. Vincent's Orphan Asylum for Boys was erected. It was later known as St. Vincent's Protectorate and finally as St. Vincent's Industrial School.

The "Utica Sunday Tribune" in 1914 recalled the feuds between the Assumption boys and those of the Academy:

"Who can forget after participating in one of them, the battles royal which took place between the boys of the two institutions during snowballing times in the big open spaces which is known as Rutger Park? The Free Academy boys were known as the 'Dudes' while the Assumption Academy lads labored under the less dignified sobriquet of the 'Micks'. When the 'Dudes' had labored long and earnestly to construct an immense snow fort in the park, it was naturally expected that before long the 'Micks' would come along in force and storm it. They were seldom disappointed and many a hot and lusty battle was waged. It was not always with snowballs alone, for the writer remembers distinctly the first 'black eye' he ever possessed handed to him from

221

the fist of a husky youngster who is now one of the leading bankers in the city."

With the development of parochial schools in Utica, in 1916, the Assumption was converted into a high school. In 1917, the Xaverian Brothers took over the Assumption and conducted high school there until June of 1932 when the last class was graduated. Shortly thereafter the old Assumption Academy was demolished and is now a parking lot. The Xaverian Brothers then took over the teaching of the boys at the new St. Francis de Sales High School on Genesee street. In 1958, the Brothers opened a new school Notre Dame, at the old Country Day School in New Hartford and in 1960 built the building on Burrstone Road.

WELSH AND GERMAN LANGUAGE PUBLICATIONS

THE original foreign language publications in Utica were those of the Welsh. "Y Cenhadwr American idd" ("The American Messenger"), a monthly, was commenced in Utica in 1832. In 1834, it was moved to Steuben and published by Rev. Robert Everett.

"Y Cyfaill O'R Hen Wiad" ("The Friend from the Old Country") was removed to Utica from New York City by Rev. W. Rowland in 1841. It was removed temporarily to New York and Rome. In 1857 it was brought back to Utica. It continued well into the twentieth century being published by T. J. Griffiths Company.

"Seren Arllewinol" ("Western Star") was commenced in Utica as a monthly in June 1844. It was transferred to Pennsylvania in 1846. "Cysell Hen Wladyn Americanidd" was published at Utica by E. E. Roberts in 1843. "Haul Gomer" ("Gomerian Sun") was commenced as a semi-monthly in 1847 and lasted one year. "Y Gwyliedydd" ("The Watchman") was commenced in Utica in 1854 with Morgan

Ellis, editor. In 1856 it was removed to New York City and united with "Y Drych".

"Y Drych" ("The Mirror") had been established in 1851 in New York City and removed to Utica in 1860 and published by J. W. Jones until January 1, 1875 when Thomas J. Griffiths became the publisher. This weekly came to be recognized as the national organ of the Welsh people in the United States, with a circulation of about 8000.

In 1872, a Welsh monthly for children called "Bloden Ye-Oes" was commenced here by T. Solomon Griffiths and William ApMadoc. It was removed to Pennsylvania in 1874. In 1875 "Y Wawr" ("The Dawn") was first issued in Utica by Rev. Owen Griffith, as a Welsh Baptist Journal, printed by T. J. Griffith. In 1881 "Y Pregethur O'R Eoboniur", a bimonthly was published for a short time. In 1887, T. J. Griffith began the "Cambrian", an illustrated monthly in Welsh, which became semi-monthly in 1909 and ceased about 1919.

On January 7, 1853, a few leading German citizens of Utica established a newspaper in German called the "Central New York Demokrat". It appeared weekly and was supplemented with a monthly publication called "Der Hausfreund". The printing took place at the house of James J. Hamlin at the corner of Columbia and Varick streets, and later the plant was moved to 35-37 Broadway.

In 1857, Paul Keiser bought the paper and changed the name to the "Oneida Demokrat". On September 1st of that year, John C. Schreiber became connected with the publication and was its guiding genius and editor for about fifty years, until his death in 1907. In 1891, the name of the paper was changed to the "Utica Deutsche Zeitung and Oneida Demokrat." It was issued tri-weekly on Mondays, Wednesdays and Fridays and the plant was located at 10 Lafayette street. In later years, the "Oneida Demokrat" was dropped from the name of the paper.

Following the death of Mr. Schreiber, Otto Poepel became the editor until 1925, when he resigned. In 1911, the business was taken over by Richard Metzler and in 1913 the plant was moved to 14-18 Elizabeth street, opposite the present School Board building, where it remained for ten years. In 1923, the newspaper was moved to the Metzler printing plant at 317 Lafayette street. In 1917, the paper was changed to a weekly. In 1934, with the number of German readers dwindling, the newspaper was taken over by the "German Zeitung" of Syracuse.

THE WELSH EISTEDDFOD
1856

THE Welsh-speaking citizens constituted a large ethnic group in Utica during the nineteenth century. They occupied positions of trust as bankers, merchants and public officials. Among mechanics and artisans, they were skillful carpenters and masons and many of the buildings and homes of Utica were constructed by them. They were deeply religious and organized their churches of various denominations. At an early period of Utica's history, their culture and love of music and literature gave us the "Eisteddfod".

The "Eisteddfod" history goes back along the line of Welsh and British literature until it is lost in the dim mists of fable and tradition. It can be established that the Eisteddfod existed in the early centuries of the Christian era as an old institution. The constant warfare, internecine and foreign, of those early centuries destroyed most early records. After the sixth century it had a fitful existence, while the nation was fighting for its life against the Saxon. In the sixteenth century, after comparative tranquility had been restored, the Eisteddfod became more and more popular. The national Eisteddfod of Wales was held with much more pomp and ceremony than its American counterpart, but it has been said that the Eisteddfod as established in America "made up in enthusiasm and spirit what it lacked in antiquity and mystic ceremony."

The first American Eisteddfod worthy of the name was held in Carbondale, Pennyslvania in 1851 and B. F. Lewis of Utica won a prize at the second Carbondale Eisteddfod in 1852. The first Utica Eisteddfod was held in what was then the Welsh church, later the Jewish synagogue, on Seneca street, January 1, 1856. It was a several day program involving choral competition, poetry and literature, as well as elocution pieces. The proceeds, after paying the expenses including the prizes awarded, were applied to charitable purposes.

In announcing the Eisteddfod for January 1, 1858, it was stated that "the price of seats had been fixed so low as to

224

bring them within the reach of all, being two shillings to the two sessions. It is the intention to give whatever sum may remain in the treasury after paying the expenses of the Eisteddfod, toward helping the poor Welsh people of the city in these hard times." The "hard times" resulted from the panic of 1857. The Eisteddfod was conducted in Mechanic's Hall until 1862, when it was decided to suspend until after the Civil War.

The next was held in 1867 in Concert Hall on John street, owing to a fire in Mechanic's Hall. When Mechanic's Hall was repaired, the annual Eisteddfod was held there until the Utica Opera House was erected on Lafayette street in 1870. The Eisteddfod was under the control of a "board of managers" from 1867 to 1869.

On January 15, 1869, a number of Welshmen met at the Welsh Methodist Episcopal church on Washington street, to discuss the advisability of forming a regular society to carry on, among other activities, the annual Eisteddfod. At this meeting, it was decided to organize "The City of Utica Welsh Literary Society". At the second session held in the office of the Welsh newspaper "Y Drych", the name was changed to "The Cymreigyddion Society of Utica". The Rechabite Hall on Franklin Square was rented for $40 per year for its meetings. An initiation fee of $1 and quarterly dues of 25 cents was adopted and the constitution provided "that an annual Eisteddfod should be held under the auspices of the society on January 1."

This society continued to flourish until the Eisteddfod of 1876 when a dispute arose between the members and at a meeting on January 26, 1876, held in the "Y Drych" office, after a very stormy session, it was decided by a majority of one to wind up the affairs of the society and auction off its effects. It was also decided to transfer the balance in the treasury to the Welsh Benevolent Society. The amount was $6.94.

This action disturbed the Welsh community and a large number of them called a meeting the next evening at the "Y Drych" office to reorganize the Cymreigyddion Society and lease the Opera House for the 1877 Eisteddfod. The annual event was continued well into the twentieth century, during which time it was conducted in the State Armory on Steuben Park.

HENRY N. MARCHISI — PYROTECHNIST

IN the early days of Utica, no celebration was considered complete without a display of fireworks at the City Garden on lower Genesee street. It is not known when Uticans first undertook the manufacture of these displays, but by the time of the Civil War, of the twenty fireworks manufacturers in the United States, five were in the State of New York, and of these, Marchisi & Co. of Utica was perhaps the leader.

Henry N. Marchisi was born in Utica September 4, 1824, a son of the Italian pioneer druggist, Jean Baptiste Marchisi. Young Marchisi was educated in the common schools and in the Utica Academy. At the age of nineteen, he went to work in his father's drug store as a clerk until 1848, when he went to New York city for five years. Upon his return, he became interested in manufacturing fireworks. His first venture was with Samuel Barnum and William M. Storrs. The city directory of 1857 lists him as a "pyrotechnist" with a factory on the corner of Jay and Second streets. For the celebration in New York City in 1858 for the completion of the Atlantic cable, he prepared $700 worth of fireworks and supervised their display, which gained him a wide-spread reputation. This factory was destroyed by fire in 1860 and in association with George A. Lane, he built a laboratory on the corner of State and Henry streets, the latter being named after him. The firm was known as Henry N. Marchisi & Co. The four distinct buildings were built of brick and surrounded by a high fence.

Disaster struck again in May 1862 when fire destroyed the entire plant. In August 1862, Henry Marchisi enlisted in the Army as a hospital steward. Upon his return, he resumed work with his father, as a maker and dealer of trusses. When his father's formula for "Catholicon" remedy was sold in 1878 to Howarth & Ballard drug company, Henry worked for them until shortly before his own death in April 1906, at the age of 82.

CITIZEN SOLDIERS PRIOR TO THE CIVIL WAR

IN the decades following the War with Great Britain in 1812, the training of the militia deteriorated. At Utica's semi-centennial in 1882, General James McQuade spoke on the "Military History of Utica" and said in part,

"My recollection of the military of Utica does not reach back to the efficient militia which existed prior to the period of independent companies. Some of you may recollect that in the earlier years while the inspiration of the last war with Great Britain still lingered, the militia was well equipped and that a certain degree of discipline obtained. The militia I remember was greatly deteriorated. Military duty was performed in a loose, shambling and disjointed way. The letter of the law was regarded so far as the assemblage at stated periods of those liable to duty was concerned, but in the matter of arms and equipment enjoined there was a lamentable breach of observance. Instead of appearing 'armed and equipped as the law directs', umbrellas were often substituted for firearms, walking sticks for bayonets, while the powder horn was represented by a flask, which although capable of producing a 'horn' was useless as a receptacle to keep the powder dry. Two days in the year were devoted to the acquisition of knowledge in the art of war. The first was the company muster, where each contingent assembled at some place within the military district, and the other, the regimental muster or general training. The largest company in Utica (except perhaps the Fourth) was that of the First Ward, which mustered in front of Trinity Church. Mott Brown, a member of the corps, familiarly known as 'Old Rosin the Bow' was Captain, I think, B. F. Ray and Fred Fargo were lieutenants. I used to sit on the steps of Samuel Stocking's house, directly opposite and view with rapt admiration the quavering and uncertain line of doughty warriors, in shirt sleeves and straw hats, who, after answering the roll-call, were wont to slip around the corner to 'see a man'.

"The general training, however, was quite an imposing demonstration. Here was some semblance of organization. As a rule the levies from the verdant hills of Deerfield wore improvised uniforms, and were the objects of

227

special youthful commendation. They had black beaver hats of the stovepipe pattern, embellished with cockades and their shoulders were ornamented with epaulets of sheepskin. Then they carried muskets and powder horns, which in a military point of view possess certain advantages over canes and umbrellas. These exceptionally fine soldiers were described by the envious and sarcastic as the Deerfield Rangers. At the general training there was an enormous consumption of sweet cider, gingerbread and honey in the comb. It was a great day for the boys."

From 1837 to 1860, various militia companies were formed in Utica: Utica Citizen Corps (1837), Utica Light Guard (1841), the Union Guard (1843), Utica City Guards (1852), the German Lafayette Rifle Company (1852), Seymour Artillery (1853), the Emmet Guards (1853), Utica Flying Artillery (1854), the Washington Continentals (1855) and the Palmer Grenadiers (1856).

BUTTERFIELD'S OVERLAND MAIL
1858

ONE of the most fascinating tales of the Old West is the story of the Overland Mail. The discovery of gold in California drew many prospectors there in 1849. The establishment of permanent settlements on the West coast turned the attention of the public to finding means of communication. Ocean travel around the tip of South America was too lengthy and dangerous. The railroads had been built to St. Louis, Missouri but almost three thousand miles separated the settled area along the Mississippi river from the coast. The only roads were wagon trails across mountain ranges and along open plains where Indians would suddenly attack and kill travelers.

In 1857 Congress authorized the federal government to

contract with private contractors for the conveyance of mail and passengers from Missouri to California. The Postmaster General drew up a proposal for twice a week delivery of mail between the two points, each trip to take not more than twenty-five days. The distance to be covered and the time limitation discouraged most private operators from bidding on the contract.

In Utica, John Butterfield, the greatest stage coach proprietor of the time, if not of all time decided to accept the challenge. He signed a contract with the Postmaster General to carry the mail, twice a week for a term of six years at $600,000 per year, the contract to take effect on September 16, 1858.

In the spring of that year, he sent his son, John Butterfield, Jr. to San Francisco by steamship to lay out a route from there to St. Louis, Missouri. John Butterfield, Jr. was born at the family home on Whitesboro street on August 20, 1827 and died here on March 9, 1909. Young Butterfield started out from San Francisco on January 7, 1858 and returned to Utica on May 2, 1858. The route he laid out was southeasterly from San Francisco through the mountains, crossing the open plain leading to Tucson, Arizona and El Paso, Texas. From El Paso, the route led across Texas to Sherman, near the northern border, and then on to Fort Smith, Arkansas, thru the Indian Territory. From Fort Smith, the route went over the mountains to Springfield, Missouri and thence northward to Bolivar and Warsaw. At the latter point it was necessary to ford the Osage river. From Warsaw there was a long swing to the northwest to Fayetteville, a town of some size and the home of Charles E. Butterfield, another of John Butterfield, Sr.'s sons. From Fayetteville, the course was due east to Tipton, the western terminal of the Missouri-Pacific railroad, 150 miles from St. Louis.

The odds against Butterfield successfully performing his contract were considerable and most business men viewed the 2,770 miles to be traveled and the time limitation of twenty-five days insurmountable. But not Butterfield, who loved challenge.

He would use lighter coaches than those generally in use. He contracted with a builder in Concord, New Hampshire to furnish what were known as "Concord Coaches", lighter than customary, with heavy canvas covering, and capable of carrying eight to ten passengers. Six of these new coaches arrived in Utica in August 1858 and were shipped by railroad to St.

Louis. These "Concord Coaches" were to be used on the best portions of the route, but until the roads could be improved with bridges over some of the streams, Butterfield would use "celerity" spring wagons made by a builder in Albany. These wagons could conveniently carry four passengers, besides 500 to 600 pounds of mail. They were covered with a canvas top and side curtains, and had three seats with backs that could be let down to form a bed for night travel. The passenger fare was two hundred dollars one way, not including meals.

To meet the time limit of twenty-five days, the distance was cut up into relays of 12 miles each. At each way station, a new driver and fresh horses would replace those of the previous relay and in order to avoid any delay, when a coach approached the end of its relay, the driver would blow his horn to inform the stablemen to have fresh horses and a new driver in readiness.

John Butterfield had a large number of employees in Utica whom he placed in charge of various portions of the operation. Henry Bates was born in Lansingburg, New York in 1817 and came to Utica as a child. As a young man he drove the Butterfield stages from Utica to Clinton, Newport and other towns. Then he became the proprietor of a livery stable on Hotel street, opposite the old Mechanic's Hall. Butterfield sent him in 1858 to Sherman, Texas and he managed the station there until 1861, when the Civil War made it unsafe for a northerner to remain in that section. He returned to Utica in 1866 and became superintendent of the horse-car lines to New Hartford and Whitesboro. He died December 17, 1884.

John Butterfield, Jr. became superintendent of the section between Tipton and Fort Smith, a distance of 500 miles.

The Overland Mail Company had made all its arrangements and was ready to begin carrying the mail on September 16th, 1858. The Pacific Railroad had completed its track 160 miles west to Tipton, Missouri. Tipton became the head city for all the mail stages in Missouri during the three years of the service that saw the departure and the arrival of the mails regularly twice weekly.

Early on the morning of September 16, 1858, the first westbound mail was made up by the St. Louis postmaster, in two small mailbags marked "Per Overland Mail" and sent to the railroad depot where they were turned over to John Butterfield, Sr. who took charge of them and boarded the train leaving for Tipton at 8 a.m. The St. Louis postmaster was somewhat skeptical about the whole affair, and he attached a stick to the first two mail bags, so that in an emergency they could be thrown over the back of a mule to be delivered to their destination. The mail arrived at Tipton one minute past six o'clock p.m., the same day. The "Utica Morning Herald" of September 24, 1858 printed a letter from a "passenger" to Butterfield's wife:

> "The Great Overland mail left St. Louis on the Pacific R R at 8 a.m. on the 16th Sept., en route for San Francisco under the personal charge of Mr. John Butterfield. When the cars arrived at Tipton 162 miles from St. Louis and the end of the railroad, John Butterfield, Jr. drove along side of the platform a new Overland Stage drawn by six beautiful bay horses. Eleven persons, including Mr. Butterfield, Senior, took passage in and upon it, and John Butterfield, Jr. had the honor of driving the first six miles the first stage ever started from St. Louis for San Francisco. We reached Syracuse (the line gave local names to the various way stations they had set up), 168 miles from St. Louis at 7 p.m. and took supper. In fifteen minutes I shook hands with your husband and your son, and they started for Fort Smith under as bright a moon and on a beautiful night as the Good Being ever granted to the sons of men. Mr. Butterfield told me, as he was getting into the stage, 'Write my wife when you get to St. Louis and tell her how well I am, and that I believe we shall succeed.' Mr. Butterfield will proceed to Fort Smith where he will meet the stage from San Francisco, and on the 10th of October he is expected on his return at St. Louis, with the first U. S. Overland Mail from San Francisco."

On the trip to Fort Smith, John Butterfield, Sr., attired in a long linen "duster" coat, wide brimmed, low-crowned brown felt hat and leather boots, had helped change horses at the way stations and had on one occasion taken the driver's seat and the reins of the four-horse team and had driven over a portion of the route.

The stage arrived at Fort Smith, Arkansas, a little after two o'clock in the morning, where the mail from Memphis was taken aboard. Here, all of the passengers, including John Butterfield, Sr. left the stage. A single passenger, Waterman Ormsby II, assigned by James Gordon Bennett of the New York Herald completed the trip. He was the only journalist to cover the event since most newspapers doubted its success.

The stage left Fort Smith, the last outpost of civilization and the next two thousand miles to Los Angeles were through rugged country with only three settlements, Santa Fe, Las Vegas and Albuquerque. The stage proceeded southwest through Oklahoma and the Choctaw territory to Colbert's Ferry, crossing the Red River into Texas and to Fort Chadbourne. From there, the stage proceeded west, through Guadelupe Pass to El Paso. Crossing the Rio Grande, it travelled 360 miles to Tucson, Arizona territory; then to Fort Yuma; then northward to Los Angeles. From Los Angeles, the stage went through the Sierra to San Francisco, arriving early Sunday morning, October 10th, 1858. The entire trip took twenty-three days, twenty-three and a half hours.

The mail from San Francisco to St. Louis had left simultaneously with the western trip and when it arrived in St. Louis, Butterfield telegraphed President Buchanan from Jefferson City, Missouri:

> "The Overland Mail arrived today at St. Louis from San Francisco in twenty three days and four hours. The stage brought through six passengers."

President Buchanan replied,

> "I cordially congratulate you upon the result. It is a glorious triumph for civilization and the Union. Settlements will soon follow the course of the road, and the East and West will be bound together by a chain of living Americans which can never be broken."

After three years, the outbreak of the Civil War brought an end to the Overland Mail. Federal troops could no longer be counted on to protect the route; Indian raids were made on the way stations; and Confederate troops destroyed the link to California. After the war, with the building of the railroads to the Pacific the need for a stage delivery of mail was eliminated.

"OLD SARATOGA"

1861

THERE are a few Uticans who will remember the old cannon which rested on the northwest lawn of the old State Armory at Steuben Park for so many years. It was placed there in December 1896 and was a relic of the Revolution. When it was first brought to Utica is unknown but at least in 1815, it was kept in a barn back of Major Bellinger's tavern on Whitesboro street and was brought out and fired on the Fourth of July each year and on other special occasions. It was fired in 1824 when General Lafayette visited Utica, and Lyman B. Adams was the Captain of the gun squad in charge of the cannon. When the Civil War broke out, the "Utica Morning Herald" of June 24, 1861 reported:

> "The old gun is a twelve pounder, manufactured in England in 1741. The weight is 2339 lbs.; its length seven feet eight inches; size of bore 4¾ inches; diameter at the breach 17 inches — at the mouth 13 inches. On the rough outside, the date of manufacture, its number and weight can be deciphered. On the upper side is a crown, with the initials 'G. R.' (George Rex).

> "The piece was brought to this country to use against the 'rebels' of '76, and Gen. Burgoyne's artillerymen had it in charge until the battle of Saratoga, in 1777, when it was reluctantly delivered into the hands of the rebels aforesaid, and afterwards brought to this city, where for years it was an inseparable appendage of a Fourth of July celebration. For a great while it was under the control of a gun squad, commanded by Capt. Nathan G. Williams, of which Dr. A. H. Colling, and perhaps others now living in the city were members, and was kept in the old engine house on Hotel street. In December 1848, the fire which destroyed the store of Owen O'Neil, on Genesee street, and the city property in its rear on Hotel street, consumed the carriage of the gun. Demounted and partially buried, it lay idle and forgotten in that vicinity, until the property and the rubbish passed into the hands of Warnick & Bryan, and continued to lay there till yesterday.

> "A few days ago, Dr. Colling recollected his old play-

233

thing, investigated and found it. He then proposed that the old gun be procured from Messrs. Warnick & Brown, remounted, and once more made to contribute its share to the noise so indispensable to the celebration of our National holiday. Messrs. W & B consented to return it to the city, upon the condition that it be suitably mounted and properly cared for. Patriotic citizens accepted it upon those conditions, and Saturday morning it was taken from the rear of the premises, No. 13 Hotel street, and removed to the carriage factory of Davis & Cosselman, who have contracted to mount it upon a strong carriage by the Fourth of July, at an expense of about $75. On the Fourth of July the gun will be taken to some place outside of the city limits, and its roar will revive recollections of the time when independence celebrations were in their infancy."

For years afterwards, the old gun was taken out and fired after each victory during the War. There is a story told that on one occasion, some of the young men of the city took it over to Genesee street and fired it in front of the Butterfield House. The shock was so great that many windows were shattered and it cost the young men $100 to repair the damage.

In 1879, the old relic was the subject of an historic and amusing confrontation between the city officials and the State military authorities. In July of that year, Colonel Edward Kent went to the office of Mayor John Buckley and demanded that "Old Saratoga" be turned over to the State as an historical item. When Mayor Buckley learned that the State wished to set it up in Central Park in New York City, he refused and the Colonel threatened to call upon the Sheriff to retake the cannon, and if that failed, the military authorities of the State would move in force to recapture the weapon. The Mayor ordered the police department to "proceed to the City Hose House and take possession of the iron gun or cannon, and hold it against any other authority, no matter who, until I arrive."

Some citizens took matters into their own hands and secreted the cannon on a farm near the State Hospital. They were persuaded to turn the old relic over to the police. The cannon was chained to the old Police Station on Pearl street and Assistant Chief McElwaine placed the following notation on the police blotter:

"Old Sarah Toga — a wicked and troublesome old gal, who plays the deuce with the affections of young and

234

old, and excites the cupidity of ravenous New York monument fiends — arrested at 9 p.m. and placed under lock and key, by order of Mayor Buckley, with directions to 'Hold the Fort' against all interlopers."

Avoiding a military confrontation, the State retreated from its ultimatum, and it remained in front of the old police station until 1885 and then was removed to the yard of the new City Library on Elizabeth street. Later it was placed on the State Hospital grounds and then turned over to the Citizens Corps, who cleaned it up and placed it in front of the Steuben Park Armory in the late 1890s. It today guards the entrance to the Culver Avenue Armory.

REGIMENTAL ARMORY ON BLEECKER STREET

1862

L ATE in 1859, a petition was presented to the Common Council by citizens asking that the old Market lot on Bleecker street be deeded to the State to build an armory for the 45th Regiment. On February 15th, 1861, pursuant to a deed of the property to the State, the Utica newspaper reported:

> "On Monday, the labor of pulling down the old Market building will be begun. The front part will be demolished first and the rear — where the Watch House is — be left undisturbed for a week or ten days thereafter. A new Watch House must be provided by the Council immediately."

The plan for the armory was furnished by H. N. White, a Syracuse architect and the contract was awarded to Messrs. Lloyd & Bond, whose bid was about $5,000. The plans called for a building of fifty feet on Bleecker street and about eighty feet deep, with a tower at the southwest corner. The building was completed in February 1862, and was two stories in height with a basement designed for the storage of artillery. It contained two drill rooms, and three ordnance rooms. The first floor was divided into eight rooms, for use as company rooms. In these rooms were stored the uniforms of the men, their knapsacks, etc. The main drill room, fifty by seventy feet was on the second floor, reached by a flight of stairs. The arms of the various companies were arranged along the walls, in racks, under letters designating the Company to which they belonged.

When the new armory was constructed by the State on Steuben Park and the old building was no longer in use as an armory, it was sold at auction. It was remodeled and a new front was put in. The first floor which was about four feet above the sidewalk was lowered and a number of stores constructed reaching out to the sidewalk line. It was found that the walls of the old building were hollow or double. The side and rear walls were allowed to remain. What had been the second floor drill hall became a dance hall. Over the dance hall was an attic. This was transformed into a banquet hall which was reached by a narrow and steep stairway located not along an outside wall, but in the very center of the house. From this stairway one went through several small rooms to enter the attic.

In 1911, the upper two floors of the building, then known as the Owen Building were occupied by Walter E. Barber as a dancing academy. On March 19th, 1911, fire destroyed the upper two stories of the building. It was replaced by a brick building, occupied by the Gem Theater and in later years by the Index Lunch and Rogers Bowling Alley.

THE CIVIL WAR GUNSMITHS OF UTICA

ELIPHALET Remington, of Ilion, New York early in the year 1816 decided to make his own rifle and from that effort grew the now famous Remington Arms Company. According to tradition, Remington forged his barrel from scrap iron. He had no machine to rifle the barrel and he came to Utica to have a famous gunsmith of Utica, Morgan James, do the work. When it was finished, Remington returned to Ilion and shaped a stock for the gun and completed it. For some time thereafter, Remington would walk the fifteen miles to Utica to have James rifle the weapons. Later, he built his own rifling machine and by 1845, standard model rifles, shotguns and pistols replaced the old custom gunsmithing. Remington then took government contracts for 5000 rifles.

When the Civil War broke out, the federal government turned to Remington for rifles and pistols. The first contract was for 5000 rifles and it took two years to complete the order. In addition, a contract for army revolvers was awarded the company. This was beyond the capacity of the Ilion plant and Remington decided to enlist the aid of the skilled gunsmiths of Utica. The "Utica Morning Herald" of

December 19, 1861 announced that the old screw factory on the corner of Fulton and Franklin streets had been leased from the Tibbitts estate.

The "Utica Observer" on December 30, 1864 reported:

"Bullets Flying in Utica. Yesterday morning, the revolving iron kettle into which the bullets of the pistols manufactured in the Remington Armory are discharged when the pistols are tested, ceased to revolve. In consequence, a hole was soon made through the metal, and a bombardment of the First Ward began. Bullets entered the saw factory of Lennebacker & DeLong, the undertaking shop of Wm. B. Monroe and the hardware establishment of J. E. Roberts. The crashing and whizzing of the leaden messengers created a sensation among those whose lives and limbs were endangered. One ball passed within six inches of a man's head, and other persons had narrow escapes. Word was sent to the Armory in double-quick time and the bombardment of Supervisor Douglas' district speedily terminated."

George H. Ferris was born at Willowvale on January 8, 1820. He was a machinist and pattern maker. About 1850, he moved to Utica and began a gunmaking business. He went into partnership with Morgan James and their gun factory was located on Fayette street, between Genesee and Seneca. At that time, James & Ferris employed about a dozen men and was one of the leading gun shops in the United States. After Mr. Ferris dissolved the partnership with James, he opened a shop on John street and then moved to No. 33 Bleecker street.

It was during the Civil War that Ferris invented a cannon which was far ahead of its day. He theorized that a greater range, increased velocity and more destructive power could be secured by using equal weights of powder and ball, instead of the previous ratio of powder being one-eighth of the weight of the ball. He built two cannons on this principle. On March 1863, he tested the cannon at Oneida Lake and in May 1863 at a farm a mile east of Deerfield Corners. The results were so startling that the cannon was taken to the Navy Yard at Washington where the shots went nearly through three plates of solid iron.

George Ferris was not to see the fulfillment of his dream. When he died on December 13, 1885, the "Utica Daily Press" wrote:

"at that time, Dahlgren was interested in a gun, which he wished to get into service, and he misrepresented the facts regarding the Ferris gun. Mr. Ferris was a man without means, and hence was unable to make any headway against those who had more money and influence. At the time of the Franco-Prussian War, the gun was tested in Paris. While the test was finished and negotiations were pending the Prussians captured the city and that was the last heard of the Ferris gun. It is supposed that it was captured and taken away by the victors. The advantages of the Ferris gun were never denied and had it received financial and influential backing would have made the owners independently wealthy."

CIRCUS DAYS IN UTICA

THE nineteenth century was the hey day of the American circus. Unlike its European counterpart which exhibited in a permanent location, the travelling show by wagon developed to meet the demands of a predominantly rural America. Uticans were among the pioneers in this field. In 1907, the "Utica Saturday Globe" wrote about the old time circus:

"The modern, mammoth circus, with its three rings, which calls at only the larger towns in special trains, has lost much of the glamour and romance which attached to the one-ring wagon circus of a generation ago. Where is the Utican of advanced years who as a small boy did not arise at 4 o'clock in the morning and hie himself to the outskirts of the town to watch the approach of the long line of wagons in the morning mist? What a thrill of ecstacy when out of the gloom advanced a great, creaking hulk, the driver sitting drowsily atop and within some terrible beast of the jungle! Then the long shadowy column of rumbling vehicles, damp with the morning's dew, would pass while one stood spellbound with the delight of it all.

"Then the gorgeous street pageant. Where is the boy

who never followed the band wagon two miles before standing still to let the parade pass? Who has never dug his naked toes into the upturned loam, while his eyes stared ecstatically at the inspiring spectacle of the heroic tamer sitting so boldly in the den of snarling lions? Where is the swain who has not, with his girl, groped for the roped way to the main entrance, or suggested stopping for the concert announced to follow the show? For this is a circus."

John Robinson, of Aberdeen, Scotland came to America about the year 1800, married Nancy Boyd and settled down in Charleston, South Carolina. A whitesmith — a worker in iron who finishes or polishes his work — he removed to New York City, where he remained but a short time before leaving for Schenectady, and thence to Utica. It is said that he had the contract for the erection of the first grist mill here. John Robinson and Nancy Boyd had four sons: John (1807), Boyd (?), James (1811-1908), and Alexander (1812-1887). The eldest son, John, always claimed to be a native of Utica but some biographical notes give Albany as the place of his birth. Alexander always acknowledged his native city as Schenectady. Be that as it may, John was an early resident here, while Alexander lived here most of his life.

A version of young John Robinson's life in early Utica was given in 1872 in a book, entitled, "Cincinnati, Past and Present":

"For some reason or other John could 'never get the hang of the log school-house,' and he would never attend unless he was obliged to do so. This, as might be expected, often brought him into collision with his father, and having a spirit that revolted at the very idea of corporal punishment, he had scarcely entered upon his teens than he began to devise means for relieving himself of parental restraint. After several ineffectual attempts, one of which was frustrated by his father overtaking him some twenty miles from home, he succeeded in reaching Albany, having traveled over one hundred miles on foot, principally at night for fear of detection."

Between the time when he left Utica and the early 1840s, when he was the most famous four-horse rider in the world, his life is obscured by conflicting versions. He became a hostler for a small circus in New England and at night secretly began to ride the baggage horses, first one, and when he mastered this, added a second, a third and finally a fourth. By 1840 John Robinson had an equestrian troupe of his own,

240

the chief attraction of which was "Little Jimmy", a child rider, known professionally as Juan Hernandez. By 1849, John Robinson was in partnership with Gil Eldred and this company continued until sometime in 1856.

From that time until 1929, the John Robinson Circus was among the leaders in the circus field. Under 'Old John', his son, John Franklin Robinson (1843-1921), and his grandson, John Gilbert Robinson (1872-1935), the troupe became one of the largest in the country, with 800 employees, an 8-pole big top tent and a 12-pole menageries tent, with the largest collection of wild animals owned by any circus. Robinson was the first to put on a big spectacle, entitled "King Solomon and the Queen of Sheba" and the first to make use of railroad cars to transport his equipment and stars. The bulk of the equipment together with the Robinson title were sold to the American Circus Company which operated a "Robinson Show" until it disposed of the property in 1929 to John Ringling.

The early life of "Old John's" brother, Alexander Robinson, is as obscure as that of his own. At his death in 1887, Alexander's age was given at 75 years, whereas the census of 1880 listed his age as 63 years which would make his date of birth 1817. The 1843-44 city directory lists "Alexander Robinson, blacksmith" at No. 8 Main street, with his residence at No. 19 First street. He is said to have learned the blacksmith trade from Hiram Rose, who had a shop on Main street. That he married a daughter of Rose is clear from the census of 1855 which lists Hiram Rose, blacksmith, age 57. It also shows that there were living with him at the time two "grandchildren", Helen Robinson, age 15 and Boyd Robinson, age 8. There were born of his marriage, three children, Helen, born in 1840, John Robinson, born 1842, and Boyd J. Robinson, born 1844. While Helen and Boyd stayed with their grandfather, both Alexander and his son, John, were performing with Uncle John's circus. In November 1855, Alexander married Mary Jane Deery. Miss Deery's first husband was named Peterson and he was one of the clowns in Robinson & Eldred's Circus and acquired considerable fame as a performer. On Peterson's death, she married Alexander and came to Utica to live.

By the winter of 1860, Alexander Robinson formed his own circus company, with wagons and equipment manufactured in Utica. He put up his tent on Columbia street and after a three day showing here, started his travels on April

22, 1861. There is no information available as to how successful the trip was, but the outbreak of the Civil War must have had an adverse effect because there is evidence that John and Alexander combined their shows as "Robinson & Brother" in 1863.

After this single year in combination with his brother, Alexander in 1864 started out as "Robinson & Deery's Metropolitan Circus" with new wagons, new canvas and new wardrobes. For the balance of their circus careers, John and Alexander conducted separate companies. John played in the South and West, and Alexander in New York, New England, Pennsylvania, and later in Canada. Alexander's winter quarters were originally in an old wooden barn near his home at No. 54 Whitesboro street. He also had another barn and practice ring on Eagle street, at the corner of Seymour.

The year 1866 was a tragic one for Alexander. His twenty four year old son John was a featured rider with John Robinson's circus. On April 26th, a gang of rowdies at Crittenden, Kentucky were denied admittance because of their conduct. Enraged, they invaded the circus tent, firing revolver shots which killed young John and wounded some others.

As the size of the circus grew and wild animals were added, Alexander found it necessary to establish winter quarters at a farm beyond the city limits, at a place called Harbor, in Herkimer county. The financial success of Alexander Robinson's Circus company continued through the seventies. In 1878, a series of disasters struck him. He was travelling through Massachusetts when an epidemic broke out among the animals. Most of the beasts were killed and heavy expense was entailed before they could be replaced. Two months later, when the show was beginning to recover from the loss, a windstorm wrecked the tents and new equipment had to be secured.

A year later, the show was placed for the first time on railroad cars and while travelling in Connecticut, a wreck occurred, and many of the animals were killed. Alexander decided to retire from the circus world. His old ringmaster, Professor William Costello came to live with him at the old house on Whitesboro street. The two old circus men reminisced about the glamour of those days, until Alexander died on February 27, 1887. Professor Costello continued to live with Alexander's widow until his own death on February 16, 1890. About 1894, she moved to No. 51 Broad street where she died on February 3, 1903 at the age of 83. Their daughter, Helen, died some years later at Harbor.

In the early days of Utica, when circuses were small in size, they were held in the open spaces about the city. The earliest were probably held at the old City Garden on lower Genesee street. As the village grew into a city, circuses were held in Chancellor Square, Columbia street, the east side of Genesee street above Hopper, the commons on Rutger street, and on High street (now Summit Place), the site of the old reservoir. Dan Rice's Circus showed in Utica on High street in September 1866 and an amusing incident occurred. In 1900, a lady who witnessed the event told the "Utica Saturday Globe":

> "A circus and menagerie exhibited there. One night about 1 o'clock the next morning a racket on the street awakened the whole family. On looking out the upstairs windows a terrible sight met their eyes. Looming up in the darkness was the largest elephant in the show with half the front fence on his back. The big pachyderm then made a raid on the garden vegetables and ate the good sized heads of cabbage as he would peanuts. The whole neighborhood was now in an uproar, fearing that he would back into or push over their homes. After enjoying his midnight meal, the elephant, like other midnight prowlers, set out to look for a drink. He loosened two or three pumps, but the water wouldn't come. Then he espied a cistern at the side of the house which he had robbed of its fence. He knocked the top covering off the cistern and inserted his trunk into the water. After getting his fill he looked up at the yelling occupants of the windows and fired about a tub of water at them. Then the circus employees appeared in sight, but it took over an hour for them to subdue the big beast. They didn't do a thing with him but prod him with a pitchfork, and pound him with sticks till he meekly took his place in the line and marched off with procession to the next town. It took several day's profits to settle that elephant's short spree."

243

THE MANUFACTURE OF CLOTHES IN UTICA
1862

PRIOR to the Civil War, the production of men's clothes was in the hands of merchant tailors, who plied scissors and the skillful use of needles for those who could afford individual attention, while the less fortunate were dependent upon the domestic skill of the females in the household.

The earliest manufacturer and dealer in clothes was James B. Martin, who began in 1836 with a factory at No. 90 Genesee street. About 1860, his brothers-in-law, Charles A. Yates and Rymer V. Yates continued the business as Charles A. Yates & Co. at No. 54-65 Genesee street. On the first floor of No. 54, they operated a retail store known as the "Great Marble Block Clothing Store" with every variety of men's coats, vests and pants. On the second floor, the "ready-made" clothing was cut out, supplied with trimmings and dealt out to the old-time thrifty German and Welsh sewing women of the city and towns. When returned to the factory, they were stocked for sale. On the third floor was the general wholesale room and in the fourth story some manufacturing was done. At No. 56, Yates conducted a "custom tailoring department" and in the rear half of the store, a "boy's clothing department" where parents could select garments already made up. It was the establishment of Charles A. Yates which had as a young clerk, Henry H. Cooper. He was born in England and came to Utica, where he learned the business which was to become his life work.

The Civil War produced a great demand for ready-made clothing in the form of soldier uniforms, and the firm of Palmer V. Kellogg & Co., located on the third floor of the Empire Block on Hotel street, was a prime supplier. Under a government contract, the firm in the middle of June 1861 completed 1003 pants, 1026 coats and 500 jackets.

After the Civil War, in 1869, Kellogg & Co. moved to Chicago, where the firm engaged in the manufacture of clothes and amassed a considerable fortune. John Owen, Philip Owen and Henry D. Pixley as Owen, Pixley & Co.

purchased the fixtures of the Kellogg firm here and gave employment to its employees, in the building in Franklin Square where Kellogg & Company had carried on their business. The original 200 employees grew to 600 to 700.

In 1870, Yates & Company was taken over by M. H. Griffith, James Roberts and J. M. Butler, as Griffith, Roberts & Butler with a factory at 15-17 Whitesboro street and the store at 54 Genesee street. Henry H. Cooper decided to strike out for himself and on January 1, 1871, Cooper, Chamberlain & Horn began as manufacturers and wholesale dealers of clothing in the upper floor of the building at 67-69 Genesee street. By this time, less work was being done in the homes, and the early system of having one worker make the complete garment was giving way to garment workers who specialized and did piece work. Shears were the usual cutting tool in the early days, but this gave way after 1870 to a long knife fastened in the slot in the cutting table. A few years later, the first power cutting machine was introduced and about 1892 electric cutting machines were perfected. Mr. Horn withdrew from the business in 1875, and the firm became Cooper & Chamberlain and moved to larger quarters in the Ballou Block on John street. The partnership of Cooper & Chamberlain was dissolved in 1877 and Mr. Cooper re-organized the business as H. H. Cooper & Co. and leased even larger quarters in the Reynolds Block on John and Catharine streets.

The firm of Griffith, Roberts & Butler which succeeded C. A. Yates & Co. continued for some time, when Mr. Griffith left that firm and built a building on Main street and became M. H. Griffith & Co. with Henry O'Neill Tucker as a partner. On the death of Mr. Griffith, the firm became Tucker, Calder, & Co. E. D. Brandegree was employed as a traveling salesman and out of this experience in 1888 was formed Crouse & Brandegee, which became one of the largest clothing firms in the country. Mr. Brandegee handled the manufacturing portion of the business and Mr. Henry P. Crouse the financial affairs.

THE POLICE DEPARTMENT
1862

WHEN Utica became a city in 1832, the police protection consisted of a night watch. In 1846, David Hess was named the first City Marshal, by William Baker, the Recorder under the Recorder's Court Act. He was born on June 23, 1810 in Otsego county and came to Utica in 1835. The city was known as a "tough canal town" and Marshal Hess and the night watch, consisting of six constables, had difficulty in keeping the peace. The watch house was in the old Public Market on Bleecker street. On one occasion, the watch, who always went about town at night in twos, was jumped upon by a crowd of sportive toughs on the Broad street bridge spanning the Basin, as it was called. One watchman was held by the toughs until the other constable was dumped unceremoniously into the dark, dirty water below. When he reached the bank, the ruffians then dropped the other constable over, and then ran off. This aroused Hess' ire and from that moment on, he showed them no mercy. They were arrested for every violation of the law he could find and they were fined and jailed. He was often seriously injured.

In 1862, the legislature established a police department for Utica by abolishing the old night watch and the city marshal and substituting a paid police force of twelve men from whom the Council would choose a chief and an assistant chief. David Hess was the first chief. In 1866, the police were given a uniform of strong blue cloth with caps modeled after the New York city police. The front was ornamented with a silver wreath within which was placed the number of the officer.

The period from 1866 to 1874 was marked by a dispute as to the control of the department. The appointments were made by the Common Council and with each change of administration, the members of the force were often changed. In 1867 the Legislature placed the police department under the control of a Board of Police Commissioners. The Common Council refused to give up control of the department and in 1870 insisted on naming special policemen. The Council in 1872 named a new police force. When a dispute arose in 1874 over the election of the chief engineer of the fire department, influential citizens asked the Legislature to remove Council control over both departments. The Legislature created a Police and Fire Commission, with sole power and authority over both departments. This commission functioned until the adoption of the Second Class Cities Law in 1908.

When the old Market House on Bleecker street, with its watch house on the second floor, was turned over to the State as a site for an armory, it was necessary to build a police station. This was constructed in 1865 and was a two story brick building on the corner of Washington and Pearl streets in the rear of the City Hall. This building soon proved to be inadequate for the needs of the growing city and in 1878, "the latest thing in police stations" took its place. It fronted Pearl street, and the first door to the right was occupied by the Chief of Police, the first room on the left by the Recorder (City Judge), and his courtroom was next south to it. South of the Chief's office was the booking room. The cell block for men was in the basement, the cells being of steel where those of the old station were of wood. The cells for the women were on the second floor, together with a room for the matron.

In writing of the old police force in Utica in the "Observer-Dispatch" of March 6, 1932, J. Soley Cole, a veteran reporter, wrote that

> "there was no police signal system at the time, nor patrol wagon, both of these important features of the service being established during the 80's. If an officer made an arrest, he had to bring his prisoner in as best he could and for that reason he was rather circumspect about seizing drunks on the outlying beats because of the time, labor and sometimes needless danger involved."

Finally in 1889, the Common Council voted to provide a patrol wagon.

UTICA WAS ONCE A SHOE
MANUFACTURING TOWN

IN early Utica, shoes were made by custom shoemakers to the order of the customer. John Cantwell was born in Ireland in 1815 and came to Utica with his family in 1837 where he followed the trade of shoemaker. He was said to be the "premier shoemaker in the State" and opened a shop at No. 3 Catharine street, where he employed a dozen to fifteen shoemakers making the finest shoes and boots in Central New York. Since Utica was then the site of a number of fine tanneries, leather and skins were plentiful. It may be said that he was the forerunner of the large shoe factories which were established here during and after the Civil War. He died on July 25, 1864 at the age of 49.

By the year 1859, Lewis Brothers had a large shoe store at No. 180 Genesee street and the firm had sixty-seven workmen making shoes. They produced two hundred pairs of shoes daily "even to the famous copper toes for children". James M. Wiswell, at No. 1 Columbia street began the manufacture of shoes in 1862. He made ladies Balmorals and Gaiters and by 1867 increased his production from sixty to one hundred twenty pairs per day, employing forty persons, including sixteen women. He was soon joined by James H. Thompson and the firm became Wiswell & Thompson. In 1866, J. Newton Cloyes purchased Wiswell's interest and the firm became Thompson & Cloyes. In 1872, Mr. Cloyes became the sole owner and by 1878 was turning out 300 pairs of shoes daily at his factory, No. 12 John street, employing 80 to 90 people. In 1880, he moved his factory to Meadow street. He retired in the middle 1890s.

By the year 1867, there were five shoe companies employing between three and four hundred workmen, making 1000 pairs per day, mostly ladies wear. Another pioneer shoe manufacturer was Case, Losee & Smith, which firm became Case, Losee & Knox, located at 34-36 Genesee street. In 1867 the firm became Case & Tallman and was producing 32 pairs per day. In the middle 1890s the firm discontinued manufacturing shoes and continued to wholesale shoes under the name of Tallman & Hurd.

William Owens' factory on the corner of John and Jay streets in 1867 employed twenty men and sixteen women, making 90 pairs per day of children's, ladies' and misses' shoes. This firm began on June 16th, 1866. Later, hard times and the failure of western customers caused Owens to give up the business. Then for some years, he conducted a retail shoe store with his son William.

The factory of Bick & Dayton was located in the Empire Block on Franklin Square in 1867. They made no sewed shoes, and all its pegged work was done by hand. They made mens' and boys' shoes, as well as ladies' calfskin shoes. It was the only wholesale house in Utica at the time that manufactured boots.

R. S. & W. H. Reynolds, at 6-8 Fayette street, started business in 1865, employing sixty-eight workmen and producing 268 pairs of ladies' and misses' shoes daily. In 1866 their brother George A. Reynolds joined the firm and in 1867 the plant was moved to 21-23 Blandina street. In 1873 this factory was partly destroyed by fire and the firm purchased the old "Military Hall" on the corner of John and Catharine streets and began the work of enlarging and remodelling the building. Their shoes bore the trademark UTK and were equal to the finest made in the country. The eldest brother, Samuel, withdrew and moved to Chicago where he had large real estate holdings. When William H. Reynolds died in 1874, George Reynolds continued the business.

On December 1, 1874, George H. Ludlow, who had been superintendent for Reynolds, formed a partnership with H. J. Holbrook and began manufacturing shoes at 9-11 John street. The firm occupied six floors and produced 700 pairs of shoes daily, with finer grades of French and American kids, principally for ladies' and misses' but soon boy's fine shoes were added.

In the 1880s the Knights of Labor began to organize the shoe workers and a series of strikes, coupled with poor workmanship and the depression of the early 1890s, resulted by 1895 in all the shoe factories closing or moving away.

THE UTICA ART ASSOCIATION
1865-1878

AS the pioneers of Utica developed trade and transportation and built their mansions, a mid-century culture began to develop. This was noted in the "Daily Gazette" in November, 1843:

> "In our good city there has been a progress in the fine arts within the last twenty years. This is developed in the science of music, of painting, and of poetry, which have within that time been quite successfully cultivated and encouraged, and in each of which we have a number of native or resident artists or proficients, who do credit to themselves and to the taste and scientific character of our citizens."

For a decade following the Civil War, Utica had regular art exhibitions in which the best artists of this country were represented. Thomas H. Wood, a man of artistic taste, began a campaign to promote an appreciation of art in the community. Through his efforts, the Utica Art Association in 1863 was made an adjunct of the annual fair of the Utica Mechanic's Association.

In 1863 there were 141 pictures and art objects exhibited; in 1864, there were 177; in 1865, 217; in 1866, there were 221 and 22 of these were sold for almost six thousand dollars. In that year, the Art Association was incorporated and severed its connection with the Mechanic's Association. However, Association Hall, in the same building was fitted up as an art gallery, and for six weeks during Lent each year, these rooms were the center of the social life of the city.

Outside of New York city, there was no public exhibition which equalled it, and many illustrious artists showed their works in this city. No exhibitions were held from 1871 to 1878. That year the exhibition was held in Carton Hall on Genesee Street and the last in 1882 was held in Liberty Hall. In 1910 the Association transferred its remaining funds, amounting to $6,576.68 to the Utica Public Library as a fund for the promotion of art in Utica.

During the exhibitions, local artists, although not as numerous as the others, were well represented. Among them were many who achieved fame as artists and sculptors.

250

Erastus Dow Palmer was born in Pompey, New York in 1817 and as a young man came to Utica where he was employed for a time as a pattern maker in the Peckham Stove Works. Then he turned his attention to making a cameo portrait of his wife. He also made out of wood a figure of a ram which was placed in front of the Steam Woolen mill, erected in 1847. When the mill was remodeled during the 1880s, this figure was so badly disintegrated by the action of the weather that it fell to pieces. About 1850 he abandoned his saws and planes and removed to Albany where he took up the hammer and chisel to fashion sculpture. He became famous and his "Angel at the Sepulcher" in Albany Rural Cemetery is one of his best known. Grace Williams, daughter of James Watson Williams and his wife, died in 1854 and Palmer in 1856-57 carved the beautiful figure of "Grace Williams" in Grace Church, Utica. Palmer died in 1904.

Mandevillette Elihu Dering Brown, known locally as "M.E.D. Brown" was born in 1810 and came to Utica as a young man. From 1843 to 1850, he studied art in Europe and returned here. He became "the lion of the town". He was a man of many peculiarities. He never married, although in his day, he was one of the leading beaux of the city. He established a studio in the Tibbits Block on lower Genesee street and no family in Utica was considered prominent unless its leading members had their portraits painted by Brown. He painted portraits of Joshua Spencer, Judges Beardsley, Denio, Gridley and Doolittle, which were placed in the old John street court house, as well as one of Judge Beardsley in the Court of Appeals Hall in Albany. After the Civil War, he suddenly dropped out of society and contented himself evenings by gathering with his companions in front of Owen O'Neil's hardware store or Warnick & Brown's tobacco shop on Genesee street. He died in his studio in the Tibbit's Block on September 1, 1896.

MUSIC AND DANCING IN UTICA IN THE NINETEENTH CENTURY

U TICA has long been known as a musical center. According to Frederick Selch, founder of the Federal Music Society, musical instrument making, printing and publishing, flourished in Utica in its early days as a village. One of the earliest American collections of instrumental music was published here in 1816, compiled by William Whitely, a local instrument maker. It was from the Whitely collection that Selch obtained two long-buried marches composed in Utica in 1815 by the itinerant band master, Joseph Curphew. The compositions were "The Utica Independent Company's March" and "March in Memory of Washington".

The Utica City Band was organized early in 1822 by Thomas Davies and for more than sixty years occupied a place of distinction in the musical world. In 1824 the band joined the Eighth Regiment of Artillery and adopted an ornate uniform. The jackets were of white and the trousers of the same color, trimmed with black. These uniforms did not serve very well, though they were adorned with gold lace and epaulets and the headgear was so ornate that it attracted attention whenever the band appeared. The mud in the streets in the days of unpaved roads ruined the white uniforms. Soon they were changed to a blue color and a new long skirted coat adopted to cover the rotundity of some of the members. In 1825, the band welcomed Lafayette when he made his triumphant tour along the newly opened Erie Canal.

James Koehl was born in Utica on July 18, 1843, the son of Jacob Koehl, a well known musician, who had led a band in the French army for seven years before coming to America. When ten years old, James began playing the violin in his father's orchestra for dances. He then developed an expertise in the French flageolet, a small wood instrument of the flute class. He became manager of the Old Utica Brass Band from 1874 to 1886, when it was disbanded because of differences among the members. Koehl and George Perkins then formed from the members of the old band, the Koehl &

252

Perkins Military Band and Orchestra in 1888. When Mr. Perkins died in 1890, George Jacobs, who managed Jacob's Military Band, joined with Koehl as Koehl & Jacobs from 1891-1893. When Mr. Jacobs moved to Rochester in 1893, the band was known as Koehl & Burton's Military Band and Orchestra. In 1894, the name was changed again to the Old Utica Band. James Koehl died in Utica on November 3, 1919.

Prior to the Civil War, there was an organization in Utica known as the Utica Musical Academy, directed by George Dutton. It was a large chorus of mixed voices and they gave concerts in Concert Hall. It lasted about ten years or more. Some years later, it was reorganized by William H. Dutton, the son of the former leader, who kept a music store on lower Genesee street. The outbreak of the Civil War disrupted this society and Bill Dutton left Utica in 1866. Another group, the Aeolian Quartette, was formed in 1856 and achieved a wide reputation for excellence.

Late in the month of December 1864 or early in January 1865, some singers, returning from a rehearsal at old Trinity Church, stopped at the Sherwood House, on the corner of Broad and John streets for a brief social hour. This resulted in the organizing of the Utica Mendelssohn Club, which group lasted until some time in the eighties.

On January 8, 1865, the Utica Maennerchor was organized, formed by the consolidation of the old Concordia and Liederkranz societies, for the purpose of promoting a love of music among the German residents of the city. The first meetings were held in a building on Columbia street which was later occupied as a public school. The Maennerchor first sang in public when Lincoln's funeral train stopped briefly at the Utica depot on its way to Springfield in April 1865. The first musical director was R. Ritz, succeeded by Professor Mitzki, Professor Sutorius, and then for many years by Professor Zarth. In 1892, the Maennerchor Society began the construction of its own Musik Halle on Columbia street.

The first chime of bells in a church in Utica was installed in St. Patrick's Church about 1870. It was played by Professor Sutorius who in addition to the Maennerchor, directed the Adelphi Barden, a German musical group from 1874 to 1877. The Beethoven Glee Club was another group that flourished from 1865 to 1875 or a little longer.

The Welsh citizens not only promoted the annual Eisteddfod but organized the Welsh Choral Society and the Handel Choral Society, having 150 mixed voices. There was also the Gwalia Glee Club, from which grew the Haydn Male Chorus, of about 75 members, which did much to popularize music in Utica for many years and won many awards and prizes.

Louis Lombard came to Utica to direct the Philharmonic Orchestra and in February 1889, he started the Utica Conservatory of Music which had over the years a strong influence in the development of Utica musically.

The Hatton Quartette was organized in May 1891. Its members were Elliott H. Stewart, a member of the Tabernacle Church choir, first tenor; Edwin H. Ballou, a member of the choir of the Church of the Reconciliation, second tenor; Charles A. Winslow, soloist at St. Francis de Sales, first bass; and Walter McIncrow, soloist at St. John's Church, second bass. This Quartette became very famous. In 1895, the name was changed to the Oriental Quartette, because its current members were all members of Oriental Lodge, Free and Accepted Masons.

Professor Franz Rath, a native of Vienna came to Utica about 1890 to teach the flute and zither at the Conservatory of Music. He also became musical director of the Utica Saengerbund. He married Rosa Mary Lukowitz, one of the most talented lady violinists at the time. In 1892, Professor Rath formed Rath's Military Band and Orchestra, which flourished as one of the best aggregations of musicians in Central New York. The orchestra, with Harry McCormick as pianist, was the house orchestra at the Majestic Theater and played for dancing at Utica Park. In 1907, Rath and his wife went to Denver, Colorado, where he died in 1921.

When the citizens of Polish descent began to grow in numbers, they established choirs. The choir of the Holy Trinity Church was known as the Chopin Choir, under Professor Narkon and that of St. Stanislaus, the St. Cecelia Choir, under Professor Czonyka. Another still famous Polish choir was organized in the fall of 1910. It was "Kolka Filaretow", sometimes called the "Filarets". For 34 years George Wald directed this group until his death in 1965. Its repertoire included secular and sacred music, Polish folk, classical and popular selections. It today numbers 37 men.

The art of dancing was early taught in Utica by "Bill" Smith in Washington Hall and in 1850 in Concert Hall. His rival and successor was Charles L. Dobson. Charles Leaf

Dobson was born in England in 1823 and came to America with his parents and settled in Westmoreland, where his father began business as a tallow chandler. The elder Dobson was a musician and he taught dancing to young Charles. The family moved to Utica in 1840, and young Charles, at the age of 19, with a total capital of 18 cents, opened a fruit and candy business on the southwest corner of Genesee and Fayette streets. He sold out to his brother, Alfred B. Dobson, in 1862 and devoted his life to teaching dancing.

While he was still in business, he began to give dancing lessons to Uticans. At first he taught in the old "City Hall", which was then on the corner of Whitesboro and Division streets, then in "Apollo Hall" on the corner of Liberty and Burchard Lane, and also in Washington Hall. He owned the point at Oneida Square, bounded by Oneida, Hobart and Genesee street and opened Dobson's Hall there. This was the scene of many dancing parties and receptions. His reputation went through Central New York. He retired in 1890 and in 1895, erected the Dobson Flats on Genesee street and Dobson Hall on Oneida street. He died January 17, 1901.

THE HORSE CAR STREET RAILROAD IN UTICA
1863

John Butterfield believed that the rapid growth in population in Utica required the building of a street railway system to connect with New Hartford and Whitesboro villages. There were only four cities in the United States which had street car service: New York City (1852), Boston (1856), Philadelphia (1857) and New Orleans (1861). He organized a company and proceeded to lay tracks up Genesee street. Finally, on September 15, 1863 the "Utica Morning Herald" was able to report:

"Opening of the Street Railroad. The thing is done! The horse cars move up and down Genesee street at last. Yesterday, about 2 p.m. three of them were in position on the lower end of the track, and filled with gentry who had been invited to share the pleasures and perils of the first ride. John Butterfield, Esq., President of the Company appeared and took the lines of the horses attached to the first car. 'Go' and they went up Genesee street on a swift trot, with their car and its dignitaries, followed by the two cars behind. The delighted people that lined the street and stood at the doors and windows smiled and shouted. The passengers were not less delighted and enthusiastic. The horses trotted all the way up Genesee street hill and proved that the grade, about which some doubt had been expressed, would answer the purpose. It was necessary to stop about fifty rods north of the Orphan Asylum (i.e. Pleasant street), as the rails had been laid no farther. The horses were immediately transferred to the other ends of the cars and went back at the same rapid pace. The treat trip was ended and the practical operation of the Utica Street railroad inaugurated. Henceforth we may ride and smile on street cars to our heart's content."

On the occasion of the 50th anniversary of the street railway in September 1913, Fred A. Cassidy recalled the trip he made as a youngster on the first trip in 1863:

"The New York Street Car Company had loaned nine cars for the occasion as the new cars had not been finished. It was State Fair week and everything had to be ready for business. Then the State Fair was on Genesee street, near where the West Shore now crosses. They started from about in front of where Williams & Morgan's store is now (No. 31 Genesee street), with 12 big mahogany bays, every one of them 17 hands high, hitched to the first car. John Butterfield, Sr. was going to drive, and when the folks got on I was standing around. My father, Patrick Cassidy, was on the car, and I started to get on, too. Someone said, 'Here, no kids allowed on this car', or something to that effect, when Mr. Butterfield put out his hand and said, 'That is all right; this is my boy', so they let me on.

"First Mr. Butterfield tried to get the horses started but couldn't make it, so he asked my father to start them. Butterfield had a short stocked whip with a 20-foot lash that he used on the Overland Route back in the '50s. Well, my dad took hold of the lines and the horses started off so suddenly that they nearly jerked him over the front of the car. Two of the men caught him and the horses went along all right until they came to Catharine street, and there six of them split off, while the other six kept on the track. Roger Rock and John Butterfield, Jr., jumped off and put the six back on the track and then my father and John Butterfield, Sr. took them over the bridge. At the four corners (that's the Busy Corner now) they split again and my dad had to straighten them out again. Then after they got beyond the corners my father insisted that Mr. Butterfield take the reins again, so Mr. Butterfield drove the first six and my father took the swing, the middle and the pole horses, and so they went up Genesee street, with Henry Chase of the 'Evening Telegram' on the brake handle.

By December 1863, the tracks had been completed to New Hartford village. In the fall of 1865, Butterfield began to lay tracks along Columbia street.

THE DEVELOPMENT OF THE KNITTING INDUSTRY
1863

AMONG the industries for which Utica was notable during the last half of the nineteenth and first part of the twentieth century was that of knitting. Utica became the center of that industry and a very large percentage of knit wares used in the entire United States came from our mills.

The knitting industry here can be traced back to the Civil War years. In 1840, Samuel Lowery, Sr. came from Belfast, Ireland and settled on a farm in Oriskany. He had five sons, John Alexander Lowery (1825-1912), Samuel S. Lowery (1832-1912), William Lowery (1834-1878), James L. Lowery (1837-1895), and Joseph Stuart Lowery (1841-1891), the latter being born in Oriskany. All five went to work at an early age in the various woolen factories in the county and learned the art of sorting and weaving wool. In 1863, Samuel S. Lowery and his brother, James L. Lowery, formed a partnership to manufacture socks in Utica. The beginning of the industry was described in the "Utica Morning Herald" of March 7, 1863:

> "Messrs. S. S. and J. L. Lowery have now fairly under way the new manufacturing enterprise — the Utica Knitting Factory. It is located on Pine street, and the buildings are those formerly known as Curtis' Machine Shop, but, of course, repaired and remodeled. The machinery is now turning out about fifty dozen pairs of stockings per day — a substantial and durable article, neatly finished, and of the ribbed pattern. The yarn is first run through Aiken's machine, which transforms it into straight ribbed hose, of any desirable length. This is cut into proper lengths, slits made in each, and heels handsomely and quickly inserted by means of the heeling machines. Other machines partially 'narrow off' the feet with white tips, after which deft and skillful fingers put the finishing touches on to the two extremities. The completed stockings are washed by machinery, then stretched on shapely pieces of wood and hung up in the drying room, and soon after are ready to be packed in bunches and sent to wholesalers and retailers of dry goods.

> "Messrs. Lowery intend to add another set of machines in their establishment and will then employ about fifty hands, mostly girls, and about twenty more at their homes — seventy in all. The knitting machinery is all in the second story. The first is noisy with the whirr of wheels, rollers, spindles, etc., whereby the wool is transformed from its raw state into the yarn that is so rapidly swallowed by the hungry and curious combinations above. The long spinning jenny winds two hundreds pounds of rolls into yarn in a day, and makes four hundred and twenty yards. Thus, it will be seen, the Messrs. Lowery have made an important contribution to the business activity and manufacturing interests of our goodly city."

For most of their lives, the Lowery brothers maintained their interest in the knitting industry. John Alexander Lowery moved to Utica in 1864 and engaged in the knitting business in Oriskany under the name of Lowery & Williams, making socks for the army until the end of the Civil War. He then engaged in the business of buying and selling wool in Utica, retiring in 1906.

Samuel S. Lowery dissolved the Pine Street firm in 1865 and in 1867 with his brother-in-law, James L. Williams, started the Lowery & Williams Knitting Mills at the corner of Franklin and Fulton streets, making knit underwear and socks. He was active in Republican politics and was State Senator from 1872 to 1876. In 1890, he left the knitting business and devoted himself to real estate with an office in the Arcade Building.

In 1865, when his partnership with Samuel on Pine street was dissolved, James L. Lowery continued the business there with his younger brother, Joseph Stuart Lowery. The Pine street plant burned in 1867 and the two men, with their brother, William Lowery, formed a partnership to engage in the cotton and waste business. The firm was located on Columbia street, then on Main street, and finally on Broad street. In 1878, William died, but the firm continued as Lowery Brothers until Joseph, who was severely wounded at Cold Harbor during the Civil War and was promoted to the rank of Colonel, died in 1891. James Lowery continued the business alone until his death in 1895. The Lowery brothers were, indeed, the fathers of the knitting industry in the city.

JUSTUS HENRY RATHBONE AND THE KNIGHTS OF PYTHIAS
1864

JUSTUS Hall Rathbone came to Utica from New Hampshire in 1819. He studied law with David W. Childs here and became the attorney for the old Bank of Utica. He was also the custodian of the first library in Utica, which was housed in his law office. His wife was Sarah Elizabeth Dwight, a lineal descendant of Jonathan Edwards and a member of the famous Dwight family of New England. The couple had five children, of whom Justus Henry Rathbone, the founder of the Knights of Pythias, was born in the town of Deerfield on October 29, 1839.

Justus Henry Rathbone attended the public schools of Utica and Cortland Academy, Carlisle Seminary and Madison University. In 1857 he went to northern Michigan and taught school there.

As a teacher, he became impressed with the story of Damon and Pythias and decided to form an order which would incorporate the ideals of purity, generosity and boldness. In 1861, he was called east by the death of his father in Philadelphia on May 27th. Justus Henry Rathbone entered federal service as chief clerk of the Hospital at Germantown, Pennsylvania. In August 1862, he married Miss Emma Louise Sanger, of Utica and was transferred to Washington, D. C. as a clerk in the War Department.

There he met Robert A. Champion, a fellow clerk, and the two men discussed the formation of a society. The first meeting of a group of federal employees who were, with one exception, members of a glee club, was held in a small room on F Street on the evening of February 15, 1864. They formed Washington Lodge No. 1, Knights of Pythias. From this initial meeting, one of the most influential societies in the United States, the Order of the Knights of Pythias grew throughout the country.

JAMES EATON & SON MATCH FACTORY
1864

JAMES Eaton, one of the pioneer match manufacturers of America, died in Utica on November 18, 1890. He was born on the Cherry Valley turnpike, a short distance west of West Winfield on November 19, 1816. He was a natural mechanic and had a shop in his home. He invented a machine for manufacturing matches and in 1845, together with Henry Stanton, established a factory about a mile and a half north of Richfield Springs. This was one of the first match factories in the United States. In 1850, Mr. Eaton withdrew from the firm and commenced business for himself at West Winfield, where he thrived until 1864, when he removed to Utica and opened a factory in the "gulf" at South street. The "Utica Daily Observer" on December 18, 1879 reported:

> "There are only seven match manufactories in the State, and but twenty five in the United States. James Eaton, the senior of the Utica firm, has been a manufacturer of matches for the past thirty years. He commenced at West Winfield, making only three gross boxes per day. From a very small beginning he developed a business that is today an industry of which Utica may well be proud. At first he bought the match sticks from a Utica concern, and afterwards sawed the blocks and cut them up by horse-power. He came to Utica sixteen years ago, locating at Third and South streets. In 1864 there was not a building in the ravine in question; now there are fifteen separate structures that cluster around the factory. Eaton & Son have recently completed a large brick addition to the box-making department. Eaton & Son employ sixty hands and in the busy season turn out 400 gross of matches every twenty-four hours."

Mr. Eaton was the first to suggest that the various match makers form a single large company. As a result the Diamond Match Company was organized and Eaton sold his business to the new company in 1881, which continued the Utica plant until 1883.

FIRE ENGINES AND FIRE HORSES

IN the spring of 1864, old fire engines two, four, and five had been in use for more than twenty years and were worn out. The Legislature authorized the Common Council to raise $10,000 for the purchase of two new "steam" engines. The prospect of a "steamer" did not excite any great enthusiasm with the volunteer firemen, who were very proud of their old hand-operated machines. In May 1864, the two steamers arrived in Utica and were tested at the canal. Washington Company No. 7 brought out its old hand machine and attempted to show that it could throw a higher steam of water. In one case they did and in the other they claimed they did, but the newspapers declined to report whether this was done or not.

For a short time after the steamers became a part of the fire department, they were drawn to fires by the members of the company to which it was assigned. The engines were heavy and the men were exhausted by the time they reached the scene of the fire. The city then contracted with the proprietors of the livery stable nearest the fire station to furnish a team of horses for the steamer at every alarm of fire. This would cause delay and often the teams furnished had no experience hauling a fire engine. The city then purchased its own horses for the steamers, for the heavy ladder trucks which were added, and for the chief's rig.

Between 1864 and 1917 when the fire department was motorized, Utica's fire horses were the pride of the firemen.

One newspaper report remarked that,

"Many a youth of those days thrilled watching the 'hitch' made in an engine house. With the first stroke of the big gong the horses came dashing from their stalls. The fire animals knew just what to do and within seconds, were standing under the harness swinging evenly over the pole of the engine. They needed no command but trotted out of their stalls and into place under the harness in perfect step. The harness fell upon their backs and the firemen snapped the collars about their necks with amazing speed. A slight pull of a cord released a catch in the iron framework that held up the harness and the framework flew up to the ceiling. The driver jumped to the seat, grabbed the reins and within seconds after the first stroke of the alarm bell, the doors flew open, and the big apparatus, weighing up to four tons or more was off to the fire, followed by the chemical wagon and hose carts.

"Three practice hitches were made each day, at 8 o'clock in the morning, at noon and at 7:15 in the evening. The last hitch was always more successful that the other two, perhaps because the horses knew that they would be fed after the night hitch. The horses could tell the difference between a real and a practice drill. They had one way of answering a false alarm and another of responding to a fire. They came at a trot, in comparison with the dash which followed a real alarm. When the horses saw the men run to the indicator box and the drivers run to the engine, they knew it was the real thing."

Even when retired, the old fire horses never forgot the meaning of a fire alarm. On one occasion, a horse who had been retired for two years was brought to the fire house to settle a dispute. He was placed in his old stall and when the alarm was sounded, he was in his old place under the harness as promptly as he had ever done in his active days.

It was a rare fire company that did not have a fire dog on active duty. Jim, the Fire Dog at Engine No. 1 on the northwest corner of Eagle and Park Avenue was recalled by a reporter in the "Daily Press" of March 19, 1915:

> "Jim was a fire-dog and one of the best. He was a big Newfoundland, coal black, with hardly a white spot on him. The men at No. 1 Engine Company made a pet of him. When the man on watch went about lighting the lanterns on the apparatus, he lit one and placed it on the floor for Jim. If the bell should hit, Jim would bound down the stairs, pick up the handle of the lantern in his teeth, and wait patiently for the horses to start out. He never neglected his duties except at certain times. Fourth of July was one, and any time during a thunder storm was the other. The dog hid under a bed in the darkest corner of the men's dormitory Independence Day, and steadfastly refused to come out. It was the same during an electrical storm. Jim obstinately refused to leave the house. The fire house was the dog's home until he died, some time in the late 1870s."

THE UTICA TRADES ASSEMBLY
1865

THE only significant activity toward the formation of a labor union in Utica prior to the Civil War was in the 1840s when a few printers formed an organization known as "Fellow Typographers". After several attempts to accomplish their objectives of raising wages and improving working conditions, the group disbanded about 1848.

By the time of the Civil War, Utica became more industrialized and employees in the more skilled crafts began to form unions. On April 19, 1863, the printers held a meeting at Temperance Hall on Franklin Square and on May 18th received a national charter as Typographical Union No. 62. In the same year, the cigarmakers held a meeting in a hall on Genesee street and organized Cigarmakers' Local No. 7. They were soon followed by the machinists, blacksmiths, carpenters, textile spinners, tinsmiths and iron molders.

On September 23, 1865, representatives of these unions held a meeting at Temperance Hall on Franklin Square to organize a federation. On October 20, 1865, the "Trades Assembly of Utica" was established and on January 4, 1866, "the Assembly decided to purchase the furniture and right of the room formerly occupied by the Young Men's Literary Society, in the Empire Block, where the different unions will have an opportunity to meet in the future." ("Utica Daily Journal", October 23, 1865).

In 1882, the American Federation of Labor was organized by Samuel Gompers, and on January 21, 1882, at Haberer's Hall on Lafayette street, the Utica Trades Assembly was organized of delgates from each of the craft unions. In later years, the name was changed to the Utica Federation of Labor.

CRICKET AND BASEBALL IN UTICA

NEAR to the hearts of the English, Scotch and Welsh was the game of cricket. Blandina Dudley Miller in the "Utica Observer" of January 4, 1904 wrote that as early as 1845, there was a cricket club in Utica, known as the "Star of the West". Their first match was with the Syracuse Club which was returning from a game with the St. George's Club of New York. The Syracuse club was short two men, and George Bryant and James G. French of the Utica Club filled in for them to provide the eleven men needed.

The Utica team consisted of William Foster, a veterinary

surgeon of Liberty street, Samuel Vines, who ran a variety store at 198 Genesee street, Charles T. Smith, a saw filer, corner of Liberty and Genesee, George Ralph, the brewer of the Oneida Brewery, Theodore Dimon, physician, 38 Whitesboro street, George N. "Top" Beesley, who ran the news room in the Exchange Building, corner of Genesee and the Canal, Orchard G. Kellogg, a lawyer at 122 Genesee street, John Hackett, provision merchant, of 176 Genesee street, Frederick J. Martin, a brass founder, of 64 Genesee street, George Stevens, who lived on Whitesboro street, and John Lindley, a cartman of 3 Spring street.

The match was played on the "common" which Miss Miller described as being a level piece of ground between Cornelia street on the east and State street on the west, O. B. Matteson's garden on the south and a fence along the south side of Burton Hurlburt's property on the north. This description places the location about where the Kennedy Towers now stand.

In the late sixties and seventies, the cricket matches were played at a "cricket patch" located where Grove Place now runs. After a while interest in the sport lagged. Uniforms and paraphernalia for the game were quite expensive and the English, Scotch and Welsh youngsters then growing up in the city preferred to play "two-old-cat" with its joyful wranglings and excitement. The more dignified game with its strict rule of conduct did not seem to appeal to them. Gradually the teams disorganized and for a number of years the game was played only intermittently.

Utica had its amateur baseball club as early at 1860, known as the Utica Baseball Club. The team consisted of E. Curran, A. S. Potter, N. C. White, S. Sicard, A. D. Crocker, L. M. Thomson, George Sicard, George S. Porter, and W. J. Doolittle. Lamott Thomson was the pitcher. They played four games with Whitesboro, winning three and losing the fourth.

In July 1860, a second baseball team was organized, called the Pastime Base Ball Club. Its roster consisted of R. F. Birdseye, first base; I. G. Craige, third base; C. D. Gillmore, pitcher; F. J. Harding, left field; J. Healy, center field; W. Hunt, Jr., second base; John D. Kernan, shortstop; B. F. Miller, catcher; D. F. Ritchie, right field. A game between the Utica Club and Pastime resulted in a score of Utica 43, Pastime 21. From 1861 to 1863, the Knickerbocker Club of Albany and the Utica team had a friendly rivalry. The early days of baseball in Utica were recalled in articles in the "Utica

Sunday Tribune" of October 25, 1891 and the "Sunday Journal" of June 23, 1900.

Then interest began to lag after the Civil War and the "Morning Herald" of June 22, 1874 lamented:

> "For the past few years the national game has not been pursued with a great deal of zeal or success in this city. Its English rival, cricket has received some attention, but the systematic, nerve-trying, muscle-straining and anatomy-destroying game of baseball has had a period of comparative rest. There is a nine of no limited prowess that sallies out from the academy occasionally under the name of the Central City's. Then over in West Utica is the Alert Club that does some good playing. By-the-by we believe these two clubs play a game tomorrow, on the river grounds."

Meadow street in Utica at the time of the Civil War was nothing but a mere lane north and west of Bagg's square that led to a farmhouse located on the present site of the Barge Canal terminal. A short time later, it was made into a baseball field, at the lower extremity of the property owned by Peter Davis. In 1877 at the suggestion of several prominent citizens, an eight club league was organized in Utica.

The games were played in Riverside Park, as it was called. There was originally no fence surrounding the playing field and the only seating arrangements were a row of plain boards placed on stakes, extending behind the diamond. An admission charge of ten cents was set and three watchmen were hired to make sure that no one got in without paying at the entrance at the end of Meadow street. During the first season, the sum of $600 was collected and this provided four prizes for the teams, paid for the uniforms for the three teams which couldn't afford to buy their own and for the balls used, and left the sum of $40 for a league banquet.

Professional baseball began in 1878 with the formation of the Utica Baseball Club. There was a professional league in existence composed of Binghamton, Syracuse and Auburn, and the Utica Club bought the Binghamton franchise. The Utica team joined the International League and had a fairly successful season the first year, but in 1879 attendance was poor and the team disbanded in early summer. For the next few years, a sort of a team played in a sort of State League with no great success.

David Dischler organized a very good amateur team in 1884, 1885 and in 1886 it joined the International League again and won the pennant, but in 1887 it was forced to disband. In 1890 Utica again joined the State League but this lasted only two years. The old field fell into decay which prompted the "Saturday Globe" on May 4, 1895 to write:

> "Utica is to have no baseball this year. We of old Pent-Up, once famous for its stars, must content ourselves with such games as the schoolboys may give us on the street lots or the enthusiastic older boys on the Utica Park grounds. Professional baseball seems to be dead here and Riverside Park, the kindergarten where some of the brightest lights of the diamond received their earliest lessons, has falled into decay and will probably never again resound with the cheers of the spectators, the crack of the bat, the shrill shriek of the umpire or the howl of the coaches. The fence and grandstand, nearly half destroyed by the floods and age, are to be taken down and the grounds transformed into farm land."

UTICA CURLING CLUB
1868

THE first curling in this area took place at Clark Mills in 1854 by a group of Scots and Englishmen who had recently settled at the site of the small textile mill.

Benjamin Allen, who died in March 1903 at the age of 85, was the "father" of curling in Utica. He was born in England and came to Utica in 1830. He learned the trade of stone cutting and cut the stone used when the Erie Canal' was enlarged. In 1845 he began the business of constructing plank and stone sidewalks. His sons joined him and the firm became Allen & Sons, with its stone yard located at the junction of Park avenue and Catharine street.

Allen, John Crook, John Ross, Thomas Savage, and "Pop" Hollingsworth formed the Utica Curling Club in 1868. In an interview in 1900, Mr. Allen said:

> "We used to play on the Chenango Canal, not far from the foot of Plant street. Then we went over to what is

known as the Sulphur Spring, where our rink is now. I bought this property and we have used it ever since."

This property in the "Gulf" was flooded and two curling rinks were laid out. About 1890, a shed was built on the same property and a three sheet enclosed rink with a large second floor club room with a plate glass view. The city condemned the property in order to fill in the "gulf". With the $16,000 received from the city for the property, a lot on Francis street was purchased and in 1915-16, a five sheet rink with a second floor clubroom was built. Artificial ice was introduced in 1937 because of the uncertainty of the weather. Here, not only the men, but their wives and daughters, and female friends enjoy the Scottish game.

WINTER PASTIMES IN UTICA DURING THE 19TH CENTURY

SKATING became very popular by the middle of the 19th century. The Mohawk river and the Erie Canal were favorite spots while West Uticans used the fourth level of the Chenango Canal. On Corn Hill, Peter Davies donated the use of a pond on his land, constructed by means of a dam thrown across a small stream. Even the girls ventured to try the sport as evidenced by a newspaper report in January 1859:

> "Late yesterday afternoon, it pleased us to see on the canal near Hotel street bridge, a number of girls — not young women — with skates strapped to their feet. They made fine use of their limbs and were as graceful as their brothers and youthful male friends. The sight was pleasing. How ladies with long skirts would have appeared we can't say; but it is a pity if skirts broad and long are to keep the young women from the enjoyment of the most invigorating and graceful of sports. We are in favor of getting the women on skates — or skates on the women — if possible."

On December 6, 1861, the Utica Skating Club was formed and a baseball field, known as Excelsior Park, was selected as the location of the sport. When it was flooded and the ice was good, a ball was raised on a pole in front of the store of Edward Curran in lower Genesee street. The "Oneida Weekly Herald" reported:

"Carnivals will occur once or twice a week for which the new City Band will furnish music, and in which, beside the host of pretty girls Utica is sure to contribute, we may expect the damsels of Rome, Little Falls, Clinton, Whitestown, Clayville and the other villages to participate. The altogether lovely presence of such loveliness should inspire blunderers to 'go down' with decorum. We trust the practice of sudden prostration before natty ankles will be dispensed with this season; there is danger in it. Our girls are not Juggernauts, nor our young fellows Brahmins; the former may be compelled to withdraw the objects of this abject sacrifice of bruised knees and elbows within some infernal Turkish trousers or such. What will worshippers do then? We do tenderly but earnestly suggest that the ladies ought to compromise by wearing shorter dresses and less hoops. The latter are non-sensical on ice, and we wonder they have not long since been discarded."

In 1867, the Butterfield Skating Park was constructed on Jewett Place. The "Utica Daily Observer" described the new park on October 25, 1867:

"It is situated at the foot of Jewett street, the second street above Mr. Howard's Green House. Leaving the cars at Jewett street, three minutes' walk brings us to the Park proper, which extends from the foot of the declivity leading to the canal to the roads running east of a parallel with the Chenango canal. This road is better known as Chenango Avenue."

The "Utica Daily Observer" of January 10, 1891 described the winter fun in Utica in the gay nineties:

"Sleighriding, coasting and skating are being enjoyed to a larger extent in this city than for many winters past. The greater quantity are indulging in coasting, and the number of young men and women, boys and girls, and even middle-aged people who are to be found congregated on First street, West and Charlotte streets, Cottage street, Cornelia and other streets, between 7 and 10 a.m. ethusiastically engaged in the exhilarating sport of gliding down the icy roadways and climbing back to the tops of the grades, only to again load up in blocks of from eight to twenty to again shoot down amid shouts of laughter and general merriment, reaches into the thousands. Long bobs, short bobs and single sleds, bobs with gongs, bobs with guiding wheels and bobs of all varieties are pressed into service. On Cornelia street one can see the sport at its best, and several evenings this week the number there coasting has been put at one thousand. The owners of the coasters are not at all exclusive, and many who go there without coasters are allowed to ride by those who own the long flyers. They get off the track, tip over, get such jolts as to throw off the riders, but with a shout and a hearty laugh all generally right themselves. Few serious accidents occur, but more care might and should be used. Cross streets should be more carefully guarded.

"While these main coasting resorts are the ones used by the older class, the small boys have short, but very steep, slides all over town in vacant lots, and wherever they can find a hill. An "Observer" reporter watched a group of happy youngsters yesterday afternoon sliding down one side of the Gulf, near Elizabeth street. The chute, for it could be called nothing else, was glary ice, and the little fellows used very primitive sleds. One used a single barrel stave, and gleefully sitting on it, shot to the bottom, all unmindful whether his maternal ancestor had any more pieces like his unmentionables or not. Another even scorned a barrel stave and made his anatomy serve as a basis to slide on. Others used old pieces of carpet, and some of them shot down the hill seated on old brooms.

"Next to coasting probably the larger number of young people are enjoying skating. In the Gulf near Elizabeth street, down in between the hills, where no wind reaches, is a fine open air rink, where large numbers gather afternoons and evenings. Adults pay 10 cents and boys 5 cents. In the canal, near John street, is another rink largely patronized. Little houses in which to adjust skates and keep warm are to be found at each. The canal, except where cleaned off by private enterprise, does not furnish good skating on account of the snow on the ice. However, a group of boys can be found almost any time under the Genesee street bridge, where they enjoy a little covered rink, where they enjoy a monopoly of their own, and often build bonfires on the ice to keep warm. The flats (Deerfield) and river do not this year furnish any good skating. One of the pleasantest resorts is Allen's Curling Rink in the Gulf at Rutger street. Here a nice class of young and middle aged people congregate afternoons and evenings. A cozy house with a warm fire is at the edge of the ice. Admittance for adults is 15 cents, and for children 10 cents. Skates are be had at 10 cents per hour. In the matter of skates a great step has been made. A few years ago, one must provide his own skates with straps all fitted up, with the buckle holes just right, etc. Now the adjustable skate is handed you, the turn of a screw adjusts it and in five minutes you are as much at home as though you had worn the skate for weeks. On the ice is an easy chair with runners, in which a child, an invalid or a lady who does not skate can be propelled about the rink by a strong skater. Polo games on the ice are also played here by the gentlemen. On this rink, the home of the Utica Curling Club, can be found every day teams of the Utica curlers contesting at that favorite Scotch game. The best approach to the rink is from Rutger street, where a well cindered path winds down the hillside. It can also be reached by way of South and Mill streets. It is a popular and pleasant resort, and is well worth visiting."

The "Utica Observer" wrote about "A Night With the Ice Skaters in Utica" on January 24, 1896:

"An 'Observer' reporter went last night to view young artists cut the double eight and do the 'grape vine', 'Dutch roll' and 'outer edge' on the ice on the West side. There is a cleared space on the Erie canal extending west from the swing bridge about 800 feet, and here is where the young people of the west end gather nightly when the ice is good condition and glide up and down the smooth surface humming 'Paradise Alley' for accompaniment. A flight of broad steps lead from the bank of the canal to the ice below, and bring one to a flat boat owned by Lorenzo V. Coleman, which is frozen in the ice. Coleman's home is nominally in Western, although he might aptly be termed a 'float' for he lives on the boat and in the summer drifts about the Erie and Black River canals to such points as he thinks he can do the most advantageous trading. The opening of the skating season and the large number of persons who went to the Erie Canal to enjoy that sport suggested to him an idea which he has since resulted very profitably. He built an 8 by 16 foot addition to his boat, put in a small stove and began business. His stock consists of cigars, cider, candies and cookies, besides a number of pairs of skates which he rents for five cents an hour. He also sharpens skates at the rate of five cents a pair, and does quite a thriving business.

271

"If the ice is badly cut up at night, Mr. Coleman devotes the forenoon of the next day to sprinkling it and getting it into condition. He has hit upon a novel method of spraying the ice, from which he gets good results. A large hogshead mounted on a sled is filled with water, which gushes out through the stem taken from a huge watering pot. The sled is drawn along the ice, and the water and the frost do the rest. On a good night when the ice is in prime condition the crowd on the canal will vary from 500 to 1,500 and Coleman's receipts are influenced accordingly.

"Just west of that portion of the canal which is so well cared for by Coleman is another stretch over which Jay Campbell presides in like manner, and beyond him is another of which Henry D'Aprix has charge. A skate which is very popular among those who enjoy the ice on the canal is the 'Hollander'. It has a wooden frame with a long narrow runner, and is fastened on by thongs. They are patterned after the old fashioned Dutch skate, and vary in length from 12 to 20 inches. It was on skates of this pattern that Phil Hammes recently skated to Rome and return in 2 hours and 15 minutes, including a brief stop at Oriskany.

"On Seymour avenue, just above the West Shore Railroad, there is an excellent open rink called the Elmhurst. It is 385 feet long and 105 feet wide — one of the largest in the city. Breastworks of wood and snow isolate the pond from general inspection and temper the winds. There is a cozy little house, almost hidden in the snow. A narrow window extends across the front; out of this aperature members of a brass band thrust their instruments and pipe merry tunes for the pleasure of the crowd that gracefully weaves and darts over the ice. The rink is an ellipse. At the axes there are electric lights. Nearby is one of the city towers, the rays from which make the scene brighter. Then there is one of those little cabins, where skaters may slack their thirst with harmless drinks or eat a toothsome lunch. Millgate Brothers, the rink proprietors, conduct the place in an admirable way.

"The Oneida Rink (the Oneida Square Bicycle Rink), where bicycles roll in summer, politicians meet in fall and skaters meet and fall was certainly smooth last evening, although that is a night when the attendance is the lightest.

"The Empire Rink, corner of James and Miller streets, is one of the largest in the city with an area of about 350 by 500 feet. It is conducted by James O'Brien, Henry Mil-

272

gate and John Foley. On favorable evenings this rink has contained from 300 to 400 skaters at a time.

"At the Steuben Rink, at the corner of Steuben and James streets, William J. Marron and R. T. Woodhull proprietors, a skating surface of 150 to 200 feet is provided, furnishing healthful sport on some evening to from 100 to 150 people. Owning to competition both the Empire and the Steuben have reduced the admission price to five cents and are open Sunday afternoons. Both are furnished with covered buildings and warm rooms for the use and comfort of patrons.

"Schremp furnished music for skating at a pretty rink on Jay street, near Kossuth avenue, last evening. Jay street rink is popular, and its popularity obtains through the good class of young people to be found in the east end of the city. The ice at this rink was in first class condition last evening, and was enjoyed by nearly 200 lovers of the popular pastime. The mangement is under Henry Wilkinson."

The winter sport of tobogganing began in Utica in the 1880s, as we read in the "Utica Morning Herald" of December 25, 1885:

"Tobogganing in Utica, now a fashionable and favorite pastime with many of our citizens, owes its prosperity if not its introduction to Dr. Wallace Clarke. The toboggan slide on Steele's hill last winter proved such an attractive resort for the scores of adventurous spirits who pioneered the toboggan, that a toboggan club has been organized and the hill much improved for this winter. A wooden building has been erected at the top of the hill, painted neatly, and warmed by stoves, as a rendezvous for the tobogganers. The hill, which is very steep, has been leveled and graded, so as to offer too exhilarating bumpers on the way down. At the foot of the hill the fences have been cleared away, and a free course made across Pleasant street and through the Jewett farm, so that the coasters will not be compelled to steer down Elm street between snow drifts and fences. There are two separate chutes down the hill, each starting from a platform at the top conveniently arranged, and the two slides will be continuously separate to Pleasant street, so that two tobogganers can slide abreast. The grounds will be in charge of a special policeman who will exercise a general care of the grounds and tobogganers and prevent intrusion by objectionable parties."

POST CIVIL WAR ARCHITECTURE IN UTICA

THE increased prosperity of Uticans as a result of the Civil War produced a new wave of building and a number of palatial mansions were erected. Egbert Bagg in an article "Architecture in Utica" which appeared in the "Observer-Dispatch" of March 6, 1932, wrote:

> "This was the period that gave us the square houses with a cupola on top, and with porches, cornices and all available space covered with jig-saw wood work, It is known to architects as 'The Reign of Terror'. Utica took advantage of it and extended her buildings out Genesee street clear to Pleasant street, over Rutger to the gulf, and over a large portion of the Corn Hill district. The interior of these houses was marked by heavy stained wood trim, heavier plaster cornices and ceiling decorations, fluted black walnut newel posts, wide hand rails and curved stairs, and gorgeous marblized slate mantles."

Perhaps the best known architect of the period was Azel Josiah Lathrop. He was born in Lebanon, Connecticut in 1814, and at the time of his death in March 1880, was in his sixty-sixth year. He came to Utica about the year 1840. He had learned the trade of carpenter and builder, and while thus engaged, he studied architecture. He spared no pains in perfecting himself and the latest and most costly works on architecture were placed in his library. At one time he carried on a school in the old Military Hall for instructing young men in drawing. The buildings erected by him were substantially built and handsome in design.

Chauncey Palmer was born in North Bridgewater, Oneida County, on August 4, 1807. He learned the trade of carpenter and cabinet maker and moved to Utica between 1825 and 1828. He established a carpenter shop on Pine street in the 1840s. In connection with his trade he needed lumber, and he joined with Lewis Lawrence about 1846 in establishing a planing mill in Seymour's Steam Block on Fulton street, near the canal, and used the first planing machine ever operated in this vicinity.

The business and commercial prosperity which attended

274

the Civil War resulted in the building of a number of new mansions on Genesee street. Although they were designed to meet the expressed wishes of the owners, a French style of architecture appeared to predominate.

The home presently occupied by the Catholic Women's Club at No. 294 Genesee street was the former Matteson-White house and in its day was perhaps Utica's most ornate house. It is a combination of two houses, the southern portion built about 1825 and the other at the close of the Civil War about the year 1865. Orasmus B. Matteson came to Utica from Verona and studied law with Bronson & Beardsley. He was elected to Congress in 1848 and served four terms. Something in his political life displeased society in Utica and he was socially snubbed. He determined to build a house which in elegance and grandeur would eclipse all the others on the street.

The interior design was French. One of the drawing rooms is almost oval in shape, the end being rounded instead of square. The windows were French, running to the floor. The glass in the windows was French plate. The mirrors at either end of the rooms were of plate glass, the frames of solid wood of Florentine design. The parlor furniture was of solid rosewood, one set upholstered in maroon damask and the other green and yellow patterned damask. On the walls were two pictures painted by M. E. D. Brown. One picture represented Rebecca and the other Ruth. The mantles were of Carrara marble. The ceiling was ornamented with a grape vine pattern, fashioned to expose the form of the grapes and leaves. The chandeliers of gas followed the same grape vine pattern.

On Mr. Matteson's death in December 1887, the house was owned by William M. White for many years and on his death in 1896 passed to the estate. It was occupied by William Pierrepoint White and John W. White until the house was sold in 1919 to the Catholic Women's Club.

Jared Eliot Warner who conducted the historic drug store at Bagg's Square from 1817 to his retirement in 1867 occupied the house at 296 Genesee street, which adjoined the Orasmus Matteson home. The property passed to G. Clarence Churchill who commissioned Azel Lathrop, the architect, in 1870 to remodel the old house which was built thirty to forty years before. The general style of the new building was French. The native wood trimmings of the various rooms were of white and black walnut, ash, chestnut, butternut and pine. The mantles were of wood, with ebony, walnut and ash trimmings.

In 1869, Charles Downer, the pioneer lumber dealer in Utica secured from Azel Lathrop a design for a new residence on the corner of Genesee and Cornelia streets. It was of brick, ornamented at the front porch with iron Corinthian columns. The building was covered by a "Mansard roof", terminating in a tower in the center, protected with red slate.

Charles A. Yates, who with his brother Rymer V. Yates was the pioneer in the sale of ready made clothing, built in the fall of 1867 a beautiful mansion on Genesee street at the corner of Cottage Place. It was designed by Lathrop and both the sitting room and dining room had elegantly designed marble mantels, from a celebrated Austrian cutter in New York city.

Thomas Buchanan, the banker, secured plans for a residence on Genesee street from Azel Lathrop. The design was purely French and described in detail in the "Utica Observer" of September 14, 1867.

> "The windows in the attic, or (strictly speaking) the French story, are designed with the most perfect taste and skill. The middle window is handsomely patterned after the 'Oriel' style, and flanked by the dormer windows, stands out in admirable relief from the comparatively plain windows below."

UTICA DRIVING PARK
1867

DURING the latter part of the 1860s, Utica was the site of the State Fair. The old fair grounds were located between Genesee street and Oneida street, near what was later to be the West Shore railroad tracks. The State Fair Racing Track was situated about where Kellogg's lumber yard was on Kemble street until its destruction by fire a few years ago.

It was the age of the "trotters" and "pacers", and many of the affluent persons enjoyed driving their "high steppers" along Rutger street. They organized the "Gentlemen's Riding and Driving Club of Utica". They proceeded to build the Utica Driving Park in East Utica, as described in the "Utica Observer" on July 11, 1867:

> "The track is one of the finest, firm, and without being too hard, splendidly curved and perfectly level. The length of 'the course' proper is 2640 feet, exactly half a mile. The 'home stretch' is 680 feet long and 50 feet wide. The 'back stretch' is 680 feet long and 30 feet wide. The 'turns', two in number, have each 500 feet of curve, and when the width of the track is taken into consideration, it will be seen that the course is one of the roomiest and at the same time perfectly safe in case of rivalry among the owners of 'two-forty's'. On the right is to be erected a large and commodious building designed for the accommodation of ladies and gentlemen. The structure will be under cover, and will possess every convenience and design of the most fashionable and popular of the eastern courses. On a line with the inside railing on the 'home stretch' will be the Judge's stand. The course is situated between two streets, which are being cut at both sides of the Park, extending from Broad to Bleecker streets. The grounds are to be appropriately enclosed, and a neat inside railing will materially add to the attractions and conveniences which the Park is to possess. As yet, the track only is finished. This is to be thrown open to the public this afternoon."

Many events were held at the Utica Driving Park, including the fairs of the Central New York Horticultural and Agricultural Society in 1873, 1874, 1875 and 1876; and the annual State Fairs in 1882 and 1886. In 1889, the New York State Lodge of Masons inspected and later purchased the site for its new Masonic Home, which today occupies the site.

Between 1890 and 1900, West Utica had its own driving park. The "Highlands" area of West Utica was purchased around 1890 from Harriett Ballou by Edward W. Mathews. He surveyed the property, laid out streets and building lots for Utica's expanding population. The area included Brayton Park Place, Churchill Avenue and Mathews Avenue. Just west of this, from Downer avenue westerly to the city line at Yorkville, was the "West Utica Driving Park", operated by John Blanch. Downer and Kellogg, the lumber dealers, owned the land where the track was located and gave their names to the streets there. Mr. Blanch purchased an old farmhouse, located on the southwest corner of Whitesboro street and Mathews avenue, moved it to the race track and converted it into a clubhouse. The "Daily Press" of June 27, 1900 described the final days of the old West Utica track:

> "Charles Faass, the owner of the West Utica Driving Park, has decided to use the place hereafter solely as a meadow. The park was at one time a very popular driving place, but now the track is overgrown with grass and weeds, and next year it will be plowed up.
>
> "Several years ago the West Utica Driving Association got control of the park and made many improvements there. Grand stands, Judge's stands and new barns were built and a number of races were held there. Then the Utica Trotting Association got the place in the Western New York Circuit and no place was left for the West Utica people. Fritz Brand, proprietor of Casino Park, has purchased the grand stand and Antoine Toussaint, a West Utica butcher, bought the hotel buildings. He has workmen engaged in tearing it down and in selling the lumber."

THE BREWING INDUSTRY IN UTICA

THE business of brewing beer began in the early days of the village. When the city was incorporated in 1832, there were four breweries in operation: Edward Bright, on Varick street near Hamilton, Joseph Goodliff's brewery at the corner of Columbia and Varick, the Gulf Brewery on Jay street at the Basin, and the Oneida Brewery at the corner of State and Court streets. About this time, Michael McQuade purchased the old "Gulf Brewery" and the "Daily Gazette" of June 29, 1848 wrote:

> "McQuade and Pond are erecting a very large building on the site of their old one, lately pulled down. While West Utica is being devoted to the manufacture of dry goods, East Utica rather leans to wet articles. The Oneida Brewery already begins to look ill at ease in a neighborhood so dry as a cotton factory. We hope its proprietors will find it for their advantage to sell out so as to leave the hill to better shape for building lots. As a brewery it has behaved with credit to itself and satisfaction to its patrons, but the corner is needed for dwelling houses and beer can work elsewhere as well."

The arrival in large numbers of German immigrants to Utica after the uprising in Germany in the 1840s, created a demand for "lager beer". The Utica breweries were producing at the time only English ale.

Charles Bierbauer was born in Bavaria in 1818 and learned the art of brewing in Munich and Vienna and came to America in 1849 and to Utica in 1850. He purchased from Michael Devereux, a tract of land on Third street near Mary and started a small brewery. About Christmas time in 1850, he offered for sale the first glass of lager beer ever brewed in Utica.

Declaring that he used only the best "hopfen and maltz" he remained on Third street for two years and then rented a small house on South Hamilton street in West Utica. A short time later he purchased land from Alrick Hubbell on Edward street, the site of the present West End Brewing Company, and erected his brewery. He also conducted an inn which was very popular. It was here, it is said, that the Utica Maennerchor was organized, with Mr. Bierbauer as one of the founders.

Charles Hutten was born in Wittenburg, Germany in 1829. In 1855, he came to Utica and was employed by Peter Vidvard who had purchased Bierbauer's old brewery on Third Avenue. In the fall of that year, he purchased the brewery in company with his father and continued brewing until he died on August 20, 1890.

When Charles Bierbauer died on August 17, 1885, his brother-in-law, John Kohler, who at one time was County Treasurer, organized, with others, the Columbia Brewing Company to continue the business. In 1880, a twenty-one year old expert in the old-world method of brewing lager beer, Frank X. Matt arrived here to become the brew master. When the Columbia Brewing Company failed after three years in operation, Mr. Matt organized the West End Brewing Company, which is at the present time, the only brewery in Utica.

The Star Brewing Company was organized in 1873 by John Myres, James O'Toole, John Quinn and Thomas Quinn. John Myres, the brewer, was the brother-in-law of the Quinns. The brewery was opened on July 4, 1874 on the corner of Mohawk and Jay streets. It turned out ale, old stock and porter. All the work was done by hand. As cold storage for beer was unheard of at the time, the beer was in a constant state of fermentation. Oftentimes the three-inch solid oak head in the barrel would be blown out when the beer worked. Even when the beer was delivered it would have to stand for two or three days before it could be tapped and drawn, and even then it would be too lively.

With modern methods of brewing being developed, the Eagle Brewing Company was organized by the same people who conducted the Star in September 1888. A substantial brick building was constructed at Third avenue and Jay street. It was the first brewery equipped with a mechanical refrigeration system. The old Star Brewery ceased operations in 1900 and the site was taken over for an apartment building.

HOSPITALS AND HOMES FOR THE AGED

EARLY in the 1850s, a building on Bridge street (Park Avenue) formerly occupied as a fur shop was taken over by the Mayor as a City Hospital. It was fitted up to contain 35 to 40 beds. A newspaper of the time said, "The hospital is far from what we want in Utica, but it is a large advance on nothing at all and we hail it as a forerunner of its betters."

The City Hospital (later known as the General Hospital) on South street at Mohawk was erected in 1856 by the city and was originally intended as a work house. Two years later it became a hospital under the Poor Master and when the Board of Charities superseded the Poor Master, the building came under their jurisdiction. The three-story building was built of brick and cost $12,000. At the Battle of Cold Harbor in June 1864, many of the wounded soldiers were from Utica and Oneida county, and the City Hospital took care of them for the following year.

On November 19, 1866, a charter was granted under the name of the "Home for the Homeless in the City of Utica" to take care of the aged, indigent and infirm women who were unable to support themselves. The home was opened in a building on Whitesboro street, opposite the State hospital, in May 1867. Theodore S. Faxton, contributed $20,000 and two acres of land on Faxton street toward the erection of a new home there. Citizens contributed an additional sum of $26,000 and B. F. Jewett and his sisters donated four lots adjoining those of Faxton and a new building was opened on December 26, 1870 at a cost of $30,000 and in 1879 an additional building was added at a cost of $6,000.

St. Elizabeth Hospital and Home was organized December 12, 1866 by Mother Bernardina, a member of the Franciscan Order. She received the first patient in a small wooden building on Columbia street which was donated by the Franciscan Fathers at St. Joseph's Church for that purpose. Through the generosity of Thomas B. Devereux, another building was added and soon afterward a third. In 1868, the old wooden buildings had to be removed to make room for the new St. Joseph's Church and a house was purchased a few doors west of the former location. This was opened for patients on

October 15, 1869. This second hospital was a wooden one of two stories but it soon proved to be inadequate. In 1887 a new hospital was built and served as such until the new modern hospital was erected on Genesee street in 1915-17.

Early in its history, St. Elizabeth's established a dispensary which was visited by the sick residents of Utica in large numbers. It was used to advantage in December of 1871 when a smallpox epidemic broke out.

There was also the Utica City Dispensary. We read in the "Utica Morning Herald" of March 5, 1872:

> "On Elizabeth street, just in the rear of the old Central Hotel property, stands a neat little white building on which is the sign 'Utica Dispensary'. Here the needy sick of our city may find the purest of medicine and the best medical advice, free of charge. The front room on the first floor is to be used as a reception room. Opening from this is the room containing the medical stores, and on the same floor are a consulting room and the sleeping apartment of the janitor."

In 1872, Mrs. James Watson Williams donated a house at 26 Elizabeth street. On January 13, 1903, the dispensary property was condemned for the site for the new Court House and the proceeds were used to purchase a house at No. 124 Mary street.

On December 23, 1869, St. Luke's Home was incorporated for the purpose of "establishing and maintaining in the city of Utica a refuge for the poor and friendless members of Grace Church parish in Utica and such others as the Board of Managers may think entitled to its benefits." On September 1, 1870, a double two-story brick dwelling adjoining the Home was purchased on Columbia street and a hospital, St. Luke's, was opened July 9, 1872. By 1886, the old building with over 200 patients was overcrowded and a larger structure of brick, costing over $15,000 was built. In 1892, an addition was added. On October 17, 1905, Mr. and Mrs. Frederick T. Proctor built and furnished a new St. Luke's Hospital on Whitesboro street.

The next hospital built was Faxton Hospital, a gift from Theodore S. Faxton, which opened in 1875. The growth of Faxton Hospital for the first ten years was slow. In 1892, a training school for nurses was established and in 1895, Dr. Fred J. Douglas was appointed the first resident physician of Faxton. In 1897, a home for the nurses was opened and in 1926 a new addition was added to the hospital.

In 1878, the upper two floors at Faxton Hospital were converted into a home for aged men. In February 1882, the Home for Aged Men was incorporated and this was amended to include their wives. In 1890, a lot opposite the hospital was secured and the new home opened on July 15, 1891.

In 1895, the homeopathic staff at Faxton withdrew and opened a hospital on Genesee street known as the Utica Homeopathic Hospital. A new building was built on the site and in 1926 the name was changed to "Memorial Hospital". It is today the Genesee Nursing Home.

FAXTON HALL — COURT AND VARICK STREETS
1867

ON the triangular plot on the north side of Court street where Varick intersects, is another historic building, now known as "St. John's Hall". Theodore S. Faxton purchased the former residence of DeWitt C. Grove and the adjoining land for the purpose of erecting a building dedicated to public use. He commissioned Azel Lathrop to design an appropriate structure. It was decided to construct a two story brick building with a stone foundation, in the French style of architecture. The plans were described in the "Utica Observer" of January 19, 1867:

> "The Hall is to be of rectangular shape, 70 feet long by 35 wide, and fronting on Court and Varick streets, with a yard in both rear and front. The height is to be 38 feet with a tower in the southwest corner which will not rise much above the main roof.
>
> "The first story is to be used as a School Room, having rear entrances upon both Varick and Court streets. It is to be divided into seven rooms.
>
> "The main Hall is to be situated in the second story, and

is to be 60 by 33 feet in size. The entrance is to be by a single staircase, seven feet wide, through the tower, with folding doors leading into the Hall. Around the outside are to be two rows of cushioned seats. These seats are to be fixed and raised slightly above the other slips. The body seats are to be movable and are to be placed at right angle to the others. The rostrum is to occupy the tower or entrance end of the room. The windows of the second story are to be circular, finished with iron caps above and below, with stone sills and iron corbels.

"The high-curved French roof will have two curved dormer windows upon each side, with one in front and rear. These, as well as the curved portion of the roof, are covered with ornamental slate in two colors — probably green and purple. The deck is to be nearly flat and covered with tin. The high French roof also forms an attic, which is to be used as a storeroom.

THE SCHOOLS OF UTICA AT MID-CENTURY

DURING and after the Civil War, there were thirteen public schools: Advanced School (1847) corner of Charlotte and Elizabeth, Whitesboro street school, at Potter street (1853), Aiken street school, west of Cornelia (1853), Steuben street school, south of South street (1851), Blandina street school, east of First street (1852), Hamilton street school, south of Columbia (1851), Catharine street school, east of Park avenue (1852), Albany street school, near the toll-gate (1858), Lansing street school, east of the Gulf (1858), Court street school, on Asylum Hill (1860), Francis street school (1867), and South street school, corner of Seymour (1867). This last building was designed by William Metcalf and was two stories and of plain Norman architecture. To this should be added the Faxton Hall school, on Varick street, donated by Theodore Faxton.

On the morning of May 13, 1865, the Utica Academy, the historic building at Chancellor Park was destroyed by fire. By permission of the County the school was opened and continued in the court house until the completion of the new building. The grounds were enlarged by purchasing the lot on the corner of Bleecker. This new building, completed in the autumn of 1867 was erected on the site of the old academy, two stories of brick, in the Renaissance style.

In January 1869, an evening school was commenced in the Faxton Hall building, and in May of the same year St. Patrick's Parochial School, which occupied a brick building on Columbia street, was placed in charge of the school commissioners. This building had originally been built by the city and sold to the parish. It was now leased to the city without rent for seven years.

In 1878, the Court street school was enlarged to twice its original size. In 1879, the Lansing street school was also enlarged. In 1880, a new school building was erected on the corner of James and Kemble streets.

The rapid growth of East Utica demanded a new school building in that area and a site was purchased in 1879, extending from Blandina to Mary streets near Jefferson avenue. A small wooden building moved from Lansing street served temporarily as a primary school and in 1881, a brick structure replaced the old wooden one.

In 1888, the old landmark, known as the Washington street school, which was first erected as a church and later converted into a school was sold and a new structure on Whitesboro street was erected by brick, with brownstone and moulded trimmings.

There were a number of private and parochial schools in Utica during the century. The Academy of the Assumption, at the corner of John and Elizabeth streets, conducted by the Brothers of the Christian Schools, educated the boys. The girls were taught by the Sisters of Charity, first in their orphanage on John street, and later on Burnet street. In August 1860, Timothy Cronin drew plans for a new Catholic school house on Burnet street in the rear of the orphanage. This in later years was known as Utica Catholic Academy. It was first known as "St. John's Select and Free School". The "Utica Daily Observer" of April 13, 1861 gave a complete description of the building, from which we note the following:

"The walls are two feet in thickness at the base and eighteen inches in the upper part. The building is 48 by 70 feet, and fifty feet in height. The front entrance is very wide, and the heavy doors are three inches in thickness. As you go through the front entrance, you enter a wide, pleasant hall, with rooms on either side, which measure 24 by 40 feet wide, and are fourteen feet high. These rooms are lighted by large windows, which have double architraves, with flaring jams and sills. These are to be the school rooms, and here from four to five hundred girls will be taught daily. Two verandahs, upper and lower, run along on the back side of the building. Two staircases lead from the hall to the story above. This story is twenty feet from floor to ceiling and will make a hall ranking with the leading public halls of the city. It is the intention of Sister Perpetua, Superior of the Catholic Orphan Asylum, to place in this story two panel partitions, thus dividing the hall into three class rooms. In one of these the older scholars will be taught various accomplishments. The partition can be removed, whenever occasion requires, and the three rooms open into one, in which public meetings may be held or exhibitions take place."

There were St. Joseph's (German) School for Boys and St. Joseph's School for Girls, each conducted in a building at No. 135 Fayette street. St. Patrick's School for both boys and girls, was taught by the Franciscan Sisters at 87 Columbia street, near the church, until it was taken over by the city in 1869.

There was a German Lutheran School conducted in the basement of the Lutheran Church until 1871 and a German Moravian School in the church on Cooper street from 1862 to 1870. In 1866, the Grace Church Parochial School for girls, known as the Ken Institute in 1868 was first conducted in the Chapel of Grace Church.

A German Free School was organized on December 23, 1867, and the classes were held in a building on Whitesboro street. About 1871, St. Luke's Church Parish School was opened on Hamilton street, on the corner of Columbia, for boys and girls.

The private, non-sectarian schools included the Utica Female Academy at No. 77 Washington street (chartered April 28, 1837). This building was burned on March 27, 1865 in a most spectacular fire. It was replaced with a new building in 1869-70 at a cost of $75,000. This was one of the finest structures in the State and the school was widely acclaimed for its educational faculty. It was long known as the "Balliol School", a boarding as well as a day school for the young ladies of Utica and vicinity. In its latter days, it was commonly known as "Miss Piatt's School".

The Utica Business College was opened in 1863 by C. A. Walworth, who conducted the school in the Butterfield (Gardner) Block, under the firm name of Bryant, Stratton & Walworth. The aim of the institution was to equip young men and women for employment in the business world. It specialized in bookkeeping, penmanship, business arithmetic, commercial law, stenography, telegraphy, etc.

There was also a Classical and Commercial School conducted by J. Williams at No. 6 Blandina Street. Among the others were: James Lombard's Private School at 230-32 Genesee street; a French & English Boarding and Day School at 19 Court street conducted by Miss Mary Tobin; a Ladies Board and Day School, conducted by Miss Caroline Backus, at 49 West Bridge street (Park Avenue); a Young Ladies High School, by Miss Harriett R. Downer, at 31 Whitesboro street; Miss Goodrich's Private School at 40 Court street, for boys and girls; the Misses Mott Private School for Girls at 5 Clark Place; Miss Collins' Private School, at 2 Faxton street; Miss Gibson's Grammar School for Boys at 85 Hart street, later at 69 Cornelia street; and Miss Gillmore's Private School for Boys and Girls, at 62 Broad street.

THE BUTTERFIELD HOUSE
1868-1911

NEXT to Bagg's Hotel, the Butterfield House possessed more nostalgic memories than any hotel within the city. It had no rival in fine appointments outside of New York city. It was a project of John Butterfield. He not only erected the Butterfield House, but also the handsome building on the southwest corner of Genesee and Columbia streets, originally called the Butterfield Block. It was later know as the Gardner Block, razed in 1974 as the site of the new Sheraton Hotel.

In the early days of Utica, when Genesee street made little pretense of becoming a business thoroughfare, the Butterfield House site consisted of beautiful rolling lawns, intersected by sweeping, well-kept driveways which ran between majestic rows of trees to a handsome old manor house. This was known as the Van Rensselaer estate, later owned and occupied by Nicholas Devereux. During a time of financial stress, he divided the estate into building lots and intersected it with streets, one of which was named in his honor. Mr. Devereux removed to a home at Chancellor Square where he died December 29, 1855.

On the corner of Genesee and Elizabeth streets, on the site now occupied by Grace Church, stood the Eagle Tavern. Just south was a two-story brick residence, and on the corner of Devereux and Genesee was located a store. In the 1840's, Amos Scranton occupied a small frame dwelling next to the Eagle Tavern, and also conducted a grocery business in the store on the corner of Devereux.

These buildings were razed in 1866 and Butterfield engaged Azel J. Lathrop, the architect to design a model hotel. It was completed and opened in July 1868. It was a four-story building, with stores on the ground floor, two on each side of the main entrance on Genesee street, and two more on the Devereux street side. An arched ground passage way connected from about the middle of the building on Devereux street with the rear of the stores. This was used for the entrance of carts and wagons.

The basement was divided into a barber shop, cigar stand, and a telegraphic office. The Butterfield barber shop, like many others in the city, had bathtubs where the more fastidious might bathe for a price. There were three tubs adjoining the shop. The barber shop at the turn of the century was considered the ritziest in town and contained six barber chairs, with barbers who collected fifteen cents for a shave and twenty-five for a hair cut. The steady customers had their own mugs and many had individual razors and brushes. The mugs arranged in a wall cabinet were decorated with names in gold letters and fancy insignia.

On the first floor was the office, a Gentlemen's reception room and the Reading room. The main entrace of the hotel was in the middle of the building on Genesee street and access to the upper story was by means of a circular stairway starting from the center of the building. It was well lighted by a skylight in the last story. The whole building was surmounted in the center by a tower, in the French style of architecture.

The original cost of the site and hotel was $175,000 and about $100,000 was later expended in additions and improvements. Despite the fact that it could accommodate several hundred guests, was elaborately furnished and had a spendid cuisine, the hotel was never a profitable operation.

During the 1870s nearly all of the exclusive social functions were held there and famous persons inscribed their names on its register. During a presidential campaign, Ulysses S. Grant visited Utica and from the balcony viewed a monstrous political parade, flanked by Utica's Senator Roscoe Conkling. President Grover Cleveland also paid a visit with his wife, and thousands of persons thronged the corridors of the hotel, all eager to shake hands with the President.

On the death of the owner, John Butterfield, the property passed to Mrs. Butterfield and Mrs. William M. Storrs. Upon Mrs. Butterfield's demise, Mrs. Storrs became the sole owner. John A. Roberts purchased the building and demolished it in 1911 and errected the famous John A. Roberts Dry Goods Store and in the spring in 1929, the J. B. Wells & Son Company relocated there from lower Genesee street.

THOMAS REDFIELD PROCTOR AND BAGG'S HOTEL
1869-1890

THOMAS Redfield Proctor, a leading citizen of Utica during his lifetime and perhaps its greatest benefactor, was born in Proctorsville, Vermont on May 25, 1844, a son of Moody S. and Betsy Nancy Redfield Proctor. His great grandfather, Leonard Proctor, a soldier in the Revolutionary War and a descendant of Robert Proctor, who settled at Concord, Massachusetts, as early as 1645, founded Proctorsville.

As a young man, Thomas Proctor enlisted in the Navy during the Civil War and was paymaster's clerk on the ship "Brandywine" of the North Atlantic Squadron, and was later transferred to and became secretary to Admiral Pearson, of the Pacific Squadron aboard the warship "Lancaster". With the end of the war, he returned to Proctorsville to manage the family business. After a year or two there, he went to Nyack, New York, and became the proprietor of the Tappan Zee House. Becoming proficient in the business of hotel management, at the age of 25, he came to Utica and purchased Bagg's Hotel.

From 1865 to 1869, James A. Southworth operated Bagg's Hotel. In May 1866, he decided to have a picture taken of the hotel to ornament his billheads and bills of fare. The Civil War had produced great improvement in photography and Mr. J. B. Smith was conducting Smith's Gallery of Art in the Marble Block of 56 Genesee street. The "Utica Morning Herald" gave this description of the taking of the picture:

> "To give the picture life and naturalness too, dashing equipages lined the curb-stones, express and baggage wagons (including Bill Dunn's mules) stood at the door; a busy populace swarmed upon the sidewalks; a small boot-black brigade were on duty in the square; and last, but not least, a worthy ex-Alderman occupied his usual, sunny position at the corner of the hotel. With affairs in this shape and a demure expression on the countenance of all, (including Dunn's mules), the sable cloth, which hitherto covered the lens of the instrument, in Bagg's Square, was removed, and, as we should say from the

negative we have seen at the establishment of Mr. J. B. Smith, one of the best and most perfect of pictures was taken. This accomplished, the dashing equipages, and the baggage and express wagons (and the mules) and the busy populace, and the boot-black brigade, etc., was allowed to move away to give room for a more paying crowd."

President Andrew Johnson came to Utica on August 31, 1866 accompanied by General Ulysses S. Grant and Secretary of State William H. Seward. A platform was erected on the north line of Whitesboro and Main streets and the President delivered an address. In 1867, David McClasky, of Albany, purchased an interest in the business and the hotel was conducted under the name of Southworth and McClasky.

When Thomas R. Proctor took over the hotel in 1869, he made such improvements that the old hotel took on new life. The "Utica Daily Observer" in 1872 commented:

"The rooms of the old hotel were comparatively comfortable, but the old fashioned style of wall paper with a border twelve inches wide, and beds so high that one could not climb into them without the aid of a chair, and wash-stands as big as one's head, were peculiar to them. Old guests who have visited Utica within the past four years are completely turned around upon being shown into the house now-a-days, but turn which way they will they cannot but remark the wonderful improvements made in the old house."

In 1890, Thomas Proctor gave up the hotel business and thereafter devoted himself to finance. On April 9th, 1891, he married Miss Maria Watson Williams, a daughter of Mrs. James Watson Williams, of Utica. A great sorrow befell the couple when their only son died in infancy.

Mr. Proctor died on July 4, 1920, and the "Saturday Globe" wrote:

"Utica has lost him, but to no man stands a more lasting memorial than the splendid parks which Mr. Proctor gave to the city. They are the people's own, forever consecrated to their use, a heritage to the thousands who will come after us when our brief stay is ended. Mr. Proctor visioned the future. He saw not only the city that was, but the city that was to be, and it was for the city of the future that he sought to provide."

THE VELOCIPEDE MAKES ITS APPEARANCE
1869

THE first cycle with pedals was produced in 1863 by Pierre Michaux in Paris. It was a monstrous affair made of wood. The large wheel in front on which the rider was perched and which furnished the motive power was in sharp contrast to the little wheel in the rear. The craze captured New York City in December 1868 and on February 18th, 1869, the "Morning Herald" reported:

> "The city was excited yesterday by the appearance upon the streets of several gentlemen mounted upon the sensation vehicle of 1869 — the velocipede. The riders were in most cases adepts and therefore met with few accidents. Occasionally, however, even the teachers of the art would turn too short a corner and lay broadside upon the sidewalk and then, of course, the crowd would laugh. These smiling men were several times invited to mount the iron horse themselves and see if they could do better. Of course, they refused. The greatest amusement, however, enjoyed in the evening at City and Concert Halls. Both of these places were almost filled with people anxious to see the great novelty. The teachers were willing to show how the thing was done and they found many anxious learners. Adepts in the art would make the circuit of the halls with the greatest speed, their legs working up and down with the regularity and even greater speed than the pistons of a steam engine. The sport was enjoyed until a late hour. Velocipedes will be the talk for the next month."

The velocipede craze reached such proportions through the city that the "Utica Observer" of May 19, 1869 reported that the City Fathers were considering an ordinance banning the vehicles from city streets since they had received many complaints that youngsters "made the sidewalks" on our back streets fairly dangerous to pedestrians; fences have been broken, steps have been mutilated; gates have been torn down from their hinges; horse blocks have been displaced, trees have been 'barked' and a very general havoc has been created by the boys and the bicycles.

THE OLD TOBACCO FACTORY ON WEST STREET
1869

UNTIL recent times, one of the landmarks of Utica was a dilapidated looking four story wooden structure on the east side of West street, just above Johnson Park — a building that was familiar to thousands of Corn Hill residents. It was successively a tobacco factory, a cigarette factory, a bed spring factory, and the headquarters for the manufacture of paste.

About 1869, Walter V. and William B. Pierce erected the building for a tobacco factory, when Utica was a leading tobacco manufacturing town. They had carried on a chewing tobacco business for some years on Bleecker street, opposite the site of the old Amphitheatre, later the site of the Colonial Theater. The history of the old building on West street was given in the "Observer-Dispatch" of June 21, 1925 and March 10, 1930:

> "R. M. Jones, of New York City, a man who had been connected for a number of years with the Sweet Caporal Cigarette Company, came to Utica and leased the building, installing machinery for the first cigarette factory upstate. This venture did not prove entirely profitable and continued but a few years when Charles Segar took over the building in 1871 and conducted a bed factory there. The Segar business was the forerunner of Foster Brothers Manufacturing Company of today. It became Segar & Foster, and later Foster Brothers, the business which started on a comparatively small scale in the old wooden structure, developing into one of the city's largest industries. In later years, the building was used by Tack Manufacturing Company, makers of paste and glue. This company failed a short time ago. Whether the structure will again figure in the city's industrial life to any great extent is doubtful."

In 1930, the structure was torn down by the American Adhesive Company and the land cut up into residential lots.

293

THE SAVINGS BANK OF UTICA — "THE IRON BANK"

1870

THE fathers of the savings bank system in the United States were the Devereux Brothers, John C. and Nicholas Devereux. At the time of the building of the Erie Canal, there were no savings banks in the country, only commercial banks. The Irish laborers distrusted these banks and deposited their savings with the Devereux firm, which invested it and paid regular dividends. A charter for the Savings Bank of Utica was granted in 1821 but it was not put into effect because of the completion of the canal. On July 22, 1839, a second charter was granted and the Savings Bank of Utica opened in the office of John & Nicholas Devereux on Bleecker street. The small banking business had grown by 1851 to the extent that the building occupied by John P. Marchisi on the east side of Genesee street just south of Bleecker was purchased.

On June 28, 1869, the Savings Bank sold this property to John Carton and engaged Azel Lathrop to design a new bank building on the southwest corner of Genesee and Lafayette streets. This was constructed with an iron facade painted white, to give the impression of a marble structure, but the public seized on the name of "The Iron Bank" as symbolical of the strength and stability of the banking institution.

On May 1, 1870, the new building was occupied by the bank and served as such until 1898, when a new site on Genesee street at what was later to become Bank Place was purchased. This site contained one of the historic mansions of Utica, the Alexander B. Johnson home, which was demolished. R. W. Gibson, of New York city designed the new "Bank With the Gold Dome" in the European Baroque style of architecture, which was popular at that time. When it was completed, the Savings Bank in 1900 moved into the new building, and the old building at Genesee and Lafayette streets was taken over by the Utica Trust & Deposit Company.

ICE HARVESTING IN UTICA
1870-1900

IN the early days, ice was harvested from the Mohawk river and the Erie canal. The pioneer was a man named James Fay who was succeeded by Hugh Hamilton and afterward by the firm of Marquise and Roberts. The ice business was operated on a small scale in the 1850s with four one-horse wagons distributing the ice to homes and businesses. This changed when the firm of Quinn & O'Hara was organized in 1856.

Thomas A. Quinn was born in Utica on December 2, 1829. He learned the trade of molder and was employed by various factories for some years. In 1854 he began the ice business and in 1856 was joined by Patrick O'Hara to form Quinn & O'Hara, which continued for forty-four years until Quinn's death on December 27, 1898.

Patrick O'Hara was born in 1832, the son of Patrick and Mary O'Hara on a farm in the town of Schuyler, Herkimer county. He came to Utica as a young man and opened a grocery store in West Utica. He married Mary Quinn, a sister of Thomas A. Quinn. He died on December 2, 1892. His son, Thomas A. O'Hara was born in Utica on April 16, 1851 and conducted a dry goods business in the Arcade for some years. When his father died, he took over his father's interest in Quinn & O'Hara and on the death of Mr. Quinn continued the business alone until the organization of the Utica Ice Company in 1906. He retired from the company in 1908 because of ill health and died April 3, 1914.

Quinn & O'Hara at first took their ice from the Mohawk and the Erie. About 1870, they began to cut ice on the reservoir. When Mr. Quinn started the business, he realized that ice in order to be kept at all must be stored underground and he went to work with a crew of men making excavations in the side of the "Gulf" on Third avenue. He erected an ice house, 30 by 80 feet and 16 feet high. From this small beginning the firm built up a total of 14 ice houses and handled about 25,000 tons of ice annually. The harvest of 1890 was described by the "Utica Daily Observer" on December 31, 1890:

"The ice harvest has commenced in earnest, and an "Observer" reporter went to the distributing reservoir near the head of Mohawk street where Quinn & O'Hara commenced yesterday to cut their annual crop of ice, with a force of about 150 men and 50 teams.

"Quinn & O'Hara have cut ice off the reservoirs about 20 years. It requires much work to clean and scrape the snow off the reservoir. The ice is now 12 to 14 inches thick, and as clear as crystal. After the ice was scraped clean, a straight line was drawn across the north side of the reservoir. A marker drawn by a horse was then put on. One blade is set in the slot marked out, and just 22 inches away and parallel with it is a blade with teeth which make a line parallel with the first, and so the ice is marked, both ways, in blocks 22 inches square. This is followed by an ice cutter or plow, which is a single bladed arrangement with teeth, which is drawn along the lines already laid out by the marker and cuts them as deep as about half the thickness of the ice. As about 500 tons are taken out in a day, there was a large space of clear water today where the ice was taken yesterday; and several teams employed in scraping, cutting, etc. work quite close to the edge with no danger.

"After the ice is cut half its depth the men split off rows of two blocks wide across the open space by driving iron bars with a wedge on one end into the cracks. It easily separates, while other men with long poles having iron hooks and points at the ends push the large cakes along in the water to the west side of the reservoir, where there is an inclined plane or chute which runs up to a loading platform. At the entrance of this chute the large rows of ice are split apart into blocks of ten cakes each, and these are hooked by tongs and horses draw them up to the platform. The teams are loaded two at a time from the platform. The teamsters have a stint of seven loads a day, and average from two to two and one-half tons each load.

"Quinn & O'Hara have four ice houses on Third street, near Rutger, four on Bleecker street and four on Mohawk street."

About 1920, mechanical refrigeration came into use and natural ice harvesting discontinued about 1950 and shortly thereafter the huge ice conveyors at the old site adjacent to the Pleasant street reservoir were dismantled.

THE BEGINNING OF AN ITALIAN COLONY IN UTICA
1870

JEAN Baptiste Marchisi was the only Italian resident of Utica for the first half of the nineteenth century. Prior to the Civil War he was joined by Alessandro Lucca, commonly called "Johnny Lucas" by the residents. He was born in Tuscany about 1820. By trade he was an image maker who went to England and married Margaret, a young woman born in Germany. They came to Canada and at the age of 33, "Johnny Lucas" arrived in Utica. The "Utica Saturday Globe" wrote in 1911:

> "A stranded canal boat, no longer fit for service was docked near the Clay street bridge and in this hulk of the Erie, the first Italian immigrants made their temporary home. An ambition to work and get ahead is the dominant trait of Italian character and Lucas immediately set forth to win bread for his family. He was a man with a talent for art and in a little while after his arrival, he began to vend plaster of Paris statues through the streets and soon his busts of Dante, Shakespeare, Napoleon and copies of the famous masters began to appear in many of the homes of the city.
>
> "Lucas made a little money and soon abandoned the canal boat and lived in a small shack on the towpath. Vending statuary was a precarious business at best. This thrifty Italian saved his small earnings and it was not long before he was running a grocery and saloon on Clay street."

In 1860, Lucas became a naturalized citizen, and in time a few other Italian immigrants arrived in Utica, including Elia Pellettieri in 1865, followed by his brothers, Salvatore in 1867 and Achille in 1869. Elia married Lucas' daughter, Margaret, and upon Johnny's death on December 12, 1874, took over the grocery and saloon, which became the principal gathering place of the dozen or more Italian newcomers.

The Pellettieri brothers were born in Laurenzana, Italy. They were: Elia, born in 1848 (Died May 1, 1910); Salvatore, born in 1858 (died October 10, 1921); Achille, born in 1851 (died January 19, 1931); and Michael, born in 1841 (died

297

September 12, 1923). Elia conducted the store on Clay street and invested his money in real estate, retiring in 1905.

Salvatore learned to play the violin and at the age of ten was earning his living as a street musician in Utica. In 1870 he went West and played for three years on the Mississippi river steamboats. He returned to Italy in 1878 and was conscripted into the Italian army. In 1881 he returned to Utica and worked in a furniture factory here. In 1886 he opened a grocery store on Kossuth avenue which he conducted for fourteen years, selling out to his nephew, Rocco Peretta & Co. in 1900. He then went into the liquor business on Nichols street and in 1902 established a furniture business on Bleecker street. He was an acknowledged leader of his ethnic group and organized and was the first president of *Progresso di Aiuto*. At the beginning of the twentieth century when the Italians began to outnumber the Irish in the old Fifth Ward, he was elected alderman in 1908-09 and 1911-12. After his death, Morehead street was changed in 1925 to Pellettieri Avenue under Mayor Frederick Gillmore.

During the 1870s, a few more Italians settled here, but it was not until 1883, when the West Shore Railroad began to build through Utica, that large numbers came to work as laborers. By 1890, the Italian population reached 500. Most of them worked as laborers in the brickyards and on construction work for small wages, carrying their picks and shovels over their shoulders. Many of them deposited their small savings at the Savings Bank of Utica, then located at the southwest corner of Genesee and Lafayette street. They would stop and chat with Achille ("Frank") Pellettieri, who operated a peanut stand on that corner. In 1912, when the old "iron bank" was to be razed by the new owner, the Utica Trust & Deposit Company, and the peanut stand had to be removed, the "Utica Sunday Tribune" wrote:

> "Probably there is not one thing in Utica that is more familiar to persons of all ages than the weather-beaten stand with its peanut roaster and shelves of jars containing candy, and its quiet proprietor, half-sheltered from the wind and rain between the end of his establishment and the steps of the bank.

> "It was more than 30 years ago that Frank sought permission to erect a stand on the corner. The Savings Bank of Utica then occupied the building, which was comparatively new and regarded as one of the best buildings in the city. The bank owned the corner, but did not occupy the entire lot for the reason that the building was

curved and on the unoccupied point Frank was permitted to set up his business. In return for the privilege he was to sweep the sidewalk in summer and shovel off the snow in winter. In addition he became the official English-Italian interpreter for the bank and when his countrymen had difficulty in making themselves understood by the bank clerks, Frank was always at hand to make their meaning clear."

Father Antonio Castelli was born in Ausonia, Italy, in the year 1829, was ordained a priest in 1854, and came to Utica in 1884 as a chaplain for St. Vincent's Industrial School and an assistant to Monsignor Lynch at old St. John's church. Monsignor Lynch gave him the use of an old school building on Catharine street owned by the church for holding services for the little Italian colony. On July 24, 1895, the church of St. Maria di Monte Carmelo was incorporated by Father Castelli, Salvatore Pellettieri and Antonio Sisti and on August 3, 1895, a lot was secured extending from Catharine to Jay streets and plans were made to build a church. Funds were scarce and when the basement was completed Mass was first held there on December 20, 1896.

The church of Our Lady of Mount Carmel was completed and opened on June 29, 1902. Father Joseph Formia was sent as an assistant at Mount Carmel and after Father Castelli's death in 1903 at the age of 74, Father Formia, a member of the Scalabrini Missionaries, became the pastor and under his direction, a school was established in 1904.

By 1905, the Italian population of Utica had reached upwards of 10,000, roughly one-sixth of the total population of the city. The "Utica Daily Press" on April 8, 1905 reported extensively on the "Italian Colony", including the following:

"Considering their number in this city the Italians are well represented in the learned professions. One of their leading physicians is Dr. Francesco Giovanni Rossi of 644 Bleecker street. Dr. Rossi was born March 8, 1874. He was educated in the University of Naples, from which institution he graduated in August 1901, in medicine and surgery. Another Italian doctor is Dr. F. Palmieri of 143 Jay street. Dr. Palmieri is also a graduate of Naples University. There is one Italian dentist, Dr. F. P. Cavallo.

"What is the employment of the Italians? The majority are day laborers and the next largest number are employed in the cotton mills. But there are about as many mechanics as among most nationalities. From three to four hundred are at work in the tailor shops, the largest two shops being conducted by Frank Brendes and Victor Pietrafese. Over a hundred are employed in the two macaroni factories. There is one ladies' tailor, who is classed as the Worth of Utica. Of the barber shops there are at least ten, with two to five chairs each. Time was when there were more employed as cooks in hotels than at present. As cooks Italians and those from the Italian canton of Switzerland rank among the best in the world. There are in this city some shoemakers and some machinists. The two Italian newspapers are set by Italian compositors. There are some hat makers and also some masons, stone cutters and carpenters and cabinet makers. There is one quite skilled wood carver and chairmaker."

The two Italian language newspapers mentioned were "L'Av Venire" (1904-07) and "La Luce" (1904).

Adolph Capecelatro was born in Naples on November 16, 1870, of the Roman aristocracy, tracing to the patrician house of Capicius, with the title of Marquis of Santo Mauro. He studied law at the University of Naples, and was employed for fifteen years in the editorial rooms of the "Naples Courier". He came to Utica in 1906 as office manager for Marrone & Lofaro. In 1913, he started "Il Pensiero Italiano" (Italian Thought), as editor and publisher. It was printed in English and Italian, "to help preserve the ideals and sacred traditions of this, our adopted country." In January 1917, "La Luce" and "Il Pensiero" were merged and under his guidance continued to be a powerful influence in the community. Mr. Capecelatro died on October 13, 1932.

SAINT VINCENT'S ORPHAN ASYLUM
1870

FOR many years, the Catholic citizens of Utica realized the growing necessity of providing for the moral care, education and physical well being of the many orphan boys who were scattered about in various parts of the city. To meet the temporary needs of the situation, the Brothers of the Christian Schools set apart a portion of the Assumption Academy on the corner of John and Elizabeth streets to receive and care for the orphan boys. The building was never intended for such purpose, and the increase in the number of boys during the Civil War years compelled them to consider an Asylum for the exclusive use of the orphan boys.

A valuable piece of property on Rutger street was purchased, five acres in extent, fronting on Rutger street, bounded by Taylor avenue, Third and South streets, It was built of brick, in the French style, two stories in height, exclusive of the basement and an attic formed by the Manard roof. The plans were made by Metcalf & Dering.

In 1876 the name was changed to St. Vincent's Protectorate and in 1885 as St. Vincent's Industrial School. A fifty acre farm adjoining furnished milk and vegetables for the school. The institution also featured an excellent drum corps of sixty pieces and two cadet companies. Professor England of the old Utica Band was in charge of the music and Captain Charles Howe, G.A.R. of the cadets.

THE NEW COUNTY CLERK'S OFFICE
1871

THE office of the Clerk of Oneida County was located for many years prior to 1871 in a little one-story building just south of the City Hall on Genesee street. The Board of Supervisors in 1870 decided that a more suitable building was required to house the deeds and records of the County. Mr. Azel J. Lathrop was asked to prepare plans for a new building on the site. In June 1870, the archives of the county were temporarily removed to the John Street Court House and the old building was torn down. The new building was built of brick, with iron girders, floors and staircases, to make it fireproof. It was four stories in height, including the Mansard roof.

The second story was reached at the northern end of the building by means of an iron staircase. In the second story, the two front rooms each 24 feet wide, were for the use of the Sheriff and the County Judge. In the rear was the Supervisor's Chamber, with a raised platform for the Chairman. The "Utica Observer" of September 21, 1871 in describing the new building wrote:

> "Eight large desks and a sufficient number of tilting, pivot chairs will be provided for the portly Supervisors who control the affairs of our county. The lobby is large enough to accommodate all who wish to attend the meetings of the Board. In the rear of this room are three or four apartments for the use of the clerks and committees. The whole cost of this magnificent building will be about $50,000, and the money appears to have been judiciously expended. The new office will probably be open for business on Saturday of this week."

When the new County Court House was opened on the corner of Charlotte, Elizabeth and Mary streets in 1909, the Genesee street building was taken over by the Utica Gas & Electric and used as its office until 1927, when its six story building was erected on the corner of Genesee and Court streets in 1926.

In 1945 it was taken over by the Bank of Utica.

THE UTICA OPERA HOUSE
1871-1900

IN March 1870, the Mechanic's Association announced plans for a new "Opera House" to be erected on the northeast corner of Lafayette and Washington streets. The first floor was to be occupied by five stores. The entrance to the main stairway to the upstairs theater would be the first doors at the east end of the front of the building. The stairway, fifteen feet wide, ascended to the lobby with three doors opening from the lobby to the main hall. The "Opera House" was to be 70½ feet by 80 feet in size. The stage was to be 60 by 42½ feet on the west side, with a 43 foot proscenium. Boxes flanked the curtain. A magnificent prismatic chandelier with its one hundred jets shed a softened light over the whole of the auditorium. Almost seventeen hundred elegantly unholstered chairs were provided for the spectators.

The Opera House opened on October 16th, 1871 with a production, *Lady of Lyons* under the managership of N. C. Forrester, a native Utican. The "Utica Observer" the next evening wrote:

> "The audience was a remarkable one, comprised as it was of members of the families representing the wealth, beauty, fashion, intelligence and usefulness of our city. By the side of the gentlemen and ladies of wealth and leisure, sat the artisan and his wife and family, and each seemed interested in the event which brought them together. Nearly two thousand persons were seated within the walls of the new Opera House last evening; and from the time when the first notes of the fine orchestra, in a selection from Fra Diavolo, were heard, until the close of the entertainment, the closest attention was paid, and the best of order preserved."

The history of the Opera House was briefly related by Carroll T. Waldron in "A Hundred Years of Amusement in Utica" (1906):

> "The new playhouse was well attended from the start, refuting the prophesy volunteered by a visiting manager (probably from Syracuse), who, glancing over the ex-

303

panse of seats, remarked that 'not in a hundred years would the town be big enough to need a theater such as this.'

"One of the early attractions was Buffalo Bill and a company of cowboys and Indians in a howling frontier drama — *Scouts of the Prairies*. This was during the early days of Colonel Cody's fame as a delineator of the Wild West and could he spread on the blood and thunder with a lavish hand. In the words of a spectator, the 'play wiped out about a dozen Indians every night'. The feature of the show was a great prairie fire, made realistic by a fearsome panorama depicting a flame-driven plain, the effect of which was heightened by pans of red fire hidden here and there behind the artificial shubbery of the scene. The Indian slaughter occurred just prior to the conflagration and the sight of the great fire sweeping nearer and nearer until it played weirdly over the very forms and faces of the warriors strewn about, was a situation to startle the most phlegmatic spectator. But it is told of the play's Utica appearance that some thoughtful soul mixed a liberal quantity of red pepper with the red fire and the pepper sputtering about the stage, wrought havoc among the slain. One after another the dead Indians would raise their heads and sneeze. And not one sneeze apiece, but several, to say nothing of sundry moans, coughs and squirms. And one corpse, crawling to a clearer breathing space close to the footlights, stretched himself at full length and conscientiously died over again. Never had the scene created such a furore. The curtain was hurried down upon the most astonished and hilarious audience that Buffalo Bill and his little company had ever faced.

"There was another wrecked performance in 1873. The occasion was the engagement of Tomasso Salvini, the eminent Italian tragedian, in his portrayal of the Gladiator. His fame had spread before him and there gathered a great audience, representative of the cultured people of Central New York. Salvini made a lasting impression; but the performance itself ended in one of the most embarrasing fiascos a dramatic star ever had to endure.

"One of the powerful moments in the play shows an ancient amphitheatre with the Gladiator down in the arena, the cynosure of every eye among the concourse of noble Romans that fill the tiers upon tiers of surrounding seats. In Salvini' production the greater part of this vast audience was painted realistically upon a drop curtain, but in front of this sat several tiers of flesh and blood spectators. Supers (extras) to the number of thirty or forty were utilized for this scene, mounted upon a platform of graded height.

"Salvini had worked his Utica audience into a tension of breathless interest, the house in a pin-drop of quiet when suddenly there came a creaking and a splintering from the direction of the platform, followed by a stupendous crash as it collapsed to the stage with its mighty burden of Fifth Ward Romans. What had been a moment of dramatic intensity now offered a scene of the most ludicrous confusion. The supers, having expected nothing of this nature, acted as supers might be expected to act; and there, in the midst of the sheepish toga-torn crowd, raved the great Salvini, in no manner improving matters by his ill-concealed emotions. Minutes passed before the chaos of supers and scantlings had resolved itself from sight. The play had been marred beyond redemption and the audience withdrew with the fourth act unacted. As Salvini spoke only his native tongue, such words of blessing as he is reported to have showered upon the struggling young amateurs, and upon everyone else within hearing distance, are lost to posterity and perhaps 'tis better so.

"But kindly as were the sentiments surrounding the old house, Uticans finally came to consider it quite out of keeping with the city's advancement. Its long flight of stairs, tolerated by a past generation, were now (1900) climbed under protest. The theater's interior construction, with the rear seats almost beyond hearing and seeing distance of the stage, began to be termed 'barn-like'."

The last offering of the old Opera House was *The Christian* and with the lowering of the final curtain, cornetist George Smith arose in the orchestra pit and sounded "taps".

THE HOUSE OF THE GOOD SHEPHERD
1873

A meeting was held in the rectory of Trinity Episcopal Church in the winter of 1872-73 for the purpose of founding an institution for infirm and destitute children. Through the generosity of Mrs. Charlotte B. Crouse and others, a small tenement on Blandina street was rented and the House of the Good Shepherd was opened with two children. Within a week this increased to twelve and taxed the capacity of the small house. A subscription was taken up and a house was purchased on the corner of Bleecker and East streets (now Tilden Avenue) which was opened June 8th 1875. It was later enlarged with an infirmary, a school-room and a chapel. By 1891, there were about 45 children in attendance and it was deemed necessary to move to larger quarters. Through the generosity of Thomas R. Proctor and others, a site on upper Genesee street, now occupied by the Pin-O-Rama bowling alley was purchased and a large building erected. It was formally opened on September 29, 1904 and the "Daily Press" of September 2nd of that year described the new building:

> "The new building is on the west side of Genesee street, just above Pleasant, and stands in the center of a plot of land about 1200 feet square. It is in the shape of a letter E, of three buildings running parallel, connected at the front by a building running transversely. The center is the administration building, while the two wings are the girls' and boys' departments respectively. The frontage of the building is 180 feet, while the depth of the center wing is 107 feet. The building is in the Elizabethan or manor house style of architecture. The architects of the building were Messrs. F. H. Gouge and G. Edward Cooper. It is built of red brick, laid in white mortar with trimmings of Indiana limestone and roof of slate. The building is two stories high besides attic, but most of the center building is three stories high, and the rear part virtually four stories high. The floors are of riff grained Georgia pine, and the interior woodwork is of cypress with bronze trimmings."

Panorama View

Detail

This bridge, designed by Squire Whipple was considered an engineering marvel in its time. The platform was raised by means of counterweights. It was erected in 1874 and was removed when the Erie Canal was abandoned.

The "Whipple Bridge" 1851-1890. This picture was taken in 1888.

The "Hump" Bridge, 1891–1923

Genesee Street Bridge Over The Erie Canal

Squire Whipple, the father of American bridgebuilding designed the first iron bridge. When the trolley cars became electrified, it was necessary to replace this bridge.

View south from the Busy Corner, 1890

The Genesee Street Horse Car

THE DEVELOPMENT OF TRANSPORTATION, 1863–1900

The top photograph shows the old "Iron Bank" on the corner with the old horse car on the Lafayette street line. Heading in the opposite direction is the "new" trolley car.

Old Pine Block   1865

This picture of the west side of Genesee street was taken about 1865 from the corner of Elizabeth street. Note the gas light in front of the old Central Hotel on the east side of the street. At the intersection of Seneca street, in the triangle which is now a park stood the Pine Block. It was a wooden structure owned by John Mulholland, dry goods merchant. His store was in the center of the building. On the left John L. Dowd and his brother made and sold cigars. The building was demolished in 1881.

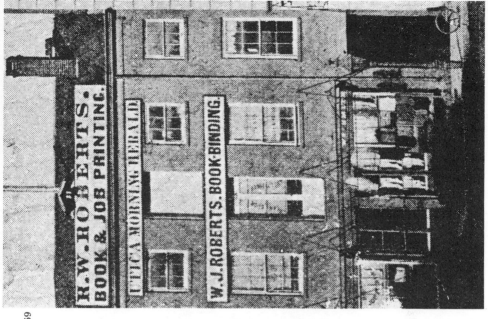

Utica Morning Herald 1869

Daily Newspapers
In the
19th Century

The Daily Observer was located on the east side of Genesee street, near the corner of Broad street. The store on the ground floor was occupied by Isaac Tiffany; books and stationery.

The Morning Herald was located on the west side of Genesee street, opposite Broad street. The building to the right was the Marble Block and the passageway between the buildings was the entrance to the City Garden.

Daily Observer c. 1869

St. Elizabeth — Columbia st. 1869

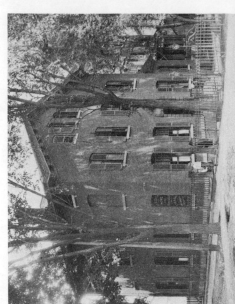

St. Luke's
Columbia st. 1870

Hospitals
In
Early
Utica

Faxton 1875

FAXTON HOSPITAL

City Hospital 1856

CITY HOSPITAL

St. John's Orphan Asylum 1853

House of the Good Shepherd 1875

Utica Orphan Asylum 1861

St. Joseph's Infant Home 1896

UTICA'S ORPHANAGES

Assumption Academy, John St., 1854–1932

St. Vincent's School,
Rutger St., 1870–1920

Utica Free Academy, Academy St., 1867–1899

PUBLIC &
PRIVATE SCHOOLS
19TH CENTURY

Advanced School,
Elizabeth St., 1847–1940s

Female Academy, Washington St., 1867-1908

NY State Armory — Bleecker street
1862-1890

City Library
Elizabeth street
1870-1904

YMCA
Bleecker street
1889-1907

Social Buildings of
Old Utica

Washington Hall   1822

Washington Hall and City Hall

   Washington Hall was erected in 1822 as Utica's first office building. Here in the early days were the offices of most of Utica's business and political leaders. Horatio Seymour's office was on the ground floor to the right where the bay window is located.

   City Hall on Genesee street was built by William Jones in 1853 and contained city offices on the first floor, the Federal Court on the second and a large hall on the third.

City Hall   1853

Court House — John street, 1852–1909

County Jail
Mohawk Street
1853-1883

Utica Police Force in 1893 in front of Police Station

Fire Apparatus in front of Engine House No. 2
on John street opposite St. John's Church
1900

Utica's Finest in the 19th Century

The police station on the corner of Pearl and Washington streets was erected in 1877 and was in use until 1928. Engine House No. 2 on John street was erected in 1874 and was in use until 1911.

Chancellor Park

Johnson Park

Steuben Park

FOUNTAINS

In 1875, Utica had three parks where its citizens might sit and gossip and enjoy the scenery: Chancellor Park (1811), Steuben Park (1827), and Johnson Park (1849). Mayor Charles W. Hutchinson decided to add these handsome fountains.

Postcards showing these fountains are collector's items today.

Liberty street about 1910. The gable-roofed building at center right is "Mechanics Hall".

Interior of Opera House, 1870-1900 taken from balcony.

Utica Park   Sept. 1903

Bicycles   1887

Utica Curling Club   1890

Sports and Recreation in the
19th Century

Utica Park was opened to the public in 1891 and located three miles from the center of Utica. It was a popular resort, with picnic grounds, a dance pavilion and other attractions. The name was changed to Forest Park in 1925 and closed permanently in 1934. The gentlemen with their bicycles are the Hammes Brothers. Philip C., Fred P. and Peter, of West Utica, were famous bicyclists of the era. The Curling Club building was in the East Utica Gulf just below the viaduct.

CARTON HALL — 1870

THE PAID FIRE DEPARTMENT
1874

THE volunteer fire companies of Utica exercised the prerogative of electing their own Chief Engineer. For a number of years prior to 1874, Wesley Dimbleby had been a very capable administrator who enjoyed the respect of the firemen. Among the many improvements he suggested was the building of a hose depot. Hose when cleaned and left flat on the ground or in reels at the various fire stations, tended to rot.

In 1868, the city opened the Hose Depot on Cooper street, one door west of the Moravian church on the corner of Cornelia street. It contained a vat in the first floor in which the hose could be soaked and cleaned before being mended and oiled. Hose that simply required a slight cleaning was washed on the floor, which was constructed so as to slant from both sides to a gutter which ran directly through the center of the floor, allowing water to be carried off.

In the rear of this room was a tower between fifty and sixty feet in height. After the hose was washed, it was hoisted to the top of the tower and hung, in fifty foot lengths, to dry. When the hose was properly dried, it was conveyed from the tower to the work room in the second story where it was mended and oiled.

On March 10, 1874, a newly elected Common Council removed Dimbleby and replaced him with its own political appointee. The fire companies announced that they were withdrawing from service and the "Morning Herald" on March 17th announced:

> "Thus it transpires that Utica today is without a fire department."

Such a situation aroused the property owners and business men, who petitioned the Legislature to establish a Police and Fire Commission for Utica, which would be independent of the Common Council. This bill was adopted and on June 1, 1874, the new commission established a paid fire department, consisting of four steamer and hose companies and a single ladder company. It appointed Dimbleby as chief engineer, a position he held with great competence until May 5,

1899, when he was appointed to the newly created position of Fire Marshal. He served as such until his death on January 14, 1903.

In early Utica's history, church bells were used to raise an alarm of fire. When the City Hall was erected, the janitor was required to climb to the tower and toll the bell. This was a slow and not always accurate process, since the janitor had to know the location of the fire in order to toll the bell the same number of times which corresponded to the ward wherein it occurred. The janitor had to rely upon a report brought to him or climb the tower and look out the windows.

In June 1878, an alarm system was completed by Messrs. Barber, Palmer & Jones. Thirty boxes were placed at various street intersections. Keys to the boxes were given to police and firemen and left at prominent places near the boxes. To send an alarm the holder of the key could turn the knob in the inner door of the box, which would transmit the signal to the police station and the steamer houses. In addition, a sledge-shaped hammer was attached to the City Hall bell. The "Utica Observer" of December 23, 1878 described the new system:

> "The Clapper of the Old Bell In The Grip of Electricity. The old system of sounding the alarm on the bell has been radically altered, and the change is one for the better. Hitherto the Janitor has been obliged to amble up six flights of steep stairs before he could reach the lever to sound the alarm of fire. The new alarm tele-graph of Barber, Palmer & Jones was last week attached to the bell, and hereafter the alarm will go direct from the boxes to the Police Station, and thence to the old iron-throated metal with electric strokes. The old clap-per remains in place as usual, and also continues under control of the lever as formerly. The power from the electric battery is concentrated on a sledge-shaped hammer that works on the outer rim of the bell. The janitor is an enthusiast on the subject of electricity, for it will save him much extra exertion in working the lever when the fire alarms are to be sounded."

POST STREET IN THE 19TH CENTURY

THE original location of the black residents in the pioneer days of Utica was at the eastern end of Main street and the little colony was called "Hayti". At that time the blacks were "hewers of wood and drawers of water." The men were employed in poling boats up the Mohawk River. One who was especially strong was Joseph Pancko, who had on his shoulders huge bunches of callouses where he set the end of the pole when he pushed the flat boat along. Others were employed as hostlers in the stage coach and livery stables, or acted as coachmen for the rich while the women worked in the laundry and kitchens of private homes, boarding houses and hotels.

In time, however, the property on Main street became too valuable as building sites for businesses and the cheapest land was south of the Erie Canal. On John Post's original purchase was a small lane running easterly from Charlotte street to Burnet street. Post street, as it was known, was through swampy land that had once been a pine forest. By the 1840s the trees had been cut but the stumps remained. History recounts that the blacks moved to Post street because

> "there they could grub from the ground the resin filled roots of the pines which made good kindlings which could be sold for a penny a bunch to the residents of Utica. Those were the days when wood was the only fuel and kindlings were in demand, for fires had to be built anew every morning." ("Daily Press", November 7, 1912).

The blacks who lived on Post street were poor but most owned the little houses in which they lived. They were a joyous people, who enjoyed music, singing and dancing.

> "There was Joe Pell, a man of giant frame and great strength, whose work by day was sawing wood and by night sawing on a fiddle. He played for dances almost every night. He was the soul of good nature and his laugh would be impossible to describe, but once heard it could never be forgotten. It was the heartiest, most vociferous laugh that ever welled up from a man's heart. The Lord had blessed him with a big family of boys, at least enough to form a baseball club, called 'The Fear-

less'. Like him they were musical. It was a social and musical neighborhood and at one time boasted of a full brass band. The street also boasted of quite a number of banjo players and the vocal music was even better. On summer evenings they filled the steps and you could sit all night and listen when the conditions were right" ("Daily Press").

The early efforts of the blacks to form religious societies had been sporadic and short-lived. During the Civil War when the numbers of ex-slaves from the South began to increase, the Rev. P. H. Fowler, then pastor of the First Presbyterian Church, took steps to establish a mission in the vicinity. He was aided by Theodore S. Faxton, Judge William J. Bacon and James Sayre, who raised funds to build a small chapel, which became known as Hope Chapel.

This little frame building, located on the north side of Elizabeth street, just east of the later erected Paul Building (originally built as a bakery by George Young) and opposite the Oneida County Court House, was in use until 1916 when its dilapidated condition made a new church edifice a necessity. Under the direction of Edward L. Wells, a lot, 60 by 150 feet, on Catharine street, between First and Second streets, the rear half of the Merritt Peckham property, was purchased for $2,000, and a brick chapel erected at a total cost of $8,500.

Post street was the enclave of the blacks during most of the 19th century, but by 1894, the encroachment of business buildings on Elizabeth street and the erection of livery stables and warehouses for the stores on Bleecker street caused a displacement of the blacks on Post street, leaving only 54 in six houses. In 1912, when the city took over the site on the corner of Elizabeth and Burnet streets for a Central Fire Station, Post street became entirely deserted as a place of residence.

THE UTICA SUNDAY TRIBUNE
1877

THE first Sunday newspaper in Utica was founded in May 1877. It had long been thought that people who considered Sunday as a day for religious observance and not worldly things would not accept the idea of a Sunday paper. The "Utica Sunday Tribune" was organized by Dennis T. Kelly, who learned the business in the office of the "Utica Observer". His partner was Thomas F. Baker, who was later to found the "Utica Saturday Globe". The first office of the "Tribune" was on the corner of Genesee street and Broad street and the first issue was May 6, 1877. It was a four page, seven column newspaper containing both telegraph and local news as well as syndicated articles of general interest.

In October 1877, Dennis T. Kelly disposed of his interest to his brother, Patrick E. Kelly, and commenced instead the "Utica Daily Republican", which continued for two years before surrendering the daily field. The office of the "Tribune" was moved in 1878 to the corner of Broad and John streets. Since there were few Sunday trains and none on the Rome and Watertown line nor on the D.L. & W., the "Tribune" ran a pony express Sunday mornings from Utica to Waterville. In the nineties, its circulation was between 7,000 and 8,000 copies.

On October 14, 1894, the "Sunday Journal" entered the competition with an eight page, six column paper, announcing "the 'Sunday Journal' will be Republican to the core." The "Journal" started on the fourth floor of the old Martin Building on Genesee street, with a small Cottrell press which could only print two pages at a time. On March 4, 1907, the Journal was bought by and absorbed into the Tribune Company.

THE AMERICAN DISTRICT TELEGRAPH
1877

THE "Utica Morning Herald" of August 18, 1877 reported a new form of communication in Utica:

"Utica's branch of the American District Telegraph Company's system will be open for messenger service today at No. 131 Genesee street over the Western Union Telegraph office and will remain open hereafter until midnight. Five messengers are now employed. They are provided with a neat uniform of indigo blue pants and jacket with cardinal cording and stripes, and a gold-plated button, a fatigue cap bearing 'A.D.T.' and the number of the messenger in varied characters. Superintendent Nightingale already has thirty boxes ready for operation in stores, factories, railroad depots and private houses, and several more are to be put in this week."

These call boxes were installed in homes and business places at a cost of $36 per year. An extra charge was made for each message transmitted. It was not a telephone in the sense that conversations could be carried on. The boxes were provided with cranks and depending upon the distance the crank was moved, the subscriber could call a uniformed messenger, a doctor, a policeman, or the fire department. The system worked rather well, except that occasionally the absent-minded subscriber would summon the firemen when he wanted a messenger, or a policeman when he wanted a doctor. The operation was soon moved to a ground floor office on Liberty street just west of the corner of Genesee. On November 21, 1877, the Utica newspapers reported that the Company had 52 boxes in operation, with eight miles of wire and the previous week had handled 210 calls, 46 of them from boxes.

When the centennial of American Independence was celebrated in Philadelphia in 1876, an interesting device called a "telephone" invented by Alexander Graham Bell was on display.

THE COMING OF THE TELEPHONE
1877-78

A pioneer in bringing the newly invented telephone to Utica was John Joseph Doyle, who was born in Manchester, England on May 3, 1850. He came to America at the age of nine, accompanied by an aunt, his parents having preceded him to Utica. The family lived at the corner of Hart and William streets and young John was educated at St. Patrick's school on Columbia street and at Assumption Academy.

He was interested in the fire department and became a volunteer with the Friendship Hook & Ladder Company at Oneida Square from 1868 to 1874. When the paid department was established, he became a stoker for Engine No. 1 at Oneida Square. He was often asked to assist E. K. Chubbuck in repairing the fire alarm telegraph system. In 1876, he attended the Philadelphia centennial exposition and saw the new "telephone" device in operation. He returned to Utica and sent to New York for one of the new instruments.

One day, Doyle's next door neighbor, General W. H. Christian told him that a New York company was offering telephones for sale and Mr. Doyle went there and obtained the agency and the right to use telephones in Oneida, Herkimer and Otsego counties. He returned to Utica and received from the Common Council a franchise to run telephone wires in the city. The first effort was to put a telephone in his own house and one in General Christian's house next door. The "Utica Morning Herald" of January 19, 1878 gave an account of the installation of the first commercial telephone in Utica from Young's Bakery on Bleecker street to Colonel George Young's house on Rutger street, by Christian & Doyle:

> "They have been quietly at work preparing to introduce the apparatus into Utica and their first patron was Colonel George Young, the enterprising baker. Yesterday, about 5 p.m., Colonel Young's residence on Rutger street was connected with his bakery on Bleecker street, seven or eight blocks or 2000 feet away. Agents Christian and Doyle handed the apparatus complete over to Colonel Young, who immediately opened business

313

communication with his establishment, as will be seen by the notice in another column. He has been suffering from lameness in the back for several days and unable to go down town. His bookkeeper received the messages quite readily, and then a reporter of the 'Herald' had a pleasant chat with Colonel Young. The telephone worked admirably, as clear as a whistle. The apparatus consists of a neat hardwood box about 12 by 5 inches, attached to the window casing. Within this box are the magnets for transmitting the vibrations from the diaphragm contained in the mouth and ear-piece. The latter is attached by flexible wires to the box. When communication is desired, a small battery is switched on to the wires, a crank is turned and the vibrating magnets ring two small call bells affixed to the face of the telephone box. After calling, the battery is detached, the party at the other end of the line answers through the telephone and conversation is kept up as long as desired. The simplicity of the invention astonishes everybody. Colonel Young is delighted with its operation, and would not part with it at any price. Now that he has introduced the telephone into Utica, there are many others who will probably follow suit."

When the first telephones were installed in Utica, there were no poles along the streets and all the wires had to be strung on the rooftops of the houses. The second telephone connected the coal office of W. E. Everts & Company on Genesee street at the bridge with the coal yard on Lafayette street near Varick. Another line was run to South street and another to Coakley's store in Albany street. No telephone company was organized, however, until some time later and then by other parties. Mr. Doyle was later employed as an engineer for the Utica Belt Line Railroad, having charge of the power house on Lincoln avenue, and then for the Utica Electric Light & Power Company, at its station on Cornelia street. He died on May 16, 1925.

The Western Union Telegraph Company, with which the local district telegraph company was affiliated, urged the local company to adopt the "Edison" telephone, which was done. As the number of subscribers increased, it became necessary to set up an exchange so that a person could talk with more than a single other person. This was established in the Arcade building. The first switchboards were primitive affairs and the process of making connections was slow. When a subscriber rang the exchange, it would cause a "drop" to fall in the central office. The boy there (there were no girls at first) would insert a plug in the switchboard and shout to a companion at the other side of the room that Mr. Jones wanted to talk to Mr. Smith. The second boy would insert another plug and push a button which would ring Mr. Smith's phone. At night the operator slept in the exchange and when a call came in the switchboard, it would ring a bell to awaken the operator, who would arise and make the connection.

It was not necessary to issue a catalogue of the first telephone subscribers. The score of names, more or less, were printed on cards and one of these was tacked on the wall beside the phone. There were no numbers. As time passed it appeared that a mistake had been made in adopting the Edison phone because the Bell company soon took the lead and in two years, the Edison telephone passed under the control of the American Bell Telephone Company and the Utica company became a subsidiary of that Company. From the Arcade, the exchange was moved to the Oneida National Bank on Genesee street and then to the telephone company building on Bleecker street, and the first telephone poles were erected on that street. In 1909, the Central New York Telephone & Telegraph Company was merged with the New York Telephone Company.

In April 1902, a new telephone company was organized in Utica for the purpose of forcing the Bell company to reduce its rates. This was called the Home Telephone Company and it erected a building on the south side of Elizabeth street, just east of Grace Church. The new company began operation on March 25, 1903. The 'Saturday Globe' of June 13, 1903 described the operation:

> "The general offices on the first floor, have the elegance of a banker's business apartments. Across the hall is the toll office, and in the rear are the testing board, the generators and the frame from which distribution of the wires is made. In the basement is a network of wires, about 7,000 of which enter the building, being part of the 7.274 miles of wire which the company owns.
>
> "On the second floor is the operating room, where 18 girls at the same time are at work on the switchboards. The switchboard contains 1,200,000 feet of copper wire, and has positions for 120 operators. There are 1,800 working telephones connected therewith. There are 35 operators, with three shifts. The 'information girl' ought to become popular. She tells you, if you call her up, who won the ball game; what the correct time is; whether or

not trains are late, and a thousand and one other things. She also wakes up railroad and commercial men with phones in their homes, who may ask to be called at any hour during the night."

The Home Telephone Company continued until March 1911, when it was absorbed into the Bell system since it couldn't successfully compete with the older company. In addition, most professional and business people had to install the phones of both companies. The old building was purchased in 1913 for the use of the Chamber of Commerce. In 1926, the company purchased the handsome Thomas Foster home on the southwest corner of Genesee street and Cornelia Place and on April 18, 1927 the colonial style building was opened as the exchange and office building for the company.

THE NEW CITY LIBRARY
1878

THE first dealer in books in Utica was George Richards, Jr., who, in November 1803, opened the Oneida Book Store on Bagg's Square adjoining Post & Hamlin's store. It is said that his store was a favorite spot for readers. There is some evidence that about that time there was a library called, "The Fort Schuyler Library," which may have been the one of which Judge Nathan Williams was librarian for some years.

In March 1825, a village library was incorporated and opened in July of that year. The books were kept in the office of Justus H. Rathbone, a lawyer, who acted as librarian. In 1834, the library was located in Knickerbocker Hall on Catharine street. The Mechanic's Association established a library in Mechanic's Hall. On December 7, 1852, the Young Men's Association was organized and a library and reading room opened. The city library was taken over by the School

Board in 1842. It was located on Franklin Square over the Central New York Bank. Francis D. Grosvenor was the librarian.

In 1856, the City Library was removed to the City Hall and remained there for more than twenty years. In July 1878, a new building was erected on the north side of Elizabeth street between Genesee and Charlotte streets for the combined use of the School Board and City Library.

The library proper was an annex situated at the rear of the main building. It was 40 by 60 feet and 47 feet to the apex of the roof. It was lighted by side and clerestory windows. It contained a gallery supported by iron brackets and reached by an iron stairway. The windows were fitted with iron shutters, while double iron doors shut it off completely from the main building.

In 1893, the library was transferred from the jurisdiction of the School Board and a Library Board of Trustees was organized to administer the affairs of the library.

THE CITY HALL OPERA HOUSE
1879 - 1895

FROM its opening in the middle 1850s, the third floor of the City Hall on Genesee street was a public hall, available for receptions, fairs and other activities. In 1879, the Common Council decided that the city might derive some revenue from its use as a theater or opera house. They proceeded to remodel the third floor, putting in a slanting floor and adding a gallery at the south end of the room. A stage was erected at the north end. The hall was furnished with plush seats with iron frames, seating about a thousand persons, five hundred on the floor and 400 in the gallery. The new hall was described in the "Utica Morning Herald" of July 29, 1879:

"The frescoing and scene painting has been done under the direction of Ludwig Berlin. The prevailing colors are drab buff, brown and other neutral colors, and the trimmings gilt, white and blue. The designs are Eastlake patterns, in which there is no showy scroll work, and no heavy or massive figures. The center piece over the chandelier is a light panel, with handsome corner ornaments. The main part of the ceiling is comprised in an octagonal figure, with very handsome ornaments in four of the corners. This figure is surrounded with a beautiful border of darker colors. The only designs on the ceiling not geometric figures, are boughs with foliage and in the center of each of these sprays is the picture of a bird of rich plumage. In the center of the top panel of the proscenium is a head of Shakespeare and at the sides of the panel, representations of musical instruments. The sides of the proscenium are ornamented with figures representing music — nude children with tamborine, violin, cymbals, etc. The woodwork of the boxes and front of the gallery are painted white, with trimmings of gilt. Crimson lamberquins are to be placed in the boxes, with plush of the same color on the railings."

The scenery comprised eleven distinct scenes. The drop curtain represented a scene in Italy, with a castle in the distance on the left, and a mountain with clouds in the background. The usual scenery of the period was included — a parlor scene of Florentine design, a prison scene with light coming through a grated window, a palace scene, a kitchen scene with fireplace, a street scene in France. These interiors were painted by William Hinney, of Kingston, Ontario. The exterior scenes were painted by Charles F. Petford, who moved to Utica from New York City.

The grand opening of the new "bijou" theater, in contrast to the larger Opera House on Fayette street, occurred on September 9th, 1879 when Miss Mary Anderson presented two plays in which she played "Julia" in the "Hunchback", and "The Countess" in Sheridan's "Love". Carroll Waldron in 1906 recalled:

"For this occasion Peter Crowe, the florist, furnished handsome floral decorations for the boxes, and Howarth & Ballard perfumed the programs. It was a cozy little theater and well lighted. The arrangement of the seats was such as to practically afford every spectator an easy view of nearly everyone else and this opportunity to display millinery and gowns gave it some popularity with that class of people who attend theaters (and churches) for no other purpose."

The new opera house enjoyed a degree of popularity until the middle of the 1890s, when it fell into disuse as a place of entertainment. In 1895, the Common Council decided to remodel the City Hall to take care of the needs of a growing city. When the new Post Office was opened on Broad street, the federal government gave up its perpetual lease of the second floor and books, which had been housed in the City Hall, were moved to the new Library on Elizabeth street.

THE ESTABLISHMENT OF THE POLISH COMMUNITY IN UTICA

IN the nineteenth century, Poland was a divided country, trisected by the neighboring monarchies of Austria, Germany and Russia. The first Polish settlers in Utica came from that part of Poland under German rule. In 1870, the community consisted of two or three families who settled in the Highlands area of West Utica. The pioneer was probably Michael Blair and his wife, Magdalena Hudacz. Michael Blair died sometime around 1885. Magdalcna, who died at her home on Mandeville street in 1914, was born in Germany on July 8, 1839 and came to Utica with her husband about 1870.

In the 1870s, the Polish immigrants coming to America were numbered in the hundreds, but from 1880 to 1890, the number reached 54,000.

"Then the great influx of Poles began. Family after family came to Utica and located. Other families settled in New York Mills and other suburbs. The majority of these families, as was generally supposed, did not come from Europe, but from the New England States, where they had been employed in the large textile plants. Of course there was, too, a large immigration from Russia and Austria, but the greater number came from down East. In the last eight years the Poles increased from 100

319

to 400 families and today [1906] in Utica alone they number over 4000 souls. In New York Mills there are 500 more and all through this section they have settled largely. The predominant trait of the Pole is his industry. He is thrifty and frugal and his most cherished ambition is to own a little home. With this end in view he has saved on the smallest of wages, and in a few years is a property owner. A good index to the character of the Polish people in this city is their generosity toward the church" ("Saturday Globe" 1906).

In the year 1889 a Benevolent Society of St. Stanislaus was organized in Utica. This society brought together the scattered Poles in the vicinity and invited a Polish priest from time to time. Without a church of their own, they worshipped in St. Joseph's church on Columbia street. The St. Stanislaus society raised a small sum of money to establish a church of their own. On August 11, 1896, a lot containing a small frame house on Chenango street (now Lincoln avenue) was purchased for church purposes. On December 23, 1896, the Rev. Simon Pniak, a native of Galicia, in Austrian Poland, who was ordained after study in Canada, came to Utica as his first assignment. He said the first Mass at St. John's school hall on Burnet street on Christmas Day 1896.

Serving as an altar boy at this first Mass was Leon Jankiewicz, who was destined to become the first Polish physician in Utica. He was born in Poland in 1878, the son of Peter and Theresa Wisniewski Jankiewicz. He came to Utica with his parents in 1884 at the age of six years, and attended St. Joseph's School. A graduate of Utica Free Academy, Leon attended St. Jerome College, Canada, for two years and was graduated from McGill University, Montreal. He began his medical studies at the University of Maryland and received his medical degree from the Baltimore School of Medicine. He began his practice in Utica on Whitesboro street where he practiced his profession until his retirement at the age of 92. Dennis Jankiewicz was the first policeman of Polish extraction in Utica and rose to the rank of Deputy Chief of Police.

The little frame building on Lincoln avenue, purchased for church purposes, was rapidly transformed into a small chapel and on the first Sunday after Christmas 1896 Polish Catholics attended Mass in their own but very small chapel. The congregation numbered about fifty families. Holy Trinity congregation immediately began to plan for a suitable church edifice and in the summer of 1897 contracts were awarded for the construction of a new church. The first Mass was celebrated in the basement of the new building on Christmas Day 1897 and the church was dedicated on June 11, 1899.

The new church was a modest one and it was to prove to be too small within the next ten years. The growing industries of Utica needed more employees, and newcomers began to arrive. The Russo-Japanese War contributed in a large measure to the increase in the Polish population in Utica. Men of military age preferred to come to a free country rather than go to war to protect the tyranical Czar of Russia. Many settled in Utica and in a short time, Lincoln avenue became the center of the Polish colony, with its stores and businesses and homes. In 1905, Father Pniak purchased three more adjoining lots on Lincoln avenue and commissioned Agne, Rushmer & Jennison to draw plans for a new granite church of Gothic design. The "Utica Daily Press" of August 18, 1905, thus described the Holy Trinity congregation:

> "Since its formation the Holy Trinity Society has had a wonderful growth surpassing that of all other church societies in the city. The Polish Church of the Holy Trinity is, in fact, the mother church or center for a large Polish population in central New York. Besides ministering to the Poles of Utica, Rev. Father Pniak looks after the spiritual welfare of the Polish residents of about fifteen towns in this vicinity. There is something doing at the church of the Holy Trinity about every day and evening in the week. There is no less than fourteen different societies connected with the church and meetings are held about every evening. One of these is a society which has a brass band connected with it, and they are making considerable progress in the mastery of the instruments. Others are devoted to St. Joseph, St. Michael, St. Albert and St. Stanislaus, the Children of Mary, the Rosary Society, the Young Men's Dramatic Society, and many others. Connected with the church is a day school with two male and one female teachers and a daily attendance of 180 children."

The present church of the Holy Trinity was completed and dedicated on May 22, 1910 and the old building was converted into a parochial school. The rapidly growing Polish population required a weekly newspaper and in 1915, the "Polish Word" began publication at 120 Lincoln avenue and "Slowo Polski" continued until recent times.

While the greatest number of Polish residents resided in West Utica, a growing colony of Poles began to locate in East

Utica to be close to the knitting mills which were developing along Broad street. On March 11, 1911, a religious congregation was organized taking the name of St. Stanislaus Roman Catholic Church and the first Mass was celebrated on December 11, 1911. Church services were first held in a private house on Nichols street and the cornerstone of a church building was laid on October 12, 1913. It at first consisted of a basement and one story, seating 450 people. A second story, to be used as a school was added in 1917 and the church was formally dedicated on November 29, 1917.

THE UTICA SATURDAY GLOBE
1881-1924

THOMAS F. Baker was born in Hartford, Connecticut on April 5, 1847, and when he was three years old was brought to Utica by his parents. Here he attended the Assumption Academy and when he was sixteen years old, entered the "Utica Observer" printing plant as an apprentice. When he had finished his apprenticeship he remained with the "Observer" until 1870, when he established the "Utica Daily Bee", which was short lived. In 1877, with Dennis T. Kelly he established the "Utica Sunday Tribune". He long had a dream of establishing a weekly paper in which, in addition to the news, the readers would see illustrations and pictures of the people and of the events of interest. The result was a journalistic wonder of the time.

He and his brother, William T. Baker, rented two small rooms on the third floor of the Thomas Building, later known as the Lux Building, on Bleecker street. There they issued the first number of the "Utica Saturday Globe" on May 21, 1881. The publishers had fondly hoped that the first issue would contain an illustration of former Governor Horatio Seymour, but the engraver in New York failed to complete the cut in time. The infant weekly was an eight page affair, of seven columns to the page, and of these, four pages were of the ready print variety, purchased already printed outside the city and containing stories and selected miscellaneous articles of general interest. The other four pages were made up of telegraph news, local news and editorials. 2000 copies of the first issue were printed, but only 700 sold.

The existence of the "Globe" was precarious from the beginning. Its entire capital had been expended in the initial issue. They were able to get out the second issue, and the Seymour illustration, three columns wide, appeared on the first page. People began to take an interest in the weekly and a third issue was produced. This featured a cut of Senator Francis Kernan, followed with one of Theodore Faxton in the fourth number. These were, of course, rather crude likenesses, but they were hailed as an innovation in journalism.

On the second day of July 1881, when the telegraph flashed the news that President Garfield had been assassinated in Washington by Charles Jules Guiteau, the "Saturday Globe" was the only publication from which the excited citizens could get the facts. The "Utica Morning Herald" did not get out an extra and the press at the "Observer" had broken down. The papers were sold as fast as they could be printed in the job printing office of Curtiss & Childs — for the "Globe" did not have its own printing press. This was the event that turned the tide for the "Globe" and it became a recognized newspaper not only in Utica but throughout the State and country.

In 1882, larger quarters were required and while the Kinney block was being built on Charlotte street, temporary offices were located in a frame building on the northeast corner of Post street and Charlotte street.

In 1885, the Bakers purchased property on Whitesboro street and commissioned Architect George Edward Cooper to design a suitable building. This building, still standing, was a three story brick affair. The paper's circulation was then about 40,000 per week. Within a year, the plant was inadequate and in 1887, the building was doubled in size.

In 1892, it became necessary to further enlarge the "Globe" plant. Another story was added and the frontage of the building increased. The western half of the ground floor contained the press room. There were eight large Campbell & Cottrell presses, with each capable of 1,200 impressions per hour. They were not fast presses, but ran slowly so that the illustrations which formed the conspicious feature of the "Globe" might be developed clearly and distinctly.

The average circulation of the "Globe" reached 180,000 copies per week, and also reached 269,000 on some occasions, when the events of the week held a special interest. For more than two score years, the "Globe" covered and illustrated cyclones, floods, conflagrations, executions, inaugurations, assassinations and all the great happenings of the day.

On January 24, 1920, the "Saturday Globe" presented "A Glance Back to the Babyhood of The Globe" and wrote, in part:

> "Along the highway leading from then to the present there are many milestones, and among these are many monuments to which we who have long been with the 'Globe' look back with quickened pulses. We flush with pardonable pride when we recall that the 'Globe' was the first five-cent paper in the world to print a half-tone cut; that we were the first to print on a cyclinder press a paper illustrated with half-tones; that it was in our office that the first half-tone was cast into a form instead of being 'matrixed'; that ours was the first newspaper to print cartoons and half-tones in colors; that ours was the only paper in Central New York to send a man to Johnstown and keep him there during those awful weeks succeeding the great disaster; that ours was the only paper in the State outside the metropolis to send a writer and photographers to Galveston when that beautiful city was destroyed by wind and wave; that in order to get the exact facts and legitimate pictures we have sent our representatives direct from the home office into more than three-quarters of the States making up the Union; that our subscribers have come from the wilds of Alaska and the teeming cities of China; that we have received personal letters of approval from Supreme Court judges, Presidents of the United States and even from Queen Victoria herself."

The founder of the "Saturday Globe", Thomas F. Baker died on May 15, 1916 and in 1920, his brother retired and the weekly was sold to the "Globe-Telegram company", formed to publish a new daily paper in Utica. This venture was not successful and lasted but a few years. On February 26, 1924, the "Utica Saturday Globe" published its last copies of the weekly.

Many of the historical facts about Utica's earlier days can be found in the old issues of the "Saturday Globe" and these are collectors' items today.

UTICA IS LIGHTED BY ELECTRICITY
1881

AFTER 1845, gas light began to replace the whale oil lamps and candles in Utica. In 1881, a new form of illumination was perfected. On October 21, 1879, Thomas Alva Edison tested the first successful incandescent lamp. The era of electric lighting had arrived and Utica business men were quick to realize that it would eventually replace the gas jet.

Publius V. Rogers, Abram G. Brower, William S. Doolittle, Henry H. Fish and Robert S. Williams organized the Central New York Electric Light and Power Company and proposed to set up the necessary machinery, string wires and light the streets of Utica by electricity. On June 28, 1881, the "Utica Morning Herald" reported:

> "Superintendent Fish is exhibiting a light from the street lamp on the corner of Genesee and Whitesboro streets and a still brighter one on the corner of Hotel and Whitesboro."

On August 23, 1881, the same newspaper announced,

> "It is pleasant to be able to announce that the electric light which has been exhibited for three evenings past in front of Sayre's store is to become a permanent institution in the city."

On June 23, 1883, the city entered into a contract with the Central New York Electric Light and Power Company to furnish

> "at an average of ten hours a night sufficient lamps, not to exceed twenty-five, as in the judgment of the Mayor and Chairman of the committee on streets shall be necessary to properly light the following streets — Genesee street, from Mohawk river bridge to the City Hall; John street from Bagg's square to Bleecker street; Bleecker street from Genesee to Mohawk street; Columbia street, from Genesee street to Varick street."

The city agreed to pay seventy cents a night for each and every light, each night the lamps were lighted. In addition, the electric company supervised the electrification by 148 lights of the Skenandoa Cotton Company's yarn mill in East Utica, which were first used September 21, 1883.

In 1886, a rival gas company was established called the Equitable Gas Light and Fuel Company of Utica. In 1887, the Utica Gas Light Company was merged with the Central New York Electric Light and Power Company to be known thereafter as the Utica Gas & Electric Company.

In 1877, John H. Hapgood, Joseph Moore and Andrew L. Soulard organized the Utica Electric Light Company and obtained a lease of the Wood & Mann building, on Cornelia street, near the Erie Canal, formerly occupied for the manufacture of steam engines, but lately used as a skating rink. Here they set up a generating plant, with eleven dynamos to produce electricity to light the streets. The "Daily Press" of January 2, 1888 reported:

> "The engines were started about six o'clock, and the lights blazed out in brilliant style. This comprised circuits Nos. 2 and 4 in which there are 150 lamps, and the tower in Bagg's square, and at the corner of Bleecker and Albany streets, corner of Bleecker and Nichols street, corner of Bleecker and East streets, corner of Albany and South streets, and at the City Hospital. The tower in Bagg's square is really an ornament to the lower part of the city and was admired by many. The company will probably place additional low lamps on Broad and Catharine streets. On Genesee street above the bridge the illumination was all that could be desired. Columbia, Bleecker and Fayette streets were lighted as they never have been before. There has heretofore been an electric light in the City Hall clock, but none shone out from that quarter last night. Some arrangements will probably be made with the company so that people who don't own a Waterbury may know when it is late enough to go home. One thing in which the new system is an improvement on the old is that it does not interfere with the telephone wires. It has often occurred at night that any conversation through the telephone was almost impossible, on account of the loud buzzing sound produced by the electric light wires wherever they crossed or came in contact with those of the telephone exchange."

UTICA DAILY PRESS
1882

IN March 1882, the printers employed on the "Utica Morning Herald" petitioned for an increase in wages, and when it was refused, they went out on strike. On Sunday, March 12th, at a meeting held for the purpose of devising ways and means to carry on the strike, someone suggested that a newspaper be started to compete with the morning newspaper and the idea met with instant favor. A job printing office at No. 3, 5 and 7 Columbia street, owned by H. M. Greene was taken over, and the printers began the task of publishing the first copy of the new newspaper for Monday morning March 13, 1882. The title for the new paper was a matter of convenience, not choice. Among the refuse in the printing office was an old electrotype "THE RENSSELLAER COUNTY PRESS". Someone found it and with a saw cut out the two middle words, leaving "THE PRESS".

On the 25th anniversary of "The Press" in 1907, that newspaper described the "first night":

> "The paper used for the first edition was borrowed from P. E. Kelly, who then owned and conducted the 'Sunday Tribune'. With the first 10 cents taken in for subscription a blank book was bought for the use of H. D. Perry, who served as an accountant. The first legal notice ever printed in the paper was given by the firm of Lindsley & Dunmore. On March 17, when five days old, the 'Press' was made one of the official papers of the city of Utica, a kindly act which at that time was of great assistance.

> "There had been no preparations in the job printing office for daily paper work, for that matter none for night work. Oil lamps were suspended from wires over the cases and there were as many different kinds of type used as if the paper were bigger and better equipped, though it was a matter of necessity, not of choice. The work began at 6 o'clock, and when the paper was ready to make up there were no chases of proper size. Friends and sympathizers were running in and out constantly all night and the wonder is that anything at all was done. A dilapidated washstand served as a desk on which to turn out copy. After a great deal of effort a little four-page

sheet 17 by 26 inches in size when folded was ready and it was 8 o'clock in the morning before it was on the street.

In a short time, the paper moved to No. 60 Seneca street.

In February 1883, a stock company was organized, taking over the paper and all its belongings. Shortly afterward, the building at No. 9 Broad street was leased and occupied in the spring of 1883. The office and press room were on the first floor, the editorial rooms on the second and the composing room on the third. The old single cylinder press was replaced by a double cylinder press, but even with this, the papers had to be run through twice, as but one side could be printed at a time. The Broad street quarters were cramped and the growth of the paper demanded improved facilities and in 1891, a lot at No. 17 Main street next to the old New York Central Depot and east of Bagg's Hotel was purchased. G. Edward Cooper, the architect, designed the new building. It was four stories, and on top of the front of the building was a brown stone panel 4 by 14 feet, with the words, "Utica Press" cut in relief. At the sides and rear of the press department were signs of wire netting about six feet high, with the words "Utica Daily Press" on the two sides and "Weekly Press" in the rear, the letters being of galvanized iron and four feet long.

In 1904, the Press had outgrown the plant at No. 17 Main street, and it was decided to erect a more modern newspaper plant across the street. The site was an historic one, No. 12 and No. 14 Main street was the location of the old Butterfield livery stables. The brick portion at No. 12 was built in the 1850s and the first floor was devoted to a blacksmith shop, with the stables in the rear. At No. 16, just east of the brick building was a wooden frame building occupied by Owen Owens as a bakery until 1855, when it also passed into the hands of Mr. Butterfield and became part of the livery business. The Main street property remained in the hands of members of the Butterfield family and was used by them until 1893. Thereafter it became a storehouse until the property was acquired by the "Press".

The new Press building, which still stands, was used by that newspaper until it was combined with the "Observer-Dispatch" in 1935 and moved to Oriskany Street East.

ROLLER SKATING IN UTICA

IN 1884, a ball-bearing wheel was patented for roller skates and the sport soon gained popular attention throughout the country. The Utica Observer on July 1st, 1884 wrote:

> "The rage of roller skating has taken possession of Utica's younger people, and after the summer vacation they will have one of the finest rinks in the State."

In April of that year the Elite Roller Skating Company, formerly of Newport, Rhode Island, leased Mechanic's Hall. The wooden floor was covered with cloth pasted down and covered with a celluloid preparation to make it smooth. ("Daily Press," April 18, 1884).

The Mechanic's Hall rink was known as the "Gaiety" and opened in July 1884. To promote attendance, Blanche Hayden, of Boston, "the lady champion skater of the world" displayed her talents. On August 12th, the "Observer" reported an exhibition of

> "fancy skating by Will G. Barnum and the whistling with piano accompaniment by Manager Olds."

Success encourages competition and J. S. Dresser and Frank J. Callanen leased the land of the Watson estate on the corner of Genesee and Hobart streets between Oneida Square and Hobart street and erected a large wooden building, which they called the "Casino". Maple flooring permitted not only roller skating but bicycling and lawn tennis as well. This new rink opened on October 16, 1884. To add class to the new establishment, the "skate boys" hired to rent the skates and help the customers wore Turkish caps, black stockings, red breeches, gray shirts, red coats and sashes.

Messrs. Segar & Spiegelberg opened a third roller skating rink on the southeast corner of Lafayette and Washington streets, opposite the Opera House on December 13, 1884. This was known as the "Lafayette". Competition was keen between the Casino and the Lafayette. One of them introduced a new sport to Utica, "polo on skates". There were seven players on each team: rusher, second rusher, back, point, cover point, goal coverer, and goal tender. The two famous Utica teams were appropriately called, "The

Casinos" and "The Lafayettes" and they not only played each other but the leading teams from other localities.

On May 13, 1885, The Casino experimented with polo on horseback. Six horses were brought into the building from the Oneida street entrance, their feet encased in rubber shoes to protect the floor. This was not very successful. The horses threw their shoes and unseated their riders. The "Daily Press" on the 14th of May concluded that the spectators

> "would probably enjoy the sport in a field where it properly belongs."

On June 12, 1885, a fire, believed to be of incendiary origin, destroyed the Casino and the proprietor in the fall of that year, leased the Wood & Mann building on the northwest corner of Lafayette & Cornelia streets near the Erie Canal. The rinks were in operation for a few years thereafter.

THE NEW TELEPHONE EXCHANGE
1888

IN the spring of 1888, the Central New York Telephone Company had its exchange in the Arcade building and the total subscribers numbered nearly 700. The old system of asking the operator to connect with a particular person was changed to a number system. The "Utica Sunday Tribune" of February 26, 1888 described the new operation:

> "The reason for the change in Utica is the removal of the Central office in this city to its new location in the third story of the Oneida National Bank Building, and the introduction there of a new switchboard on the multiple system from the Western Electric Company.
>
> "Under the new system every subscriber will be numbered. Supposing that the 'Tribune' is No. 50, you ring the Central and say, 'Hello, give me 50'. Then you sim-

ply stand still with the hearing thing at your ear, and the young lady in the Central office does all the calling for you, and after she has taken out a plug from one place and put it in another, and pressed a button which rings a bell, which calls the man who owns the phone, you are standing metaphorically face to face with the 'Tribune' office and may ask with perfect safety, 'Who wrote the item?' After you are through conversing, you will be expected to give the crank a turn which will drop a little shutter called an 'enunciator' in the exchange, thus indicating to the operator that you are through and the line will immediately be disconnected.

"The cables for the outside will consist of fifty wires each, encased in paraffine and lead. Of these, some three or four miles will be strung in the central part of the city, consequently doing away with a network of unsightly wires. These cables will be strung on the tops of the tall poles now being erected on Genesee street, and will consequently be out of the way in case of fire, as they will loom above the tops of our highest buildings. The poles are beautiful specimens of pine timber and were purchased near Chittenango, at a cost of nearly $100 each."

EDISON'S PHONOGRAPH MAKES ITS APPEARANCE
1889

THE first practical phonograph was invented by Thomas A. Edison in 1877. The record was a sheet of tin foil wrapped around a cylinder. A needle placed in the center of a diaphragm which vibrated traced a pattern on the foil. The first sounds ever recorded were "Mary Had a Little Lamb." In 1885, an improvement was made by coating the cylinder with wax. Then in 1887 Emile Berliner developed the gramaphone which changed the direction the needle vibrated from up and down to sideways. Utica was given the first demonstration of the new devices on January 29, 1889 when John P. Haines and William S. Hatch, of New York City brought three machines here. They invited a number of prominent persons including Thomas R. Proctor to attend a meeting in Parlor C of Bagg's Hotel. The next morning, the "Utica Daily Press" reported:

> "The instruments were three in number. One was on a sewing machine table, and the power was furnished by the ordinary treadle, and the other two were on common tables, the power being supplied by a storage battery and electrical motor.

> "The instruments were explained, and then Mr. Hatch talked into one, and what he said was accurately repeated. This was the sewing machine phonograph, and the guests took turns in hearing it through a rubber tube with a contrivance to be placed in the ear. The next trial was on the Edison phonograph, and Mr. Williams did the talking, taking as his topic the rumor that James G. Blaine was to be Harrison's Secretary of State. A big tin horn, painted brown with yellow stripes on it, was then hung up at the mouth of the machine, and it repeated in a loud voice what Mr. Williams said. After that Mr. Fred Fincke was induced to show that the phonograph hath an ear for concord and sweet sounds by singing a stanza. The tin horn was again put in front and the wheels set in motion, when the song was accurately reproduced with the applause, the 'bravo' and the whole business."

STONE RESIDENCES IN UTICA
1889-1900

BY the mid-eighties, the aristocratic old Broad and Whitesboro streets were being abandoned to business and commercial interests and the new residences were being built on Genesee street above Oneida Square. This period was marked by an increased use of stone in home construction, most of it quarried at Higginsville. A stone house was built for Professor George R. Perkins in 1873 on the northwest corner of Genesee street and Barton avenue, then the road to New Hartford. This is the location today of Our Lady of Lourdes Church. George R. Perkins was a noted educator, born in Otsego county on May 3, 1812. He was principal of Utica Free Academy in 1838 and died in Utica August 22, 1876. The Perkins residence was built of limestone.

In 1889, three new stone houses were built in Utica. The Baker brothers, Thomas F. and William T. were the successful publishers of the "Saturday Globe". Each built houses on the west side of Genesee street at the intersection of Jewett Place. They were of colonial style of architecture and marvelous examples of the style of the period. G. Edward Cooper, the architect, designed identical houses. The "Sunday Tribune" of January 20, 1889 wrote:

> "T. F. Baker's house covers 48 by 80 feet of ground and an imposing structure it is especially when viewed from the south side, where two immense chimney breasts come into view, with numerous pleasing angles, porticos and abutments. The mansion is constructed almost entirely of Higginsville stone, of a grayish color. The entrance is hidden under a massive portico of stone and leads into a reception hall. Double doors to the right disclose a drawing room. Sliding doors to the left open into a cozy parlor, one corner of which rounds out into a commanding bay window. Back of this is Mr. Baker's library. The second and third floors are divided into ten large bedrooms. On the third floor is a billiard room and a nursery.

> "So far as pertains to views, modern improvements and the like, William T. Baker's mansion will be the exact

counterpart of his brother's. It is slightly different in architecture, pertaining more to the ornamental and not so much to the massive. Higginsville stone of a blue shade has been used liberally in its construction. The same general plan in the laying out of the lower floor is followed as in the other house."

Thomas E. Kinney was born in Canada in 1841 and came to Utica, where he studied law under W. & J. D. Kernan and was admitted to the Bar in 1867. He had the unique distinction of being elected Mayor of Utica on four occasions: in 1885 as a Democrat; in 1886 as an Independent; in 1887 as a Democrat; and in 1898-99 as a Republican. He died November 4, 1899. In 1889, he commissioned Jacob Agne to design a stone house for him at the eastern end of Rutger Park. His home is today the headquarters of Local Union No. 182, International Brotherhood of Teamsters.

The house was constructed of blue stone with brown stone trimmings. The main building was 59 feet front by 34 feet deep. The wing in the rear was 16 feet wide by 23 feet deep. The front of the building had an attractive stone porch, 10 by 36 feet. The main hall was 14 by 24 feet, arched in the center, and in the rear a staircase reaching to the third floor. To the east of the main hall was the library, 18 by 15 feet, and the dining room of the same dimensions, with a bay window in the rear. On the westerly side of the entrance hall was the drawing room, 18 by 31 feet, and out of it opened a large tower in the corner, which extends the height of the building. In both the library and drawing rooms are large fireplaces. The second floor contained six bedrooms and a large sitting room.

In the fall of 1898, Utica's most palatial residence was built for Robert McKinnon, the owner of the McKinnon Knitting Mills in Little Falls. The site selected was the old Philo S. Curtis home on Genesee street. Mr. McKinnon purchased the adjoining lot at the southeast corner of Genesee and Faxton streets, the present site of the First Presbyterian church.

YOUNG MEN'S CHRISTIAN ASSOCIATION
1889

O N February 10, 1858, a group of men met in the lecture room of Westminster Church and organized the Utica Young Men's Christian Association. The first president was Edward Curran. A series of prayer meetings was held in various churches, including the Bleecker street Baptist Church, on the corner of Charlotte and Bleecker streets. In May of the same year, the Association secured rooms on the third floor of the Tibbitts block on lower Genesee street — consisting of a sitting room, a reading room or library, and a hall. During the Civil War period, and for a short time thereafter, interest in the organization waned. In the eighties, a new spirit revived the organization and funds were raised to build a YMCA building. When the Bleecker street Baptist Church moved to and became the Park Baptist Church at Steuben Park, the old church was razed and a cornerstone for the YMCA building laid on October 8, 1883. While the new YMCA building was being erected, the Association occupied rooms in the Arcade building.

The new building was finished and occupied on November 1, 1889, at a cost of $105,000. It was a large, splendidly equipped building, with ornate pillars, cone shaped roofs and ornamental spires. For eighteen years, this building served as the headquarters of the YMCA and among the many accomplishments during that time was the introduction of the game of basketball to Uticans. On March 1, 1907, the building was completely destroyed by fire in one of Utica's most spectacular blazes.

The association began an immediate campaign for funds and secured pledges of $75,000 to secure a new building. Early in 1908, the Young Ladies Seminary, then known as the Balliol School, at 726 Washington street was purchased for the sum of $40,000.

In the years from 1908 to the mid fifties, a gymnasium was added. In 1951, a modern gymnasium and swimming area were built. By 1956, the old building had outlived its usefulness and was razed to give way to a new and modern Y.M.C.A. dedicated in 1958.

COMMISSION TO STRAIGHTEN THE MOHAWK RIVER
1891

"A great many years ago Tom Moore, the Irish poet, who had been visiting in this country wrote these lines, 'From dawn of day till set of sun I've seen the mighty Mohawk run.' To the man unfamiliar with the ribbon of water that stretches from the northern part of Oneida county down between green slopes to the Hudson, these lines would convey the impression that the Mohawk is a great and well-behaved stream entitled to respect and admiration, and that it deserves a more conspicious place in geography than the men who supervise the making of books on this subject generally give it. But folks who know the Mohawk have always believed that Moore's Muse was not in normal condition the day he wrote these lines and some think that liquid inspiration gave the stream an exaggerated importance to the eyes of Erin's melodious minstrel. No one in this vicinity has ever bestowed many admiring glances on the river. ("Saturday Globe", February 2, 1901).

In 1891, the U-shaped portion of the flatlands lying within the town of Deerfield was annexed to the city of Utica and by the stroke of the Governor's pen, two hundred and forty-nine acres of land and a thousand residents were added to the city. In March 1891, the Legislature authorized the creation of a commission to straighten out the Mohawk river by eliminating the U-shaped channel. Delays followed and nothing specific was accomplished until the Common Council voted in December 1901 to dig a new river channel to provide land upon which the New York Central railroad would eliminate the grade crossing at Bagg's Square and add new tracks and build a new station and freight facilities. There were further delays and the work came to a standstill for lack of funds and the bankruptcy of the contractor. Funds were provided in 1907 and the work was completed by Harry W. Roberts and water was turned into the new channel to the north on June 24th and the project was accepted by the State on July 28, 1909.

THE BUILDING OF THE GENESEE "HUMP BRIDGE"
1891-1895

BY the middle 1880s, the street railway built by Butterfield was almost useless as a means of transportation. It consisted of a few dilapidated, slow moving horse cars traversing our principal streets once each half hour, its finances almost in bankruptcy. The city council and mayors complained about storing the cars about Bagg's Square, which was necessitated by the tearing down of the old City Garden in 1870, where for a few years the company stored its cars when not in use. At this juncture, A. D. Mather & Co., the private banking firm, obtained control of the stock and proceeded to revitalize the old line. In 1886, the Utica Belt Line Railroad Company was organized. It leased the New Hartford and Whitesboro lines of the old company; doubled the track on Genesee street; and began the construction of the South street and Blandina street routes. It erected a two story car barn and repair shop on Main street, with five tracks on the ground floor for storing cars and washing them, and with stalls for 150 horses. The Belt Line was electrified in March 1890. The first trip was made on March 10th at night, so that if anything went wrong, there would be few people to notice it. The "Morning Herald" the next morning reported:

> "At 11:19 last night electric motor car No. 20, brilliant with electric light, started out from the Main street depot of the Belt Line company on its first trip to Whitestown. The connections were completed, the car was shoved out on the tracks, the trolley was sprung against the wire, and in less time than it takes to tell it, the car was jammed with people. Harry G. Floyd, who has had charge of the construction, took his position at the brakes and turned on the current. There was a whir beneath the car and amid the cheers of the passengers, car No. 20 started on its first journey.
>
> "When the car moved into Genesee street and took the run up over the Genesee street bridge at a speed of seven miles an hour, there was another cheer. It was not until the car got into Columbia street that Mr. Floyd let

on the strength of the current. A speed of 15 miles per hour was attained there. In going over the switches the speed was diminished quickly and easily. The car arrived at the old terminus in Whitesboro at 11:59. During the trip many street passengers hung on to the car for short distances in order to have the distinction of having ridden on the first trip of electric cars in Utica."

The weight of the new electric cars put a strain on Whipple's bridge over the Erie Canal at Genesee street, and the State on September 11, 1890 condemned the old bridge, prohibiting the passage of the new trolley cars across it. The result was that the street railway company had to suspend at the north side of the bridge, its cars running from the depot on Main street. Passengers then had to cross the bridge on foot and take the car at the southern end. This caused a serious disruption in traffic and the city had to devise a way to rebuild the bridge to take care of the street cars. James F. Mann suggested that the design include a permanently built raised "hump" in the center over which the street cars could pass and a lift bridge on each side for carriages and wagons as well as a raised footpath. This was adopted.

On May 6, 1891, the State appropriated $30,000 and authorized the city to raise $15,000 in corporate bonds for the construction of the new bridge. The plans were drawn by Dean & Westbrook and the contract was awarded to the Hilton Bridge Company and work commenced November 30, 1893. Traffic on Genesee street was seriously disrupted for many years because of the difficulties in getting the lifts to work properly. In the spring of 1895, the new bridge was given its first test. The lifts were operated by compressed air, activated by water power taken from the canal and discharged into the John street sewer. This proved unsatisfactory in the fall when the water was low. A scheme for operating the air compressor by electricity was devised.

The total cost of the bridge when completed was $96,000 of which $73,000 was borne by the State and $23,000 by the city. In 1918, the old Erie Canal through Utica was abandoned and in 1920, the canal lands were given to the city. By 1923, the canal bed had been filled in and leveled off and the old "Hump" bridge was removed and the level lowered.

MOTHER LAVENDER — ANGEL OF MERCY
1892

IT was to sing at a camp meeting at Halleck's ravine on Oneida street, later called "Little Coney Island" that Lizzie Lavender came to Utica. Five years later, about 1892, she came here again and, in a public hall, told her story as a slave in Dixie. Among the persons attending the meeting was Edward Curran, then Charity Commissioner, and he suggested that she should remain here and do her work as a missionary among the poor.

Lizzie Lavender, known affectionately as "Sister" Lavender and in her advancing years as "Mother" Lavender was born in Georgia in 1841. She was born a slave and one of nine children. When she was eleven years old, her mother and the nine children, six boys and three girls, were sold at auction, each to different persons in different locations. Freed toward the end of the Civil War, she came to Albany and determined to devote her life to missionary work among the poor, black and white.

For many years, Mrs. Lavender kept a rooming house on Elizabeth street, just east of the present County Courthouse, but after 1920 she lived at 630 Broad street. To the public she was best known for her annual dinners for the poor on New Year's Day in her home. In making preparations, she

> "would greatly appreciate any contributions of money or food to enable her once more to greet the stranger within her gates in the name of the Master."

On September 8, 1928, the citizens of Utica mourned the death of this angel of mercy and charity to the poor and down-trodden. She was not a lady of great wealth but a poor black woman who throughout her life exemplified the true spirit of Christian charity. Mother Lavender was truly one of Utica's greatest and most humane citizens.

GEORGE YOUNG'S BAKERY
1893

GEORGE J. Young in 1893 conducted a large wholesale bakery and biscuit plant on the north side of Bleecker street between the old Clinton House on the east and the old Armory on the west. On January 11, 1893, fire broke out in a stock room on the third floor, evidently originating in the flues which ran from the ovens on the first floor to the roof. Nine hours later, the building was largely gutted. Young determined to rebuild.

He purchased the lot on the northeast corner of Charlotte and Elizabeth streets running back to Post street. On the southeast corner of Post street was the Hutchinson Block, today a parking lot, and the new building was built around that block. The portion that extended from Elizabeth to Post street was 100 feet deep. The architect was G. Edward Cooper, and the four story high building was built of brick, with brownstone trimmings. This building today is known as the Paul Building. The "Utica Daily Press" of February 18, 1893 described the new building:

> "The retail store will be on the corner of Charlotte and Elizabeth streets. The offices will also be along Elizabeth street. The balance of the first floor will be used as a shipping department. The second story will carry the brick and iron fire-boxes, which will stand against the east wall. The balance of the floor will be used for packing purposes. The ovens will be directly above the fire-boxes and will therefore be on the third floor. This floor will also be used for manufacturing purposes as will the fourth. The material is first received at the basement, sent to the fourth floor, where it becomes dough, then to the third floor, where are located the machines and ovens, then down to the second, the packing room, and finally to the shipping room on the first floor. The front portion of the third floor will be used as a candy shop."

Later, Mr. Young died and the business was sold and the property came into possession of John L. Maher, who renamed it for "Paul" Maher, his son.

ST. JOSEPH'S INFANT HOME
1894

IN 1892, Sister Stanislaus, the superior at St. John's Orphan Asylum, suggested to the religious lay people of Utica that since her institution was not authorized nor had the facilities to take care of infants under the age of two years, a separate organization be founded for their care. The result was the formation of St. Joseph's Infant Home. On November 1st, 1893, the Home was incorporated with a Board of Trustees and on January 4, 1894, the home was opened in a small house on Cottage Place. The need for larger quarters was soon apparent and on April 4, 1894, a house on the north side of Rutger street, east of the viaduct and between Morris and Mohawk streets was rented for $40 per month. It was a two story and attic frame building. In 1894, Father O'Callahan, director of the Mother House of the Sisters of Charity, granted permission for the Sisters to staff the home and on February 20, 1895, the first three Sisters arrived to take over the active work at the home. The home then had about 44 infants and the need for larger quarters was again apparent. On September 4, 1896, the property at 1211 Green Street in West Utica, known as the old Dr. Gray residence, was leased with the privilege of purchasing it later. The residence was opened on January 1, 1897, and on February 4, 1899, the purchase of the property was completed. From 1905 to 1910, an addition to the front of the building was made and other additions were made in 1911 and 1915.

The old Gray residence had historical interest and the "Utica Daily Press" on January 2, 1897 presented a detailed history of the site:

> "The formal opening of St. Joseph's Infant Home, under the auspices of the Sisters of Charity, occurred yesterday. The house which the managers have been so fortunate to secure, is one of the oldest in the city and when built was probably the handsomest house here. It still retains much of its old-time elegance and has quite a history.

> "Jason Parker came to this city in 1794. He was the pioneer in establishing stage lines running between

Utica and Schenectady and Utica and Canandaigua. He was afterward joined in the transportation business by Theodore S. Faxton, Silas D. Childs and John Butterfield. Mr. Parker died in 1830, but before his death he had amassed quite a fortune. He bought a farm in the western part of the city, running from Pleasant street to the Mohawk River. On a portion of this farm the State Lunatic Asylum was built. Mr. Parker's son, Milton D., obtained quite a portion of the farm which was then located in the town of New Hartford. A year or two after his father's death he determined to put up a fine residence, and for this purpose he chose the bluff on the west, overlooking the city. It is said the brick for the building was imported from Scotland, and certainly no money was spared to make it the finest residence hereabouts. In 1833-34 Rev. Andrew Reed, D.D., and James Matheson, D.D., were sent as deputation from the Congregational Churches of England and Wales to visit the churches in America. In the narrative of his travels, published in 1836, Rev. Dr. Reed thus refers to the Parker House, at Utica:

'I was referred to a dwelling of special pretensions and was told that it was built in imitation of an English cottage. Greatly would they be deceived who would take it for a sample. Of this English cottage the body is Gothic, the parapet of no style and the portico Grecian. But what of this! It is only such a combination as we see in the neighborhood of Westminster Hall.'

"No one at this late day will deny the accuracy of the description, but certain it is that the interior of the house was very elegant for those days. It was before the day of stoves, so the heating was by fireplaces. The mantle in the reception room was of mahogany, in the dining room of gray marble and in the back parlor, now used as a children's nursery, of Egyptian marble. Two of these remain. On the first floor the ceilings had deep stucco moldings in leaf patterns and heavy center pieces, although gas was then unknown. The stairway had a rail of mahogany terminating in a lion's claw, and in the hall where the stairway turns were niches with statuary. At the entrance were Corinthian columns, and just inside the vestibule were other columns. Most of these things remain to the present day.

"Mr. Parker married Catherine Tracy, daughter of William G. Tracy of Whitesboro, and sister of William and Charles Tracy, and moved into the house in December 1834, or January 1835. The city then had been chartered a little over two years. The State Lunatic Asylum, now the Utica State Hospital, had not been thought of, much less built. Of the factories that made West Utica, the first was the steam woolen mill, but that was not built until 1846. On Nail creek which runs through West Utica, was the only manufacturing establishment, a nail factory in which the bellows was run by dog power.

"Mr. Parker went into the wholesale grocery business with John Hastings of Clinton, their store being on the west side of Genesee opposite the north line of Catharine street. West Utica was considerable of a wilderness and when the creek was high and Whitesboro street about impassable, the house was reached via Pleasant street and York street. Mr. Parker removed to the city after three or four years, locating on Lafayette street. He died in 1839, leaving two daughters. The only one of these now living is Mrs. Osgood Field of Rome, Italy. Mr. Parker's wife was drowned in the Hudson river in the steamer Swallow disaster. Her mother, Mrs. Rachel Tracy, had bought the property and owned it for some time."

The article in the "Press" then gave details of the subsequent owners, including Rev. Chauncey E. Goodrich, a Presbyterian minister, whose wife was Margaret Tracy, a sister of Mrs. Parker. He was chaplain at the hospital and also was interested in horticulture and agriculture and made many experiments in the raising of peaches and grapes. The property was then occupied by a Mr. Bradt, a farmer, who raised strawberries, corn and peas. In 1860 Doctor John P. Gray purchased the property and took off the balustrade which hid the roof, added a third story to the main part and a second story to the wing. In 1873, Dr. Theodore Deecke was appointed pathologist at the hospital and had his chemical laboratory in the house. The article then concluded:

"York street, which is nearest, was formerly known as 'Lover's lane' and under the stately elms and along the tall hedges many lovers have wandered. Opposite the entrance there was a hedge of white hawthorn, which is now removed. On the slope of the hill toward City street, there were three or four apple trees, and the children of the house as well as those who came up from the city to visit them thought they were the best apples in the world. Just back of the house the lilacs have bloomed regularly for more than half a century. A little further south on the same farm, at the head of Walnut street, is a ravine where peppermint and cress are gathered still.

"With its cool shades, its flowers, fruit and nuts, its

stately trees and long hedges filled with singing birds, the place has always been an attractive and pleasant one for children. So may it continue to be for many years while it is occupied by the Sisters of Charity and the little waifs under their care."

St. Joseph's Infant Home continued well into the 20th century when its charges were transferred to the St. John's Orphan Asylum on Genesee street and the institution became St. John's and St. Joseph's Home. Unoccupied for some years, it was taken over, the building razed, and the Michael Walsh Apartments, a cooperative project for middle income families was erected on the site.

THE STEUBEN PARK ARMORY
1894

THE National Guard in Utica after the Civil War consisted of four companies attached to the 26th Battalion: Company A (1869 "Veteran Zouaves"); Company B (1869 "Fire Zouaves"); Company C (1873 "Dering Guards"), formed from members of the old Hutchinson Light Guards; and Company D (1875 "Conkling Corps").

A major reorganization occurred in March 1881, when the 26th Battalion was mustered out of service and Companies A and D disbanded. Company B continued in service as the 24th Separate Company, until it was disbanded on March 23, 1887. Company C became the 28th Separate Company, with Joseph Remmer as Captain. On September 27th, 1887, some of the members of the old Citizens Corp, which had continued as a separate military group, were mustered into service as the famous 44th Separate Company. Their armory was transferred from Chubbuck Hall to the old Bleecker street armory.

By the early nineties, the old Armory had outlived its usefulness for military purposes, and in 1891 the Legislature authorized an appropriation for a new armory in Utica. In December of that year, the Williams property on the southeast corner of Steuben and Rutger streets was purchased. The cornerstone was laid August 10, 1893. The armory was completed and accepted by the State on December 23, 1894 and the companies moved from the old Bleecker Street armory, which was abandoned as a military building.

During the Spanish-American War, the 44th Separate Company enlisted as Company E of the First New York Volunteers and sailed for the Phillipines. The 28th Separate Company was not called into service as a company but many of its members joined separate companies of the 202nd and 203rd Regiments and served in Cuba. They returned from service in 1899.

BICYCLING IN UTICA IN THE NINETIES

THE invention of the chain and sprocket and the pneumatic tire resulted in the bicycle replacing the old velocipede as a mode of travel. It is generally acknowledged that Lawson's bicylette of 1879 was the first design for a bicycle with a chain drive to the back wheel. The front wheel of the first bicycle was forty inches in diameter and the back wheel twenty-four. Gradually the disparity between the wheels was lessened.

The only form of cycling suitable for women in the 1880s was the tricycle but this presented problems for the ladies. Their dresses were constantly riding over their knees, each alternate stroke lifting them higher. Then a few bicycles with dropped frames appeared on the market and by the middle of the 90s, women began to ride them. The "Saturday Globe" in 1895 wrote:

> "Almost every day parties of young women on bicycles can be met on Utica's streets and that they enjoy it is evident from their beaming looks and happy smiles. The question of a becoming dress is a serious one. So what,

they ask, shall we do? Shall it be bloomers or what? A reporter asked the opinion of this matter from a prominent cycling woman in Utica and was answered thus: 'Bloomers, I can see no objection to bloomers on any ground save that of their ugliness; they are simply hideous and yet one can't wear skirts without the danger of becoming all tangled up and getting severely hurt.' Knickerbockers were suggested as a possible solution and the young woman replied, 'Well, knickerbockers might be better. In fact I'll tell you something if you'll promise not to tell. Some girls are thinking of knickerbockers. There's nothing so dreadful in them when you get used to it; it's just the idea. I have just come from New York and there I saw dozens of women in bloomers and a few in knickerbockers. I am bound to say, however, that the latter class was much more interesting.' The reporter thought he would find them most interesting too."

The new asphalt pavement on Rutger street, the first such in Utica, was the favorite spot for bicycling. Lucy Clark, in "Town Topics", November 1931 wrote:

"On Sundays it was the mecca of bicyclists from all parts of the city and suburbs. Oh, the ladies in shortwaists, sailor hats and short skirts — 'short' meant at the shoetops in those days — and, a few daring ones in bloomers. The men in caps, blouses and odd, skimpy knickers. What a picturesque pageant they made, pedaling past those dignified houses, from which an occasional horrified occupant peeped out the parlor window, bewailing modern contraptions. But youth is ever indifferent to the pangs caused by the passing of old time ways, and the boys and girls of Rutger street's best families were mingled in that gay wheeling throng — many a smart debutante looking very sweet 'upon the seat of a bicycle built for two.' "

Albert J. Seaton conducted a bicycle academy in the old armory on Bleecker street in 1895 and he was enjoying such popularity that Welch Brothers built a bicycle rink on a vacant lot on Oneida Square, just south of Pegg's Tavern. It was a frame building 144 feet deep, two stories in height, with towers on either end. The bicycle rink was in the rear, 76 by 140 feet in dimensions. There were platforms at the side upon which spectators could sit. The rink opened on June 19, 1895. The Academy was open daily and each evening as well. The rates were: Admission without riding, 10 cents; admission for people having their own wheels to ride,

20 cents; admission and wheel for one hour, without instruction, 30 cents; single lesson with instructions for half hour, 40 cents; course of six lessons, $2. Wheels could also be rented for road riding.

The Oneida Square Bicycle Rink was also used for ice skating and political rallies. During a presidential campaign in 1900, Teddy Roosevelt's oratory rang in its precincts and Senator Chauncey M. Depew's wit entertained a great audience gathered at the same meeting. The rink was sold in October 1901 at foreclosure.

MECHANIC'S HALL RELIVES ITS DAYS AS A THEATER

WHEN the Opera House of Lafayette street opened in the seventies, old Mechanic's Hall was quite inactive except for a few lectures and an occasional use as a roller skating rink during the eighties when that craze hit Utica. From December 1892 to March 1895, it was transformed into the Wonderland Theater, interestingly described by Carroll Waldron in the "Utica Sunday Journal" of December 16, 1906:

> "In December 1892, there flashed upon us that brilliant young luminary of lesser showdom, the only, the original Arthur E. Seymour — he of the wavy locks, the voluble tongue and the broad expanse of immaculate shirt-front. Mechanic's Hall had been opened as Wonderland by an out-of-town firm, and Arthur was on hand the second week, managing his father, the truly mystifying mind-reader, Andrew J. Seymour. Arthur's genius as a publicity promoter, coupled with his sire's sensational performances, packed old Mechanic's as it had never been packed before. The Seymours were loath to leave pastures so verdant, and leave they did not. Within a week of his arrival Arthur was announced as manager of the house, and shortly thereafter,

perhaps before the original owners had time to fully grasp the situation, he had seated himself at the desk of the 'sole proprietor'.

"Wonderland comprised a Curio hall and a 'family theater'. In the theater department were given variety performances. Curio hall had an array of 'freaks' and acts such as make up the regulation circus side-show. Big Eliza, the 720-pound black woman, was an early attraction, followed by such celebrities as Jo-Jo, the dog-faced boy; the 'half horse, half-man' prodigy; the Ossified Man; Colonel Coffey, human skeleton; Baldwin, the man with a broken neck; and Laloo, the double-bodied Hindoo. Another gentleman there was who danced with bare feet upon broken glass, ate nails, pen-knives, needles and Paris green — and swore he enjoyed life.

"Not the least of the attractions was Seymour himself. Tall and of a certain forceful bearing to dignify the special policeman's badge that glistened at his lapel, Arthur was a personage to engage the attention of his adult patrons and to hold in terror the small boy who might be tempted to keep his cap on or who might hiss, stamp or jab pins in the shins of the Ossified Man.

"Wonderland's policy was several times changed — from freaks to drama, from drama to variety, and from variety back to freaks. Between seasons in 1893, fire — that demon that seems ordained to feast at least once upon every playhouse — visited Wonderland and made a $25,000 meal of the building's interior. Seymour was on hand to open the reconstructed New and Greater Wonderland in the fall of 1894, however, and the place boomed as before.

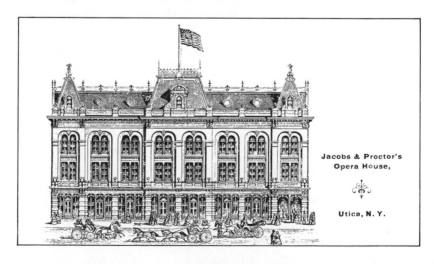

Jacobs & Proctor's
Opera House,

Utica, N. Y.

"But with the close of the season in sight, Seymour one Saturday night took French leave of the city and the little troupe of stranded performers were not the only ones who had reason to bewail his departure. But beside his creditors there were others who missed Seymour. He had made a practice of taking his troupe to the State Hospital for the entertainment of its inmates once a week, and the unfortunates had come to look forward with keenest anticipation to these visits of the stalwart gentleman with his merry company. They missed him sadly. And he and his show were missed by the children of the city, at least by those whose life circumstances were such as to give each nickel the appearance of a cartwheel. For among those he had been prodigal with free tickets. And again, had he not one day flung thousands of pennies from Wonderland roof down into the street, that they might claw each other in the maddest 'scramble' the town ever knew? Assuredly, Seymour was missed."

THE VANISHING GULF IN EAST UTICA

IN the early days of Utica, Ballou creek meandered down through East Utica from its source in the southern hills and emptied into the Mohawk river at Park avenue and Broad street. The newly built Erie Canal crossed Ballou creek at this point and the Miller family and other prominent citizens viewed this as an ideal location for the creation of a harbor around which manufacturing establishments might be erected. The city directory of 1829 referred to the "Public Basin":

"This work, which is to connect with the Erie canal where it crosses Ballou creek, will be 150 feet wide and 1400 feet long. The bridge just erected across it at Broad street, is 48 feet wide and 165 feet long. A weigh-lock, on the lever principle, opposite the basin, is nearly completed."

This basin was also known as the "Big Basin" and "Miller's Basin" and was filled with water from the canal until it extended southward between Third and Mohawk streets to a point beyond South street. With the exception of the Gulf Brewery and the flour mill and a few other structures, it never developed as planned and was the "Shantytown" of Utica, because of the numerous abandoned houseboats anchored there and the rude huts lining its banks. In addition, the existence of the basin made Utica a "pent-up" city since the east-west streets with the exception of Broad street ended at the basin.

In 1852, two streets east of the gulf were in existence as related in the "Daily Gazette" of May 31, 1852:

> "Beyond the Sulphur Springs 'gulf', two other avenues are opened, parallel to those on the west side — Mohawk street extends from the river at Miller's Bridge, to within a quarter of a mile of the Slaytonbush road, a distance of over two miles. We recollect some half dozen years since, that it was considered almost an imposition to sell lots on the upper part of this street, but it is now built up almost its whole length, has a fine plank sidewalk, and is surrounded by a growing settlement of off-shooting streets. The Mohawk street settlement is popularly known as 'Texas'.
>
> "Kossuth avenue, opened this year through the High School farm (old Utica Gymnasium), is at present the easternmost street of our city. It requires some exercise of faith to look forward to the time when the territory which it lays open, will be required to accommodate the growth of the town."

Gradually through the ensuing years, the city built culverts to connect the streets on the west with those on the east. This was done at Bleecker, Elizabeth, Blandina, Mary, South and Eagle streets. When these culverts were first built, they were made only wide enough to allow a fill to be made over them sufficient to allow teams to cross. In the course of time sidewalks were found to be necessary and the culverts were extended to a width sufficient to form a foundation of the sidewalks. This was done on Bleecker, Elizabeth, Blandina and South streets. In June 1893, the people of Mary street sought the same improvement, but it was vetoed by the Mayor on the ground that it would have to be built on a trestle.

Older Uticans will remember the viaduct on Rutger street spanning the Gulf. This was prompted by the building of the

350

Masonic Home at the end of Rutger street and the necessity of furnishing access from the city. The contract for the construction of the Rutger street viaduct was awarded in April 1890 to Dean & Westbrook, for the sum of $25,500. It was built of iron and was in use until 1916.

The "Saturday Globe" of September 30, 1905 wrote "The Old Gulf is Vanishing":

"The time is still remembered when the territory beyond the Gulf was virtually a suburb of the city. Now it is an important part and as it spreads more and more so does that natural dividing line made by Ballou's creek tend toward obscurity. It is still there, with many of its picturesque features, but much of it has vanished and the generation which is making Utica one of the busiest muncipalities in the State will see the day when the Gulf will have completely disappeared. It is safe to predict that the Rutger street viaduct which must some day yield to the touch of time, will never be replaced. When its usefulness is ended there will be a culvert and filling, with an asphalt top, just as there is at some other streets. What are some of the changes which have taken place in that time along this very Gulf? In 1890 riding along Bleecker street in the snail-like horse cars, there were no buildings to shut off the view north and south. The few structures were one-story or one-and-one-half story dwellings. To the north, Shantytown, as the section in the immediate vicinity of Jay street was known, loomed up with its little houses, one of which rested partly upon a tree trunk growing out of the gulf. A trestle-like sidewalk spanned the ravine, and beyond could be seen the remains of the old basin, where the boatmen gathered at Jay Campbell's place and the older fellows assembled at Horatio Rickard's stables and talked politics and other things. That area has metamorphosed and the sons of Genoa and Naples sleep and gossip where two decades ago the merry songs and jest of old Erin were rehearsed. To the south from Bleecker street not so many years ago, you could see the youth of East Utica playing ball along the edge of the creek in midsummer and sliding down Gallagher's hill when the coasting was good. There was an almost unbroken stretch of ravine from Bleecker to Rutger street, with no intervening culverts, except at Blandina street, and no viaduct. The latter came when the Masonic Home was built in 1891.

Now there are not only crossings at all the streets — Elizabeth, Mary, Blandina and Lansing street — but the ravine itself is being filled up between streets, and it will not be long before houses are standing where recently was a dismal swamp.

"South of Rutger street the Gulf retains much of its former character, though this too is undergoing change, particularly beyond South street, where the city has made improvements by building contagious disease hospitals and by filling in at Eagle street. In this section there is a picturesque ruin — the old jail building, whose front is on Mohawk street and whose decaying rear walls and towers and fallen roof give it the appearance of an abandoned fort on the Gulf side."

The "Utica Daily Observer" of May 9, 1916 reported:

"Commissioner of Public Works Hayes will tomorrow close the viaduct crossing the Ballou Creek at Rutger street. The viaduct has been in a very dangerous condition for nearly two years. Recently, two of the supporting columns of the bridge gave way entirely and for some time there has been absolutely no support for the west end of the bridge. About five months ago it was found necessary to close the northern half of the bridge to traffic and pedestrians, as the supporting columns had rotted away and that part of the bridge was in imminent danger of collapse. Therefore for the safety of the public, Commissioner Hayes has decided to close the bridge entirely. Coincident with the work of removing the viaduct, the task of filling in the gulf at Rutger street will be pushed with great vigor."

On July 5, 1918, the "Daily Observer" reported:

"Rutger street was opened to traffic yesterday at the former Ballou creek viaduct just west of Mohawk street. The street at this point has been closed to traffic since May 1, 1916, and the viaduct was removed by Thomas Smith in June of the same year. In the same month, the work of extending the Ballou creek culvert at Rutger street began, and the deep gully has since been used as a place to dump all the ashes and refuse of the city. The place has now been filled in so that a fairly good passage way, level and sound, has been made, so that the thoroughfare can now be used for travel both by vehicles and pedestrians. The new roadway will in the near future be paved."

BASKETBALL COMES TO UTICA
1896

THE game of basketball was "invented" at the International YMCA Training School (later Springfield College) in Massachusetts in 1891 but was largely a local game. In 1896, Doc Newhall, physical director of the Utica YMCA introduced the game in the old Bleecker street building. The game proved so interesting that Doc Newhall formed the Iroquois League, composed of the Sadaquadas, Yahnundasis, Cayuga and Senecas. George Esmay, of the firm of Esmay & Daggett Co., was the captain of the Senecas and romped away with the silver cup, which was later destroyed in the YMCA fire. A year or two later, Nick Weaver organized the old YMCA Independents.

The first game of basketball ever played in Utica by ladies was held at the Female Academy, then known as "Mrs. Piatt's School for Girls", on March 6, 1899 between the Monday night class of girls, who were not pupils of the school but working girls being instructed by Mrs. Piatt, and the Women's Auxiliary of the Waterville YMCA. The costume of the players included a divided skirt of dark blue. Utica was victorious by a score of 10 to 6.

THE POLITICAL MARCHING CLUBS

DURING the nineteenth century, political parties promoted their respective candidates for President by organizing marching clubs to parade about the city. In the campaign of 1880, when Garfield and Arthur were the Republican candidates, the club was known as the "Reynolds Guards" in honor of Major Reynolds, the shoe manufacturer who funded the purchase of the uniforms. Another marching group, known as the "Lewis Lawrence Cadets" was sponsored by Lewis Lawrence of Utica, a close friend of Roscoe Conkling, and it marched during the campaign of 1880. Incidentally, Mr. Lawrence lived in the Lawrence mansion on the northeast corner of Rutger and Steuben Park. In later years, this mansion was the home of the Republican Club.

At a meeting of the Reynolds Cadets in the City Hall, those present were divided as to the selection of a uniform. Many were dissatisfied with the one then worn and wanted a more showy one. The result was that a number of the members withdrew and formed what was known as the "Republican Continentals." They purchased elaborate old-fashioned continental uniforms and attracted much attention.

In the campaign of 1884, Blaine was the Republican nominee and Grover Cleveland the Democratic. The Continentals continued their club and secured beautiful uniforms. Another group, "The Plumed Knights", were commanded by Isaac Bielby. They wore flashing white uniforms with German cavalry caps. The name was taken from the title of the famous speech of Robert Ingersoll nominating Blaine. During 1884, the Lawrence Cadets did not march as a body, but some of the members paraded as the "Fourth Ward Pioneers."

The Utica Jacksonians was the principal Democratic marching club, first organized in 1880. They marched in the fall of that year and also in the elections of 1884, 1888 and 1892.

In 1888 the Lewis Lawrence Cadets formed the nucleus of a new organization which was called the "Conkling Unconditionals". Their first parade under Major Charles Horsburgh was held on October 14, 1888, the group wearing black uniforms and helmets. The organization paraded in every presidential campaign from 1888 to 1924, inclusive, and attained a national reputation. In 1892, the uniform was changed to white, with black and gold trimmings and a headgear called a "shako". In 1896, the club wore a stylish white cutaway coat, with gold trimmings and a white shako. In 1900 the outfit was of khaki, after the style of the Spanish-American war uniform.

The "Utica Saturday Globe" of October 13, 1904, described the uniform of the Jacksonians:

"The uniforms are stylish. The coat is of the straight frock pattern, single breasted, similar to the National Guard full dress coat. It is made of white duck, with black oil cloth trimmings, and has a black belt and a brass buckle. The trousers are of white duck, with a wide black stripe down the sides. The leggings are of black enamel, with white trimmings. The headgear consists of a black fur shako with gold tassel and white braided ornamentation. The fatigue cap is of white duck, with gold strap. The officers and staff uniforms are of the same material as those of the privates, but are trimmed with gold oilcloth, shoulder straps and aigulets, while the headgear is a chapeau of white with black feathers. The rank and file carry lanterns on staffs, in red, white, blue and green. The staff and officers carry hand lanterns in colors. White gloves complete the outfit."

In its next issue on October 22, 1904, the "Saturday Globe" described the uniforms of the Unconditionals, of 130 men:

"The uniform consists of white duck coats and trousers, trimmed with black bars, braid and collars, black leggings with white trimmings and a white cap of the new United States army pattern, trimmed with black. The line carry lanterns on long sticks and the variegated colors give a pleasing effect. The staff carry hand lanterns which lend themselves to pretty effects, particularly in the "open order" formation, with hands joined and lanterns raised. The officers' uniforms differ from those of the line and staff in that they are trimmed with gold."

After 1924, changing conditions and the advent of automobiles made political marching clubs only a memory of the days when "There'll Be a Hot Time in the Old Town Tonight" thrilled the hearts of political partisans.

THE DEVELOPMENT OF THE PARK SYSTEM

DURING the 1890s, the city was expanding in all directions. In spite of agitation to add a park system, the city fathers were reluctant to expend the funds necessary to acquire the land. It was then that public-spirited benefactors came forward to give Utica one of the most extensive public park systems of any city of its size in the country.

James Connor Greenman, the only son of Silas C. and Elizabeth M. Greenman, was born on November 14, 1859, in the old Greenman homestead on Seneca street. His grandfather, Hiram Greenman, came to Utica from Oxford, New York, in the pioneer days of the village. In 1823, he kept a public house on the Erie Canal near the Washington street bridge. Later he became a packet boat captain on the canal and made a modest fortune in the stock of the boat companies and the early telegraph lines. He died in 1850. James Connor Greenman succeeded to the estate of his grandfather, which consisted of real estate and Western Union stock. In 1879, he married Miss Anna L. Olmstead, and in 1887 purchased the fine residence of Ellis H. Roberts at 263 Genesee street, moving there from the old Greenman residence.

He was a great lover of sports and upon his death on July 22, 1894, his estate was placed in trust, to pay the income to his wife during her lifetime and at her death to purchase, lay out and maintain one or more plots of grounds, within or near the city of Utica, to be used as a public park or playground, particularly for the children and youth of the city. It would be some years before this fund would be made available for this purpose.

On October 4, 1895, John D. Kernan and his wife conveyed a park of one acre, more or less, south of Rutger street at the West Shore crossing. Mrs. Thomas R. Proctor and Mrs. Frederick T. Proctor, in memory of James Watson Williams, donated to the city in 1897, six and one half acres, Watson Williams Park, lying between Steuben street on the east, Elm street on the west, James street on the the north and

Elmwood Place on the south. Subsequently a fountain was erected, as well as a pond which was used for skating in the winter.

When the Masonic Home was built in 1892, the city decided to extend Rutger street east across the old Gulf and continue it to the entrance of the Home. In the spring of 1899, Thomas R. Proctor threw open to public use sixty acres of the old Bagg's Hotel farm lying just westerly of the Masonic Home grounds. He did not give it outright to the city at that time, because it was not prepared to appropriate the money necessary for its maintenance. Of the sixty acres, thirty-five were cleared and twenty-five were wooded.

On June 15, 1907, Thomas R. Proctor presented to the city Horatio Seymour Park, 14.66 acres, lying on the corner of Sunset avenue and what was then known as Pleasant street (now Burrstone Road), west of Genesee street and back of the House of the Good Shepherd; Addison C. Miller Park, 15.28 acres, lying across the D L & W and O & W railroad tracks at York street; and J. Thomas Spriggs Park, of slightly less than an acre, a point of land lying between Whitesboro and Erie street, at their junction.

In the same year, 1907, Mrs. Proctor decided that the plot of land on the southeast corner of Eagle and Genesee street and extending along Eagle street to Park avenue be made into a small park to beautify Genesee street. The land contained the old Palmer residence and was overgrown with weeds and grass. She purchased the old mansion; tore it down and put landscape gardeners to work to transform it into what is known as "Christmas Tree" park.

On February 3, 1908, deeds of these parks to the city were filed with the city and at the same time, Frederick T. Proctor and his wife deeded the land on which St. Luke's Hospital originally stood on Columbia street, to be known as Truman K. Butler Park.

It was in April 1904, that Thomas R. Proctor made his first purchase of lands on what has come to be known as the Parkway. He purchased one farm after another until the total acreage contained about 380 acres. He engaged Frederick Law Olmstead, the well known landscape architect, to lay out drives and paths, and plant trees. On the summit of the hill, there was erected a tall flagpole. Nearby a huge 20 ton boulder was placed upon which a bronze tablet dedicating the park in honor of Roscoe Conkling was attached. In July 1909, both Roscoe Conkling Park and Thomas R. Proctor Park were dedicated to use of the citizens.

In the same year, to give access to the new park, the city completed the construction of the short stretch of the Parkway from Genesee street to Elm street. In 1911, it was extended to Mohawk street and in June 1919 its extension from Mohawk street to Welsh Bush road was authorized by the council.

On the Parkway at the head of Elm street in December 1910 was placed the Swan Memorial Fountain, donated by the late Mrs. Joseph Swan. It was the creation of MacMonnies, America's great sculptor. The base was a monolith, six by ten feet and surmounting the column was the figure of the god Pan — the Grecian divinity, who was considered the patron of flocks and shepherds, hunters and fishermen ("Saturday Globe", December 24, 1910). On July 9, 1921, the statue of Thomas R. Proctor, the gift of the school children of Utica, was unveiled in the park.

Among the many monuments along the Parkway, the "Hiker" monument at the intersection of Oneida street and the Parkway was erected in 1915, dedicated to the memory of the veterans of the Spanish-American War. The sculptor, Allen G. Newman, caught the spirit of the trooper in an inspiring manner, with soft hat slanted at a tilt, flannel shirt wide open at the throat and arms bare above the elbow. It is a dashing figure and a finished work of art. The huge boulder upon which it stands has a history of its own.

It was discovered near Trenton and a trucking company was engaged to haul it to the city. Early in January 1915, the trip began, but the big sled became stuck in the snow and was abandoned until the snow melted in the spring. The most difficult part of the journey was in getting the 17 ton load down the incline of Deerfield Hill for three miles to Deerfield corners. The trip was resumed with two teams hitched to the wagon and a third with block and tackle attached to trees. The task was completed however, in time for the dedication of the monument on July 5th, 1915.

THE AUTOMOBILE INDUSTRY IN UTICA

THE automobile was not invented by a single individual, but evolved from experiments in attempting to achieve locomotion with whatever power devices were available. The steam carriage was the pioneer automobile — a term applied by the French. Stored electric power in the form of a battery became available by 1892, and in 1893, Duryea Brothers of Springfield, Massachusetts, built the first successful gasoline automobile in America, a one-cylinder affair. In 1895, they produced a two cylinder. Until the year 1900, most of the vehicles were either "steamers" or electrically operated, a type favored by the wealthy ladies of the period.

In the spring of 1900, Walter Jerome Green owned the first horseless carriage in Utica, which he drove along Utica's asphalt pavement on Rutger street, the first in Utica. It was a Locomobile "steamer", a one-seater, propelled by a small, gasoline-fueled steam engine under the seat. When the boiler was hot enough to produce steam, the unheard-of speed of twenty miles an hour could be achieved, scaring horses along the way. The State by 1907 found it necessary to regulate the speed to ten miles per hour in heavily populated sections of a city, fifteen miles in other parts, and twenty miles on rural roads.

Since it was necessary to build bodies for these cars, it was inevitable that the manufacturers would turn to the carriage and wagon makers. Utica possessed many such shops with skilled workmen. The Utica Carriage Company was organized in 1893 and produced rockaways, surreys, cabriolets, phaetons and traps of many kinds at its factory on Dwyer Avenue. Edward A. Willoughby was a well-known carriage maker in Rome and when a fire destroyed his manufactory there on March 4th, 1897, he came to Utica and took over the management of the Utica Carriage Company in its red brick, four story building, 100 yards west of the city line. This became, with William H. Owen as a partner, the Willoughby, Owen & Co. This company received in 1899 two contracts, one for 75 and the other for 60 carriages for the Columbia Automobile Company of New York. A reporter for the "Utica Sunday Journal" described the operation of the factory:

"The finished brougham, hansom or other style of vehicle is longer by a few feet than its brother, which is drawn by horses. In the hansom the driver sits behind just as he does on the carriages now in use. Where before he had the appearance of being about to drop off the main part of the vehicle, he is now supported beneath by a box about three feet long and eighteen inches high. In this box is put the storage battery. The wires run from the battery to the motors, which are attached to the axles, just as the motors of a trolley car are attached to the track. The motors not alone turn the wheels, but they also run the various appliances. The driver on his perch on the box with his hand on the lever makes the automobile go fast or slow at will. With a foot on a spring he can turn on the electricity which will reverse the wheels immediately. With his other hand he steers the vehicle. This steering is one of the features of this new carriage. The back wheels only turn. With a touch so light that it makes no more effort than a writer uses in lifting his pen, the wheels may be turned. Much has been said about the difficulty with which the automobile is managed. The difficulty is that only a light touch is needed where a heavy hand is often used. Inside the carriage are a reading lamp, call bell, feet warmer, all run by electricity, while outside are two coach lamps also lighted by incandescent lights."

These electric cars would run about 25 or 30 miles on a battery charge and since the charging plants were extremely few, this was a nuisance and these electric cars were mostly used for short distances in the city by the ladies. The men preferred the "steamers" or the new gas engines. By 1901, the idea of owning an automobile as a status symbol was catching on and interest grew rapidly. The first Locomobiles cost about $750.00. Other vehicles began to make their appearance, and the business of selling them was soon taken up by various individuals. Miller & Mundy, located on Pearl street, and later at Oneida Square, had the agency for the Mobile and White "steamers" and the Autocar and Pierce "Gasoline" machines. The Autocar was a two-cylinder, four passenger car, steered by a lever at the left of the driver. It sold for $1,700. The Pierce "motorette" was a single cylinder motor mounted close to the rear axle and was a rather noisy, clumsy looking vehicle, which sold for $900. In 1901, the Utica Automobile Club was organized among the owners.

Utica had the potential of becoming a manufacturing center for the new automobile industry which was beginning to develop. The Willoughby, Owen & Co. made excellent bodies for automobiles, and on Lincoln Avenue, near the later Burrstone Bridge, the Weston-Mott Wheel Works produced all types of wheels, mostly bicycle at the time. Charles J. Mott was induced in later years to move his plant to Michigan and eventually became a Vice President of General Motors. Utica, however, was a "mill town" and little encouragement was given to those who attempted to establish a new industry which would cut into the cheap labor force in the area.

The Remington Automobile and Motor Company was organized as a New Jersey corporation by Philo Remington, the gun manufacturer of Ilion. He induced the Chamber of Commerce to find a suitable location here and to have its members invest in its capital stock. It opened in May 1901 in the three story, 35 by 100 foot building on the east side of First street, between Mary and Blandina streets, a factory previously occupied for the manufacture of furniture by Wager Brothers Company. The company announced that the "Remington motor so well adapted for propelling automobiles is equally well adapted for propelling launches" and when permanent quarters were obtained, they would manufacture boats.

In March 1902, Remington purchased the factory buildings in East Utica bounded by Niagara, Broad and Ontario streets. This was formerly the Lathrop Manufacturing Company property and consisted of a one story, 80 by 200 foot building and some smaller shops. The bodies were produced by Willoughby, Owen & Co. and the wheels by Weston-Mott. In its new factory, the Remington Company proceeded to finish 10 complete carriages, 10 complete motors and from 3 to 5 complete launches a week. The automobile did not measure up to its claims, and finally in 1904, the company became bankrupt and closed.

W. H. Birdsall designed the "Buckmobile", a car with the running gear of a buckboard, a two cylinder motor, which was comfortable and possessed considerable merit. The Buckmobile Company was organized in 1901 by A. Vedder Brower and others and began the manufacture of these vehicles on Catharine street, at the corner of John. It enjoyed initial success and in 1903 moved to a location on Sunset avenue, at what is now Shepherd Place, to the south and rear of the old House of the Good Shepherd. The "Daily Press" of July 8, 1903 reported:

"The new building is a one-story structure, 100 by 30 feet and 15 feet high inside. The old plant in the rear will be used as an assembly and store room. The new plant will make possible an output of one complete machine a day, twice the present capacity."

When the Remington ceased business in 1904, the Buckmobile merged with the Black Diamond Automobile Company of Batavia and produced Buckmobiles at the old Remington plant and also at its Sunset avenue location. In 1903 the vehicle was a sensation at the Madison Square Automobile Show in New York and orders poured in, taxing the capacity of the company. By 1905, the company was in need for funds for expansion and when these were not forthcoming, the Buckmobile became only a memory to Uticans. Utica's opportunity to become the automobile center of the East vanished.

IT WAS INDEED MAJESTIC — THE NEW THEATER
1900

WHEN Sam S. Shubert took over the lease of the old Opera House on Lafayette street, a new and even greater era in theatrical entertainment began. During the summer of 1900 the Opera House was torn down until little but the side walls remained intact. Within these was built the Majestic Theater, a dream of splendor. There were two entrances, one off Lafayette street, leading to the ground floor and balcony, and another from Washington street, leading to the gallery on the third level and to the gallerette on the fourth level. From the main entrance on Lafayette street three sets of double doors opened into a lobby floored with mosaic tile and wainscotted with Italian marble. The lobby continued upward through two floors and contained two large French block plate mirrors. On the second floor was a balcony looking down into the lobby. This was intended for use as a promenade for the balcony proper. Arches opening the whole width of the lobby gave access to the foyer, or open space back of the seats on the ground floor.

The auditorium itself was 67 feet wide and 78 feet deep. Four hundred and twenty seats were arranged on the sloping floor, and were divided into three sections. The ceiling, 57 feet high, was frescoed with figures typical of the dawn and of the histrionic art in bright colors. Stucco work enhanced these decorations, some of it representing figures in mythology. The boxes were twelve in number, six on each side and were entered from the first floor. No two boxes on a side were on the same level and this gave the occupants of each box the unobstructed view of the stage. Above the boxes a number of cupids were placed. The opera chairs were upholstered in Nile green tapestry.

From the lobby a marble stairway, with fancy marble newel and balustrade of wrought bronze led to the balcony above. At the north end of the promenade in back of the ground floor seats was a second marble stairway also leading to the balcony. The balcony was 50 feet deep front to rear and extended across the building. It was finished in maroon and green, and had 425 seats.

The gallery, which was one floor higher was reached from the Washington street entrance. Three flights of steps led over the dressing rooms of the stars, to the third floor, on which were the gallery seats, nine rows of open bottom benches and two rows of reserved seats. Five hundred could be seated there. The gallerette was a unique feature of the house. It was on the fourth floor and immediately in front of the seats in the gallery. There was a single row of seats in the gallerette, seating 75 people and standing room for as many more. There were brass rails along the front of each of the three balconies. There was a large sign on the exterior, spelling "MAJESTIC" in one hundred lights or more. The stage was forty feet in depth, sixty-seven feet wide and a height of sixty-five feet to the rigging loft. There were fifteen complete sets of scenery, which could be raised or lowered from the rigging loft without the shifting which was a noticeable feature of the old Opera House. From the opening of the new theater, the employees were dressed in uniforms of green, with gold braid and plain gold buttons.

Under the Shubert proprietorship, the Majestic furnished

a great array of attractions, the greater part of the best contemporary theatrical offerings of the time.

One early evening soon after the Majestic opened in 1900, a big yellow dog strolled into the alley and made friends with Fred Waldron, the stage carpenter. From that time until he died, old "Blutch" as he was called by Waldron, became as famous as the theater itself. In 1915, one Utica newspaper made him the subject of a news story:

"Blutch is known from coast to coast by the foremost actors and actresses of the profession who have crossed the threshold of the stage door of the Majestic Theater within the last fifteen years. He is the pet of the boys who work about the theater and the mascot of the firemen at No. 3's. An example of the manner in which this unusual dog has taken a hold upon the affections of those in the vicinity of Washington street is often shown by the taxi drivers who slow up and even come to a dead stop when they see feeble old Blutch attempting to cross the street. In many other ways consideration is shown Blutch in his advanced years. In his younger days he was a dandy.

"Among his actor friends are John Drew and Lawrence D'Orsay. Upon one occasion, John Drew sent Blutch a handsome collar which he purchased at Strauss' in New York city. Blutch proudly sported it for a time until someone stole it. Among Blutch's peculiarities is the habit of snoozing about the stage until the call of 'overture' which is the signal for the actors to be ready for the raising of the first curtain. At this call, he retires to the wings or to a dressing room to remain until the fall of the final curtain. He shows a dainty preference for the star dressing room because of its nice, soft carpet, and he is always given a cordial welcome.

"Blutch knows the length of a show. His instinct in this direction is unexplainable but he knows when 'overture' is called and he can tell within a minute which is the final curtain. The length of the show, whether two, three or four acts makes no difference to Blutch. Blutch has an ear for music, especially the bass drum. There has been no minstrel show or 'Uncle Tom's Cabin' show here in years, whose band has not marched through the streets of the city with Blutch in line, generally at the head of the band.

"While setting the stage of the theater with palms or ferns, stage hands have often watched Blutch walk under them so that the overhanging ends just touch his back. He seems to enjoy having these ends draw slowly over his back but is very careful and has never been known to upset any of the plants. He sleeps back of the stage in the theater at night but is on hand for roll call at the firehouse in the morning.

"The only pedigree he has is the one made for himself and that is a noble one. Like many another actor, his star is waning, but when he leaves his friends it will leave behind him a record such as no blue ribbon, high brow dog has ever done before."

When the Majestic Theater was built in 1900, the space over the stores on the northeast corner of Washington street was fitted up as an auditorium, long known as "Assembly Hall." The entrance was from a flight of stairs from Washington street. These led to the auditorium itself, underneath a balcony. The auditorium was 100 feet long and 32 feet wide with a stage 33 by 35 feet. Paul F. Kallies did the decorative work. A series of clusters of American beauty roses were painted on the ceiling in the center of the room, and an allegorical picture representing comedy and tragedy occupied the space over the proscenium arch and extended up the coved ceiling. The only exposed wall was on the Lafayette street side, and light during the day was obtained from the number of large windows there. In this hall, Wilmer & Vincent began their long successful career as theatrical agents and proprietors.

Sidney Wilmer and Walter Vincent were vaudeville actors when the former came to visit his sister, Mrs. E. W. Wright, who resided in the Olbiston apartments early in 1900. During his visit, he received a proposition from Seymour D. Latcher, agent for Owens Brothers, owners of the Majestic Block, to take over the Assembly Hall and operate it as a vaudeville house. They took a lease at $2000 rental per year and opened it on January 19, 1901 as "The Orpheum", enjoying great initial success.

They had to struggle to overcome the opposition of the clergymen of Utica and lost some $3000 the first season. The "Sunday Tribune" which devoted several pages to theatrical news, was prompted to come to the defense of Wilmer & Vincent:

"There seems to be a question in the minds of many as to the kind of house Messrs. Wilmer & Vincent are conducting. It is not a concert hall in any sense of the word, but a high class vaudeville (a French word meaning a diversified entertainment) theater, in which none but refined acts will be played. No drinking is allowed nor

smoking except in the gentlemen's smoking room and
none but ladies and gentlemen are desired as patrons."

During the following summer, after breaking the theatrical ice in Utica, Wilmer & Vincent persuaded the owners of
the building to knock out two stores on the Lafayette ground
floor and give them an entrance on that street. From that
time on, the Orpheum became a pronounced success. They
did so well that Owens Brothers offered the Majestic to
Wilmer & Vincent when Shuberts lease was running out in
1905. The lease for the Majestic had been the second in their
chain, which later included theaters in Pennsylvania and in
Virginia.

In the "Observer-Dispatch" of March 13, 1949, there appeared the story of a humorous incident at the Orpheum in
1903 while Eugene L. Koneke was the manager:

"Do you remember the old Orpheum Theater? It was an
upstairs house on Lafayette street, about where the
Pershing stands. It had no stage entrance. All scenery,
baggage, props and impediments had to be sent in
through the gallery entrance which was on Washington
street.

"Sidney Wilmer made the bookings for the theater. He
booked a bareback rider and toe dancer who called
herself Mlle. Theo, Parisian equestrienne. The act was a
twosome. The second half was Theo's trained horse
'Prince'. Wilmer broke the news to Koneke. He assured
him the horse was trained to go up and downstairs as
daintily as the family cat. Koneke reminded Wilmer that
it was not just stairs that would have to be negotiated.
From the gallery loading entrance there was a flight of
stairs. Then the route led down center aisle and over a
runway which bridged the footlights of the stage.
Wilmer was positive that 'Prince' would leap over every
obstacle.

"Monday of the week of the horse act came. So did
Theo, 'Prince', and his personal groom. The horse was a
handsome white gelding with a broad, fat back. He
trotted to the gallery door and there he stopped. It was
more than a balk. It was a definite blockade. Finally they
blindfolded him. He still refused to begin the climb.
They padded the stairs with blankets and started him
up. He surprised them. He bolted and ran up.

"Koneke had been assured that the horse would be
brought to the theater each afternoon before the
matinee and taken out after the final evening performance. Accommodations had been reserved for him in
the Mansion House Stables. They stayed vacant.

"The act played the opening performances and was a great success. It was novel and interesting. Theo was young, pretty, a good bareback rider, and she finished with a toe dance routine on a pad on the horse's back, while he was circling the ring. The curtain went down; the house lights were dimmed; the specially made runway was placed in position over the footlights. Prince approached, sniffed and backed away. He would not put a foot to the planks. Says Koneke: 'We converted a corner of the Orpheum stage into a box stall and the horse spent the week there.'

"On Saturday night, when all the actors, their baggage and belongings had gone, the stagehands entered the arena once more. They were a patient crew, but about 2 a.m. they were ready to quit. Koneke told them to bed the horse down once more and to report back Sunday morning. Sunday morning's clammy dawn changed to noon's brilliance, but there was still a dim and dubious outlook back stage. In desperation, Koneke decided to route the horse the royal way — down the front stairway.

"This was in two sections, with a landing half way up. The top half of the stairway was carpeted and padded but the lower half was sheer white marble. The horse was blindfolded. The crew practically lifted him down the first half of the steps. They struck the marble stairs. The horse slipped and rolled over and over. When he struck the tiled floor of the lobby 'Prince' rolled across that. He brought up short with his feet against the wooden stiles of the doors. He got to his feet and followed the groom quietly to the railroad and his box stall on wheels. Koneke then made a rule. He would take dogs, monkeys, bears, pigs, cats, birds, seals, and even lions, but no more horses."

Wilmer & Vincent continued to operate the Orpheum until May 1, 1915, when it was taken over as a motion picture house by William P. Donlon. He was a native of Amsterdam, who came to Utica in 1907 at the age of 16; purchased the candy concession at the Majestic and in a few years was assistant manager of the Majestic. The Orpheum continued to enjoy a popular patronage until 1917. About five o'clock in the morning of March 20th, 1917, fire extensively damaged the building and it was not thereafter used as a theater. A second floor motion picture theater was no longer acceptable because of the danger of fire.

THE UTICA PUBLIC LIBRARY
1904

IN 1893, a charter was granted by the Board of Regents to a Board of Trustees to administer the "city library" in the old location on Elizabeth street. By 1899 the old building was inadequate and the need for larger quarters became evident. William Pierrepont White donated $1,000 to a building fund. Mr. and Mrs. Thomas R. Proctor and Mr. and Mrs. Frederick T. Proctor purchased and donated the Hutchinson property on Genesee street. This house had been originally built by Samuel Farwell, a prominent Utican and railroad builder, whose firm built the Flint & Pere Marquette railroad in Michigan. After Farwell's death, the property was occupied by Charles W. Hutchinson.

Bonds to finance the construction of the new library were issued and construction began, with the cornerstone being laid on May 4, 1903. It was built of Indiana limestone and New Haven brick and was designed by Arthur C. Jackson, of New York city, a native of Utica. The library was opened to the public on December 10, 1904.

To serve the needs of a growing city, on November 10, 1910, the Potter branch was opened in the abandoned Whitesboro street school. This branch was discontinued in 1918 and replaced in 1920 with a branch in Faxton Hall, on Varick street for some years.

On November 11, 1913, the East Utica branch opened in a building donated by Frederick Towne Proctor. The site had been purchased by him and the building constructed at a cost of $6,000, from a design made by architect F. H. Gouge. In 1932, a lot adjoining the property was donated by Mrs. Maria Proctor.

Library service began in North Utica in 1924. A deposit station was opened in the back room of O'Connell's drug store on North Genesee street. The next year, it was moved to Doyle Hardware on Auert avenue. In 1928 it was moved to the new fire station No. 10 on Trenton avenue and late in 1960 to Jefferson School. In 1969, it was again moved to the former Fire Station No. 10 on Trenton avenue.

THE ETHNIC ENRICHMENT OF UTICA IN THE 20TH CENTURY

A S the twentieth century dawned, Utica became even more cosmopolitan in character. The "Saturday Globe" in November 1900 reported that the Election Bureau had released figures of the foreign born voters in Utica in 23 of the 26 election districts in the city (missing were the two districts of the Sixth Ward, with mostly German residents, and one district of the Fourth Ward). There was a total of 3282 foreign born voters. The Germans were the most numerous, 999. The Irish were next with 653, followed by the Welsh 384, English 383, Italians 277, Polish 218, Canadians 88, Scottish 62, Swiss 59, French 39, Austrians 37, Danes 20, Hungarians 4, Hollanders 4, Greeks 2, Swedes 2, Syrians 2, Australian 1, and Belgian 1.

In 1893, the Lithuanian residents of Utica formed the St. Casimira Society with nine members, which increased to 40 or 50 members by 1911. In 1910, they formed another society, the St. Anthony Society with an equal number of members. In 1911, the "Saturday Globe" reported that there were 125 Lithuanian families in Utica with a population totalling 500. They were employed as tailors and in the various trades and many were employed in the textile mills. They originally worshipped in St. Joseph's Church, but by 1911 they decided to have their own church building. They purchased the colonial house at 97 Lafayette street from Richard A. George and converted it into a church. The Rev. Anthony Dekanis, an assistant at Holy Trinity Church, took charge of the services of the St. George (Lithuanian) Catholic Church. It was dedicated on September 17, 1911, with 100 families as parishioners. A picture of the old house was shown in the "Saturday Globe" of April 8, 1911.

The Syrian colony in Utica was small at first. The "Saturday Globe" of April 7, 1900 reported that there were about 100 in Utica and that Father Michael Khouri, a Greek priest would celebrate Mass for them as a guest of Monsignor J. S. M. Lynch, the pastor of St. John's Church.

The "Saturday Globe" of April 18, 1903 reported:

"The Syrian colony in Utica is small, not over 100. Of these, 35 live in New York Mills and Whitesboro and are

369

employed in the mills there. Of the remainder, some are employed in the West Utica mills and some on the East side of Utica. A considerable number are engaged in peddling. All the Syrians in Utica are from the Levant. Three are engaged in business, two of them Joseph Tady and Acee M. Acee conduct dry goods stores on Bleecker street. Another is a merchant, John Nessen, on Sunset avenue."

By 1910, there were about 600 persons of Syrian extraction in Utica. Anthony Deep had a restaurant on Bleecker street and a meeting there resulted in the organization of the Church of St. Louis of Gonzaga, built on the corner of Albany and Elizabeth streets.

THE THEATORIUM
1907

THE first motion picture house to open in Utica as a nickel theater was the "Theatorium" at No. 206 Genesee street, on the east side just south of Hackett's Block and opposite the old Butterfield House. It opened on September 26th, 1907 with continuous performances from 2 to 5 and 7 to 10:30 p.m. Admission 5¢. This theater burned out on February 19, 1910 and the building was completely destroyed. Herb Young in the "Observer-Dispatch" on September 3, 1933 gave an interesting description of it:

> "Pat Clancy, who is no stranger to Uticans, was the manager and singer, and he would arrange to run four shows an hour. Many funny incidents happened then, as everything was crude and undependable. Sometimes, while in the middle of a picture, the machine would get so hot that it would set up and make it impossible for the operator to turn the handle. That meant he had to stop the machine and wait for it to cool. In the meantime a sign would be flashed upon the screen, which would

read 'One minute please', but it was a good many minutes in some cases before the machine would be ready to start again.

"The film in those days would be running into a galvanized can on the floor, and it would sometimes fill the can and overflow on the floor, where it would wind itself around the operator's feet, which would mean another stop, and another 'one minute please' sign. Another cause for a stop occurred when the jaws holding the carbon would fall out, and, of course, no light. Then the house would be in darkness. This would necessitate the manager to step forth on the small stage to make an announcement, saying that the machine was out of order for the time being. This announcement would usually bring forth much stamping of feet, catcalls and whistling, much to the manager's embarrassment.

"A small machine was used in the booth. It was hooked to a tripod, which was fastened to the floor. When the machine would get hot and set up, they had to use another machine in its place. All the employees in the theater at that time had to help in the booth to get the machine going when it got balky. The machine was operated on a 220-volt current and would have to be stepped down to 110 volts. To accomplish this, a home-made carburetor (as it was called in those days) was used. It consisted of a big chunk of iron in a barrel of water, with a wire attached to it. This was not always successful as it sometimes would cause all the fuses in the theater to blow out.

"While we think we have talking pictures these days, it must be recalled that talking pictures were the thing back in the good old days. The manager and singer would do the talking from behind the screen. Back of the screen they would have a home-made prop bench, where they had all the effects on it. They could give the effect of a horse trotting, a telegraph set clicking, a door closing, etc. and most any sound that the picture would call for. The talking was never rehearsed. They would make up the talking as the picture went along, so in all the first showing of it was their rehearsal, and they had a new show each day.

"The screen used then was composed of a large frame which stood on four legs and the interior of the frame was covered with a heavy canvas coated with calcamine. The screen had to be coated frequently as it would not hold up. The new sound screens of today have a special composition on them which lasts a long time.

"Most all of the nickelets then had the bold front with colored lights decorating the entire front of the theater. The admission price appeared on the window of the box office in letters about two feet high. You could not miss it. The interior of the house was generally dark and dingy. The seats consisted of about 300 folding chairs. They would take six or eight chairs and nail them together and place them in rows down the center of the theater. All the other chairs would be placed along both sides of the theater. Many a person had his feet stepped on, as the interior lighting was not so good. This was also the time of the merry widow hat and many a person went to the show and came out disgusted, and you know why."

THE DECLINE OF BAGG'S SQUARE
1910

BAGG'S Square, the cradle of Utica's infancy, began to lose its old time appearance after the Mohawk river was straightened out. In the fall of 1909, the city deeded the old river channel to the New York Central Railroad and work commenced on March 29, 1910 to fill it in, preparatory to constructing the overhead crossing. The "Herald-Dispatch" of April 8, 1910 reported:

"Historic Bagg's Square is today in a state of dishevelment and mourning that her doom is near. It is being torn up on both sides, while great mounds of earth and timber, a big stationary engine and other contractor's material, cover most of the square which is boarded off to the south and the two sides, excepting for a thoroughfare on the east side just wide enough to allow teams to pass each other on their way to and from the railroad crossing. On the east side, the big trench to allow the foundations of the retaining wall being built has reached the great stone staircase, formerly the main entrance to historic Bagg's Hotel."

The "Utica Observer" of August 16, 1911 reported:

"The overcrossing is a massive affair as can be seen at a glance. The bridge proper from abutment to abutment is 425 feet long. The south approach is 212 feet long and the north approach 600 feet in length. The roadways are 21 feet each in width, exclusive of the sidewalks. The work of building the overcrossing was begun in the spring of 1910."

On the afternoon of November 21, 1911, the doors of Bagg's Hotel were closed for the first time in a period of one hundred and seventeen years.

On June 13, 1913, work on the new Union Station was commenced and this was opened to the public on May 14, 1914, at a cost of one million dollars. In the same year the overhead crossing was completed at a cost of half a million dollars.

UTICA'S FIRST WIRELESS STATION
1910

F. W. Schiller, a former employee of the Utica Gas and Electric Company, built for his own amusement the first wireless station in Utica in 1910 in his home on Seymour avenue. The "Utica Sunday Tribune" of October 16, 1910 reported:

"Utica is now in the wireless zone, thanks to an amateur operator who with great care and at no small expense has erected a station which picks up messages from as far east as Cape Cod and as far west as Port Huron. Persons who pass along Eagle street, Neilson street, Seymour avenue, and adjacent streets can easily see a high pole from which are strung a number of stout guy wires and suspended from which are parallel lines of antennae, between which are flashed the electric waves. Those who live in the immediate vicinity have already begun to get familiar with the crackling of the wireless apparatus, and the erection of the plant has so stimulated the boys in the vicinity that several crude wireless plants have been built. Some of these are sufficiently well equipped to allow the youngsters to communicate from house to house and to pick up the messages sent from the more perfected plant."

While Schiller was able to receive snatches of long distance message, his wires were not high enough to avoid local disturbances. He sought a higher location, and on March 27, 1911, the "Utica Daily Press" reported:

"Towering about 170 feet above the level of the street, a wireless telegraphic instrument has been placed on the roof of the Kanatenah by Louis R. Mather and F. W. Schiller of this city. The pole is about 73 feet in height and is held in position by numerous wires, which are in turn fastened to the roof of the building. At the top of the pole is an arm from which wires run to the attic of the Lorraine (apartment house) where the instrument for sending the message and which makes audible the messages picked up, are placed.

UTICANS GET THEIR FIRST VIEW OF AVIATION
("Utica Daily Press" September 18, 1911)

"NATURE never was in a more gracious mood than Saturday, when the afternoon rays of a warm September sun touched lightly the upturned faces of thousands of Uticans, who voiced their pleasure in hearty cheers as they watched Eugene Godet, Curtiss aviator, sweep into the air for the first flight of his exhibition. This was the long expected event. Interest whetted by previous disappointments drew a crowd of perhaps 25,000 persons to the Parkway for this demonstration of aerial skill and the long pent-up enthusiasm burst forth in cheers as the nervy

Frenchman manipulated the machine that moved so easily it seemed alive.

"It took until shortly after 4 o'clock to get the motor tuned up so that it was ready to venture into the air and by that time, the breeze, which had been rather brisk during the afternoon was beginning to die away. The humming mutter of the motor as it whirled the propeller blades about 1,000 times a minute announced to the crowd that he was off and as he swept down the Parkway the crowd cheered wildly.

"As he picked up speed he tilted the plane and slowly the machine began to climb, making the long, graceful ascent as a swallow swoops down to the surface of the water and then sweeps upward in a long, easy swing. Once fairly off the ground he began to rise more rapidly, as the machine gathered headway, and without delay he headed toward the setting sun.

"There he was — way off to the west — a little speck in the sky, and then he began the return sweep that took him over the city. Over the buildings in Utica he flew, staying fairly high so as to avoid as much as possible the counter currents met in the lower strata of air. For this was his first flight over a city, and housetops are not particularly good to light on.

"As he passed the Parkway, although more than a mile north of it, the crowd could see the machine very plainly and they watched his progress with keen interest as he swung down toward the Masonic Home and then started back to his landing place. Straight as a homing pigeon he came and when he took the first sharp dip and then straightened out to glide gently to the earth he got a tremendous reception. Easily the machine settled to the ground and ran along for a hundred yards before it came to rest. And while the people applauded Godet hopped out, unconcerned, to busy himself with his machine."

THE PASSING OF THE STREET MUSICIANS

FEW Uticans will today remember the days of the street musician carrying his hand organ or dragging his street piano. He was usually accompanied by a monkey with a little hat, whose antics attracted attention and whose outstretched hand and hat enticed donations of a penny or two. The "Saturday Globe" of July 9, 1910 wrote:

"The organ man is a fixture in the land and holds a place in the heart of childhood second only to Santa Claus. Nor are they children alone who enjoy the music of the street. The tunes may be old and commonplace — and some of them are as old almost as the hills — or they may be recent 'classics' from the concert halls; but old or recent, they inject a little sentiment into life and life without sentiment is not life at all, but mere existence.

"The children know this. Their eyes sparkle with joy. Their cares are forgotten, and to the strains of the Wearing of the Green or Old Grey Bonnet they are transported from the hot, dusty pavement up where the butterflies play, up where the clouds trace their imagery on the sky, up where the eternal stars nightly assemble as world sentinels.

"Some of the congested sections of Utica would be less joyful were it not for the organ grinder. While to some he may be a nuisance and his music ear-torture, to childhood he is dear, and as long as he makes the rounds the pennies of the children will find their way into his pocket."

From 1910 to 1913, however, the hand organ grinder business began to decline. We read in the "Utica Daily Press" of July 25, 1913:

"Time was, back in the halcyon days of the organ grinder and the 'monk', when the dispenser of various and sundry moans and grunts, coming under the head of music, was welcomed on every hand. As the years rolled on, this brand of melody suffered a jolt as the street piano made its appearance, until now the organ and the monk are rare sights. And if the combination retains any attraction whatever, it is furnished by the antics of the monk.

"But just as the hand organ business declined, so has that of the street piano, until today fewer than ever are heard. Whether it is the increased use of the phonograph in the home, or the possibility of owning your own piano, the fact remains, the hurdy-gurdy is seemingly destined to the eternal and everlasting brink. As a final stroke in the business in this city, the police now have instructions to drive these musicians to silence after 9:30 p.m. At any rate, the hurdy gurdy man is gradually disappearing and one of these days will be a thing of the past."

THE CAVALRY ARMORY — HALCYON HALL

A troop of cavalry was organized in Utica in 1912, composed of a number of Uticans dubbed the "Gentlemen's Riding Club". They began with four or five horses, owned by the men, and they drilled in the old Munson Brothers' foundry on Broadway at the Erie Canal. They were incorporated as Troop G of the New York National Guard on June 12, 1912. As the numbers grew, the State leased in August 1915, Halcyon Hall on LaFayette street, just west of Sayre Alley.

The site was orginally occupied by the residence of Julius Spencer. This house was torn down about 1875 for a new building erected by Wheeler & Bailey as a foundry for the manufacture of stoves and heaters. When Wheeler & Bailey moved from the site, the foundry was converted into a hall and was used for political meetings and athletic events and, in later years, as a bowling alley and finally as a roller skating rink.

The troop took over the property on April 30, 1916 and a temporary drill hall was provided in the Pfluke property immediately in back of Halcyon Hall. This was 62 by 70 feet in dimension and the floor was laid with tanbark composition.

On June 19, 1916, the troop was mobilized and sworn into federal service for duty on the Mexican border during the trouble with Mexico. The troop reached McAllen, Texas on July 7, 1916 and put in nine months patrolling the border. It arrived back home on March 12, 1917 but its stay here was short. It was called back into service on July 15, 1917. The fact that the Savage Arms Company in Utica held the rights to manufacture the Lewis machine gun resulted in its reassignment from a cavalry troop to a machine gun battalion. Its members were divided into Companies B and C of the 106th Machine Gun Battalion and sailed for Brest, France on May 17, 1917. There they were assigned to the British Second and Fourth Armies and fought on the Somme and took part in the breaking of the Hindenburg Line. After the war ended, they returned on March 18, 1919 and were mustered

378

out of federal service. They resumed their cavalry status and continued to use the old armory on LaFayette street until 1927 when the old building became dangerous and was abandoned. Troop G went out of existence on October 1, 1927 with the formation of the new 121st Cavalry Regiment of the New York National Guard, and its members became Troop A. A new cavalry armory was then erected on Culver avenue.

JAMES S. SHERMAN — VICE PRESIDENT OF THE UNITED STATES

JAMES Schoolcraft Sherman was born October 24, 1855, the son of Richard U. and Mary Frances Sherman at a house on the corner of Eagle and Kemble streets. In 1884, the house in which he was born was moved to Lincoln Avenue. "Jim Sherman" was graduated from Whitestown Seminary in the spring of 1874 and the following year entered Hamilton College in the Class of 1878. There he distinguished himself as a public speaker and debater.

Upon leaving college in 1878, young Sherman studied law in the office of his brother-in-law, Henry J. Cookingham in Utica, and was admitted to the Bar in 1880. Like his father before him, he was interested in politics and in the spring of 1884 he was elected Mayor of Utica, at the age of twenty-nine. He declined renomination after his one year term and in 1886 was nominated by the Republican Party for Member of Congress and was elected. The Congressional district then comprised the counties of Oneida and Lewis. He proved to be an effective Congressman, and an able parliamentarian. He became a warm friend and supporter of both Presidents McKinley and Roosevelt.

At the Republican National Convention in Chicago in 1908, James S. Sherman was nominated for the office of Vice

President of the United States on a ticket headed by William Howard Taft. He returned to Utica on July 2nd and was greeted by great crowds at the railroad station. He was escorted to his home with a great parade up Genesee street. On August 18th, a platform was erected in front of his home on Genesee street and he was formally notified of his nomination. He was elected on November 3rd and went to Washington for the next four years. The Conkling Unconditionals, the Utica marching clubs, were invited to participate in the inaugural parade in Washington but, delayed by a snow storm, arrived too late in the day. They did parade the next day however.

In the summer of 1912, he was renominated together with Taft for a second term. He did not live to see the ticket defeated in November. He died October 30, 1912. In 1923, the statue of Vice President Sherman on the Parkway facing Genesee street was unveiled with speeches by Mayor Fred J. Douglas, Warnick J. Kernan and Elihu Root.

UTICA'S PENNY POSTMEN

IN the early days of Utica, residents called at the post office to pick up their mail. It was not until 1863 that the first free delivery of mail system was adopted. There were no corner mail boxes in which letters could be placed. Every letter had to be taken to the post office which was first located on lower Genesee street, and later in Mechanic's Hall on Hotel and Liberty streets. As the city grew, the penny postman made his appearance. The "Oneida Morning Herald" of November 15, 1850 contained the following announcement:

> "Penny Post. Many of our city readers will be glad to learn that the ancient and useful office of 'Penny Post' — formerly filled with great acceptance by the late William Richards — has been revived. The new incumbent, Hugh Smith, now goes his daily round, delivering such

letters as are not regularly called for, at the trifling compensation of 2 cents extra per letter. Newspapers gratis. Mr. Smith has established boxes for the reception of letters destined for the mails at the store of Cooley & Clark on Corn Hill, and at Henry Lewis', corner Columbia and Varick streets, West Utica. Mr. Smith's office will be a great public conveyance and we hope it will be well sustained."

When free delivery was adopted in 1863, twelve letter carriers were appointed and James Barnum was named the superintendent of mails. He was born in Utica on October 11, 1828. His father and brother, Levi and Charles Barnum kept a hat store at 38 Genesee street and he learned the hatter's trade. In 1861 he secured the post of penny postman at the post office. His duty was to sort out letters by street and begin delivering them. Utica had 22,000 residents and extended from Bagg's Square to Jewett Place on the south and from the State Hospital grounds on the west to the old "gulf" on the east. He would start out delivering letters at 7 a.m. Except for a brief lunch at home, he walked until 5 p.m. when he returned to the post office. He received a new batch of late mail and began a second delivery, pausing for supper, and continuing until 9 p.m. His compensation averaged $3.00 per day and he walked on an average 25 miles per day.

Mr. Barnum continued as Superintendent of Mails from 1863 to 1885, when President Cleveland came into office and appointed a new superintendent. In 1889, Ellis H. Roberts as Assistant Secretary of the Treasury appointed Mr. Barnum as mail clerk at the New York sub-treasury office. He served in that position until early in 1896 when he resigned and returned to Utica, where he died in October of that year.

ARTHUR SAVAGE INVENTS A RIFLE
1892

ARTHUR W. Savage was born in Kingston, Jamaica, British West Indies on May 13, 1857, the son of John and Jane Henderson Savage. He went to England for his education at Leeds and was a student at South Kensington Art Academy in London (1871-74). He sailed for Australia where he engaged in the cattle business for about eleven years and there married Anne Bryant. He then returned to Jamaica and operated a coffee plantation for two years. In 1888 he came to New York where he was employed by Munn & Company, publishers of scientific papers and magazines.

Shortly after that, Mr. Savage came to Utica where he became an employee of the Belt Line Railroad and did much to improve the service. The Thompson-Hueston Company, interested at the time in the Belt Line, sent Savage to Saratoga Springs to take charge of the street railroad there (1891-92), during which time he electrified the lines and placed them on a substantial basis.

Arthur Savage began to exercise a talent for invention while he was a cowboy in Australia. When he returned to Jamaica, he learned that the British government wanted an improved firearm and he set about to produce it. He devised a gun, the rights for the manufacture of which he sold to the Hartley & Graham Company. When he returned to Utica, he entered his new Savage 1892 military rifle in the military trials of that year on Governor's Island. It was placed No. 35 and no United States contract was obtained. On February 7, 1893, he secured a patent on his rifle and organized the Savage Repeating Arms Company (1893-97). Since he had no factory, he arranged with John Marlin of the Marlin Firearms Company of New Haven, Connecticut, to make the first group of rifles. In 1895, Savage developed the .303 caliber lever-action rifle, and began their manufacture in a small plant in Hubbell street, Utica. In 1897, the Savage Arms Company (1897-1917) was incorporated and a site on Tilden avenue was purchased and buildings erected.

In 1905, Mr. Savage sold his interest in the corporation

and went to California where he engaged in the orange growing business. His inventive genius included, in addition to magazine rifle improvements, a knowledge of munitions, and he designed the dirigible torpedo. During World War I he resigned as an officer of the Savage Tire Company, a five million dollar corporation he founded to engage in war work with the government, and was assigned to work with the British Minister of Munitions. He died at the age of 83 in San Diego, California on September 22, 1938.

The Savage Arms Corporation was a major supplier of arms during both World War I and World War II and during the first war furnished over seventy thousand machine guns of the Lewis type to Britain to contain the German advance.

THE SHUBERT THEATER
1906

IN 1905, Wilmer & Vincent secured the lease of the Majestic Theater when Shubert's lease expired. Lee Shubert was not about to move from Utica and announced that he would build a new theater at a cost of $200,000. The site eventually chosen was on the north side of Bleecker street, between Charlotte and Culver streets. This was the site of Utica's first theater, the Amphitheatre. Shubert's intention was to call it the "Garrick", but by the time it opened, it was named the "Sam S. Shubert Theater" in honor of one of the brothers who died in 1905 in a train accident in Pennsylvania.

The new theater was four stories high, built of pressed brick. There were two stores facing on Bleecker street, between which was the entrance to the lobby. On the Charlotte street side was the entrance to the "Rathskeller", which occupied most of the basement of the building. This was an innovation in Utica and for years it was a popular thirst-quenching emporium.

The new theater opened on December 17, 1906 with Eddie Foy in the popular musical comedy, "The Earl and The Girl". The "Herald-Dispatch" described the opening:

"A big curtain slowly ascended until it was lost to view. Instead of its picture of the child Beethoven astonishing his elders around a piano, flesh and blood personages in an English scene were presented to the spectators. Prof. Franz Rath, down in front of this, directed his musicians in an accompaniment to a catchy chorus. The personages in flesh and blood referred to became animated like mechanical toys suddenly started working. They filled the place with the voice of song and the Sam S. Shubert Theater was open.

"Some of the songs in the 'Earl and The Girl' were whistled and hummed by the audience as they went out. 'How'd You Like to Spoon With Me?' and 'I Would Like to Marry You' in which the members of the chorus wing out over the orchestra, were among the prettiest. Lights were used with good effect on the swings in the darkened theater. It seemed odd to see, after the show, the many carriages gathered about Bleecker, Charlotte and Culver streets, and the interurban cars waiting in that vicinity for a theater crowd."

Wilmer & Vincent took over the Shubert Theater in August 1912. The name was changed to the "Colonial" and was sold by Wilmer & Vincent in August 1922 to Nathan Robbins.

MOTHER MARIANNE OF MOLOKAI

I N the late nineteenth century, on a barren promontory
that lay between the forest clad cliffs and the sea, on a
wedge-shaped Pacific island called Molokai, lived the
outcasts of humanity, the lepers banished there by the royal
government of the Hawaiian Islands. Never allowed to return to their homes, these poor unfortunates had a desperate
longing for someone to minister to their spiritual and tem-
poral needs — someone to show that they cared. This need
appealed to a Belgian peasant priest, Joseph Damien de
Veuster. He was moved to join their banishment and administer to them. This he did for years and by reason of his
daily contact with the victims of the dreaded disease, he
became himself a victim and died in mid-April, 1889.

Barbara Kopp, daughter of Peter and Barbara Witzen-
backer Kopp, was born in Heppenheim, Hesse-Darmstadt,
Germany around 1838 and came to Utica with her parents in
1840. The city directory of 1850-51 lists "Peter Coop, laborer, 10 Schuyler, south of Columbia." It is believed that he was
a laborer either in the textile mills or in a brewery and that
Barbara in her youth worked in the mills. The family joined
St. Joseph's Church and being drawn to the religious life, she
joined the Franciscan Order in Utica on September 7, 1862
and received the habit on November 19, 1862, taking the
name of Sister Marianne. She went to Syracuse, New York,
and taught at the Assumption School there and later at St.
Peter's in Oswego. She was recalled to Syracuse to take
charge of St. Joseph's Hospital there and in 1882 was chosen
to be the provincial of the Order.

During her second term as provincial, she received a plea
from the Bishop of Hawaii to send nuns. She responded
herself and with six other sisters left Syracuse in October
1883. They took charge of a leper receiving station and two
years later, they were operating a school and a hospital for
non-lepers as well. Determining that Father Damien needed
help at Molokai, she went there and for more than thirty
years took care of the lepers and helped Father Damien
during his life. She died in August 1918 without ever having
contracted the disease. She never returned to this country.
Little is known of her brothers and sisters, except that a

sister, Mrs. Eva Lehrscholl died in Utica on March 22, 1916 and that at the time of Mother Marianne's death, she was survived by a sister, Mrs. Kate McPhaill, of Beverly, New Jersey.

The cause for the canonization of Mother Marianne is pending in the Vatican.

THE CONSTRUCTION OF APARTMENT HOUSES IN UTICA

THE development of Utica in the last half of the 19th century resulted in an innovation in housing — the apartment house type of construction. The pioneers in Utica were Milton H. Northrup and his son-in-law, Seymour D. Latcher. Milton H. Northrup was born in Hamilton, New York, in 1835 and came to Utica at an early age. He established a candy and confectionery business, first on Liberty street and later on Columbia street and was financially successful. Seymour D. Latcher was born in Northville, Fulton County, in 1866 and came to Utica in 1883 as a bookkeeper for Hugh Glenn & Co. and later A. S. & T. Hunter. Later he joined his father-in-law in the confectionery business.

About 1888, the two men became interested in real estate and decided to erect apartment houses in the growing city. Their first was the Bellevue Flats on the southwest corner of South and Steuben streets, which were later to be known as the Chelsea and then the James Apartments. Their biggest venture was the "Genesee Flats" which were opened in 1892 on Genesee street at Clinton Place. It was a mammoth seven-story building with balconies, towers and bay windows, and was considered the biggest structure for residence purposes in this part of the State. Tragedy was to befall the structure four years later.

386

In the early dawn of March 5, 1896 a janitor shoveling snow saw flame and smoke bursting through the first floor from the basement and up an elevator shaft. The fire department responded, but within a half hour, the huge building was a mass of flames. Many of the 200 tenants were forced to fasten bedsheets to the balconies and lower themselves to the street. Watchers saw one woman lose her hold on the thin rope and turn over and over in a plunge to the walk below. The lives of three other tenants were lost and nothing remained of the building but the front wall and portions of the north and south walls.

The "Genesee Flats" were soon rebuilt and renamed the Olbiston, built on the same design. Within two years, nearly all of the original tenants were back in the new building. In 1895, the Reynolds house on Genesee street was removed to Oswego street, and the firm began the construction of the Kanatenah, which still stands. To their string of multiple dwellings were later added the Lorraine and Oswego Apartments on Oswego street and in the early 1900s the Milton Apartments, adjoining the latter two.

Mr. Northrup died on November 21, 1903 at his home in the Lorraine building and Mr. Latcher died on December 24, 1916 at his apartment in the Kanatenah.

ICE CREAM AND SODA FOUNTAINS

ICE cream was first served in the United States at a dinner in the White House by Dolly Madison, during her husband's term as President. Soda water contained no soda but was distilled water charged with carbon dioxide gas which caused the water to bubble. It was first introduced in this country in 1807. When mixed with flavorings it produced "soft drinks" as distinguished from alcoholic beverages. The soda water fountain was introduced into America shortly after the Paris Exhibition of 1867, and P.E. Cassidy, the confectioner whose store was on lower Genesee street, purchased a magnificent Puffer soda water fountain, made expressly to his order, containing six different kinds of marble, and costing $1,500. The "Utica Observer" of May 18, 1885 reported that the fountain furnished fifteen syrups and four mineral waters.

> "Mr. Cassidy has also arranged a novel contrivance whereby cream will be frozen on the counter and taken from the freezer for such as wish cream soda. Persons wishing a quart of cream for use at home can have it at 30 cents a quart. This is lower than the same quality of the article was ever before offered at in Utica. A handsome upright piano has been placed in the Ice Cream Department, and a talented player will furnish music for the patrons of the establishment."

Cordon Hackett, the caterer, in 1872 built the Hackett Block on the west side of Genesee street, affectionately leaning its northern wall against the southern wall of the Gardner Block on the corner of Genesee and Columbia. One of the ground floor stores was occupied by him for his cake and ice cream parlor. The "Daily Press" of September 27, 1887 wrote:

> "An attractive feature in the store is one of Tufts elegant soda fountains, cost $2,000. It is of Italian marble and very beautiful. It has 24 taps for syrups and 13 draft tubes."

The ice cream soda revolutionized the drug store business and any store worthy of the name installed the most elaborate fountain obtainable. The "Sunday Tribune" of August 6, 1899 concluded:

"It was but a few years ago that the soda was taken from fountains, which, in comparison with the gorgeous affairs of today, looked like a twenty dollar gravestone beside the ten thousand dollar tomb in a fashionable cemetery. The average soda fountain with its slabs of polished marble and the little silver plates with the names of the flavors and extracts does somewhat suggest the style of architecture and the material thereof in use in burying grounds."

SOLDIERS AND SAILORS MONUMENT AT ONEIDA SQUARE

THOUSANDS of Uticans pass the Soldiers and Sailors Monument at Oneida Square, but except perhaps for Memorial and Veteran's Day, few note its details and the beauty of the design. It was erected in 1891 at a cost of $32,000, from a design by Karl Gerhardt, a sculptor from Hartford, Connecticut. The "Morning Herald" of October 13, 1891 gave a description of the monument, from which the following is excerpted:

"The monument consists of a group of figures upon a graduated base, from the midst of which rises a short, solid pillar, forming the main shaft, which is capped by a dome and surmounted by a figure, representing the city of Utica. On the front of the dome are carved in high relief the heraldic shield and coat of arms of the municipality of Utica. The fiture is one of dignity and beauty. It represents a female figure, clothed in classic drapery, with bold and striking folds falling gracefully to her feet and partly looped in her girdle. Over her shoulders and falling from them is a cloak, which gives a military semblance to the figure. In her left hand is a sword, held out by the scabbard. The right hand is raised and points significantly with open palm to southern battlefields.

"The base is octagonal in form. Three granite steps ascend to the monument proper. Here a secondary base or pediment of three parts supports the structure. This pediment is raised in outline to give support to the bases of four allegorical figures at the corners of the monument. The figure fronting Genesee street is that of a soldier standing easily at 'arms a-port' in an attitude calculated to receive a challenge or repel an attack. Opposite, and facing west stands the image of a sailor — bold, determined, grand — a fine specimen of the fearless Yankee tar. This figure is, in the opinion of many, the best on the monument. Facing south beams the figure of Peace, beautifully executed. Victory, dignified of mien and of graceful bearing, looks toward the center of the city.

"The main shaft rising between the figures rests upon a round pediment of three parts. Upon the upper of these is a selection from Oliver Wendell Holmes' 'Voyage of the Good Ship Union'. Below this is a frieze of bronze, representing in spirited figures the departure of the volunteers and the return of the veterans. On the southern side of the monument, is the dedicatory language, 'We keep in memory the men of Utica who risked their lives to save the Union' and on the reverse side, 'From Sumter by land and sea to Appamattox.' "

THE BARGE CANAL REPLACES THE OLD ERIE

IN 1918, the new Barge Canal was opened to traffic with harbor facilities in North Utica. The original plan of the State was to permit the old Erie to be continued from Rome to Mohawk through Utica, to bring grain and building supplies to the warehouses here. It was soon found, however, that there was not sufficient water available to keep the old channel navigable. Between 1918 and 1920, the Erie canal channel became a mudhole and a dumping ground for rubbish. It served to divide the city in two sections, "above" and "below" the bridge. There were 17 bridges within the city limits, seven of which were of the lift-bridge type. At the instigation of the business men of the city, Governor Smith signed in May 1920 legislation abandoning the old canal. A price of $511,364 was established by the State for the four and one-half miles and 70 to 71 acres of canal lands. The City issued bonds and commenced the task of filling in the channel and removing the bridges.

In June 1922, the old Genesee street "hump" bridge was taken down and parts of it were reassembled for use near Boonville. The old "weigh lock" at John street was demolished and in July 1922, plans were drawn to use the canal bed for a broad boulevard, known as Oriskany street. Many of the old structures along the canal were demolished. A notable exception was on the northeast corner of John and Jay streets. This building was finally demolished when the East-West arterial was built in the 1960s, along the old route of the canal. The "Utica Saturday Globe" of July 2, 1904 gave this description.

> "The building in years gone by was the mecca of canal boatmen. From its spacious interior they secured equipment and supplies. When purchases were completed they sat or lounged upon the dock which stands beside the sturdy walls of the structure. At the weigh lock of the canal just west of John street their boats were tied up, while the owners paid toll and then went over the Maginn's to buy supplies.
>
> "In 1858 Mr. Whitman erected the present brick structure and the store at the time was quite widely patronized. Edward Maginn worked as a clerk for Mr. Whitman and later purchased the business from the latter. Numbers of boatmen crowded the wharf, swearing in the picturesque and expressive language of the canaler or chafed Maginn on his high prices. The lowering of the John street bridge in the later 80s and the dwindling of the traffic on the canal made a great change in Maginn's business. And now the store has been closed for about four years."

THE WELCOME HOME ARCH
1919

CONGRESS declared war on Germany on April 5, 1917. The National Guard companies in Utica were part of the First New York Infantry since 1905 and consisted of Company A (old 28th Separate Company), and Company B (old 44th Separate Company). In addition, Troop G, First New York Cavalry, was mustered into Federal service and eventually distributed into newly created machine gun companies.

On May 3, 1917, a depot battalion was formed in Utica to replace the departing companies. This group was ordered on August 7th to active service guarding the New York city aqueduct. Another group was the Utica Military Police. The organization started under the name of the Home Defense League but the name was changed to avoid confusion with another home defense group in the county. The uniform of the Military Police consisted of a khaki suit, blouse, breeches and cap, leather puttees, and for winter duty, a heavy oilskin green woolen overcoat with cap to match. Each member was sworn in as a special police officer of the city of Utica and provided with a shield. The men carried carbines and the officers 38 caliber revolvers. The company, 250 men, guarded the Savage Arms plant during the strike in 1918. The company was disbanded on January 29, 1919.

In January 1919, Mayor James D. Smith approved a "Welcome Home Arch" for the returning soldiers and sailors. It was erected in front of the City Hall just south of the intersection of Blandina street and almost in front of the southerly entrance to the City Hall. It spanned Genesee street with a great curved arch surmounting two high standards. The arch was 60 feet from pillar to pillar on the curbs and 38 feet high. The top of the arch was emblazoned with the words, "Welcome Home" and there were electric lights on the heavy bases of the semi-circle of the arch. On the arch supports at the top of the pillars were red crosses and blue stars, the latter signifying service in the army or navy. The columns or pillars which supported the arch were four feet square and were painted white, while the arc of the circle of the arch was

392

in red with the words "Welcome Home" in white electric lights. The cross was of course in red and the service stars in blue. At the tops of the columns were placed the flags of the Allied nations and on the top of the arch the American flag flew. The sign was designed by George W. Allen of the Fraser store.

The Welcome Home Day was held on September 15, 1919 with a parade of three thousand veterans up Genesee street, and a huge clambake at Roscoe Conkling Park. Among the speakers was Franklin D. Roosevelt, then Assistant Secretary of the Navy.

INDEX

395

V

W

Y

ACKNOWLEDGMENTS

Miss Helen Dirtadian and the entire reference staff of the Utica Public Library devoted many hours in research.

The Oneida Historical Society and its Director, Douglas Preston made available its files and photographic material.

Edna Sisti Cook, John Passiatore, Allan Benedict and Marian Williams supplied photographic material used herein.

The Dodge-Graphic Press and, in particular, Betsy Mack supplied the expert advice and assistance required for the production of this book.

Bibliography

Jones, Pomroy. *Annals and Recollections of Oneida County.* Published by the Author. 1851

Bagg, Moses M. *The Pioneers of Utica.* Curtiss & Child, Publishers. 1877

Durant, Samuel W. *History of Oneida County.* Everts & Ferris, Publishers. 1878

Bielby, Isaac P. *Illustrated History of Utica.* D. Page & Co., Publishers. 1890

Bagg, Moses M. *Memorial History of Utica, New York.* D. Mason & Co., Publishers. 1892

New Century Club. *Outline History of Utica and Vicinity.* L. C. Childs & Co. 1900

Cookingham, Henry J. *History of Oneida County.* S. J. Clarke Publishing Co. 1912

Miller, Blandina Dudley. *A Sketch of Old Utica.* Fierstine Printing House. 1913

Utica Public Library. *A Bibliography of the History and Life of Utica.* Goodenow Printing Co. 1932

Clarke, T. Wood. *Utica For a Century and a Half.* Widtman Press. 1952

Utica
in 1832

UTICA 1832